The New Russia

The New Russia
Transition Gone Awry

Edited by

LAWRENCE R. KLEIN

and

MARSHALL POMER

Stanford University Press
Stanford, California

Stanford University Press
Stanford, California
© 2001 by the Board of Trustees of the
Leland Stanford Junior University

Printed in the United States of America on acid-free,
archival-quality paper.

Library of Congress Cataloging-in-Publication Data
The new Russia : economic transition reconsidered / editors Lawrence R.
Klein and Marshall Pomer.
  p. cm.
 Includes bibliographical references and index.
 ISBN 0-8047-4127-1 (alk. paper)—ISBN 0-8047-4165-4
(pbk. : alk. paper)
  1. Russia (Federation)—Economic policy—1991– 2. Russia
(Federation)—Economic conditions—1991– I. Klein, Lawrence R. II.
Pomer, Marshall I.
HC340.12.N48 2000
338.947—dc21   00-034443

Original printing 2001
Last figure below indicates year of this printing:
10 09 08 07 06 05 04 03 02 01

For
Wassily Leontief,
Stanislav Shatalin, and
Yuri Yaryomenko

to honor their memory
and advance their hopes

Contents

Acknowledgments

This book is the culmination of the efforts of the Economic Transition Group, an informal group of Russian and American economists alarmed by the direction of Russian economic reform. Oleg Bogomolov and Alexander Nekipelov were instrumental in garnering the interest of the Russian Academy of Sciences. John Kenneth Galbraith and James Tobin, who have bewailed American failure to respond wisely to the ending of the Cold War, provided invaluable encouragement.

We are grateful to the members of the Economic Transition Group (see Chapter 2, footnote 5) and others who have provided both moral and intellectual support for this collaborative Russian-American effort. We wish to thank in particular: Severin Ashkenazy, Abram Bergson, Alexander Bogomolov, Alberto Chilosi, Frank Durgin, James Gavan, Constantin Gehriger, Sara Gordon, Leonid Grigoriev, Gregory Grossman, Jack Hain, James S. Henry, Peter M. Holmes, Daniel Kazmer, Henrik Konarkowski, Alla Leydman, Richard Lotspeich, Gerry Mandel, Margaret McNally, Jacqueline Mertz, Anton Moissev, Joseph Montville, Jacques Sapir, Robert Stadille, Marat Uzyakov, and Steven Wegren. We also thank Igor Kondrashin for serving as interpreter and translator.

Foreword

Mikhail Gorbachev

Readers, before you is a book whose authors are alarmed by the course of Russian reform. I welcome their opposition to the Washington Consensus and their realistic optimism. I share their conviction that my country can become an organic part of the world economy and exercise a constructive role in its ongoing processes.

"Shock therapy" did irreparable harm. Most dangerous are the social consequences—the sharp drop in standards of living, the enormous inequality of incomes, the decline in life expectancy—not to mention impoverishment of education, science, and culture. All of this was bound up with deeply flawed privatization, a flare-up of crime, and moral degradation.

At the end of the 1980s and the beginning of the 1990s, I was accused of indecision. Similar sentiments have been expressed in the memoirs of some of my Western partners. Of course, as the leader of the nation during those years, I bear a certain responsibility for what occurred later. Miscalculations and mistakes allowed the opponents of a prudent transition to spoil its realization.

I did not accept the imposition of a market model which already belonged to the past of the leading countries. I was not willing to ignore the social factor, nor disdain the fates of living human beings. It was obvious that shock methods would bring enormous harm and lead to irrecoverable losses. Finally, it is important that society itself comprehend and accept the transition to the market. It was not permissible to bring the people to heel as was done by the Bolsheviks.

My conception, formulated as part of the democratization of the Soviet Union, entailed the search for a humane and just economic system. By 1989–90 a sufficiently broad consensus emerged in support of a socially oriented market economy. In Houston in the summer of 1990, my message to the G7 (Group of Seven) laid out this conception and expressed the determination of the Soviet leadership to put it into practice.

The strategy of step-by-step movement to the market was subjected to sharp criticism. The West called for a "more decisive" approach. A team of Russian economists presented a 500-day program for the "great leap to the market." Even this was rejected for not being bold enough by activist young economists who were influenced by neoliberal allies abroad.

The possibility of reasonable consensus—as well as the fate of the Union government, the maintenance of which was a prerequisite for the success of the reforms—fell victim to political struggle. Conservative, reactionary forces were pitted against radical neoliberals. Nonetheless, an anti-crisis economic program was worked out, and received the support of almost all republican governments in the Soviet Union.

During this responsible and dramatic period, I met with the leaders of the G7 in London. They displayed varying degrees of capacity to understand the problems facing my country. Urging us to move toward the market was akin to breaking down an open door, inasmuch as our choice had already been made. Though virtually all of them recognized this, their suggestions as to the tempo and methods of transition were astonishing.

I was struck in particular by Japanese Prime Minister Toshiki Kaifu. One could have imagined that his remarks were from the representative of a country with no government economic regulation. Similar views were expressed by U.S. President George Bush, Canadian Prime Minister Brian

Mulroney, and British Prime Minister John Major. On the other hand, the statements of French President François Mitterrand, Italian Prime Minister Giulio Andreotti, and European Commission Chair Jacques Delors were very different. They bore witness to the social factor and the regulatory role of the government.

When Mitterrand said that the economies of all the nations represented at the meeting carried socialist traits as well as capitalist ones, several of those present did not disguise their astonished reactions. But this thesis is axiomatic, even though it contradicted the economic orthodoxy of the day. Nonetheless, the G7 leaders did not try to deny our right to determine for ourselves the appropriate forms and tempos for carrying out the transition to the market.

Soon after, *perestroika* was brought down. The attempted reactionary *putsch* of August 1991 provided Boris Yeltsin the opportunity he sought. He overstepped the results of the referendum on preserving the Union and, to the applause of the West, undertook a shock program of transition. It can be summed up as follows: yet another attempt to force Russia into utopia, utilizing once again the Bolsheviks' methods of "shoving down the throat." The consequences of this vicious, authoritarian approach have been economic collapse and catastrophic political events, including the assault on parliament in 1993. The very prospects ffor democratic government, the rule of law, and a civil society remain at risk.

The financial collapse in 1998 was the culmination of negative economic processes with which the authorities were incapable of coping, and it laid bare the full inadequacy of the reform program. The effort to explain the collapse as a consequence of the Asian economic crisis, or to say that the Duma members interfered with the reformers, speaks only to the fact that the reformers lost touch with the reality of our economy and our society.

In contrast, the authors of this book are realists. They recognize that economic leadership from the state—or government, as it is customarily referred to in the West—is significant in countries with mature market economies, and even more significant in the transition from a command economy to the market. *(Translated by Nicholas N. Kozlov)*

Preface

Joseph E. Stiglitz

This century has been marked by two great economic experiments. The out-come of the first set, the socialist experiment that began in its more extreme form in the Soviet Union in 1917, is now clear. The second experiment is the movement back from a socialist economy to a market economy. Ten years after the beginning of the transition in Russia: How do we assess what has happened? What are the lessons to be learned? Surely, this is one of the most important experiments in economics ever to have occurred, a massive and relatively sudden change in the rules of the game. As rapidly as Russia announced its abandonment of communism, so too did Western advisers march in with their surefire recipes for a quick transition to a market economy.

The contrast with China may be instructive. Over the decade beginning in 1989, while China's GDP nearly doubled, Russia's GDP almost halved; so that while at the beginning of the period, Russia's GDP was more than twice that of China's, at the end, it was a third smaller. Not only did Russia stagnate during this past decade, but it succeeded in turning the theoretical trade-off of inequality and growth on its head—in the process of shrinking its GDP, Russia also doubled its inequality (as measured by the Gini coefficient). Recent data contained in the 1999 World Development Indicators paint an even bleaker picture, with poverty—defined as $4 a day —rising from 2 million to over 60 million by the middle of the decade.

Why the Failure?

The question that we need to ask is, why the failure? Not surprisingly, those who advocated shock therapy and rapid privatization argue that the problem was not too much shock and too little therapy, but that there was too little shock. The reforms were not pursued aggressively enough. The medicine was right; it was only that the patient failed to follow the doctor's orders! Other defenders of the recommended reform programs argue that the failures were not in the design of the reforms, but in their implementation.

One variation on this theme is to blame the failure of the shock therapy reforms on corruption and rent seeking at every turn. But corruption and rent seeking may itself have been increased by the manner in which the reforms were conducted, which both destroyed the already weak social capital and which enhanced opportunities and incentives for such activities.

Historians may well wonder how the programs implemented by the architects of the Russian privatization could have led to the present system of economic oligarchy and disorganization. One of the theories that promoted privatization is the "grabbing hand" theory of the government. The state is seen as the primary source of the problems: interfering in and preying on firms. The emphasis is on government failure, not market failure. Privatization of enterprises and of economic life are the overarching policy goals. The grabbing-hand theory sees the state as being irredeemably corrupt, while the private sector is viewed through rose-colored glasses. The resulting program of transferring assets to the private sector without regulatory safeguards ("depoliticization") has only succeeded in putting the "grabbing hand" into the "velvet glove" of privatization. The "grabbing hand" keeps on grabbing with even less hope of public restraint. The rapid liberalization of capital accounts allowed tens of billions of dollars to be spirited out of Russia each year while the architects of capital account liberalization negotiated more billions of international debt to be repaid by taxpayers. Economic and political forces—incentives—are at play, with far different outcomes than predicted by the proponents of the grabbing-hand theory. Incentives led to asset stripping, not the predicted wealth creation. And why should we be surprised? It is not the first time that strong vested interests have used political processes to maintain and strengthen their economic interests. What is remarkable about this episode is that economists, who should have known better, had a hand in helping create these interests, believing somehow—in spite of the long history to the contrary—that Coasian forces would lead to efficient outcomes, even if one could ignore the social consequences of the new "Kapitalism." The "theory" (in quotes, because the argumentation seldom reached the level of analysis normally expected of a set of assertions that aspires to that name) was that once property rights were established, there would be a demand for a "rule of law" and for the institutional infrastructure required to make a market economy work.

While privatization was supposed to "tame" political intrusion in market processes, privatization provided an additional instrument by which special interests, and political powers, could maintain their power. For instance, in a variety of dubious arrangements, political allies of the reformers "bought" assets (e.g., with money borrowed from the government or from the banks to which the government gave charters), with part of the "profits" generated thereby being recycled to support the political campaigns of the reformers.

A part of the problem also rose from confusing means with ends: taking, for instance, privatization or the opening of capital accounts as a mark of success rather than a means to the more fundamental ends. Even the creation of a market economy should be viewed as a means to broader ends. It is not just the creation of market economy that matters, but the improvement of living standards and the establishment of the foundations of sustainable, equitable, and democratic development.

At its root, this was the most fundamental failure; there was no concept of—or perhaps even concern for—the kind of society that might emerge, other than that it be characterized by "private property" and some form of electoral process that was more democratic than the previous regime. There was a certain irony in all this. Many advocates of the radical reform strategy[1] argued that it was political economy concerns (e.g., rent seeking and incentives within the public sector) that provided the most compelling arguments for rapid reform. After all, conventional economics had little to say about dynamics and especially about complicated processes of systemic economic transformation. But their judgments about political forces proved perhaps even more questionable than those concerning economics.

Misunderstanding the Market Economy

The failure of the reforms in Russia reflects misunderstanding of the very foundations of a market economy, as well as a failure to grasp the fundamentals of reform processes. At least part of the problem was an excessive reliance on textbook models of economics. Textbook economics may be fine for teaching students, but not for advising governments trying to establish from anew a market economy—especially since the typical American-style textbook relies so heavily on a particular intellectual tradition, the neoclassical model, leaving out other traditions (such as those put forward by Schumpeter and Hayek) which might have provided more insights into the situations facing the economies in transition.

In *Whither Socialism?* (1994), I argued that the failure of market socialism arose in part from a failure to understand what makes an actual market economy function—a failure arising in part from the neoclassical model itself. If the Arrow-Debreu (AD) model had been correct, then market socialism might have fared far better. But while the AD models capture one essential aspect of a market economy—the information conveyed by price signals, and the role that those price signals serve in coordinating production—the information problems addressed by the economy are far richer. Prices do not convey all the relevant information. I want to suggest here that those advocating radical reform, with its focus on privatization, similarly failed because they failed to understand modern capitalism; they too were overly influenced by the excessively simplistic textbook models of the market economy. But we should be less forgiving of those failures. While Hayek and Schumpeter had earlier in the century developed alternative paradigms, views that had not been well integrated into the mainstream of the Anglo-American tradition, by the time the postsocialist economies faced their transition, the modern theory of information economics had shown the striking limitations of the AD model.

The information requirements for, and transactions costs involved in, implicit and explicit contract enforcement are typically different, so that the two should best be thought of as complements rather than substitutes. The problem in the economies in transition was that both enforcement mechanisms were weak: the state's legal and judicial capacities were limited, while the very process of transition—high institutional turnover, high shadow interest rates, and short time horizons—impairs the effectiveness of implicit contracts. Thus, even if institutions did not need to be created, the very process of transition provides impediments to the workings of a market economy. The success of a market economy cannot be understood in terms of narrow economic incentives: norms, social institutions, social capital, and trust play critical roles.

It is this implicit social contract, necessary to a market society, that cannot be simply legislated, decreed, or installed by a reform government. Some such "social glue" is necessary in any society. One of the most difficult parts of a transformation, such as the transition from socialism to a market economy, is the transformation of the old "implicit social contract" to a new one. If "reformers" simply destroy the old norms and constraints in order to "clean the slate" without allowing for the time-consuming processes of reconstructing new norms, then the new legislated institutions may well not take hold. Then the reforms will be discredited and the "reformers" will blame the victims for not correctly implementing their ill-considered designs.

Privatization is no great achievement—it can occur whenever one wants —if only by giving away property to one's friends. Achieving a private, competitive market economy, on the other hand, is a great achievement, but this requires an institutional framework, a set of credible and enforced laws and regulations. Do this, and the larger politically sensitive privatizations can be attended to when the needed institutional infrastructure was ready, while in the meantime privatization of small- and medium-sized firms (which have less potential for abuse and require simpler regulatory structures) could go forward apace.

The Reform Process

Since a major theme in my research is that informational problems make the actual world strikingly different from conventional economic theory, it should be no surprise that I have always had misgivings about what Albert Hirschman has called an ideological, fundamental, and root-and-branch approach to reform as opposed to an incremental, remedial, piecemeal, and adaptive approach (gradualism). I have no great quarrel with "shock therapy" as a measure to reset expectations quickly, say in an anti-inflation program. The controversy was more about the attempted use of a shock therapy approach to "install" institutions.

It is almost as if many of the Western advisers just thought the Bolsheviks had the wrong textbooks instead of the whole wrong approach. With the right textbooks in their briefcases, the "market Bolsheviks" would be able to fly into the postsocialist countries and use a peaceful version of Lenin's methods to make the opposite transition. Only a blitzkrieg approach during the "window of opportunity" provided by the "fog of transition" would get the changes made before the population had a chance to organize to protect its previous vested interests. This mentality is a reincarnation of the spirit and mindset of Bolshevism.

Those who worried about the sequencing and pacing of reforms were also concerned that without the appropriate reform strategy the likelihood of success was limited, and a failure of reform could indeed undermine its sustainability. Success, rather than speed, is of the essence. Indeed, failures are reinforcing: if reforms are not viewed to be sustainable, then investors will not have an incentive to make the long-term commitments required for growth; one could get caught in a low-level equilibrium trap. Successful transition strategies have to have the property of time consistency, including political sustainability.

In hindsight, it is clear that many of the political forecasts of those involved in the reform process were far from clairvoyant; many of their worries seem, by and large, not to have materialized, while political developments which should have been of concern were not anticipated. Nor can one separate "principles" from how they are, or are likely to be, implemented. Policy advisers put forth policy prescriptions in the context of a particular society—a society with a particular history, with a certain level of social capital, with a particular set of political institutions, and with political processes affected by (if not determined by) the existence of particular political forces. Interventions do not occur in a vacuum. How those recommendations are used, or abused, is not an issue from which economists can simply walk away. And this is especially so in those instances where one of the arguments for the economic reforms is either failures in the political process or their impact on the political process itself. It is time for the doctors to rethink the prescription. But in doing so, they will have to take the patient as he is today, not as he might have been had history taken a different course. The point is not to refight the old battles, but to learn the lessons of the past, to help guide the future.

Note

1. I use the term "radical reform" rather than the more frequently used term "shock therapy" since the latter is sometimes used to discuss the necessity of rapidly bringing down hyperinflation. Poland had "shock macro-therapy" but followed a more incremental process of reform (including privatization).

Introduction

Marshall Pomer

Soon after becoming head of state in 1985, Mikhail Gorbachev launched *perestroika*. Whether due to idealism or fear of losing the Cold War, he sought to create a "democratic market system." He promised that his initiatives would make Russia "a socialist beacon for all mankind" (Gorbachev 1987). They led instead to the collapse of the very system that he wanted to invigorate.

His successor fared little better. Following Western advice, Boris Yeltsin championed immediate transformation of Russian socialism into laissez-faire capitalism. However noble his intentions to eliminate oppressive government control, he pushed Russia, after over 70 years of communism, toward another failed utopia. Instead of the anticipated unleashing of economic potential, impoverishment and crime became hallmarks of the economic transition.

Western advisers, including officials at the International Monetary Fund and the United States Treasury, applied a narrow conception of economics and underestimated the difficulties of transition. Dismissive of Russian capabilities, they unwittingly contributed to the weakening of the economy.

Western loans supported an overvalued ruble that was destructive to industry and spurred massive capital flight. Thus Russia was saddled with an
oppressive foreign debt burden. The foreign credits made it possible to
perpetuate unrealistic economic policies that facilitated transfer of the
wealth of the nation to a corrupt few.

This book charts a new course. Optimistic about Russia's potential, the
Russian and American contributors propose a balanced approach to economic reform, steering equally clear of both unrealistic free-market ideals and
excessive government control. Given its natural wealth and well-educated
populace, Russia should expect to have a flourishing economy.

Laying the groundwork for the chapters that follow, this introduction first
reviews past Western counsel to Russia and then presents an overview of
the book. Much of the pragmatic advice offered here pertains as well to
other nations in their efforts to fashion prosperous and equitable market
systems.

Advice from the West

When he introduced his economic program, President Yeltsin was reacting
against decades of authoritarian government. He was also responding to
intense Western pressure. The capitalist West, confident after its triumph
over Soviet socialism, pressured Russia to adopt laissez-faire policies so
extreme that they would not have been tolerated at home. To wit, even
convicted felons were able to open banks. Of all the superficial economic
reforms, most fateful was the reckless privatization process.

Western governments had long supported the headlong rush to the free
market. At the July 1990 economic summit in Houston, the heads of state
of the seven major industrial countries issued a joint communiqué offering
to help the Soviet Union make the transition to a market system. Soon after,
Soviet President Gorbachev, acknowledging that "there is no alternative to
shifting to the market," outlined an incrementalist (gradualist) strategy for
dismantling centralized control (IWOE 1990, 11–14). The program gave
priority to putting government finances in order, and called for privatization

and price decontrol to proceed at a moderate pace. The initial emphasis was on privatizing service enterprises and allowing the market to determine consumer prices. Imports and currency conversion would continue to face restrictions, and government would help fund investment. State guarantees would be provided to protect and encourage foreign investors.

The International Monetary Fund (IMF), the World Bank, the Organization for Economic Cooperation and Development (OECD), and the European Bank for Reconstruction and Development (EBRD) criticized the gradualist Soviet plan and declared their unwillingness to extend support. In a harshly worded joint report in the autumn of 1990, they discounted the need to first stabilize government finances, which could have been facilitated by international aid, and called for quick removal of import barriers. Conceding that "radical reform" would cause an immediate drop in output and intense inflation, they nevertheless predicted that output would start climbing "within two years or so" and that "growth in productivity and output would likely exceed that of most mature market economies" (IWOE 1990, 18).

In contrast, among Russian economists there was nearly unanimous support for gradualism (Åslund 1992, 172). The program advocated by Yegor Gaidar, Yeltsin's main economic adviser in the fall of 1991, was originally too gradualist to satisfy Western economists (Åslund 1995, 65). Gaidar had intended to liberalize prices and foreign trade rapidly, but not all at once, and he had planned to continue to restrict currency convertibility and maintain some government support for enterprise investment. These departures from the free-market ideal would have partially sheltered Russian enterprises from foreign competition, helped maintain government revenues, and restrained capital flight—thereby mitigating transition shock.

But just two weeks before the dissolution of the Soviet Union, December 11, 1991, Yeltsin and Gaidar had a fateful meeting with seven foreign economic advisers. Jeffrey Sachs, the leader of the advisory group, promised that "it would be possible to mobilize fifteen to twenty billion dollars per year in international support" if Russia adopted a "big bang" approach to transition (Åslund 1995, 332).

On January 2, 1992, eight days after the dissolution of the Soviet Union, President Yeltsin implemented the "shock therapy" advocated by Western advisers. By presidential decree, coordination of the economy by central planning was terminated. Most price controls were suddenly lifted, the doors to foreign trade and capital flows were thrown open, and government spending was cut sharply. The goal was immediate transition to unfettered markets, thereby allowing the market to guide the economy without government interference.

Rather than propel the economy forward, sudden liberalization precipitated severe contraction. According to official statistics for 1992, (real) per capita personal income fell in half while hyperinflation of 2500 per cent decimated the savings of millions of Russians. By 1994, industrial production fell to only about half its 1990 level, and investment declined by two thirds. [These and other statistics mentioned in this chapter can be found in the tables and figures of the Statistical Appendix.]

Amidst the debacle, the National Bureau of Economic Research held a conference to evaluate the transition programs in Central and Eastern Europe (Blanchard et al. 1994). The proceedings illustrate the mindset of the Western economic advisers, who are still setting policy toward Russia.

Stanley Fischer, previously chief economist of the World Bank and now first deputy managing director of the IMF, had been assigned the task of evaluating the reform program in Russia. Rather than look closely at the crisis, Fischer focused primarily on Russian history. He argued that the New Economic Policy (NEP) in the 1920s under Lenin demonstrated the power of economic liberalization. Reinforcing complacency about the course of reform, Fischer noted that the NEP program succeeded in a situation far more adverse than the present one. But he failed to mention that liberalization under NEP was more restricted in scope and that its success depended on strong government. While he conceded that liberalization prior to stabilization and privatization was problematic, Fischer nevertheless supported, without substantive rationale, "moving as fast as possible on all fronts" (Fischer 1994).

Lawrence Summers, who from the outset of the Clinton administration had primary responsibility for economic policy regarding Russia and who later became secretary of the treasury, gave a complimentary assessment of Fischer's analysis:

> Stanley Fischer's thorough paper does an excellent job of articulating what might be labeled the "economists' consensus" view of the situation in the former Soviet Union. Despite economists' reputation for never being able to agree on anything, there is a striking degree of unanimity in the advice that has been provided to the nations of Eastern Europe and the former Soviet Union. The legions of economists who have descended on the formerly communist economies have provided advice very similar, if less nuanced, than the advice provided in this paper. (Summers 1994, 252)

And the essence of that advice is:

> The three "-ations"—privatization, stabilization, and liberalization— must all be completed as soon as possible. (Summers 1994, 253)

These three components of the "magic triad" were regarded as ends rather than means. Instead of cautious evaluation of options and concern for public acceptance, there was a revolutionary spirit among Western advisers. As suggested in the Foreword by President Gorbachev and in Chapter 10 by Georgi Arbatov, who was dismissed early on from President Yeltsin's economic counsel, the reformers used the communist revolution as a model for dismantling communism. Thus one Western adviser wrote:

> It is the nature of revolutions to be heedless of costs, to pursue their ends with a self-justification that mocks any effort at the rational calculation of costs and benefits. This was the case of the French Revolution which, too, destroyed human and physical capital in prodigious quantities, and with the communist revolutions in Russia and East Europe, and so it will be with the current revolutions. Whether enduring benefit can emerge from these events is beyond our ability for calculation, but not beyond our capacity for hope. (Brada 1993, 108)

Jeffrey Sachs, the most influential foreign adviser to the Russian government, dismissed criticism of radical reform as "politically motivated rather than analytically sound." Attributing the difficulties to "the legacy of the old regime," he said that the inefficiency of the Soviet system implied that "enormous scope exists for increases in average living standards within a few years" (Lipton and Sachs 1992). According to Sachs, the key was to end inflation by government austerity "accompanied by rapid privatization of enterprises and swift opening of international trade."

When Sachs presented this assessment before a panel of eminent economists, several questioned the emphasis on speed. Alan Blinder, soon to be appointed to President Clinton's Council of Economic Advisers, asked what could be learned from the gradual transformation in China. Sachs said there was "little relevance" since Russian industry was more developed and government control over the economy was more pervasive. These realities, however, suggest that Russia had more capability than China to guide transition in a deliberate manner and that radical change would be more destructive to the productive capacity that was already in place.

Edmund Phelps, who had studied corporate governance in Eastern Europe for the EBRD, published an extensive comment on Sachs's presentation. Phelps gave a prescient warning that hasty transition could make Russian enterprises into "Frankenstein monsters" lacking "suitable control mechanisms" (Phelps 1992, 273). Nevertheless, he did not break ranks with Westerners advising high-speed transformation. Inexplicably, he concluded that "it is better to privatize in advance of good governance mechanisms than to wait for everything to be in place." Indeed, ignoring his own warning, Phelps congratulated Sachs for his incautious advice:

> I yield to no one when it comes to admiration for Jeffrey Sachs and his team in Russia. The talent and range of competence are extraordinary in a profession suffering from long overuse of mathematics as a sort of steroid. (Phelps 1992, 273)

As described by Georgi Arbatov and Oleg Bogomolov in their chapters, prominent reform-minded Russian economists were pushed aside by Western-supported neoliberals. According to Nelson and Kuzes (1994, 35–41), Anders Åslund, a Western adviser noted for his "unrivaled knowledge of the Russian economy" (Layard and Parker 1996, 93), was influential. He alleged that Russian economists "do not understand what a market economy is," and he attributed support for gradualism to "lack of intellectual comprehension" (Åslund 1992, 177). Åslund unabashedly called for unregulated, "wild" capitalism:

The conclusion is that the Soviet Union should adopt much more liberal conditions than usually exist in the West. Demands on the state should be reduced to a bare minimum—to the essential issues, such as law and order, basic state institutions, providing fiscal and monetary balance, an infrastructure and a social safety net. State revenues should be reduced accordingly, which will happen more or less automatically. Naturally, this will imply that a pretty wild capitalism will develop, reminiscent of Charles Dickens' Britain in the 1840s or a wild west economy. (Åslund 1992, 176)

Despite economic depression, intensified corruption, and widespread impoverishment, reformers managed to find encouragement not only in revolutionary change but also in the economy itself. After 1994, output continued to fall but at much reduced rates. The declines in GDP and industrial production for 1995 were 4 and 3 percent, respectively, compared with declines of 13 and 21 percent for 1994. The dollar value of merchandise exports in 1995, albeit mostly natural resources, was up an impressive 60 percent from the level in 1991.

Western economists authored well-received books that extolled the reform program, including *How Russia Became a Market Economy* (Åslund 1995), *The Success of Russian Economic Reforms* (Granville 1995), and *The Coming Russian Boom* (Layard and Parker 1996). The costs of transition were dismissed as the necessary price of past socialism, or were attributed to continued failure of government to relinquish control. In suggesting that action by the Russian government would only make matters worse, these advisers encouraged Yeltsin's team to put its hopes in Western benevolence.

It is self-serving to blame the past rather than scrutinize the transition program. However well-intentioned, Western aid enticed Russia into adopting ill-conceived, pro-Western policies (Wedel 1998). Metaphorically, Russia played helpless child, with the West as the omnipotent adult. Free flow of goods and capital was expected to win favor with the West. The policy of minimal government was predicated on the expectation that foreign investment, in league with the automatic self-adjusting properties of the market, would provide the impetus to transform the Russian economy

(Sedaitis 1997). But total foreign direct investment for the six years from 1994 to 1999 was only $17 billion, as compared, for example, to over $30 billion in Brazil during 1999 alone.

Once liberalization and privatization had been largely accomplished, stabilization of the ruble became the primary goal of economic policy. By 1996, inflation was a relatively moderate 22 percent and in 1997 only 11 percent (compared with 2509, 840, 215, and 131 percent for 1992–1995).The policies used, including high interest rates and a sharp real appreciation of the ruble, were costly for the economy. Nevertheless, Western advisers pointed with pride to privatization and the drop in inflation (Shleifer and Treisman 1998). With the IMF taking the lead, Western nations in July 1998 put together a $22.6 billion aid package to maintain the stable, convertible ruble that was deemed essential to attract foreign investors.

This "stabilization" strategy remained in place until Russia, unable to obtain still more foreign loans, could no longer defend the ruble. On Black Monday, August 17, 1998, the central bank allowed the ruble to fall, and the government defaulted on its debt. Only then did the strategy of minimal government lose its hold (Henry and Pomer 1998a, 1998b).

After failing to win parliamentary approval for the reinstatement of Viktor Chernomyrdin, President Yeltsin appointed Yevgeny Primakov as prime minister with the support of the Communist Party. Yuri Maslyukov, who was head of Gosplan under Gorbachev and a leading member of the Communist Party, was made deputy prime minister in charge of economic policy. By year's end, the U.S. deputy secretary of state publicly acknowledged, " 'Reform' and 'market' had gone from being part of the vocabulary of triumph and hope to being, in the ears of many Russians, almost four-letter words" (Talbott 1998, 54).

The Primakov-Maslyukov team, with the support of parliament, defied conditions previously set by the IMF while Western economists predicted hyperinflation and economic collapse. IMF approval, however, remained a priority to obtain a write-down of Russian debt and to encourage inflows of capital and technology. In May 1999, apparently supported by Western leaders opposed to activist government, President Yeltsin dismissed Primakov, whose rising popularity had made him Yeltsin's likely successor.

The prime minister following Primakov, Sergei Stepashin, was summarily dismissed after only three months in office. He was replaced by Vladimir Putin, a little-known figure from internal security who was later overwhelmingly elected President in March 2000 on a nationalist platform of restoring respect for the state. Yeltsin's dismissal of four prime ministers in less than a year and a half further eroded the credibility of the free-market program that he championed. After Primakov, and continuing under President Putin, the shift toward more active government was maintained in response to the demands of parliament, albeit in a hesitant manner because of the need for IMF approval to negotiate concessions with Western holders of Russian debt.

Thus Russia began to ignore the ideas and immediate interests of the West. Western investors in ruble-denominated debt were forced to accept large losses, currency conversion was made more restrictive, deficit spending went unfinanced, and taxes were imposed on exportation of natural resources. Notwithstanding the decimated banking system and the continued withdrawal of foreign capital, the economy began to expand in early 1999 without accelerating inflation. For 1999, (real) GDP grew 3.2 percent with industrial production rising 8 percent, a remarkable performance in comparison with the rest of the decade. This progress came in spite of the financial implosion, the reduction in international support, and continued corruption.

An Alternative View

Sharing the best intentions of the radical reformers, the economists in this book laud the collapse of the authoritarian Soviet state and acclaim the goals of a free-market system. But shock therapy, violating reason and experience, was an ill-advised attempt to replace one utopian program with another. While this strategy brought short-term benefits to the West, it was punishing to the Russian people and highly destructive to the Russian economy.

Russia now functions as a source of raw materials and as a market for foreign-made goods. This process of de facto colonization, somewhat reversed by the 1998 devaluation, jeopardized Russia's technological potential. Lack of controls spurred capital flight and fomented corruption. Consider, for example, the well-publicized multi-billion dollar inflow to illegal accounts at the Bank of New York.

Given Russia's highly educated labor force and vast natural resources, a coherent development program could create a rich dynamic economy founded on modern technology. For example, a rational government program could ensure investment funds and customers for aircraft manufacturing, which is now nearly defunct. After nominal privatization, agriculture is still organized on the basis of huge, inefficient collective farms. Government-mandated decollectivization in one region could be used as an experiment to be analyzed, a program to be adjusted, and a model to be applied elsewhere.

Attaining balance is difficult. During much of the Soviet era, totalitarian control, with great human cost, did produce rapid economic growth until about 1970. In the 1930s, when the Soviet economy seemed impressive relative to other economies, there was a shift in the West in favor of government intervention. After World War II, reinforced by the temporary dominance of Keynesianism, activist government underpinned the recovery of Europe and Japan and yielded robust rates of growth in much of the developing world. However, after the Reagan-Thatcher conservative revolution, the IMF and other international agencies sought to minimize government involvement.

While minimal government is no solution, activist government can do more harm than good. Once systems of government control are in place, they tend to perpetuate themselves and can propagate endless restrictions, as Soviet totalitarianism demonstrated. Government command of resources tends to prevent rather than promote competition, undermining the very basis for a market system. In the wake of drastic economic contraction, government has interfered with market discipline, with the impetus mostly from local governments in the form of special favors that suppress competition and shelter inefficient enterprises from bankruptcy. The challenge is to achieve a rational balance between market and government.

The analysis of economic policy presented here is broadly applicable. While appreciation of the benefits of free markets, reinforced by the Soviet collapse, has accelerated global economic integration, government guidance of national economies is needed to ensure that this process is beneficial. Part One of this book provides a critique of narrow economic orthodoxy. Part Two describes the ill effects of the laissez faire approach to economic transition in Russia. Part Three presents policy recommendations.

Part One: Economic Role of Government

In the first chapter, I discuss the rudimentary competitive-equilibrium model, which stands at the core of orthodox economic thinking. This model is used in two ways: first, to explain the rationale for the shock therapy strategy; and second, to identify factors to be taken into account in implementing a strategy for transition and development. I also present a simple empirical model that clarifies government's potential role in Russia's transition.

In the next chapter, Oleg Bogomolov gives background on the genesis of this book. A leading force for liberalization during the Gorbachev era and a member of the Duma during the Yeltsin era, he describes the careless embrace of shock therapy.

It is an overreaction to Soviet authoritarianism to accept the presumption that government is incapable of acting in the public interest. This cynical but understandable sentiment is countered by Leonid Abalkin. An influential reformer during the Gorbachev era, Abalkin provides a Russian conception of a viable and humane market economy.

Cautioning against economists' glorification of self-interested behavior, James Tobin emphasizes that unfettered opportunism—whether of criminals and corrupted officials or of managers and employees—is socially and economically destructive. He points out that economies with well-established market institutions did not rely solely on the market to make massive wartime reallocations. Tobin points out that activist government was also vital to the recovery of Western Europe and Japan after World War II.

Lawrence Klein contrasts the free-market and command economy ideals with each other and with reality, and he notes socialist features of all successful modern economies. He maintains that macroeconomic stability, broadly defined, is a prerequisite for effective restructuring and transition. Comprehensive macroeconomic stability would encompass more than deficit control and price stability. As Klein explains, equitable wealth and income distributions and adequate public services would have positive effects on human capital formation and on the demand for Russian production. He notes that such social welfare interventions are necessary for politically sustainable development.

Kenneth Arrow also uses the competitive-equilibrium model as a point of departure. Focusing on the effects of a radically altered price structure, he identifies impediments to investment and growth that arise as a consequence of rapid change. He stresses the need for government to help finance economic restructuring.

Victor Polterovich refutes the proposition that efficient market institutions will arise spontaneously. He identifies a variety of "institutional traps" that have hobbled the Russian economy as a result of unguided transition. He explains that narrowly conceived macroeconomic policies have contributed to the formation of socially inefficient institutions.

Irma Adelman uses South Korea to illustrate the importance of government leadership in economic development. She shows that discrepancies between the existing Russian economic system and a dynamic market system should be reduced gradually so that undue disruption does not cause systemic breakdowns along the way. Castigating the "Washington Consensus," she praises Korean industrial policies including subsidized credit, tariff protection, and foreign exchange controls.

Part Two: Economic Crisis

Russian parallels with Weimar Germany are troubling. Few then foresaw that the austerity imposed by a misconceived peace settlement would give rise to fascism. As noted by John Maynard Keynes, the good intentions of American President Woodrow Wilson were for naught due to lack of awareness of the actual economic conditions in vanquished Germany.

Part Two delineates the economic crisis in Russia. In the first chapter, I provide historical perspective by reviewing the rise and fall of the Soviet command economy with particular attention to *perestroika*. Gorbachev was intent on revitalizing socialism by decentralizing the economy and introducing market forces. He stumbled, not because of gradualism per se or because of opposition within the Communist Party. Rather his hasty and inconsistent initiatives, along with blind refusal to allow prices to be market-determined, resulted in an incompatible mix of government and market.

Georgi Arbatov, an original member of President Yeltsin's economic advisory council, criticizes foreign advocates of shock therapy for ignoring the characteristics of the system they sought to eradicate. Endangering not only Russia's economy but also its fledgling democracy, the failings of radical reform provoked resistance to further reforms and spurred a resurgence of the Communist Party.

The next chapter was written by Sergei Glaziev, the minister of foreign economic relations who resigned in the wake of the shelling of the Duma in 1993. Providing a historical overview of economic relations between Russia and the West, Glaziev argues that the influx of foreign goods may cause an irreversible erosion in Russian technological potential.

Yevgeny Gavrilenkov surveys macroeconomic developments up until the financial collapse in August of 1998. He shows that the flaws in the "stabilization" program impeded economic restructuring and growth.

Andrei Belousov and Lance Taylor draw parallels to economic transition in China. They highlight large-scale capital flight from Russia and the failure to channel savings into domestic investment. Emphasis is given to the three-way interface of financial institutions, business enterprises, and government.

The laissez-faire approach facilitated thievery on the part of a corrupt new elite. "Mafia" extortion operates as a substitute tax system that drains off resources which might otherwise be tapped by the treasury. The largely parasitic banking system, oriented toward speculation and the financing of imports rather than long-term investment, was the recipient of large subsidies, including high rates of interest on government debt reserved exclusively for Russian banks. Even more worrisome is the veiled transfer of Russia's mineral wealth to a well-connected few, along with tax evasion on the profits from that wealth. Michael Bernstam and Andrei Sitnikov describe the development of a malignant banking system. Svetlana Glinkina, Andrei Grigoriev, and Vakhtang Yakobidze look more deeply and broadly at the entrenchment of an unprincipled elite.

It is to be expected that any radical change in the social and economic order would be chaotic and painful. Vladimir Mikhalev shows that the costs of economic transition have been borne very unequally. A marked decline in real wages has been accompanied by widespread poverty, especially in rural areas not blessed with natural resources. Amidst dislocation and criminalization, redistribution in favor of an unprincipled elite spurs capital flight and luxury imports rather than investment in the economy.

Part Three: Policy Agenda

Rather than a minimal-government strategy, we propose a balanced approach. On the one hand, government should not stifle competition and undermine market discipline. On the other hand, it has the responsibility to create an institutional framework and macroeconomic context favorable to private enterprise, as well as to ensure that the benefits of the new economic order are widely shared. Moreover, there is much that government can do to protect and support the development of particular industries, though it is no less vital not to coddle obsolete legacies of the past, impeding the emergence of dynamic new businesses.

In the first chapter of Part Three, I provide an overview of the case for activist government. One overriding concern is for government to ensure adequate aggregate demand for Russian goods, which is a daunting challenge in the context of an open, criminalized economy with an obsolete capital stock. I also discuss the potential and hazards of development policy and recommend the creation of a development council to upgrade the competence, integrity and accountability of government.

Privatization alone will not suffice to modernize Russian industry. David Ellerman, Dmitri Kuvalin, and I propose restructuring agencies to set in motion procedures for dismantling enterprises and revitalizing viable components. Suitable institutions of corporate governance must be put in place to attract capital and install competent and responsible managers.

Stanislav Menshikov addresses the problem of aggregate demand in a transitioning economy. He fits a Keynesian-Leontief macroeconomic model to Russian data for the period from 1990 to 1998. While the parameter estimates can be questioned, the model clarifies the case for intentional widening of the budget deficit in the short run. He provides evidence that reduction in the value-added tax would not only lead to higher levels of capacity utilization but would also soon bolster government revenue.

The severing of close economic ties between Russia and the other Soviet Republics was a major factor in the economic deterioration of the 1990s. Ruslan Grinberg explains how fears of renewed Russian domination have thwarted efforts to create a trading bloc that would restore trade flows. Advocating substantial economic reintegrations, Grinberg emphasizes the importance of stable exchange rates, reliable payments mechanisms, and compatible legal institutions.

The banking system aside, the most subsidized sectors of the economy have been agriculture and coal. Geliy Shmeliov, Bruce McWilliams, John Giraldez, and Alexander Vedrashko analyze the plight of the agricultural sector. Although the decline in agricultural output has been less than the decline in industrial output, it should be noted that the agricultural sector receives a larger share of government subsidies than industry, excluding government support for military suppliers.

Alexander Arbatov and Edit Kranner examine the coal industry. This heavily subsidized and politically powerful industry is a liability rather than an asset for Russia. Only about half the coal mines would have economic potential even after extensive layoffs and major new investments.

Eric Martinot and Vladimir Usiyevich show what the government can do to accelerate adoption of technological opportunities to conserve energy. Enormous energy resources made extremely wasteful practices possible under the Soviet system. With energy prices now at world levels, improved efficiency is essential for Russian industry to become competitive. Energy conservation would also help government and households better afford expenditures necessary to raise living standards.

Dwight Jaffee and Olga Kaganova next describe real estate markets in Russia. Numerous institutional obstacles and requirements must be dealt with before real estate markets can facilitate renovation and construction of non-luxury housing. The authors illustrate the need for government to be not only more constructive but also less obstructive.

While Yeltsin sought to divest government assets, apparently in part to build a base of wealthy supporters, the Russian parliament resisted. Some enterprises have not been privatized, and the state has substantial stakes in many privatized enterprises. Alexander Nekipelov provides a scheme whereby the government becomes an active shareholder to spur improvement in the quality of management.

Despite its high literacy rate and notable accomplishments in science and engineering, post-Soviet Russia has done surprisingly little to preserve and build its own human capital. Michael Intriligator, Serguey Braguinsky, and Vitaly Shvydko direct attention to the potential for the science and technology sector to become a leading force for the revival of the overall economy. They favor a government program to support, in particular, information technology.

The final chapter presents recommendations developed by the Economic Transition Group (ETG), a network of economists critical of the shock therapy approach. In the five sections of the chapter, ETG:

(1)   suggests ways to improve the institutional framework and government capacity;
(2)   proposes measures to combat criminality;
(3)   presents principles for a favorable macroeconomic context;
(4)   addresses development policy (industrial policy broadly conceived); and
(5)   lays out social requirements for a democratic market system.

Balanced Approach

The aim of economic transition is for the market to replace government as the primary mechanism for coordinating economic activity. Yet government is an integral element of any economic system. Only government can establish social order, without which productive interactions among economic agents are stifled. It is the responsibility of government to build market-enhancing institutions, to establish favorable macroeconomic conditions, and to invest in both economic infrastructure and human capital. Activist government, needed to oversee an orderly transition, has the potential to ensure equitable distribution and spur economic development.

Contrary Western advice served the myopic self-interest of the West: the weakening of a long-standing adversary, the opening up of a reservoir of natural resources, and the creation of a new market. Later chapters examine specific ways in which quick liberalization-privatization-stabilization catered to Western interests.

It appears that some proponents of shock therapy may have had their own interests in mind as well. Consider, for example, the primary adviser on Russian privatization, Harvard economist Andrei Shleifer. Between 1992 and 1997, the U.S. government disbursed to Shleifer's research institute more than $40 million for advising the Russian government. Shleifer influenced the terms of privatization for oil and other companies in which he gained ownership interests. Shleifer and Harvard are now being sued by the U.S. Justice Department for alleged improprieties, including failure to provide "impartial, unbiased advice" (Robbins et al. 2000). Corrupt Russian insiders also profited while the Russian nation, on the advice of Western economists, forfeited its wealth at pennies on the dollar.

Of course the transition strategy adopted by Russia was not simply a consequence of Western misadvice. Russian reformers, after the inhumanity and inefficiency of Soviet rule, were led astray by yet another utopian vision imported from the West—this time capitalist rather than communist. Contemptuous of the existing system, utopianism obstructs adaptation to current realities. Presented here instead is a balanced approach that accepts the mixed capitalist-socialist nature of modern market economies.

Given the deterioration of the Russian state, skeptics may feel that our policy suggestions for activist government are utopian in today's context. We take a more affirmative view and give priority to revitalizing rather than dismantling the state. A balanced reform strategy, along with improvement in government capability, will allow Russia to achieve widely shared prosperity.

References

Åslund, Anders. 1992. "A Critique of Soviet Reform Plans," in Anders Åslund, ed., *The Post-Soviet Economy: Soviet and Western Perspectives*. Pp. 167–180. London: Pinter Publishers.

————. 1995. *How Russia Became a Market Economy*. Washington, DC: The Brookings Institution.

Blanchard, Olivier J., Kenneth A. Froot, and Jeffrey D. Sachs, eds. 1994. *The Transition in Eastern Europe: Vol. 1, Country Studies*. Chicago and London: University of Chicago Press.

Brada, Josef C. 1993. "The Transformation from Communism to Capitalism: How Far? How Fast?" *Post-Soviet Affairs* 9(2): 87–110.

Fischer, Stanley. 1994. "Russia and the Soviet Union Then and Now," in Olivier J. Blanchard, Kenneth A. Froot, and Jeffrey D. Sachs, eds., *The Transition in Eastern Europe: Vol. 1, Country Studies*. Pp. 221–252. Chicago and London: University of Chicago Press.

Gorbachev, Mikhail. 1987. *Perestroika: New Thinking for Our Country and the World*. New York: Harper and Row.

Granville, Brigitte. 1995. *The Success of Russian Economic Reforms*. Washington, DC: Brookings Institution.

Henry, James S., and Marshall Pomer. 1998a. "Can Russia Save Russia?" *The Nation* 267(8): 5–6.

————. 1998b. "A Pile of Ruble." *The New Republic* 219(10): 20–21.

International Monetary Fund, The World Bank, Organization for Economic Cooperation and Development, European Bank for Reconstruction and Development (IWOE). 1990. *The Economy of the USSR: Summary and Recommendations*. Washington, DC: World Bank.

Layard, Richard, and John Parker. 1996. *The Coming Russian Boom: A Guide to New Markets and Politics*. New York: Free Press.

Lipton, David, and Jeffrey D. Sachs. 1992. "Prospects for Russia's Economic Reforms." *Brookings Papers on Economic Activity* 2: 213–265.

Nelson, Lynn D., and I. Y. Kuzes. 1994. *Property to the People: The Struggle for Radical Economic Reform in Russia*. New York: M. E. Sharpe.

Phelps, Edmund S. 1992. Comment on Lipton and Sachs (1992): 273–276.

Robbins, Carla Anne, Gary Fields, and Steve Leisman. 2000. "U.S. to File Suit Against Harvard Over Russia Foreign-Aid Program." *Wall Street Journal*, September 26: A4

Sedaitis, Judith B., ed. 1997. *Commercializing High Technology: East and West*. Lanham, MD: Rowman & Littlefield.

Shleifer, Andrei, and Daniel Treisman. 1998. *The Economics and Politics of Transition to an Open Market Economy: Russia*. Paris: OECD.

Summers, Lawrence H. 1994. Comment on Fischer (1994): 252–255.

Talbott, Strobe. 1998. "Dealing with Russia in a Time of Troubles." *The Economist*, November 21: 54–56.

Wedel, Janine. 1998. *Collision and Collusion: The Strange Case of Western Aid to Eastern Europe 1989–1998*. New York: St. Martin's Press.

PART ONE

Economic Role
of Government

1

Transition and Government

Marshall Pomer

It is tempting to attribute the disappointments of Russian economic reform to bad implementation of good policy. Part One of this book offers a more sweeping critique. Russian reformers, placing too much faith in the free market, gave too little attention to government's role.

At the core of Western economic orthodoxy is the competitive-equilibrium model (the "neoclassical paradigm"), which provides an individualistic and ahistorical conception of the market economy.[1] Applied superficially to the challenge of economic transition, this idealized image of an economy promotes exaggerated expectations for the free market. Influenced by Western advice founded on the neoclassical paradigm, the architects of Russian reform underestimated the requirements of successful economic transition.

This chapter directs attention to the potential role of government during economic transition, and afterward. The first section introduces the competitive-equilibrium model and explains its misuse in justifying shock therapy. The second section examines the limitations of the neoclassical paradigm in light of the challenges of transition. The third section considers a broad range of institutional factors that affect the functioning of a market system. The fourth addresses macroeconomic factors. The fifth considers industrial policy—intervention to support particular sectors of the economy. (A more general term would be "development policy.") The final section presents a taxonomic model that summarizes government responsibilities.

Economic Orthodoxy

A powerful analytical device,[2] the competitive-equilibrium model formalizes the "invisible hand." By assumption, the economy is always in a state of equilibrium with everyone maximizing their own self-interest through acts of buying and selling. Under ideal assumptions, it can be logically deduced that the market, affording freedom to engage in mutually beneficial exchanges, automatically transforms pursuit of self-interest into material abundance.

The essence of an economy, according to this model, is market-mediated interaction among firms and households. With profit as motivation, competition forces firms to respond to household preferences. Prices direct all economic agents to minimize their use of those resources that most need to be economized. In addition, price adjustments ensure supply-demand equilibrium in all markets, implying that all resources are fully utilized and nothing is wasted. Thus the market system, or rather the ideal form represented by the model, is efficient.[3]

There is no place for government in the basic competitive-equilibrium model. The model suggests that if there is a problem with the economy the reason is that government is intruding. Thus the primary challenge of economic reform, whether in the context of economic transition or economic development, is to take government out of the economy. Government's role is limited to either eliminating discrepancies from the neoclassical assumptions or correcting market failures caused discrepancies that cannot be eliminated.

Thus the competitive-equilibrium model, applied superficially, supports the shock therapy strategy.[4] Presumably, if government would only get out of the way, then the free market would allocate resources efficiently and create prosperity. Some reformers apparently welcomed destruction of the administrative capacity of the Russian government (Stavrakis 1993).[5]

Transition to capitalism requires three steps:

(1) *liberalization*—ending price controls and lifting constraints on international trade and capital flows;

(2) *privatization*—transferring public assets to private owners; and

(3) *stabilization*—stabilizing the value of the currency, primarily by cutting government spending.

To the extent these steps are taken, it can be said that the free-market ideal embodied in the competitive-equilibrium model is realized. Liberalization provides the freedom, privatization the incentives, and stabilization the environment so that private enterprise can thrive.

The proposition that the market would adjust on its own without activist government proved fallacious in Russia. Foreign competition and a radical shift in the price structure stunned industry. Amidst a sharp drop in standards of living, rash privatization transferred the assets of an inherently wealthy country to a politically powerful elite. Narrowly conceived stabilization, which rationalized government nonpayment of wages, encouraged corruption and the de-monetization of the economy (Woodruff 1999a). The collapse in investment and loss of technological potential has transformed Russia into a source of raw materials rather than a modern industrial economy.[6]

Limitations of the Paradigm

The competitive-equilibrium model usefully identifies the three essential elements of a market system: market-determined prices, profit maximization, and competitive markets. In the Soviet command system, as in a market system, prices guided consumers and producers to economize on scarce resources, but prices were determined by government rather than by the market. While in a market system businesses produce whatever maximizes profit, in the Soviet system government authorities decided what was to be produced. The Soviet economy relied on government oversight, rather than market competition, to curb malfeasance and incompetence.

The shock therapy strategy assumed that the three essential elements of a market system would emerge spontaneously once the command system was terminated. This did not happen. Government needs to take deliberate steps to foster the emergence of a functional market system. Government also must play a major supplementary role until the market system is well developed, and a complementary role even after the three essential elements are fully in place.

Prices

As a matter of social policy, during the Soviet era food staples and housing were priced far below cost. Energy was kept very inexpensive relative to world standards in order to support diversion of resources to the military-industrial complex. The effect of prices on producers was muted because they were allowed to violate their budgets if necessary to fulfill quotas set by the central plan. Since government-set prices so poorly reflected economic costs, it was falsely assumed by many economists that decontrolling prices would allow the Russian economy to leap forward. Price controls discourage supply and stimulate black market activity; therefore social safety nets would have to serve as the primary line of defense for those adversely affected by price shifts.

During *perestroika,* increased enterprise autonomy in the face of inflexible government-set prices spelled disaster (Chapter 9). Acute shortages became endemic and the black market flourished. On January 2, 1992, the sudden removal of price controls promised a quick fix. Inventory did reappear on store shelves, but price increases were enormous, putting many goods out of the reach of all but the newly rich. The alignment of input prices with world levels hobbled industry, which operated with technology designed for a very different price structure (see Chapter 6 by Arrow). Because price changes sharply lowered industrial profits, government revenue fell.

The violent shift in the price structure and the rapid inflation could have been mitigated if price increases had been temporarily restrained, though not frozen, by government controls during an interim period. The "ruble overhang" (the build up of savings deposits because of shortages in goods and the absence of securities) could have been addressed by temporary restraints on large withdrawals and by mandatory conversion of a percentage of large deposits into long-term government debt. Apart from the merits of temporary price controls to restrain inflation and to slow change in the price structure, price regulation is imperative for monopolies and "essential facilities" (Van Siclen 1996).

Profit

Impressed by the postwar recovery of Western Europe, Soviet leaders came to realize that decentralization together with profit maximization could bring economic benefits to socialism. Starting in the 1960s, they increased enterprise autonomy and began using profit as a measure of performance and as a partial basis for managerial and worker compensation. However, profit maximization was far subordinate to plan targets, and the two other essential elements of a market system—market-determined prices and competitive markets—were absent. Thus the weakening of government controls neither improved economic efficiency nor stimulated innovation (Brus and Laski 1989). Likewise, in the absence of proper conditions, increases in enterprise autonomy under *perestroika* and subsequent privatization during shock therapy contributed to the further worsening of economic performance.

Efficient use of resources has been secondary to the struggle for control over previously state-owned enterprises and their assets, including natural resources (Kleiner 1998). Managers have given first priority not to maximizing profits but rather to expanding their ownership, while malfeasance and mafia intrusion have led to asset stripping and embezzlement (Blasi et al. 1997). Where privatization has given workers significant ownership stakes, managers have continued costly paternalistic practices in order to maintain worker allegiance (Standing 1996). Profitability actually interferes with managerial efforts to obtain shares from employees at minimal prices. High profits also increase the risk of extortion, invite hostile takeovers, and attract the unwelcome scrutiny of tax inspectors.

As we shall discuss, the requirements for a well-functioning market system include more than market-determined prices, profit maximization, and competitive markets. Autonomous profit-maximizing firms, even in competitive markets, do not automatically serve the public interest. (Consider MMM and other Ponzi-type investment funds that swept through Russia in the mid-1990s.) The unstable, criminal environment in Russia has encouraged tax evasion and a short-term time horizon inimical to investment.[7] Particularly harmful has been a criminalized banking sector, which has not only undermined financial intermediation but also has resulted in an unreliable payments system (see Chapter 14). Suitable institutions—including corporate governance, government controls, and even the moral compunctions of owners and managers—are needed to channel profit maximization to serve the public interest.

Competition

In the Soviet economy, most products were supplied by monopolies. There were no wholesalers to provide backup inventory, and the black market came to be relied upon to remedy unplanned shortages. With shock therapy, it was hoped that competitive markets would emerge overnight.[8] Instead, organized crime has flourished and new anticompetitive structures have evolved, spearheaded by banks controlled by "the oligarchs" (Chapters 14 and 15).Without competition, firms are not compelled to be efficient, to invest, or to be responsive to customers; and they are inclined to respond to increased demand by raising prices rather than by increasing production.

Wholesalers and middlemen are important not only to forestall shortages but also to mitigate the power of monopolies. One important role of government early in transition is to encourage the growth of wholesalers and middlemen and protect them from criminal infiltration. There is also a government role in dismantling monopolies that are legacies from the Soviet era (see Chapter 18) and in disallowing mergers that would substantially reduce competition. To avoid favoritism and increase competition, it is vital to minimize licensing requirements for new businesses and open all government contracts to public bidding. Opening the economy to capital inflows will enhance competition so long as foreign investors are not attracted primarily by the prospect of eliminating Russian competitors.

While in general it is crucial to encourage competition, in some circumstances it may be beneficial to support the formation of conglomerates or other semi-monopolistic structures (see Chapter 7). Economies of scale may require a single or a few producers. Limited competition facilitates profitability, thereby generating "franchise value." The creation of franchise value aids the emergence of responsible financial intermediaries. Profitability encourages long-term time horizons and discourages both capital flight and excessive speculation. In general, firms need ample profits to survive demand fluctuations and make investments. With external financing unavailable for most Russian firms, healthy profits are needed not only to finance investment but also to maintain working capital.

Beyond the Paradigm

The complications regarding prices, profit maximization, and competition show that a laissez faire approach is not promising. To comprehend more fully the challenges facing the Russian government, it is helpful to consider drawbacks of the orthodox economic model that go beyond lack of realism. The neoclassical paradigm diverts attention away from critical issues in economic transition. Government initiatives are needed to address problems of change, criminalization, de facto colonialization, and inequality.

Transition is necessarily about change. Fundamental to the competitive-equilibrium model is the notion of equilibrium, which is inherently static. As Professor Arrow emphasizes in his chapter, the rudimentary competitive-equilibrium model does not consider time to be a factor, and even the most elaborate neoclassical models slight its importance. Professor Klein suggests that the "dynamics of disequilibrium," an erudite neoclassical topic, has nothing pertinent to offer to understanding economic transition. The applicability of the notion of equilibrium is also diminished, as Professor

Tobin notes, because of the sheer magnitude of the economic reallocations required for successful transition.

While theft, extortion, and malfeasance have major economic effects, they do not exist in the competitive-equilibrium model. It is assumed that income results only from providing value to others. The assumption that all exchanges are voluntary and mutually advantageous allows criminal activity to be seen as a consequence of prohibitions interfering with the free market. Since firms preyed upon by criminals are less able to survive market competition, it is also argued that criminality is self-eliminating.

While the neoclassical model reveals the benefits from a single world economy, it ignores the hazards of merging disparate economies and the social costs of "economic colonization." The imposition of a new price structure can be crippling, and demand for domestic production can collapse. While advantages to the recipient developed countries, cross-border capital flows facilitate tax evasion and asset stripping; encourage speculation that jeopardizes currency stability; put upward pressure on interest rates; and discourage real investment.

The neoclassical paradigm disregards inequality. The theoretical proof of the superiority of the market economy is dependent on the Pareto definition of optimality, which does not take distribution of income, or wealth, into account. (A society in which a small elite lives in splendid munificence and all others struggle near subsistence might be ranked higher by the Pareto criterion than one in which prosperity is widely shared.) A theorem of neoclassical economics posits that an initial reallocation of endowments can ensure an equitable distribution, but this notion of an initial redistribution has little relevance to a real world that evolves on the basis of existing conditions. Furthermore, the ideology of a free-market system is inconsistent with progressive taxation and social spending. Also, highly unequal accumulation of wealth may enable a powerful few to prevent government action that does not serve their ends.

Finally, the competitive-equilibrium model directs attention toward characteristics of individuals—tastes (needs and wants), technology (capabilities of economic agents), and endowments (resources owned by economic agents). More crucial, especially for guiding economic transition, are the characteristics of the economic context within which individual maximization takes place. A market system will produce widely shared prosperity and properly integrate Russia into the world economy only if the institutional framework and macroeconomic conditions are sound.

Institutional Framework

Functional markets and well-performing firms do not exist in a vacuum. The institutional framework facilitates market interactions and channels self-interested behavior in productive directions, both within and outside of organizational structures. In the absence of suitable institutions, pursuit of self-interest leads to uncooperative behavior, criminalization, and social disorder. Even advocates of shock therapy now acknowledge that Russian transition has been obstructed by the lack of institutional infrastructure (e.g., Sachs and Pistor 1997; World Bank 1999).

Only government can define property rights, provide genuine security for private property, and ensure enforcement of contracts without the use of criminal violence. Institutional checks and balances within government are crucial to minimize corruption as well as to prevent predatory government intrusion in the market. An effective system of taxation, including mechanism of tax compliance, requires extensive legislation, a strong bureaucracy, and the development of compatible social mores.

Institutional formation is a gradual process in which the new is fashioned out of the old, a consideration that supports adoption of a gradualist strategy to economic transition (Elster et al. 1998, Murrell 1995). It took centuries to evolve the laws, norms, and organizational structures that allowed Western economies to develop. [9] In Russia, where private enterprise was banished for seventy years, centralized mechanisms of social order and economic coordination were dismantled without putting new trust-enhancing institutions in their place (Hendley et al. 1997).

Soviet managers had relied on illegal methods to fulfill the central plan, making them vulnerable to corruption charges that were never brought so long as loyalty was shown to their superiors. Thus the Soviet system was built less on high moral standards than on shared guilt and vulnerability—a cynical principle that is also used by the Russian mafia (Handelman 1997). Lack of legal institutions coupled with the vestiges of the old power structure caused a highly corrupt and criminalized environment to emerge once institutions of government surveillance were dismantled.[10] Managers and owners are now routinely subjected to violence from criminal organizations seeking tribute (Sergeyev 1998).

Entry of new businesses has been impeded by fear of criminal demands and by corrupted networks inherited from Soviet times (Hendley et al. 1997). An environment conducive to lawful, new businesses is crucial since the dynamism of a transitioning economy comes largely from such firms (Kornai 1993). The rule of law and cooperation based on trust are fundamental to an innovative market economy.

Financial intermediation, a prerequisite for robust investment, requires not only trust but also an information-rich environment (Caprio 1994). Government has the responsibility to prevent fraud, promote supply of valid information about products, enforce modern accounting standards, and foster creation and dissemination of knowledge relevant for technological progress.[11] Viable bankruptcy procedures are also critical in order to encourage lenders by making collateral meaningful.

Managerial performance is a key institutional concern, whether to stem incompetence and malfeasance or to provide innovative leadership. In the Soviet era, government ministries were supposed to oversee managerial performance. Today Russian managers are largely insulated from stockholder action or hostile takeovers (Buck et al. 1998). Sound rules of corporate governance and strict disclosure requirements are vital to strengthen stockholders' rights to demand accountability. In mature market economies, strong financial intermediaries also play a major role in overseeing managers (Aoki and Kim 1995). Dismissal of corrupt managers, allowing transfer of control to law-abiding and competent owners, requires an effective legal system.[12] Tax authorities also can help by prosecuting managers and owners who engage in tax evasion and illegal capital flight.

Multinational corporations, a major institutional feature of modern economies, dominate world trade and already have a major presence within the former Soviet bloc. To hold her own, Russia will have to develop such corporate organizations, which are typically conglomerates. A key question is how to foster such entities without further giveaways to connected insiders (Chapter 7, Amsden et al. 1994). The development of competitive Russian multinationals depends also on attracting the capital and expertise of foreign partners (Chapter 17).

The neoclassical paradigm, extolling the benefits of unbridled self-interest, bolsters an individualistic ethic that can impede the functioning of the market.[13] Without a culture that fosters trust and cooperation, potential market transactions, including long-term contractual arrangements, are stifled. As Tobin points out in Chapter 4, the glorification of self-interest also conflicts with the need for leaders and voters to support economic policies that serve the nation as a whole. Given that the new Russia is in a formative stage, regard for the common good is all the more vital.

Macroeconomics of Transition

The neoclassical paradigm is ahistorical and focuses on the supply side of the economy (productive efficiency). In contrast, macroeconomic conditions are shaped by historical developments, and macroeconomic analysis emphasizes demand rather than supply.[14]

In 1990, severed control over Eastern Europe destroyed the Soviet trading bloc CMEA (Council of Mutual Economic Assistance). Demand shocks continued as other markets were lost with the breakup of the Soviet Union the following year. Aggregate demand for Russian goods was further eroded by a massive inflow of imports, sharp cuts in both social and military spending, and cessation of government funding for enterprise investment. The closure of obsolete Russian enterprises, though essential to reallocate resources, meant loss of demand for their suppliers and loss of household income. A gradualist approach, taking into account interdependence of economic activity, would have mitigated the problem of inadequate demand

(Murrell 1993). Escalating corruption and economic inequality also sapped demand by concentrating purchasing power in an elite oriented toward capital flight and imported luxuries.[15]

Despite the contraction in aggregate demand, inflation was a serious problem during the 1990s due to cost-push factors and supply bottlenecks.[16] The collapse of the Soviet trading bloc, the breaking apart of the Soviet Union, and the canceling of the central plan disrupted supply channels. In a healthy market system, a price rise for a particular good will stimulate supply and reduce demand; but severed supply channels, monopolies, and criminal interference inhibited output response to price increases. The shift to world prices created additional inflationary pressures, especially from higher costs for energy and raw material inputs. Each price increase tended to cause subsequent increases in related products as part of a staggered cost-push process. In some cases, rising prices incited fears of impending shortages and perversely shifted demand upward.

Macroeconomic policy gave priority to reducing inflation rather than to maintaining aggregate demand.[17] This strategy not only reflected failure to recognize the cost-push basis for inflation but also showed bias against government action. The main elements of the policy were: cutting government spending, ending unfinanced deficit spending (seigniorage),[18] and guaranteeing the exchange rate (see Chapter 12). This so-called stabilization policy included the short-sighted practice of reducing the deficit by withholding government salaries, a practice that invited corruption. Given the emphasis on attracting foreign investors, little was done to restrain capital outflow or limit the inflow of unstable short-term capital. The intent was to reduce the risk premium on Russian debt in world financial markets.

Dramatic real appreciation of the ruble through 1995,[19] which made Russian products less competitive, helped stem inflation. It also made foreign assets cheaper and created fear of a collapse in the exchange rate. The resulting capital flight, including a stockpiling of foreign currency, further eroded demand. Inflation steadily declined after 1995, and by mid-1997 it could no longer be regarded as serious. But the stabilization proved illusory when large short-term capital inflows reversed direction in the wake of the 1997 financial crisis in Southeast Asia. Exorbitant interest rates and an overvalued ruble, suppressing the real side of the economy, eventually created an unsustainable burden on government finances (Malleret et al. 1999). On August 17, 1998, unable to secure additional loans from the West, the government allowed the exchange rate to fall and defaulted on its ruble-denominated debt. The ensuing inflation, once again cost-push, was attributable to a tripling of the ruble price of imports.

Expansionary Agenda

The devaluation of the ruble in 1998 offset the contraction of aggregate demand and its diversion into purchases of foreign goods. In the wake of the failed stabilization program, the printing presses were used to reduce government arrears in payment of wages and pensions and to bailout banks so as to maintain some functioning of the nation's payments system. In spite of predictions of doom, devaluation and unfinanced deficit spending boosted demand for Russian goods, thereby providing the basis for economic recovery (Sapir 1999).

Higher public investment would further stimulate recovery and growth. Such spending, which might necessitate deficit spending if prices for fuel exports were to fall, would directly increase employment and have a multiplier effect on aggregate demand. Well-designed public investment would improve international competitiveness and provide a supply-side means for combating inflation. (Former coal miners, for example, could build roads to transport farm produce that would otherwise spoil; see Chapters 21 and 22.)[20]

Presumably, growth will stimulate investment that will in turn generate more growth. Suitable market institutions, combined with a government strategy to increase public and private investment, are needed to foster long-term time horizons (Pikhomirov 2000). Then investment-led economic expansion would be self-reinforcing as Russia modernizes its economy. But large-scale private investment may require government support, as discussed in the next section.

Industrial Policy

Government's potential role extends well beyond policy initiatives to combat criminalization and reduce inequality, the management of macro-economic conditions, and the creation of market institutions. Industrial policy—government intervention to foster development of particular sectors of the economy—also merits consideration.

From a neoclassical perspective, industrial policy is regarded as unwarranted intrusion in the market (Itoh et al. 1991). Presumably no sector has special importance or needs that warrant government guidance and assistance. Industrial policy can become the garb to hide the soft budget constraints of enterprises with political clout, thereby fostering rent seeking and stifling adjustments and innovations. An obstacle to globalization, industrial policy can impede the international flow of products and capital; and it can lead to isolation from the world economy. Free trade theoretically maximizes world output, providing a basis for a higher standard of living for all (Edwards 1993).[21] Removal of limitations on inflow and outflow of capital presumably is important to attract foreign investors (Ries and Sweeney 1997).

The very idea of industrial policy is in apparent conflict with the liberalization-privatization-stabilization requirements of transition. Complete liberalization would prohibit any restraints on international flows of goods and capital.[22] Total privatization precludes government support for enterprise investment. Austerity for the sake of stabilization disregards the evidence of insufficient demand for industrial production.

Despite the apparent conflict with economic transition, there is another story to be told about industrial policy (see Chapter 8 by Adelman on the "Korean miracle"). Virtually all successful modern economies have relied upon government intervention to support industrialization. In the nineteenth century, the United States and Germany caught up with England by protecting nascent industries with high import barriers. An important feature of the resurgence of Europe after World War II was strict restraint on imported consumer goods. Japan, Southeast Asia, and China all had their growth spurts while providing government finance to industry and maintaining high trade barriers.

In light of the problems of change from one economic environment to another and the transformation of the economy into little more than a source of raw materials, there is a strong case for industrial policy in Russia. It is a rational response to the economic crisis to provide assistance in the short run so that industry can become internationally competitive in the long run. In any case, until market institutions strengthen and industry rebounds, industrial policy is here to stay. Realistic design, conscientious implementation, and careful evaluation are vital, with adjustments made on the basis of results.

The best way to mitigate international competition is to ensure that the exchange rate is not high (Bruton 1998), and thus the radical devaluation of 1998 has been salutary. Government help with the financing of investment through some form of development bank, if prudently administered, would also be beneficial. Industrial policy, broadly conceived also involves restrictions on currency convertibility and capital outflows to increase availability of funds for investment in domestic industry; development and price regulation of basic economic infrastructure, including transportation, communications, and utilities; and support for science and education, including incentives to encourage research and development.

A Simple Empirical Model

The rudimentary competitive-equilibrium model does not distinguish one commodity from another. In the real world, however, the potential role of government is far different for a barrel of oil than for a shoeshine. This section presents a simplified empirical model of the Russian economy that distinguishes four spheres of production:

- basic industry and agriculture
- mineral wealth
- government services and market infrastructure
- small business

Unlike the neoclassical model, the four-sphere model provides an analytic framework that directs attention to actual economic conditions (Pomer 1999). In each sphere, the challenges facing government are categorically different.

Sphere One: Industry and Agriculture

Sphere One consists of the capital-intensive core of the economy: manufacturing, construction, and agriculture. The largest of the four spheres, it accounts for close to two-fifths of employment. Given the human costs and democratic demands, the acute crisis in this sphere necessitates government assistance. Moreover, due to its size, the revival of Sphere One is key for increasing demand in other spheres, especially the service sector (Sphere Four).

According to the competitive-equilibrium model, restraints on competition and controls on prices undermine the efficient operation of a market system. However, the opening of the Russian economy to foreign competition and the introduction of a radically changed price structure contributed to the devastation of Sphere One. Industrial output fell by more than half during the 1990s, and investment dropped by close to 80 percent.[23] Faced with sharps decline in output, employment, and productivity in agriculture, rural Russia has been devastated (Wegren 2000). Much of post-Soviet Russia now consists of economically depressed settlements built around huge obsolete factories, farms, or coal mines.[24]

Failing to revitalize the economy, privatization entrenched managers not well attuned to a market environment and facilitated mafia infiltration (Sergeyev 1998). Privatized enterprises, lacking marketing capabilities and financial resources, have done little long-term investment. Typically overstaffed, many remain burdened with paternalistic social costs inherited from the Soviet era (Standing 1996). Those able to survive have depended upon interenterprise arrears, barter, nonpayment of taxes and wages, and ad hoc subsidies (McKinsey 1999). For many companies, government connections are a way "to protect themselves against the market rather than. join it" (Gaddy and Ickes 1998, 54).[25]

Rather than prop up firms lacking potential, it would be better to facilitate the movement of labor and capital to lawful, dynamic businesses (Clarke 1998). However, market discipline, even with improvements in the macroeconomic and institutional contexts, will not suffice to revitalize Sphere One. As discussed in the previous section and in Part Three of this book, intelligent industrial policy is needed as well.

The sharp devaluation in August 1998 radically altered the macro-economic context and has been vital in starting a revival of this sphere.[26] Substantial energy export taxes, which the IMF had previously prevented Russia from using, have also made for a more expansionary macroeconomic context by lowering domestic energy prices below world levels (see Sphere Two).[27]

Sphere Two: Natural Resources

The competitive-equilibrium model misses the essential issue in Sphere Two: Who is to benefit from the nation's vast inherent natural wealth? Basic to the neoclassical paradigm is the idea that private ownership is superior to public ownership. This presumption provided cover for the virtual giveaway of Sphere Two, which consists of enterprises that control Russia's natural resources, including abundant reserves of energy and valuable ores. Many of the state-owned enterprises that extract, refine and market Russia's natural riches were privatized through rigged auctions in conjunction with the loans-for-shares program (Blasi et al. 1997).[28] Notwithstanding its limitations, continued public ownership would have provided a direct mechanism for government to capture the gains from exporting the nation's mineral wealth.

Until the mid-1980s, oil was Russia's most valuable natural resource, but by 1990 natural gas had eclipsed oil in importance (Dienes et al. 1994).[29] With a sharp drop in investment during the 1990s, oil production has fallen steadily while equipment and pipelines have deteriorated (Bater 1996). Foreign companies have been eager to furnish technology and financing, but Russian capitalists have been leery of losing control. Fearful of being taken advantage of by the West, parliament has been reluctant to facilitate foreign partnerships.

To avoid creation of monopsonies as a result of having departments privatized separately, the government ministry responsible for the gas industry was turned into one giant firm, Gazprom. By some estimates, Gazprom is the world's largest firm in terms of assets. Also, the government has maintained a dominant portion of the ownership shares, making it possible to carefully monitor revenues, though in the first years of transition government was passive. While a major rationale for privatization is to spur investment, the narrower scope of privatization in the gas industry, in comparison with the oil industry, has resulted in much higher rates of investment.

Resolute strengthening of government control is required to tax fully the economic rents from natural resources. In some cases, renationalization might be advisable, with subsequent privatization in which the government's stake is gradually reduced and careful monitoring is maintained. In any case, strict monitoring of firms in Sphere Two is necessary to ensure full taxation.[30]

Sphere Three: Public Services

Sphere Three encompasses vital services, often provided by monopolies, that government either directly supplies or strictly regulates. For such services, the invisible hand has limited applicability. This area of the economy accounts for almost one-third of employment. Maintaining and upgrading vital services are integral to establishing a healthy institutional framework for the economy. During the formative stages of economic transition, when competition is weak and sources of supply unreliable, government oversight of privately provided public services is especially critical.

Spanning eleven time zones, Russia is highly dependent on reliable, low-cost transportation and communication. Electric power, water, and sanitation utilities generally remain state-owned, typically by municipal and regional governments. An effective federal regulatory framework would place appropriate limits on both managerial autonomy and interference on the part of regional governments (Slay and Capelik 1998, Slay 1996). Unless regulation is effective or competition is intense, businesses that provide essential services are likely to throttle economic development by charging high prices while operating inefficiently.

Banks and other financial institutions are also properly regarded as market infrastructure. Strict regulation is necessary to create stability, attract deposits, and help channel private savings into capital investments. Thus far, Russian banks have failed to provide significant financing for restructuring and growth (Chapter 14). Government must regulate the banking system so that the nation will have an operative payments system and mechanisms to fund real investment. So long as the banking is underdeveloped, there is a strong case that government responsibility should extend to subsidizing private investment.

There are other public services that both affect the viability of the economy and are basic to the quality of life. These include health care, education, public safety, law, and environmental protection. A major thrust of reform has been the dismantling of social services and protections, including guaranteed employment, housing, medical care, education, and child care. An important consequence of privatization has been the curtailment of those social services that enterprises previously provided (Standing 1996, 173–184). Elimination of these obligations was expected to increase labor mobility and make enterprises more attractive to outside investors (Boycko and Shleifer 1995; Lazear and Rosen 1995). These expectations have only been partially fulfilled, while little has been done to set up a "safety net" to replace the previous comprehensive system of social support (Chapter 16).[31]

Sphere Four: Small Business

The competitive-equilibrium model has greatest applicability to Sphere Four, which covers small businesses, which are predominately in the service sector. With economies of scale less of a factor and barriers to entry low, there is a relatively high degree of competition. In accordance with the competitive-equilibrium model, it is appropriate that the role of government be more limited in this sphere than elsewhere. Indeed, excessive registration and licensing requirements, complex taxes, and restraints on terminating employees have impeded entrepreneurship (Silliman and Kayukov 1998).

Beginning in 1991, small private retail operations were started at a rapid pace in the service sectors of the larger cities. In 1992 and 1993, thousands of other service sector enterprises were converted into private firms. After 1993, formation of new businesses slowed as extortion, intimidation of competitors, and bribery became endemic (Intriligator 1997).[32] To a substantial degree, mafia tribute has displaced government taxation (Korolenko and Klein 1998). Private businesses typically require a mafia "roof" to shelter them from other mafias and from harassment by bribe-seeking government officials.

One example of government obstruction in Sphere Four is continued government control over housing. Many municipal governments, despite privatization of apartments, are still responsible for providing upkeep and maintenance and tend to hire former state enterprises that have been privatized. If each apartment building were individually responsible there would be more opportunities for new maintenance businesses to compete.[33] Discontinuing government responsibility for housing services will not stimulate growth of legitimate small businesses, however, unless organized crime is curbed (Anderson 1995).

While limiting the reach of government is consequential for the growth of Sphere Four, deliberate government action in the three other spheres is no less important. Since the spheres are intertwined, improved conditions in any one would inevitably benefit the others. It is especially critical that Sphere Two (Natural Resources) deliver the financial resources to Sphere Three (Public Services) so that it, in turn, can provide the lawful economic environment and functional market institutions essential for Sphere One and the rest of the economy. Favorable macroeconomic and institutional contexts are crucial for Sphere Four (Small Business) as well as for Sphere One (Industry and Agriculture). A government program responsive to all spheres would build market institutions, maintain aggregate demand for Russian goods, and provide judicious support for economic development.

Conclusion

Minimizing government is not a workable strategy. We used the competitive-equilibrium model as a point of departure to better our understanding of the responsibilities and potential of government in creating a healthy market economy. We scrutinized three essential elements of a market system identified by the competitive-equilibrium model (prices, profit, and competition), noted four critical factors obscured by the model (change, criminality, de facto economic colonization, and inequality), and examined the macroeconomic and institutional context. To counter the highly abstract idealization provided by the competitive-equilibrium model, we considered a simple descriptive model of the Russian economy that highlights questions whose answers will define the future of the Russian economy: Is the industrial collapse reversible? Who will benefit from Russia's abundant mineral wealth? Will public needs be met?

Encouraged by Western economic orthodoxy, Russian reformers regarded liberalization-privatization-stabilization as an instant recipe for successful transition. An appealing but superficial explanation for the failures of transition is that this shock therapy approach was incompletely implemented (McKinsey 1999, OECD 2000). Admittedly, non-transparent central bank credits, cheap energy, and arrears have allowed nonviable enterprises to stave off bankruptcy. However, ad-hoc government support, draining resources and inviting corruption, is in part a reaction to the economic and social difficulties exacerbated by the shock therapy program.

Belatedly, it is increasingly recognized that Russian reformers moved too quickly and too narrowly. Even the IMF now admits that insufficient attention was paid to institutional and legal prerequisites for liberalization and privatization (IMF 2000). However, despite the clear benefits from the devaluation of the ruble, proponents of shock therapy still downplay growth-oriented macroeconomic policy, and they continue to dismiss industrial policy out of hand (e.g., Fischer and Sahay).

The remaining chapters of Part One emphasize that the competitive-equilibrium model, superficially understood and carelessly applied, can foster antigovernment ideology, which had great appeal at the time of the

Soviet collapse. There is no doubt that the Soviet command system was oppressive and inefficient. It resulted in an economic structure that required radical change, but it also left a positive legacy of a relatively equal distribution of income along with a high level of health care and education. As is shown throughout this book, government leadership as well as market discipline is required to overhaul the economic system without squandering human resources.

Notes

1. The basic concept was developed by Adam Smith (see Chapter 4 by Tobin). The formal competitive-equilibrium model was introduced by Léon Walras in 1874 (Walras 1954). It represents the economy as a system of simultaneous equations (see Chapter 5 by Klein). For an authoritative presentation, see Mas-Colell et al. (1995). Neither Smith nor Walras were uncritical supporters of laissez faire. Smith in his *Theory of Moral Sentiments* emphasized the importance of social mores, and Walras in *The State and the Railways* emphasized the need for government regulation.

2. The analytical power of the neoclassical model derives from its methodological individualism. Not only does the model ignore government and political factors, but also it disregards sociological phenomena—including socialization and collective action. There is no interdependence or interaction among individuals or businesses except via purchases and sales in the market. Externalities (e.g., pollution, congestion, and technological spillovers) and public goods (e.g., defense, libraries) directly violate this assumption of no interdependence. While recognized in extensions of the model, such departures from the rudimentary assumptions are usually regarded as anomalous or are overlooked altogether. Implicit assumptions, addressed later in this chapter, are perfect information, complete markets, no barriers to entry, no indivisibilities or economies of scale, and no criminality. For all but the most conservative economists, violations of the assumptions justify governmental arrangements to support the market or substitute for it. However, the need for government action is likely to be more obvious without a neoclassical mindset.

3. More precisely, it is "Pareto optimal" in that the market equilibrium cannot be changed without making someone worse off. The achievement of a Pareto

optimum is predicated on the unrealistic assumption that there are no economies of scale. The convenient standard assumption of constant returns to scale obscures income distribution because it implies that firms do not make any profit other than a market-determined rate of return on capital.

4. The shock therapy approach to economic transition has been characterized as an expression of the "mood of mindless anti-governmentalism" that prevailed worldwide in the early 1990s (Heilbroner 1996, 205; see also Chapter 2 by Bogomolov). For noteworthy criticisms, see (in addition to chapters of this book) the works cited in footnote 29 of Chapter 9. For defense of shock therapy, see Layard and Parker (1996), Åslund (1995), Boycko et al. (1995), Granville (1995), Blanchard et al. (1994), Brada (1993), and Sachs (1991). Ironically, these economists stress political rather than economic considerations: the necessity to weaken the Russian government and rapidly transfer state assets to private hands in order to forestall a resurgence of communism.

5. See, for example, Shleifer and Vishny (1998). They develop the thesis that predation is the dominant feature of government involvement in most any economy, and they tout the shrinkage of the state as the primary accomplishment of the liberalization-stabilization-privatization program in Russia. They claim that any required market institutions will emerge spontaneously as a consequence of the self-interested behavior of Russian citizens, including demands by business interests that politicians establish needed government functions. On the collapse of the administrative capacity of the state, see Nagy (2000).

6. All chapters in Part One support the thesis that economic orthodoxy has misled transition policy. See also the Preface and Stiglitz (1999).

7. To further illustrate the naïveté of presuming that privatization and profit maximization would automatically benefit the nation, consider Gazprom, a privatized enterprise that controls most of Russia's huge reserves of natural gas. While Gazprom tops the list of enterprises with tax arrears, its general director, hardly wealthy during the Soviet era, made Forbe's list of billionaires. Full disclosure and strict government control are required so that the profit from Russia's mineral wealth can be taxed for the benefit of the country as a whole.

8. Bardhan and Roemer (1993) propose measures to restrain political interference in the case of state-owned enterprises. Pressing issues include the allocation of profits and the design of managerial incentives. The drawbacks

of government ownership, including bureaucratic tendency to retard innovation, are less consequential if entrepreneurs are free to establish competing firms. Efforts to implement a market system with a predominance of state-owned enterprises have not been successful (Stiglitz 1994).

9. North (1990 and 1994), who is critical of the neoclassical paradigm, ties economic development to evolution of institutions that foster productive behavior.

10. Chapters 14 and 15, emphasizing the "oligarchs" and the banking system, provide details on the criminalization of the Russian economy.

11. A potential buyer needs to trust the seller, or some other party, to provide information about the product. When information requirements are high, trust becomes more significant, as in finance (Stiglitz 1993). Thus the neoclassical assumption that all relevant information is embodied in prices (i.e., the assumption of perfect information) blatantly disregards the importance of trust. Arrow (1999) discusses the need for government to support production and dissemination of economically useful knowledge, including sanctioning temporary monopoly profits for innovators as incentives for the creation of knowledge.

12. A number of economists have given attention to the separation of ownership and control, and more generally, individual opportunism within organizations, which are issues neglected by the neoclassical model. Stiglitz (1999), taking this into account, advocates restructuring former state-owned enterprises using a radical decentralization strategy (cf. Chapter 18).

13. An individual who, in accordance with the neoclassical paradigm, is concerned exclusively with his or her own self-interest is not trustworthy. An integral feature of any society is the "socializing" of the young to have concerns other than self-interest. Fukuyama (1995), who castigates the neoclassical view that people are exclusively concerned with self-interest, develops the thesis that trust fosters economic development.

14. Shortage of demand is ruled out by the neoclassical assumption that idle resources will immediately result in price declines that quickly stimulate buying. See Tobin (1996) for further discussion of the incompatibility between the competitive-equilibrium model and Keynesian analysis focusing on the need for government to maintain an adequate level of aggregate demand.

15. Abalkin and Whalley (1999) show that the new Russian capitalists, in the absence of effective currency controls, have accumulated foreign assets rather

than invest their profits to modernize production. Chapter 17 presents a macroeconomic model in which criminality and tax evasion engender capital flight and depress aggregate demand.

16. High inflation, especially if it varies unpredictably, makes prices less informative, diverts resources into hoarding and other unproductive activity, and pushes real interest rates upward. All of these factors inhibit investment. In the extreme, foreign currency will be used as the medium of exchange; or barter will replace monetary transactions.

17. Macroeconomic policy was guided by monetarism, which appends the quantity theory of money onto the competitive-equilibrium model and generally holds that the economy will self-correct so long as there is no inflation. Its main thesis is that the money supply determines the price level, and deficit spending is regarded as invariably destructive.

18. Equivalent to "printing money," seigniorage is unfinanced government spending. In Russia it takes the form of either credits from the central bank or purchases of government debt by the central bank.

19. The index for the real exchange rate (real rubles per US dollar) went from 343.2 in December of 1992 to 60. 5 in December of 1995. It stayed close to this level until the ruble depreciation in the second half of 1998 brought the real exchange rate to 112.3, the same value as in December 1993. See Statistical Appendix, Table A7.

20. The Great Depression provides perspective. Herbert Hoover claimed that the market would self-correct, while Franklin Roosevelt launched major public investment projects. Ill-advised tax increases and monetary constraints offset the macroeconomic stimulus, and it took massive wartime deficit spending to extricate the nation.

21. Non-economists are more likely to argue that free trade conflicts with social goals and democratic national sovereignty. (e.g., Mander and Goldsmith 1996). Adjustment costs are typically severe, with losers seldom fully compensated by winners. In less developed countries, free trade can destroy the viability of indigenous cultures and communities. In developed countries, free trade tends to weaken the power of unions and environmental groups.

22. Prior to the financial collapse in August 1998, so much attention was given to the sensibilities of foreign investors in Russian government debt, that to even talk about industrial policy was regarded as a threat to Russia's future. At a seminar in February 1998 in Moscow, Brian Pinto, chief economist at the

Russian office of the World Bank, presented a "policy maker's checklist" (Buckberg and Pinto 1997) which made no mention whatsoever of industrial policy. The IMF has also consistently opposed industrial policy. For example, in March 1996 it forced Russia to cancel a scheduled tariff increase as a condition for an IMF loan (*New York Times*, 3/26/96).

23. With the Soviet economy overly concentrated in military production and other heavy industry, one might have expected expansion in light industry (e.g., food processing and textiles). To the contrary, the most resilient part of industry has been the processing of raw materials, including production of steel and aluminum. Thus Russian raw materials no longer demanded by Russian industry are now used abroad, including in the foreign manufacture of products imported back into Russia (Kotz 1997, chapter 11).

24. The coal industry is included in Sphere One because it, unlike other industries that extract mineral resources, is more of a liability than an asset to the nation (see Chapter 22). Most coal mines have no potential of being profitable due to depletion of easily accessible deposits and increases in railway costs. As is typical of Sphere One, demand is severely depressed, and deteriorating equipment is lowering productivity.

25. While Gaddy and Ickes (1998) usefully direct attention to "value-destroying enterprises," their analysis and prescriptions are simplistic (Sapir 1999; Woodruff 1999b). A critical omission is the impact of the exchange rate. For a more balanced analysis that follows Gaddy and Ickes in giving first priority to market discipline, see Ericson (1991, 1998).

26. Henry and Pomer (1998), critical of the effort to maintain a high exchange rate for the rule, predicted that devaluation would prove beneficial

27. Woodruff (1999b) rebuts the IMF contention that it is an unjustified violation of market discipline for the price of natural gas in Russia to be below world levels. The fuel that Gazprom provides to Russians cannot be exported at a higher price because the pipelines are already at full capacity.

28. The so-called oligarchs have used their political influence and media control to ensure their continued control over these resources (see Freeland 2000 and Klebnikov 2000). Media reports attributed the dismissals of Prime Ministers Sergei Kirienko and Evgeny Primakov to actions by oligarchs who objected to reductions in their control over Sphere Two (Chapter 15).

29. Production of natural gas caught up with crude oil in 1987 (in fuel equivalent). In the next eight years, gas production grew by 20 percent while oil production fell 35 percent (World Bank 1996, table 6–3).

30. Gavrilenkov (1995) examined the differentials between what producers report as their selling prices and what consuming firms report as their fuel costs (adjusted for transport costs, arrears, and sales taxes). He found that income amounting to several percent of GDP had been disappearing each year into a "black hole."

31. Startling demographic changes reflect serious deterioration in social services since 1991, including health care and public safety. Life expectancy of males has declined by six years to only about 58, and the rate of natural increase (the birthrate minus the death rate) has declined from plus two to minus six per thousand persons (Goskomstat 1997).

32. Blasi et al. (1997, xvii-xix) report annual data on new businesses. Overall growth of the service sector is reflected in Goskomstat data on expenditures by type of purchase.

33. The elimination of government responsibility for housing and utilities is important for budgetary reasons, though unless offset by other social support it would intensify the poverty problem (Struyk 1996).

References

Abalkin, Leonid I., and J. Whalley, eds. 1999. "The Problem of Capital Flight from Russia." *The World Economy* 22(3): 421–444.

Amsden, Alice, Jacek Kochanowicz, and Lance Taylor. 1994. *The Market Meets Its Match: Restructuring the Economies of Eastern Europe.* Cambridge: Harvard University Press.

Anderson, Annelise. 1995. "The Red Mafia: The Legacy of Communism," in Edward P. Lazear, ed., *Economic Transition in Eastern Europe and Russia: Realities of Reform.* Pp. 340–366. Stanford, CA: Hoover Institution Press.

Aoki, Masahiko, and Hyung-Ki Kim, eds. 1995. *Corporate Governance in Transitional Economies: Insider Control and the Role of Banks.* Washington, DC: World Bank.

Arrow, Kenneth J. 1999. "Knowledge as a Factor of Production." Keynote Address, Annual Bank Conference on Development Economics, April 28. Washington, DC: World Bank.

Åslund, Anders. 1995. *How Russia Became a Market Economy*. Washington, DC: The Brookings Institution.

Axelrod, Robert. 1986. "An Evolutionary Approach to Norms." *American Political Science Review* 80(4): 1095–1111.

Bardhan, Pranap K., and John E. Roemer, eds. 1993. *Market Socialism: The Current Debate*. New York: Oxford University Press.

Bater, James H. 1996. *Russia and the Post-Soviet Scene: A Geographical Perspective*. New York: Wiley.

Blanchard, Olivier J., Kenneth A. Froot, and Jeffrey D. Sachs, eds. 1994. *The Transitions in Eastern Europe: Vol. 1, Country Studies, Vol. 2, Restructuring*. Chicago: University of Chicago Press.

Blasi, Joseph R., Maya Kroumova, and Douglas Kruse. 1997. *Kremlin Capitalism: The Privatization of the Russian Economy*. Ithaca and London: Cornell University Press.

Boycko, Maxim, and Andrei Shleifer. 1995. "Russian Restructuring and Social Benefits," in Anders Åslund, ed., *Russian Economic Reform at Risk*. Pp. 99–118. London: Pinter.

Boycko, Maxim, Andrei Shleifer, and Robert Vishny. 1995. *Privatizing Russia*. Cambridge: MIT Press.

Brada, Josef C. 1993. "The Transformation from Communism to Capitalism: How Far? How Fast?" *Post-Soviet Affairs* 9(2): 87–110.

Brus, Wlodzimierz, and Kazimierz Laski. 1989. *From Marx to the Market: Socialism in Search of an Economic System*. Oxford: Clarendon Press.

Bruton, Henry J. 1998. "A Reconsideration of Import Substitution." *Journal of Economic Literature* 36(2): 903–936.

Buck, Trevor, Egor Filatotchev, and Mike Wright. 1998. "Agents, Shareholders and Corporate Governance in Russian Firms." *Journal of Management Studies* 35(1): 81–104.

Buckberg, Elaine, and Brian Pinto. 1997. "How Russia Is Becoming a Market Economy: A Policy Maker's Checklist." Mimeo.

Caprio, Gerard, Jr. 1994. "Banking on Financial Reform? A Case of Sensitive Dependence on Initial Conditions," in Gerard Caprio, Jr., Izak Atiyas, and James A. Hanson, eds., *Financial Reform: Theory and Experience*. Pp. 49–63. New York: Cambridge University Press.

Clarke, Simon, ed. 1998. *Structural Adjustment without Mass Unemployment?: Lessons from Russia*. Northampton: E. E. Elgar.

Dienes, L., I. Dobosi, and M. Radetzki. 1994. *Energy and Economic Reform in the Former Soviet Union: Implications for Production, Consumption and Exports, and for the International Energy Markets.* New York: St. Martin's Press.

Edwards, Sebastian. 1993. "Openness, Trade Liberalization, and Growth in Developing Countries." *Journal of Economic Literature* 31(4): 1358–1393.

Elster, Jon, Claus Offe, and Preuss Ulrichk. 1998. *Institutional Design in Post-Communist Societies: Rebuilding the Ship at Sea.* Cambridge: Cambridge University Press.

Ericson, Richard E. 1991. "The Classical Soviet-Type Economy: Nature of the System and Implications for Reform." *Journal of Economic Perspectives* 5(4): 11–27.

———. 1998. "Restructuring in Transition: Conception and Measurement." *Comparative Economic Studies* 40(2): 103–108.

Fischer, Stanley, and Ratna Sahay. 2000. "The Transition Economies After Ten Years." IMF Working Paper WP/00/30 (March).

Freeland, Chrystia. 2000. *Sale of the Century: Russia's Wild Ride from Communism to Capitalism.* New York: Times Books.

Fukuyama, Francis. 1995. *Trust: The Social Virtues and the Creation of Prosperity.* New York: Free Press.

Gaddy, Clifford G., and Barry W. Ickes. 1998. "Russia's Virtual Economy." *Foreign Affairs* 77(5): 53–67.

Gavrilenkov, Yevgeny. 1995. "Macroeconomic Stabilization and 'Black Holes' in the Russian Economy." *Hitotsubashi Journal of Economics* 36(2): 181–188.

Goskomstat. 1997. *The Demographic Yearbook of Russia.* Moscow: State Committee of the Russian Federation on Statistics.

Granville, Brigitte. 1995. *The Success of Russian Economic Reforms.* London: Royal Institute of International Affairs.

Handelman, Stephen. 1997. *Comrade Criminal: Russia's New Mafia.* New Haven: Yale University Press.

Heilbroner, Robert. 1996. "Epilogue," in Leonard Silk and Mark Silk, *Making Capitalism Work.* New York and London: New York University Press.

Hendley, Kathryn, Barry W. Ickes, Peter Murrell, and Randi Ryterman. 1997. "Observations on the Use of Law by Russian Enterprises." *Post-Soviet Affairs* 13(1): 19–41.

Henry, James S., and Marshall Pomer. 1998. "A Pile of Ruble." *The New Republic* 219(10): 20–21.

International Monetary Fund (IMF). 2000. *World Economic Outloook,* September. Washington, DC: The Fund.

Intriligator, Michael. 1997. "The Role of Institutions in the Transition to a Market Economy," in Tarmo Haavisto, ed., *The Transition to a Market Economy: Transformation and Reform in the Baltic States.* Pp. 222–240. Brookfield, VT: Edward Elgar.

Itoh, Motoshige, Kazuharu Kiyono, Masahiro Okuno-Fugiwara, and Kotaro Suzumura. 1991. *Economic Analysis of Industrial Policy.* New York: Academic Press.

Klebnikov, Paul. 2000. *Godfather of the Kremlin: Boris Berezovsky and the Looting of Russia.* New York: Harcourt.

Kleiner, George B. 1998. "Russian Enterprise Inefficiency: An Elasticity Test for Incomplete Profit Maximization," in Steven Rosefielde, ed., *Efficiency and Russia's Economic Recovery Potential to the Year 2000 and Beyond.* Pp. 209–217. Brookfield, VT: Ashgate.

Kornai, Janos. 1993. "Market Socialism Revisited," in Pranap K. Bardhan and John E. Roemer, eds., *Market Socialism: The Current Debate.* Pp. 42–68. New York: Oxford University Press.

Korolenko, Dmitri, and Steven H. Klein. 1998. "Russian Tax Collection Practices." *International Tax Journal* 24(4): 48–61.

Kotz, David (with Fred Weir). 1997. *Revolution from Above: The Demise of the Soviet System.* New York: Routledge.

Layard, Richard G., and John Parker. 1996. *The Coming Russian Boom: A Guide to New Markets and Politics.* New York: Free Press.

Lazear, Edward P., and Sherwin Rosen. 1995. "Publicly Provided Goods and Services in a Transition Economy," in Edward P. Lazear, ed., *Economic Transition in Eastern Europe and Russia: Realities of Reform.* Pp. 322–339. Stanford, CA: Hoover Institution Press.

Malleret, Thierry, Natalia Orlova, and Vladimir Romanov. 1999. "What Loaded and Triggered the Russian Crisis?" *Post-Soviet Affairs* 15(2): 107–129.

Mander, Jerry, and Edward Goldsmith, eds. 1996. *The Case Against the Global Economy: And for a Turn Toward the Local.* San Francisco: Sierra Club Books.

Mas-Colell, Andreu, Michael D. Whinston, and Jerry R. Green. 1995. *Microeconomic Theory.* New York: Oxford University Press.

McKinsey Global Institute. 1999. "Unlocking Economic Growth in Russia." Moscow: McKinsey & Co.

Murrell, Peter. 1993. "What Is Shock Therapy? What Did It Do in Poland and Russia?" *Post-Soviet Affairs* 9(2): 111–140.

————. 1995. "The Transition According to Cambridge, Mass." *Journal of Economic Literature* 33(1): 164–78.

Nagy, Piroska Mohácsi. 2000. *The Meltdown of the Russian State: The Deformation and Collapse of the State in Russia.* Northampton, MA: Edward Elgar.

North, Douglass C. 1990. *Institutions, Institutional Change, and Economic Performance.* New York: Cambridge University Press.

————. 1994. "Economic Performance Through Time." *American Economic Review* 84(3): 359–368.

Organization for Economic Cooperation and Development (OECD). 2000. *OECD Economic Survey: Russian Federation 2000.* Paris: OECD Publications.

Pikhomirov, Vladimir. 2000. *The Political Economy of Post-Soviet Russia.* New York: St. Martin's Press.

Pomer, Marshall. 1999. "Activist Government." *Studies on Russian Economic Development* 10(1): 66–70; "Ukreplenie roli gosudarstva v ekonomike Rossii v perekhodnyi period." *Problemy prognozirovaniia* 10(1): 94-101.

Ries, Christine P., and Richard J. Sweeney. 1997. *Capital Controls in Emerging Economies.* Boulder, CO: Westview Press.

Sachs, Jeffrey D. 1991. "Poland and Eastern Europe: What Is to Be Done?" in Andras Koves and Paul Marer, eds., *Foreign Economic Liberalization: Transformation in Socialist and Market Economies.* Pp. 233–246. Boulder, CO: Westview Press.

Sachs, Jeffrey D., and Katharina Pistor, eds. 1997. *The Rule of Law and Economic Reform in Russia.* Boulder, CO: Westview Press.

Sapir, Jacques. 1999. "Russia's Crash of August 1998: Diagnosis and Prescription." *Post-Soviet Affairs* 15(1): 1–36.

Sergeyev, Victor M. 1998. *The Wild East: Crime and Lawlessness in Post-Communist Russia.* Armonk, NY: M. E. Sharpe.

Shleifer, Andrei, and Robert W. Vishny. 1998. *The Grabbing Hand: Government Pathologies and Their Cures.* Cambridge: Harvard University Press.

Silliman, Emily, and Edward Kayukov. 1998. "New Company Formation in Russia: Legal Regulation," in Judith B. Sedaitis, ed., *Commercializing High Technology: East and West.* Pp. 329–353. Lanham, MD: Rowman & Littlefield.

Slay, Ben, ed. 1996. *De-monopolization and Competition Policy in Post-communist Economies.* Boulder, CO: Westview Press.

Slay, Ben, and Vladimir Capelik. 1998. "Natural Monopoly Regulation and Competition Policy in Russia." *Antitrust Bulletin* 43(1): 229–260.

Standing, Guy. 1996. *Russian Unemployment and Enterprise Restructuring: Reviving Dead Souls*. New York: St. Martin's Press.

Stavrakis, Peter J. 1993. "State Building in Post-Soviet Russia: Chicago Boys and the Decline of Administrative Capacity." Occasional Paper 254. Washington, DC: Kennan Institute for Advanced Russian Studies.

Stiglitz, Joseph E. 1993. *Information and Economic Analysis*. New York: Oxford University Press.

———. 1994. *Whither Socialism?* Cambridge, MA: MIT Press.

———. 1999. "Whither Reform? Ten Years of the Transition." Keynote Address, Annual Bank Conference on Development Economics, April 30. Washington, DC: World Bank.

Struyk, Raymond. 1996. "The Long Road to the Market," in Raymond Struyk, ed., *Economic Restructuring of the Former Soviet Bloc: The Case of Housing*. Pp. 1–69. Washington, DC: Urban Institute Press.

Tobin, James. 1996. "The Invisible Hand in Modern Macroeconomics," in *Full Employment and Growth: Further Keynesian Essays on Policy*. Pp. 5–16. Cheltenham, UK: Edward Elgar.

Van Siclen, Sally. 1996. "The Essential Facilities Concept, A Background Note." Competition Policies Roundtables, No. 5, OECD/GD 113.

Walras, Léon. 1954 (1874). *Elements of Pure Economics*. Translated by W. Jaffe. Homewood, IL: Richard D. Irwin, Inc.

Woodruff, David M. 1999a. *Money Unmade: Barter and the Fate of Russian Capitalism*. Northampton, MA: Edward Elgar.

———. 1999b. "It's Value That's Virtual: Bartles, Rubles, and the Place of Gazprom in the Russian Economy." *Post-Soviet Affairs* 15(2): 130–148.

Wegren, Stephen K. 2000. "State Withdrawal and the Impact of Marketization on Rural Russia." *Policy Studies Journal* 28 (1): 46–67.

World Bank. 1999. *Entering the 21st Century: World Development Report 1999/2000*. New York: Oxford University Press.

———. 1996. *Statistical Handbook 1996: States of the Former USSR*. Studies of Economies in Transformation, No. 21. Washington, DC: World Bank.

2

Neoliberalism

Oleg Bogomolov

Gorbachev's intent to transition to the market was met by the West with beguiling offers to share knowledge and experience. A steady stream of economists arrived from abroad, bringing advice avidly assimilated by young reformers. Chicago School neoliberalism was in vogue. Russian admirers, hastening to disown the communist faith, were won over. Many of these proselytes became even more orthodox than their new ideological heroes.

The ascent of neoliberal ideology was a relatively recent phenomenon. After the Second World War, Western European governments relied on extensive state intervention to restore production. Keynesianism, which regarded effective demand as a controllable factor key to economic revival, was a mainstay of economic policy. Foreign trade, exchange rates, and the movement of capital were regulated, and the transition to free conversion of currency took decades. Government regulation of key prices, as well as subsidies and price supports, were retained for just as long; and in agriculture and power generation extensive controls remain in effect.

But once Western Europe recovered, denationalization and deregulation became the order of the day, and neoliberal economists urged the elimination of state guidance. Thus, the methods which the West proposed for economic transformation of the Soviet Union were couched in neoliberal terms.

In July 1990, the participants at the Houston meeting of the Group of Seven (G7) commissioned the International Monetary Fund, the World Bank, the Organization for Economic Cooperation and Development, and the European Bank for Reconstruction and Development, in cooperation with the European Commission, to establish criteria for Western financial support of Soviet economic reforms. The report, released in early 1991, contained detailed recommendations.

With leading Soviet research institutes contributing to the analysis, the G7 report acknowledged the importance of a broad range of measures to facilitate adjustment. These included support for the hardest-hit social strata and for enterprises overwhelmed by sudden shifts in prices. The report stressed strict government oversight of privatization. It also gave urgency to agricultural reform and the introduction of legal and accounting institutions.

Yet priority was put on fast action, and the measures to ease adjustment were downplayed. The main concern of the more active Western advisers was to make the reforms irreversible as soon as possible. Within a year of the G7 report, President Yeltsin put into effect "shock therapy."[1]

Reform was reduced to three elements set as conditions for Western cooperation: (1) stabilization (deficit reduction and strict limits on central bank credits), (2) liberalization (abolition of price controls and the removal of restrictions on foreign trade and financial flows), and (3) privatization (Group 1991). According to the Washington Consensus,[2] as soon as these tasks were accomplished and the state got out of the way, the market would reallocate resources effectively and ensure economic growth. Such a policy appeared to be simple enough, with a few economic indicators (primarily the money supply and the budget deficit) serving as the basis for government decisions.

The reform program was directed by Western advisers holding official status in the Russian government.[3] They drew on the authority of international organizations and dominated Western public opinion. Time and again, Russia was told that it had no alternative to "big bang" liberalization and that this choice was supported by the entire Western world. Supposedly, the burden of reform had to be borne in anticipation of inevitable success. Proposals for more gradual, phased transformation were branded as antireform or procommunist.[4]

The West remained staunchly in support of Yeltsin despite his erratic behavior, evidently in fear that withdrawing support would increase the threat of communists coming to power and invite criticism of their own Russian policy. A few extracts from my own rebuttal in 1994, which I sought in vain to publish in the West, may be of interest:

> The slightest rejection of the ideals of U.S. liberalism is deplored with undisguised bitterness. . . . The radical liberals are indignant at the idea of intensifying state intervention to stop the crumbling of production, to prevent social cataclysm, chaos and further criminalization of the economy, and to support entrepreneurship. This idea instantly raises complaints about a return to the command system and provokes an outcry about making concessions to conservative directors in industry and to "Red Barons" in agriculture.

> Meanwhile, world experience especially during WWII and the postwar period shows that when destructive processes in an economy and society have gone as far as they have in this country, it is unrealistic to expect market self-regulation alone to stop them. Let me add that the successes of the Japanese economy and subsequently of the newly industrialized countries of Asia, are largely connected with the guiding influence of the state on market relations and with step-by-step reforms. . . . In removing the state (government) from the sphere of economic regulation under the impact of liberal theory, Russia has in many areas gone much farther than other capitalist countries. . . . It is now much more difficult to recreate a viable state administrative mechanism not infected with corruption and bureaucratic practices, to recreate it not as a counterweight to the market, but precisely for the sake of building a civilized and socially oriented market. (Bogomolov 1994)

On the initiative of Alexander Nekipelov and Marshall Pomer, the Economic Transition Group (ETG) was set up in 1994. It brought together prominent economists from Russia, the United States, and elsewhere who sought to develop an alternative strategy.[5] Our credo is to minimize harm in human terms and contribute to the strengthening of democratic government.

The key is neither the speed of reforms nor the degree of monetary and fiscal restraint. It is essential to avoid economic instability and build properly functioning institutions. This requires both an understanding of economic realities and a willingness to endorse activist government. There has been an underestimation of the need for adequate effective demand, a competitive environment, a functional system of commercial and investment banks, and market-compatible accounting and law.

ETG produced a widely noted, though much disparaged, joint statement addressed to the future Russian president on the eve of the 1996 elections.[6] Entitled "A New Economic Policy for Russia," it was signed by the heads of leading economic research institutes within the Russian Academy of Sciences and by seven American economists, including five Nobel Prize winners.[7] It called for a reorientation of macroeconomic policy to stimulate economic growth and the formation of a socially oriented economy. This was followed later in the same year by *Reforms as Seen by American and Russian Scientists* (Bogomolov 1996). A precursor in Russian to the important current volume, it critically examined the early Yeltsin years and set forth new directions for economic policy.

We are bound by restraints on setting a new course. Our freedom is limited by what was inherited on one side from communists and on the other side from radical neoliberals. Moreover, demands of the International Monetary Fund and international financiers pressured us to adhere to narrow prescriptions. Now that the erroneous nature of the neoliberal strategy has become so apparent, the Russo-American analyses and recommendations in this volume will no doubt enhance our courage to adopt a sensible course of reform.

Notes

1. Yegor Gaidar, acting prime minister in 1992, was initially in charge of the design and implementation of the new variant of postcommunist neoliberalism. According to an apt remark by Gregor Kolodka, one of the architects of Polish reform, Russia professed "the world's worst post-Communist neoliberalism" (*Izvestiia*, December 9, 1998).

2. The "Washington Consensus" refers to the standard set of policy recommendations worked out by agencies of the United States government, the International Monetary Fund, and the World Bank. Joseph Stiglitz, chief economist of the World Bank, caused a sensation in January 1998 with a lecture at the World Institute of Development and Economic Research (WIDER) in Helsinki (Stiglitz 1998) when he became the first major Western official to question the basic premises of the Washington Consensus.

3. The most visible of them were American Professor Jeffrey Sachs, British Professor Richard Layard, and Swedish Professor Anders Åslund.

4. Perhaps, as Julietto Chiese (1998) asserts, there is "only one reason: anti-communism. Furious anticommunism. The negation of any ideas or concepts related to socialism, to social democracy. A striving for 'ideal' capitalism."

5. The mission statement of the Economic Transition Group was published in *Problemy prognozirovaniia*. The signatories are: Leonid Abalkin, Institute of Economics, Russian Academy of Sciences (RAS); Irma Adelman, University of California, Berkeley; Alexander Arbatov, Committee for Natural Resources (RAS); Georgi Arbatov, USA–Canada Institute, RAS; Oleg Bogomolov, Institute of International Economic and Political Studies, RAS; Paul Davidson, University of Tennessee; John Kenneth Galbraith, Harvard University; Sergei Glaziev, Federal Council of the Federation of Russia; Ruslan C. Grinberg, Institute of International Economic and Political Studies, RAS; Michael D. Intriligator, University of California, Los Angeles; Viktor V. Ivanter, Institute of Economic Forecasting, RAS; Dwight Jaffee, University of California, Berkeley; A. B. Levintal, Administration of Khabarovskii Krai; Dmitri S. Lvov, Central Economic-Mathematical Institute, RAS; Valery L. Makarov, Central Economic-Mathematical Institute, RAS; Pavel A. Minakir, Center of the Far East, RAS; Alexander D. Nekipelov, Institute of International Economic and Political Studies, RAS; Nikolai I. Petrakov, Institute of Market Problems, RAS; Yuri A. Petrov, Central Economic-Mathematical Institute, RAS; Marshall Pomer, Macroeconomic Policy Institute; Stanislav S. Shatalin, Department of Economics, RAS; Nikolai P. Shmeliov, European Institute,

RAS; Stepan A. Sitarian, Institute of Foreign Economic Relations; Martin K. Spechler, University of Indiana; Lance Taylor, New School for Social Research; Lester K. Thurow, MIT; James Tobin, Yale University; Yuri V. Yaryomenko, Institute of Economic Forecasting, RAS. Other participants include: James K. Galbraith, University of Texas at Austin; Lawrence R. Klein, University of Pennsylvania; Nicholas N. Kozlov, Hofstra University; Robert McIntyre, Bowdoin College; and Geoffrey Shepherd, University of Massachusetts at Amherst.

6. The statement was published on the front page of *Nezavisimaya gazeta* July 1, 1996, and signed by Russian economists Leonid Abalkin, Oleg Bogomolov, Viktor K. Ivanter, Dmitri S. Lvov, Valery L. Makarov, Stanislav S. Shatalin, and Yuri V. Yaryomenko; and by American Nobel economists Kenneth J. Arrow, Lawrence R. Klein, Wassily W. Leontief, Robert M. Solow, and James Tobin; and by Michael D. Intriligator and Marshall Pomer. Revised version in English was published as "A New Economic Policy for Russia," *Economic Notes* 25(3): 407–410. Reprinted in 1997 in *Economics of Transition* 5(1).

7. *Komsomolskaia pravda* published a front-page, lead article sympathetic to the Economic Transition Group entitled "Does Russia Need Nobel Prize Winners?!" (Zavorotny 1996). The writer was subsequently forced to leave the newspaper.

References

Bogomolov, Oleg T. 1994. "Reforms After Gaidar." *Nezavisimaya gazeta*, February 8.

———. ed. 1996. *Reformy glazami amerikanskikh i rossiiskikh uchenykh.* Moscow: Rossiiskii ekonomicheskii zhurnal, Fond "Za ekonomicheskuiu gramotnost."

Chiese, Julietto. 1997. *Proshchai, Rossiia.* Moscow: Geya Ltd.

———. 1998. "Experiment on a Living Country." Interview in *Tribuna*, November 3.

Economic Transition Group. 1994. "Zaiavlenie o namereniiakh." *Problemy prognozirovaniia* 3: 60–63.

———. 1996. "A New Economic Policy for Russia." *Nezavisimaya gazeta*, July 1.

Group of International Experts of the IMF, IBRD, OECD, and EBRD (Group). 1991. "USSR Economy: Conclusions and Recommendations." *Voprosy ekonomiki* 3.

Stiglitz, Joseph E. 1998. "More Instruments and Broader Goals: Moving toward the Post–Washington Consensus." 1998 Wider Annual Lecture, Helsinki.

Zavorotny, Sergei. 1996. "Na figa Rossii nobelevskie laureaty." *Komsomolskaia pravda,* December 17.

3

A Balanced Approach

Leonid Abalkin

The market is one of the greatest achievements of civilization. Its vitality is proved by world experience; there are no extant examples of a flexible, developed economy without the market.

Government, nevertheless, is more fundamental. It provides the basis for social order and the foundation for the market. Myriad government activities are essential to enable a market economy to function effectively. With grievous results, neoliberal reformers, prompted by the International Monetary Fund among others, pushed the Russian state out of the economy. They sought to abolish its role in promoting the country's development. Focusing on monetary methods, they made the elimination of inflation an excuse for neglecting the nation's needs.

Economic Role of Government

It is hardly sufficient to assess government's economic role by simple indices, such as the share of state property, the share of GDP distributed through the state budget, or the quantity of purchases made by the state.

More essential are actions to regulate and promote the functioning of the market.

Government has two classical functions to perform in a market economy: defending property rights and providing a stable national currency. Even these functions have been questioned by radicals who countenance private guards replacing the police and the dollar replacing the ruble. Other basic economic functions of government, all of which Russia has been pressured to forfeit, include stimulating business activity, stemming monopolistic tendencies, and controlling external economic relations. The last of these encompasses a customs system, capital controls, and temporary protection for fledgling industries. To meet Russian realities, it is urgent to coordinate and supplement these economic functions of government with an industrial policy that prudently reinforces the flow of resources into promising areas for technological development.

The weakening of government's economic role is at variance with global tendencies. The increasing international fluidity of capital makes it all the more imperative that domestic financial institutions, including banks and capital markets, be strictly regulated and monitored. According to recent evaluations, most world trade is under the control of transnational corporations. Astute policies are needed to ensure transfer of technology and emergence of international competitors based in Russia. The formation of large well-financed corporations, which are present in all modern economies, requires the attention of government.

When we determine the scope of government, we need to remember our situation. We are talking about an economy that is in transition and is stricken by a deep crisis. The production slump, not simply cyclical, is overgrowing into destruction of the economy itself. Reproduction links are broken, and the loss of markets obstructs renewal. Barter, low tax-collection, and wage arrears cannot be remedied separately. They reflect a disequilibrium that low inflation will not cure.

General Considerations

Government involvement in the economy, its scale and forms, necessarily reflects a country's economic circumstances and stage of development. Geography too, including size and location, is also important. There is no perfect, universal scheme. The task is necessarily creative, requiring sensitivity to traditions and culture. It is far more complicated than finding a point in a single, state-market continuum.

National interests are not only the object in international relations but also in setting economic policy. Economic policy needs to be independent of groups and corrupt insiders that pursue partisan advantages. Any corporation is obligated to coordinate its activity with the national interest. It is incumbent on citizens to demand, and for leaders to remember, that the proper calling of government is to be an instrument for the nation as a whole.

The appropriate role of government is more extensive at the stage of forming a market economy than at the stage of an already formed and efficiently performing market system. Any process of self-regulation, including market self-regulation, is most feasible for stable systems and not at the stage of transition from one system to another. On one hand, self-regulation leads to strengthening of conservative tendencies and the return of old traditions. On the other hand, absence of regulating functions during transformation causes chaotic processes. Both of these tendencies, chaos and conservatism, are observed in the contemporary Russian economy.

The responsibility of the state lies not only in creating conditions that enable the market to function effectively. It is necessary to reestablish the social contract between government and the people. According to the constitution of Russia and every other democratic country, the people are the highest sovereign. The authority of government is based on the credit and trust of the people, and this credit cannot be timeless. It implies government obligation to fulfill its promises, including the maintenance of law and order, defining minimum standards of living, and promoting fair distributions of income and wealth.

Investments in people (human capital) are the most efficient investments in the long run, for human potential is the most important factor in socioeconomic development. Government is responsible to ensure health care and nutrition, as well as education and fundamental science. It is up to the state to regulate relations between labor and capital, including setting rules for union activity. There need to be health and safety regulations, and there is a government role in establishing a minimum wage, an overtime differential, and guaranteed vacations.

The solving of ecological problems provides a compelling final example of the positive role of government. Witness the aversion of tragedy for Lake Erie in the United States, or the cleaning of the Rhine, which was formerly the gutter of Europe. The market led toward ecological catastrophe, and the state had to put it in order.

Conclusion

We cannot agree with those who overstate the role of the market and underestimate the role of government. But those who exaggerate what the state can do, or who deny the role of market self-regulation, are also mistaken. The answer is to find a rational, appropriate balance of market and government.

Everyone should agree that it is necessary to foster a capable state with control over national resources. To implement economic polices for the benefit of the country as a whole and to achieve a successful transition, Russia must set its priorities and clearly specify the goals and instruments of government policy. This effort will succeed only if based on thorough analysis leading to national consensus.

4

False Expectations

James Tobin

Celebrating the collapse of communism—its economic statism, its political despotism, and its military threat—the West hailed the fall of the Soviet Union as a historic victory for free-market capitalism. The 150-year clash of ideologies symbolized by the names Adam Smith and Karl Marx was at long last over. Adam Smith had won.

In the euphoria felt as the Cold War was ending, the West expected the ex-communist countries to prosper under free-market capitalism. After all, it could only be their disastrous economic system that kept living standards of Soviet citizens so far below those of their Western neighbors. In Western countries themselves, right-wing antigovernment politics had gained in strength even before the end of the Cold War. Thatcherism and Reaganomics stand out. The collapse of communism increased the confidence and conservatism of these movements, and they cited the failures of extreme dirigiste regimes behind the Iron Curtain to promote their political agenda.

The Invisible Hand

Adam Smith's most famous passage is this: "As every individual . . . endeavors . . . to employ his capital in the support of domestic industry, and so to direct that industry that its produce may be of the greatest value . . . [he] necessarily labors to render the annual revenue of the society as great as he can. He . . . neither intends to promote the public interest, nor knows by how much he is promoting it. . . . [He] is in this, as in many other cases, led by an invisible hand to promote an end which was no part of his intention." The Invisible Hand is certainly one of history's Great Ideas. Competitive markets in which prices, rather than queuing or rationing, equate demand to supply are marvelous mechanisms of social coordination. Like the wheel, the market is a widespread ancient human invention.

It's easy to see the powerful energy of self-interest working for the best when Henry Ford mass-produces cars, Edison lights the world, and Bill Gates designs computer operating systems. The social benefits are well worth the fortunes these inventor-entrepreneurs garnered along the way. But as Adam Smith, a moral philosopher first and a political economist second, was well aware, there are perils to counting too heavily on the beneficent results of unmitigated self-interest. The Invisible Hand theorem has to be modified; governments in capitalist societies play essential roles in economic life. The market system works within social institutions that channel and guide self-interested energies into constructive activities. Without those institutions—which can never be perfect and may be weakened and perverted by crime and corruption—we are stuck with Hobbes's war of every man against every other, with outcomes quite different from the Invisible Hand theorem.

Laws and police are part of the answer, but a civilized society cannot survive if obedience to laws and other social norms becomes solely a matter of self-interest. It cannot survive, for example, if people pay taxes only if hedonistic calculus reveals that the probability-discounted penalty of being caught exceeds the probability-discounted gain from the violation. The glorification of self-interested behavior and the denigration of government in recent years bear some responsibility for recent trends. The anything–goes–if–you–can–get–away–with–it mentality is a recipe for anarchy. Enterprise can take the form of extortion by threat of violence. Alas, this kind of capitalism appears to be flourishing in Russia.

The Invisible Hand depends not only on preventing criminal activity but also on competition to convert self-interest into socially optimal outcomes. Undisciplined self-interest impels individuals and businesses to seek and protect monopolistic positions. Who would not like to control a toll booth through which economic traffic has no choice but to go? Maintenance of competition requires eternal vigilance in enforcing "anti-trust" laws.

Governments often do economic harm by misguided interference with markets for the protection of particular interests and for the benefit of politicians and bureaucrats themselves. But blind campaigns for retrenchment of government expenditures and taxes are also very damaging. Wholesale destruction of the public sector in Russia, however understandable as a reaction to communism and its privileged bureaucracy, has been catastrophic.

Modern technologies are making constructive public sector activities more essential than ever. Public education must train workers in the skills needed in high-tech industries. Government coordination is required to create modern national and international systems of transportation and communication.

Individual and societal interests diverge in the case of "externalities." These are costs or benefits of an economic transaction that fall on neither buyer nor seller, but on persons not involved in the transaction. Businesses and individuals do not consider those spin-offs in deciding what and how much to produce and consume. Environmental damages resulting from production processes or from the use and disposal of products are well-known examples. Often these consequences cross national borders. On the other hand, businesses that train workers or invent new techniques or products may spin off to others valuable by-products for which they cannot enforce payment. It is an important function of governments to manage, when feasible and appropriate, these external costs and benefits.

Reallocation of Resources

In Russia, workers and other productive inputs must be substantially reallocated—shifted from activities where they are no longer needed to activities of social value. Immense reallocations are both today's necessities and tomorrow's hopes. Resources released from obsolete activities must be redeployed into new industries, new technologies, new products. Swords must be beat into plowshares, guns must be supplanted by butter. The winding down of military production is not the only reallocation required. As the civilian sector grows, its composition will be quite different. The goods and services freely chosen by consumers will diverge radically from the menu offered by Soviet planners.

It is a fallacy to expect this reallocation to occur on its own, much less quickly enough to satisfy the aspirations of an impatient public. That does not happen even in Western countries, with well-established capitalist and democratic institutions. Redeployment may be of immense social value eventually, but its initial impact is devastating to the many people who depend on the old activities for their livelihoods.

The United States also faces difficult and painful reallocations, though by no means as severe as those of Russia. We have political trouble shutting down the production of nuclear submarines, stealth bombers, and aircraft carriers. We have similar troubles making trade agreements with our neighbors, Mexico and Canada, because freer trade might cost some jobs, even while it generates others.

The local pains, vested interests, and political perils that obstruct such reallocations must be even greater in the ex-communist countries. Shock therapy strategy would suddenly create mass unemployment and leave it to spontaneous private enterprise to create new enterprises and new jobs. The new jobs would not happen very fast, and meanwhile the depression in aggregate demand would discourage potential entrepreneurs and investors. The scenario is not politically or economically viable. In the absence of positive programs to provide jobs for displaced workers, it is not surprising that workers continue to be employed and paid in obsolete and unproductive activities.

Consider what Jean Monnet did for France, Germany, and Western Europe immediately after World War II. Devastated by the war, their economies were in shambles. For the most part they had not been doing very well before the war either. To revive the crucial industrial complex straddling the French-German border, Monnet conceived and organized the Coal and Steel Community. Industries and governments cooperated on concerted, consistent plans to expand peacetime production capacities. These plans envisaged optimistic but feasible levels of demand for coal and steel products, which the expansionary activities of those very industries would help bring about. To put the matter simplistically, coal companies were induced to invest in expanded production capacity because they became confident the steel industry would buy more coal; steel companies similarly raised their capacity because they became confident the coal industry would buy more steel. All the firms raised their sights above what they would have expected without coordination.

In the same spirit, Monnet developed for France itself a system of "indicative planning." Private industries and public sectors worked out mutually consistent plans of production and investment. These then could serve as wholly voluntary guides for individual industries and enterprises. As in the coal-steel case, each sector could expand without fearing it would be overextended because the rest of the economy would lag behind. Periodic exercises in indicative planning were useful in concertedly lifting the sights of French entrepreneurs for two decades after the war, but the device became unnecessary later.

Monnet's institutional inventions could be useful in transitions from communist to market economies. But the animus against Communism and controls is so strong that anything that involves government participation and seems to be "planning," however indicative and voluntary, is rejected out of hand.

Finance

A mature capitalist economy contains an immense variety of markets, some well organized and others quite informal. Some are for goods and services, others for paper assets and debts. Those financial markets are very exciting. They attract many of the best brains. The fantastic development of computer and communications technologies has multiplied the speed, scope, and sophistication of financial transactions. The sun never sets on trading in currencies, equities, and bonds. Derivative instruments, offering new opportunities for arbitrage and speculation, are invented, it seems, almost every day. Developing countries once regarded their own steel industries and airlines as sources of national pride. Now the prestigious symbol is a stock exchange.

The 1980s in the capitalist world was the decade of the paper economy, encouraged by deregulation of both domestic financial institutions and cross-border financial transactions. Speculators and deal makers who hit jackpots came to rival multimillionaire sports stars as heroes to college students. It is no wonder that Russian youths equate capitalism with finance, deals, speculation, and brokering.

The rush to incorporate Russia into Western financial markets was premature and damaging, except to those of whatever nationality who knew how to work the system for their own advantage. Western advisers stressed making the ruble fully convertible and the creation of unregulated financial markets, open to foreigners as well as to residents. Instead it would be better to follow the precedents of the 1940s and 1950s, the days of the Marshall Plan and the early IMF.

While it is important to ensure that foreigners who invest and sell in Russia are able to convert their ruble proceeds, it should not be guaranteed that everyone, resident or foreigner, can do the same at the commercial exchange rate. Foreign currency should be husbanded for use in purchasing investment goods.

The collapse of trade among Warsaw Pact countries and particularly among the republics of the Soviet Union has to do with uncompetitive industry. In similar circumstances in postwar Western Europe, the European

Payments Union was set up. It allowed the Marshall Plan countries to discriminate collectively against the dollar, facilitating multilateral trade among themselves. This system, which worked extremely well, might be a model even at this late date. This, of course, does not justify restoring the inefficient Warsaw Pact trade mechanism or exchanging goods at uneconomic prices.

Foreign advisers and lenders also insist on government policies of financial stabilization. In practice, this means balancing government budgets, restricting central bank credit and currency issue, deregulating financial transactions, and stabilizing the foreign exchange value of the local currency. It certainly is important to keep inflation within limits. But the faith that monetary stability is a sufficient condition for reviving production, re-orienting industry, and achieving the essential resource reallocations is a dangerous fallacy. The Russian central bank has been deservedly condemned for fueling hyperinflation by exorbitant printing of rubles. The purpose of its unrestrained issue of currency is equally deserving of condemnation. It is to enable old state enterprises to meet their payrolls even though they are now producing little of social value. The result is that Russia manages to maintain "employment" while producing less and less gross domestic product. The bank should be, directly or indirectly, channeling credit to promising new ventures.

We should never forget that the overriding purpose of economic activity and of markets is to produce goods and services of value to individuals and to society. Financial markets are means to that end, not ends in themselves. The title of Adam Smith's 1776 book, *The Wealth of Nations*, conveys its principal message. Wealth does not consist in paper claims or even gold and silver per se, but in commodities useful to consumers or capable of producing consumer goods and services. Smith sought to overcome the mercantilist instincts of sovereigns who geared their nations' economies and foreign trade to maximize accumulations of precious metals. Ex-communist economies need to produce real goods and services and develop markets where they can sell them. Excessive emphasis upon finances can be counterproductive, especially in adolescent capitalist economies.

From the Ashes

In the euphoria of the moment, Western advisers all too often forgot that the economic victory in the war of systems was not won by ideologically pure free-market regimes but by "mixed economies" in which governments played substantial and crucial roles. They forgot too that elaborate structures of laws, institutions, and customs, which evolved over centuries in existing capitalist countries, are essential foundations and frameworks for market systems.

Unfortunately, Westerners offering professional advice on the management of transitions to market capitalism—economists, financiers, business executives, politicians—encouraged false expectations. Their confidence in free markets and private enterprise had been reinforced by the political and ideological success of conservative antigovernment movements in their own countries. Their advice was in that same spirit: dismantle your government controls and regulations, privatize your enterprises, stabilize your finances, get governments out of the way, and just watch a new market economy rise from the ashes. It turned out not to be so easy.

5

What Do Economists Know about Transition to a Market System?

Lawrence R. Klein

It is very questionable to depend on what works in any given country's economy and apply the same processes to the economic environment of another country. There are some lessons or experiences to be transplanted, but first we ought to look at the issues from a theoretical point of view.

To begin, let us look at the polar extremes. At one end of the scale, we have the tightly controlled system of central planning, and at the other end the complete free market of perfectly competitive capitalism.

The central planning extreme was theoretically based on Marxism-Leninism, though the two thinkers had much more to say about capitalism and imperialism than about socialist planning. But their concepts of the labor theory of value influenced social accounting, which is a planning tool. The theory of complete state (public) ownership of the means of production (capital) was used to organize details of goods output, labor input, and rigidly set prices of individual goods. Inflation could not manifest itself because prices were not allowed to change except by administrative decision. There was hidden or supressed inflation. The result was that excess demand was prevalent. In the USSR, public debt was financed by printing paper money; since prices could not rise very much, if at all, the visible aspect of inflation was long queues, waiting lists, and money hoards. In the USSR, this gave rise to the "ruble overhang."

Key projects, buildings, the military establishment all got produced because the plan allowed it. The planned economies were largely closed, internationally, except for intra-CMEA trade, at negotiated or fixed prices, frequently in barter terms. This system produced a great deal (arts, music, scientific achievement, athletic prowess, and many other things), but it delivered levels of living that were not up to world standards.

In pure theory, intelligent central planners, equipped with powerful computers, could have sought better economic outcomes, but they did not do so and probably had an inferior conceptualization of how the entire economy functioned. At the other extreme, we have a theory of a completely competitive economy in which each household and each firm (some households are also firms) pursue their own interests, households optimizing their consumer patterns and firms maximizing their profits. The individual nations in this part of the world economy are assumed to continue their optimizing behavior in a completely free-trade environment among countries.

The French economist Walras theorized that such an economy could be described by a system of simultaneous demand and supply functions for all the goods and services available in the economy. Through the equating of all supplies and demands,

$$S_i(p_1...p_n) = D_i(p_1...p_n),$$

the n market prices could be determined. This is called market clearing, because supplies are equated to demands, and the price system accomplishes this by finding that set of prices $p_1...p_n$ that satisfies these equations.

This formal mathematical statement needs a great deal of elaboration. First, we can contrast this view with that of detailed central planning in two respects. Under central planning, there is generally excess demand. In practice, it was easy to observe. Theoretically, the equating of supplies and demands in all markets is the same thing as finding the prices that make all excess demands zero.

Market clearing prevails under the price system, and this means that excess demand is eliminated. Also, the market is, in theory, cleared for all services as well as goods, but under strict socialist, central planning many services are considered to be nonproductive, and criteria are developed mainly for material products.

We should judge the properties of the market system in its most favorable light to establish its features. The system of equations of market clearing does not provide a solution for the absolute level of prices. This system determines only relative prices, which can be looked at as ratios of goods or service prices to the general price level, P. The general price level is a weighted average of individual prices.

In classical economic theory, the general level of prices, P, is assumed to be proportional to money supply, M, which is determined by the central monetary authority. The classical rule, at the polar extreme, is for the market economy to let relative prices be set by market clearing, and the absolute level of prices to be set by monetary control. The rate of change of P is a measure of inflation; therefore the monetary authority determines inflation, while the market determines relative prices.

This is an attractive intellectual proposition because it means that the market acts as an automatic (analog) computer, while the central planning authority would have to operate its computer hardware and, then, only in an approximate sense. The silent market analog computer operates efficiently as an "invisible hand."

Finally, there is one other intellectual property of the market solution, namely, if all the supply and demand equations that make up the system are based on optimal, individualistic behavior by households and firms, the solution to the equation system can be shown to exist in a mathematical sense and to be (Pareto) optimal for the entire economy in an economic sense. Pareto optimality is not a strong property, but it has some attraction. It says that the equilibrium solution for the equation system defines a set of prices and quantities for all the economic participants such that the system cannot be moved to another position without making some economic agent worse off.

While this property has a certain degree of attractiveness, it has a major deficiency in the sense that the solution is not unique. For every distribution of wealth, or initial holdings, among society's agents, there is such an optimum, and the market system does not tell us how the distribution should be selected; i.e., the solution is optimal, subject to the choice of a wealth distribution. For the socialist planned economy, the central planners can select a socially equitable (not equal) distribution.

In addition to the fact that the market clearing solution provides no information about either inflation or wealth distribution, it is based on very restrictive assumptions:

(i)   free entry/egress in all markets;

(ii)   equal access by all to economic information;

(iii) rational decision making by all agents;

(iv)   absence of monopoly or monopsony power;

(v)   absence of natural disturbances (weather, physical environment, etc.); and

(vi)   full employment of people and resources.

There should be no interference with a smoothly working economy. Also, it is a static system with an equilibrium solution, but the economy is rarely in the neighborhood of equilibrium, and the transition process that we are studying involves the dynamics of disequilibria. What happens during the transition is likely to be far removed from either of the polar extremes.

The socialist planned economy rarely, if ever, functioned as assumed in the polar extreme. Incentives faded after a vigorous early start; equitable distributions of wealth gradually became more and more inequitable; corruption was prevalent; technical change warranted fresh prices that did not appear; people were dissatisfied in comparison with what other countries had achieved.

Similarly, the conditions for efficient functioning of the market economy did not prevail; income distribution deteriorated in recent years (in the sense of becoming more inequitable); the business cycle introduced a lack of stability in the system; unemployment has reached intolerable levels and persisted for long periods of time.

Neither system functioned according to its best theoretical case. In fact, each functioned in practice as a mixed economic system. There are planning and socialistic aspects to all economies that regard themselves as primarily capitalist. Similarly, there are market and private capitalist aspects of socialist planned systems. Both systems are imperfect in their real-world implementation, and it becomes a matter of judgment where they will end up in any transition process. The practical question facing the world economy at this time is where the former centrally planned economies will come to rest, as the transition process runs its course.

The Concept of Market Socialism

Oskar Lange and Fred M. Taylor argued more than 50 years ago that it would be theoretically possible to introduce market pricing into a socialist economy—one in which there would be widespread state ownership of the means of production. They based their analysis on a famous, abstract paper by E. Barone, who showed with general Walrasian methods that a rational solution for prices in a market economy would exist, in a mathematical sense, even if the means of production were socially owned and if the economy were to be guided by a central planning board. The board, however, would not fix prices and would respect market solutions.

Actually, the rule for practical application of the central planning board can be simply stated. In markets where there are surpluses, prices should be lowered, and in markets where there are unsatisfied demands, prices should be raised. The board should keep changing (not fixing) prices, in an iterative manner, until all markets are cleared. Also, the board should allow consumer choice (consumer "sovereignty") and require cost-effective operation by producers.

The concept of market socialism had been challenged by Ludwig von Mises, among other conservative economists, as being illogical. He felt that it would not be possible to find rational price calculations for capital goods in a socialist society. Other conservative economists argued that market-based socialism would be difficult to implement in practice. It is now accepted that market socialism is theoretically possible, but many modern economists, especially those following or working closely with the transition in the former CMEA economies, dismiss it as uninteresting and inferior to private ownership with market clearing. They do not want to modernize or liberalize socialism; they want to remove all socialist aspects during the transition period and aim for a system that resembles typical OECD countries as much as possible. To them, one of the most important steps in the transition period is to convert state enterprises to capitalistic enterprises owned by individuals or groups of individuals, either domestic or foreign.

They are simultaneously introducing a market system and selling or distributing state enterprises to private persons. It is their opinion that privately run enterprises are always more efficient than state-run enterprises. Issues of social equality, justice, or wealth distribution play little role in their thinking. Another approach, based on a different set of values and attitudes, would be one that takes the theoretical structure of market socialism seriously and follows more closely along the lines of a mixed economy objective.

The China case became known before the middle of the 1980s, and it followed a very different pattern. The stated objective has been to modernize by having market socialism, not to move in a sudden, massive direction to private ownership. Agriculture and small-scale enterprises were freed up or liberalized. There was some degree of privatization, but that was not the centerpiece. Market pricing and personal decision making in some sectors were the important features.

Agricultural output responded almost immediately and registered above-average growth for most of the decade of the 1980s. Similarly, service output—frequently small-scale—also grew fast in this period, mainly at double-digit rates. A significant innovation was the creation of the so-called town and village (government) enterprises. After the impressive gains in agriculture and service-related activities took hold, manufacturing grew strongly.

Stability Criteria

An economy in transition should not initiate immediately the process of reaching its ultimate goals; it should first try to achieve a certain degree of macroeconomic stability. In the former CMEA countries, for example, an alternative route could have been to stabilize the economies in an overall sense and then set about restructuring.

Macroeconomic stability, broadly conceived, can be characterized by:

(i)   keeping inflation in restraint—preferably well under 10 percent,

(ii) maintaining a high level of employment,

(iii) maintaining strong output growth,

(iv) keeping the income/wealth distributions equitable,

(v)   providing basic social services for the population,

(vi) building up the country's infrastructure,

(vii) keeping the balance of international payments near equilibrium (current account near zero),

(viii) keeping the internal fiscal balance near zero, and

(ix) keeping money supply under control—on a moderate growth path.

These are not easily attainable targets, but they imply that the public deficit should not be monetized and that the deficit should be kept small so that it is capable of being financed without straining the economy. The problem of financial irresponsibility of government cannot be solved by having the central bank finance the budget deficit by directly crediting the government. If the economy can be kept on a strong expansion path, and there are enough cases where this has occurred to know that it can be done, then job offers will exist in large enough quantity to keep unemployment from rising rapidly during transition.

The emphasis on rapid privatization is likely to make the income/wealth distribution highly unequal in a quick fashion; this is to be avoided because cooperation of all people working together is needed to make the system function well, both during and after transition. A noted feature of many of the successful developing countries in Asia is that they have maintained fairly equitable income/wealth distributions.

The infrastructure contributes to smooth working of the industrial and agricultural sectors. Fast transportation, instant communication, healthy workforces, well-educated workforces, and many other population attributes stem from good infrastructures. The elimination of bottlenecks and the overall enhancement of the infrastructure will lead to strengthened productivity and sharpened competitiveness of industry. These things should be put into place as soon as possible, with higher priority than economic restructuring, such as privatization.

Economic stability encourages private investment. It is also helpful to take action to lower the cost of capital to law-abiding private enterprises, for example by introducing accelerated depreciation and investment tax credits. Tax rate reductions on business should be combined with measures to curtail the "shadow economy."

Some Transition Procedures

It is easy enough to call for attainment of the various macroeconomic criteria mentioned in the previous section, but it is quite another thing to devise practical procedures that will help to realize these criteria. Of the economies using shock therapy (quick resort to market clearing, large-scale privatization, rapid exchange depreciation) very few have begun to realize macroeconomic gains. The main results have been inflation, unemployment, deficit and output decline, not to mention crime.

There is much to be said for stabilizing and improving economic conditions at the outset. Once economic stability has been attained in an overall sense, detailed economic reforms can be introduced. This is not a unique pattern and will not be suitable in every instance, but it does seem to work where it has been carefully introduced. The most impressive aspect of China's reform, restructuring, and liberalization is that it took place without putting the economy through major recession. Quite differently from shock therapy, economic reform proceeded gradually and the economy expanded in record-breaking proportions.

What are some of the more noteworthy procedures, techniques, or other transition features in the Chinese case?

(i)   the target has been one of a mixed economy, with some private ownership, private decision making, and some state ownership (market socialism);

(ii)   implementation of openness for trade and technology;

(iii)   creation of special economic zones;

(iv)   introduction of modern economic education; and

(v)   the absorption of quantitative methods from econometrics and statistics in preparation for application to economic planning.

Market socialism. The transition in Russia was distanced as far as possible from market socialism. This was an immediate reaction and adopted without hesitation. It is often said that Russia had no option, but had the issues during the 1980s been carefully studied, some steps for more gradual transition could have been put into place. Russia had China's example to study, long before the CMEA systems broke down.

Openness. To develop export-import relationships on a multilateral basis, Russia should adhere to the rules of the World Trade Organization. While free trade should be the eventual target, gradual opening of the economy to foreign competition is preferable to precipitous removal of all barriers. A special institution, similar to the Export-Import Bank in the United States, should be created to support Russian exports. To avoid corruption and encourage competition, any trade protection must be precisely formulated and transparent.

Openness is important for more than direct trade enhancement; it is important for facilitating capital flow. Most of the transition economies are badly in need of international capital imports, not only to finance straightforward activities but also to facilitate transfer of technology. Joint ventures with foreign partners, licensing agreements, and other mechanisms for transferring technology are some of the most important things that transition economies can do, in order that they can move into advanced technologies. Every economy that has tried to be self-sufficient has lagged in economic development; therefore openness is a necessity. At the same time, a cautious approach to inflow of foreign portfolio investment is critical, as illustrated by the Mexican and East Asian experiences.

Special economic zones. A particular form of openness is to attract international business to a transition economy through tariff concessions, subsidies, special rights in protected areas, and by furnishing ample resources for transportation, telecommunications, and whatever business facilities are needed for contemporary practices worldwide. One attraction of the special zones is the provision of inexpensive labor and available raw materials.

Some form of economic zone has worked well for Taiwan, Israel, Korea, and Mexico, as well as China. It is natural that large urban centers, ports, financial centers, and other key areas be liberalized first. They can absorb the ideas of modernization more readily. After the economic changes get established in principal areas, it is to be hoped that they can be moved throughout the country, to areas that have been less in touch with the outside world.

Modern economic education. Very few transition economies were open to modern economic ideas before the 1960s. On individual bases, in separate countries, modern economics was taught to representatives from CMEA countries. During the late 1960s the process began, and during the 1970s there was a steady flow to major universities and research centers. I, personally, had students and visiting scholars from the USSR, Poland, Czechoslovakia, Yugoslavia, and Hungary. The scale was not large, but it was well placed, in the sense that a corps of scholars and researchers in modern economics was developed.

In China, the process was different. Contact was made in 1979 by a team of economists from the United States (representing the Social Science Research Council and the National Academy of Sciences). In 1980 there was an econometric workshop, and after that an entire program covering many economics subjects. The China case was of unusual significance because modern economics was little-known for 30 years. The Cultural Revolution silenced those who had studied in the international community prior to the Liberation; therefore an entire generation of modern economists had to be created, and this was accomplished during the 1980s. Shock therapy would have been disastrous in this period, and the gradual, step-by-step process was extremely well suited to the Chinese case.

Economic analysis, economic ways of thinking, and economic methodology were developed in step with the modernization of the economy. This gave appreciation, understanding, and meaningfulness to the transition.

Quantitative methods. It is one thing to teach and absorb ideas from the general subjects of economics in order to give interpretation to the transition economy and its eventual targets. It is quite another thing to teach the specific methods of econometrics and of general statistical method and to develop experience with the tools for economic planning in the form of data banks, computer software, model building, and simulation studies for policy formation.

Meaningful, quantitative policy analysis depends on the development of useful quantitative information systems. In Russia market systems and privatization were rushed into immediate implementation without appropriate documentation. Chaotic conditions obstructed buildup of time series samples, cross-section surveys, and special indicators vital to intelligent economic planning. Again, this is a situation in which gradualism is much to be preferred.

6

The Role of Time

Kenneth J. Arrow

We have been witnessing a sequence of remarkable changes in the nature of economic systems, a revolution which will, in retrospect, be compared with the emergence of capitalism from feudalism. These changes rely on market-oriented forces and the removal of government controls. If the market system is so good at achieving efficiency, why not immediately abolish all price controls, remove all trade barriers and privatize everything? To a considerable extent, that is more or less what happened in Russia. According to theory, we should have seen a marked upsurge in efficiency, more goods being produced with the same labor and capital. Yet the last few years have hardly brought forth the hoped-for gains.

Looking back over history can be illuminating if done carefully. Radical changes in economic systems over large parts of the earth did not begin with 1989 but have been going on ever since 1946. Many of the ex-colonial countries, certainly influenced by the Soviet model and the experience of the Great Depression, committed themselves to extensive state direction. In many cases, bureaucratic controls spawned predatory rent seeking elites and failed to spur sustained growth. But I want to emphasize that in the more successful transformations to prosperous market economies, governments have, on the whole, not functioned by abandoning all role in the economy. Countries which developed from a very low economic level, such as South Korea or Taiwan, though relying in many ways on market incentives, did not hesitate to guide their economies through capital allocation, export subsidies, and protection. The process of favorable economic progress took time, not measured in generations or centuries, but rather in decades. Even in the economic miracle of postwar Western Europe, which took more time than is generally realized, governments were committed to some form of planning and to full employment policies.

The Market System

Economists argue for the superior efficiency of the market system using a theory that, at least in its rudimentary form, abstracts from time. I am particularly concerned that well-oriented government direction depends on a deeper understanding of the element of time in markets.

Under the assumptions of the competitive-equilibrium model, firms buy inputs and sell outputs at recognized prices that are the same for all buyers and sellers. The firms have to be able to cover their costs by the receipts from their own sales, not, for example, by subsidies. The price that a firm is willing to pay for any input is then governed by its value to the firm. It is argued from this that when one firm buys from another, it in effect values the good it buys at more than it costs the seller. Hence every transaction achieves a net social gain. This argument must be stated with far greater precision, and there are many qualifications, but this is the essence of the argument for the price system.

The concept of markets is something more than acceptance of the price system. It presupposes that the individual firms and households make their own decisions. In the command economy of the Soviet Union, many of the decisions were made by central ministries; there were output quotas to be achieved and limits on the use of certain inputs. One could imagine a different command-and-control system based on prices. But under ordinary circumstances the individual firm knows much more about the outputs that are possible and the inputs that are needed than any faraway ministry. Hence, efficiency demands that decisions be made by those most informed.

Time

There is a past and a future as well as a present in economic life. That the past influences the present is obvious. That the future influences the present seems like a violation of our ordinary laws of causality. What is really meant is that our expectations of the future will affect what we do in the present.

A productive firm is an ongoing institution, which has had a past and expects to have a future. Capital equipment was installed in the past on the basis of expectations held then of prices, input availabilities, and output needs. What is done today is based on the firm's present beliefs about what will happen in the future. This is most obvious with respect to investment, whether or not to expand by adding plant and equipment or to contract by closing down, or selling off, part of the business.

1. Price expectations are decisive. If the firm plans to expand, it makes a difference at what prices particular products will sell. The particular machines the firm buys depends also on the prices expected for different inputs. If, for example, energy prices are expected to rise, then the firm will buy equipment which minimizes energy usage.

A radical restructuring of the economic system is designed to change everything about it. This includes the whole system of expectations for the future. Supplies that were once guaranteed by central planning now depend on markets about which there is great uncertainty. Assured buyers are gone. Before, imported goods were closely rationed, now they compete with domestic products, creating opportunities for buyers and competition for sellers. During the Soviet period, energy prices were well below the world market, and oil was readily available; as a result, energy was used in an extraordinarily inefficient way. With Russian oil and gas sold freely on the world market, domestic users now must pay much higher prices.

Previously, prices reflected policy, not costs. Productive equipment was underpriced, and the use of capital was not charged with a suitable rate of interest. Therefore, firms had excessive amounts of capital. Moreover, they did not really have to meet their costs; the central bank was available to save them from the consequences of mistakes. In the terminology of the Hungarian economist Janos Kornai, the budget limits on the firm were "soft."

The difficulties of transition are compounded by the need for institutional change. Just as the readjustment of the capital stock necessarily takes time, so the readjustment of institutions is an extended process. They cannot simply be imported as ready-made copies of those in the United States or Western Europe.

The world of markets is in part a world of contractual relations among self-sustaining enterprises. Contracts played at most a subordinate role in an economy where allocation was primarily carried out by central planning authorities. Credit instruments, stocks and bonds, and mortgages are essential for the working of a market system. All such legal instruments require a whole range of government as well as private activity. Entrepreneurs have to learn their meaning. Institutions which function well in market economies adjust and evolve over long periods of time. In Russia, institutions have to adjust to a particular set of conditions; history matters a good deal.

Privatization

It is usually argued that privatization is an inseparable concomitant of the market system. But, as was first discussed by Italian economists Enrico Barone and Vilfredo Pareto, private ownership is logically distinct from acceptance of the price system or even markets. During the Soviet period, some socialist economists, to no avail, repeatedly urged the replacement of the command system by a market system.

In the proper institutional environment, privatization ensures the viability of markets, and we may take for granted privatization of the bulk of industry as a long-term goal. But we need to consider carefully the pace of privatization and, perhaps even more importantly, the road to it.

Privatization amounts to a transfer of the accumulated savings of the Russian people. Rapid privatization makes impossible a fair value exchange, since there is no well-defined fair value under such conditions. To value a productive enterprise requires some expectations of its future profitability. These in turn require expectations of the prices which will prevail in the economy in the future. But in a transition the basis for these expectations is lacking. Hence, there will be tremendous uncertainty as to the value of firms, and their sale will become very much a matter of luck.

Privatization requires preparation in the form of what has come to be referred to as restructuring. In particular, the pieces to be privatized do not exist ready-made but must be planned for. We have to move away from thinking of all parts of the economy as needing the same treatment. The difficulties of creating markets and privatizing industry are by no means the same for all productive activities. Transition policies should recognize these differences and make use of them. Without proper preparation and careful implementation, there is no reason to suppose firms will wind up in hands capable of running them efficiently.

The most serious problems of privatization arise in the capital-intensive industries, which are characterized by huge monopolies. A large accumulation of private capital is needed to purchase them. Monopolies, which simplified central control, are unsuited to the needs of the market since the best operation of a market system requires competition to hold prices close to costs and to punish technological backwardness.

Prior to privatization, enterprises should be divided into viable operating firms. The restructuring would serve several purposes: the firms should be competitive whenever possible, they should form natural and manageable economic units, and they should be capable of privatization if they prove profitable. The government initially owns these, but they should be separate corporations with the government as stockholder. With appropriate precautions, it could then sell off the stock of those firms whose success permits a sale. This should be carried out in such a way that units which have suitable capital goods and management are able to emerge as viable units under private ownership.

Change to private ownership is likely to be smoothest in businesses with low capital requirements and owner participation in day-to-day operations. Thus it is less problematic to rapidly privatize service industries, particularly those concerned with distribution and trade, and light manufacturing.

New Entry

The term "privatization" is misleading. Transformation is not necessarily a matter of taking existing state-owned industries and selling them. What is really desired is to replace existing enterprises and capital assets with new enterprises and assets. We are seeing and will continue to see new firms being created and entering into production. In some cases, they have bought out the physical assets of an existing state enterprise, but this is not at all essential.

Over time, products and methods of manufacture change. Even for mature economies, there is every reason to argue that existing capital assets and enterprises have no special place in the future. This is especially true in the transition from the socialist systems where incorrect incentives led to a highly inefficient capital structure. The German experience is most illuminating. Even under conditions far more favorable to orderly privatization than in Russia, most East German equipment is being scrapped.

Economic growth in modern market economies frequently takes the form of entry of new firms, especially in less capital-intensive industries. In this manner, fresh ideas and innovative managerial skills appear. Most employment growth, in fact, is due to new and expanding small businesses. By the same token, the development of the less capital-intensive industries in the transition need not be a highly planned operation. The state does have to play a facilitating role in creating suitable infrastructure, including telecommunications, transportation, and a modern credit system.

In Russia, this process is made easier by the fact that commerce, distribution, and light industry were neglected. Soviet ideology emphasized material production over distribution, and heavy industry over light. As a result, investments in stores and wholesale businesses have been profitable.

Encouragement of new entry merits higher priority than change to private ownership of enterprises adapted to the former regime. Here the establishment of a legal framework and modern accounting methods is especially important. Insofar as regional and municipal governments actively retard entry, there is a role for the central government in preventing such actions.

Gradualism

Not everything can be changed at once. The economy started on the path to a market system with institutions and capital equipment attuned to expectations wildly out of line with the present. Gradual transition, allowing conditions and expectations to change more gradually, renders less of physical and institutional capital useless at any given moment.

A slow transformation is potentially reversible. At each stage, there are losers as well as gainers, and the losers may stop or reverse the changes. In the Soviet Union there were several failed attempts at moving closer to a market system, or at least some incentive structure, but they were undermined because there was no belief that reforms would be permanent. Enterprises unable to cover costs could expect to receive relief rather than go under as a market system would require. Today expectations of possible reversal may inhibit commitments by entrepreneurs, and thus transition must be highly credible for the evolution of the market system to progress.

It is not surprising that the Russian economy goes stumbling and blinking into the new world of greater light. The economy cannot take advantage of the new opportunities created by markets except over a period of time. Readjustment and creation of institutions is necessarily an extended process. Privatization is fraught with political hazards and distributional risks. Although the role of government in directing economic activity in a healthy economy is limited, transition does require guidance. The only source of general guidance for the economy is the state, and there is no denying that appropriate policy and leadership could considerably smooth transition.

Author's Note: This is a previously unpublished paper that I wrote in 1993. The general analysis, in my estimation, remains valid, though there are specific statements that may be less appropriate today.

7

Institutional Traps

Victor M. Polterovich

Two myths have harmed many economies throughout the world. One is the theory of absolute advantage of central planning over the market mechanism, and the other is the belief that efficient markets develop spontaneously and quickly enough if appropriate economic legislation is established. Volumes have been written to debunk the first myth. The falsity of the second needs to be better understood.

The problem is that inside of any legislated change there exists room for development of different institutions, or behavioral norms, and it is not simple to predict which direction will be chosen by an economy. The hypothesis that efficient institutions must arise because of natural selection does not prove to be truthful. Inefficient development can be self-supporting and stable. The supporting mechanisms were systematically investigated by Arthur (1988) for technological changes. North (1990) pointed out that the same mechanisms played an important role in the evolution of institutions. The most striking examples can be found in the economic reforms of Russia and Eastern European countries.

This chapter uses the ideas of Arthur and North to describe a general scheme for the formation of inefficient yet stable norms or institutions, referred to herein as institutional traps.[1] The scheme is substantially based on the concepts of transaction costs, transformation costs, and transitional rent. The theory developed is applied to explain the emergence in Russia of barter, mutual arrears, tax evasion, corruption, and other institutional traps. Implications for reform strategy are explored. The analysis shows that the formation of institutional traps is a major risk in any reform process, and avoidance of these traps is an urgent task during transition.

Institutional Traps

A norm is a rule which large groups of people obey, or can or must obey. In any area of life and at each moment in time, a multitude of alternative norms is available, and many factors influence the norm-forming process. For example, either corruption or honest service can be the norm in a bureaucratic system. Which of the two stereotypes will be prevalent depends on fundamental factors such as the size of wages earned by the bureaucrats in comparison to other citizens; organizational factors such as the system of control over, and punishment for, corrupt practices; and societal factors such as the readiness of colleagues and clients to cooperate under extortionist pressure or, on the contrary, to resist corruption. For other norms of behavior one can also find these three types of norm-forming factors: fundamental, organizational, and societal.

Transaction Costs and Institutional Transformation Costs

Two concepts, transaction costs and institutional transformation costs, are important for analyzing the evolution of norms.[2] In this chapter, the term "transaction costs" is understood as the costs of an agent's interaction with partners within the framework of a certain behavioral norm. For example, the possibility of being caught while taking a bribe would cause a transaction cost component for an official who has chosen corruption as the norm.

I refer to the costs of transition from one norm to another as institutional transformation costs, or transformation costs for short.[3] Amidst large-scale reform, transformation costs are incurred by both the state and individual firms. One can list the following major articles of transformation costs:

(1)   Drafting a transformation project
(2)   Project lobbying
(3)   Creating and sustaining interim institutions to support the project
(4)   Implementation of the project
(5)   Adapting the system to the new institution

Any transformation, especially a large-scale one, leads to some kinds of system disruptions (see discussion below) that aggravate the transformation costs. Any reform must include an assessment of the relevant costs.[4] Despite the obviousness of this point, when Russian reforms were proposed, the issue of costs was neglected.

Norm Stability and Norm-Fixing Mechanisms

For a behavioral norm to be stable, individuals should feel that it would be unprofitable or disadvantageous for them to deviate from it. In other words, stability should be ensured through the use of some kind of stabilizing mechanism—a mechanism with negative feedback. Such a mechanism can rely directly on the structure of individual preferences. For example, the "wash your hands before each meal" norm is supported by personal hygienic considerations. Another mechanism has to do with punishment for a norm's violation that may be envisaged under the law or supported by the local tradition. A third and far more interesting type of stabilizing mechanism is based on the so-called coordination effect secured by a type of externality. According to the coordination effect, the more consistently a norm is observed in society, the greater the costs incurred by each individual deviating from it. For example, the coordination effect takes place if a personal probability to be punished for a rule-breaking activity depends negatively on the number of people involved in the activity.

With time, the prevalent norm becomes fixed as a result of the agents learning to be more efficient in terms of that norm's observance and thus perfecting their implementation skills. If the payment of taxes is considered the norm within a society, the taxpaying habits of its members will improve. If, on the contrary, tax evasion is the norm, then the relevant techniques will develop first and foremost. This is what is called the learning effect (although, perhaps, perfection effect would be a more relevant term),[5] which slashes transaction costs as a result of public compliance with the norm.

No less important is another phenomenon, herein referred to as the linkage effect. With time, an established norm finds itself linked with a multitude of other rules, and becomes part of a system of other norms. Therefore, non-observance of this norm would be sure to trigger a chain of other transformations and, consequently, lead to high (linked) transformation costs. By increasing transformation costs, the linkage effect, too, contributes to a norm's fixation.

There is yet another norm-fixing mechanism, cultural inertia, which denotes agents' reluctance to review those behavioral stereotypes that have already proven viable. Inertia effects may be supported by a formal or informal system of punishments and awards for past behavior. For example, a person with a good reputation tries to maintain it by following the respectable norms of conduct.

When a norm undergoes transformation, the relevant transformation costs are distributed among the agents unevenly. This, together with cultural inertia and uncertainty about the amount of the transformation costs, leads to the emergence of conservative pressure groups resisting any change to the norms that are effective at the moment.

In cases where two or more different norms are not equivalent, one norm may be Pareto dominated. In many situations, however, Pareto comparisons are not sufficient to weigh norms against one another; they should be assessed based on other criteria, such as social utility or efficiency. We will henceforth refer to an inefficient stable norm (inefficient institution) as an institutional trap.[6] As with any other norm, an institutional trap's stability means that a system absorbing a small external impact will remain in the institutional trap, having perhaps slightly changed its parameters, and will return to the former state of equilibrium once the source of destabilizing pressure is removed.

An individual or a small group of people loses if it deviates from an institutional trap. However, the simultaneous adoption by all agents of an alternative norm would help raise the level of public well-being.

The emergence of institutional traps is a major source of risk associated with any reform process. The universal mechanisms described above, the coordination, learning, and linkage effects, as well as cultural inertia, are responsible for institutional trap formation as well.

The structure of stable norms depends on transformation costs. Although it would appear that such costs should only enhance a system's stability by leaving the norms themselves intact, a closer look at the problem shows that transformation costs can lead to the emergence of new stable equilibria—namely, mixed norms of behavior. In a state of mixed equilibrium, the advantages of one norm over another are reduced to nil by the transformation costs, and agents can partially follow several patterns of conduct.

Transformation costs are increased through the linkage effect and can support an originally inefficient norm even when the coordination effect stops working. Once having fallen into an institutional trap, the system chooses an inefficient path of development, and with time, returning to efficient development may not make sense any longer. Moreover, a system with a prevalent efficient norm, if strongly disturbed (with the set of equilibria, however, remaining structurally unchanged), may fall into an institutional trap in which it will remain even after the disturbing factor is removed. This so-called hysteresis effect[7] is characteristic of all norm-forming processes.

Institutional Traps in Russia

The large-scale reforms pursued in Eastern Europe in the 1990s have clearly shown the need for better understanding of institutional economic change. Russia has had a particularly bitter lesson to learn. The consequences of the transformations were unexpected by experts, whatever aspect of the reform process one looked at. Once freed, prices began to rise steeply and continued to soar for a longer period of time than most experts thought they would. The rush to bring prices under control produced a system of mutual arrears and provoked a shift toward barter trading, which actually meant that a non-monetary economy took shape on a new basis. Attempts to change the tax-collecting system gave a boost to shadow economy development. The slackening of state control over cash flows, a measure expected to create a competitive economic environment, fueled corruption. The "shock privat-ization" campaign, instead of producing efficient private property holders, gave birth to inefficient organizations, such as open-end stock companies owned by their employees. All of the above changes were accompanied by an unforeseen and uncommonly sharp production decline.

Many of these unexpected phenomena are institutional traps. They are responsible for the misfortune of the Russian economic reforms. Using the concepts discussed above, one can explain their emergence to extract lessons for the future.

Barter

Barter is often an attending circumstance of rapid inflation. In modern economies, barter is associated with higher transaction costs than monetary transactions. Because of this, barter exchanges are rather scarce today. When the inflation rate increases, paper money loses its value. Economic agents try to diminish their losses and seek to accelerate the rates of money circulation, which means an increase of their transaction costs. The transaction costs of monetary exchanges may grow very rapidly, if the finance system fails to cope with the rocketing number of transactions.

In economies with advanced banking systems, the share of barter is rather modest even when inflation is high. But after price liberalization in 1992, Russia proved to be ripe for barter (Polterovich 1993). With the banking system still unformed, money transfers within Moscow could take up to two weeks, and beyond the capital, over a month. It sometimes made more sense to carry bags of cash from city to city by plane than to transfer money from one bank account to another. Many firms soon found that barter transaction costs were lower than those for monetary exchange. Moreover, the transformation costs of a shift to barter looked acceptable, given the old-time direct links between supplier and consumer that had been the pride of the centrally planned economy. The search for prospective counterparts and the process of trade negotiations were facilitated by the spread of sophisticated means of communication. The larger the number of firms choosing barter, the lower the barter transaction costs for a fixed barter volume, since it was easier to find partners and put together barter chains (a coordination effect). In those conditions, as the share of barter exchanges increased, even more companies became involved.

Thus the environment conducive to barter had been created by changes in fundamental factors, such as the rate of inflation and the risk of arrears, which radically changed the ratio of monetary exchange transaction costs to barter exchange transaction costs. The coordination effect triggered rapid formation of the relevant norm. Later the transaction costs of barter exchanges continued to decrease due to the learning effect: companies learned to design elaborate chains of barter exchanges. The newly established norm gave birth to a new institute of barter exchange intermediaries and proved to be an efficient instrument of tax evasion (linkage effect).

By 1997, inflation in Russia had gone down dramatically, and monetary exchange technology had notably improved. Barter practices, however, were not dropped altogether.[8] Barter-driven behavior is supported by the coordination effect; it has been fixed through learning, linkage, and cultural inertia. Any agent deciding to break out of the barter system would be exposed to inevitable transformation costs: sever the long-established connections, look for new partners, and be ready to come face-to-face with the tax-collecting authorities. That is why imposition of legal sanctions for barter practices may lead to a temporary additional decline in production, and a high level of social transformation costs.[9] The barter intermediaries, who would lose their chief sources of income if barter practices were eliminated, are definitely a potential pressure group for perpetuation of the relevant norm.[10]

Price liberalization and the subsequent inflationary shock exerted cumulative pressure on the system, causing institutional changes. However, when inflation and monetary exchange transaction costs diminished, the system did not return to its initial state.

What we see here is the hysteresis effect mentioned earlier. Depending on the size of transaction costs, a company may choose to barter one product and sell another for money. One should consider also the mixed norms of behavior that may prompt a company to do so. At a mixed equilibrium, the difference between marginal costs of barter and monetary exchange may fail to offset the marginal costs of transformation, thus making both increased and decreased monetary exchanges unprofitable.

The above analysis suggests that price liberalization requires an economy with sufficiently advanced monetary institutions, thus securing low-level transaction costs even when inflation is high. Otherwise the system is susceptible to a barter trap.

Arrears

If an enterprise fails to pay its suppliers, it undermines their solvency and risks triggering an avalanche of mutual arrears. In developed economies, avalanches of this kind can be averted by efficient credit institutions and enforcement mechanisms that are in place, such as bankruptcy proceedings, factoring, or company restructuring. When prices were freed in Russia in 1992, inflationary shock emptied company bank accounts. As noted earlier, transaction payments lagged severely, the credit system worked by fits and starts (although with a negative real interest rate), and there were no bankruptcy laws or restructuring mechanisms at all. Coming under the effects of those fundamental and organizational factors, most enterprises found that instead of waiting until the buyers of their products paid in full, they, too, could offer only partial payment.[11] Underpaid suppliers of materials would be unlikely under the circumstances to terminate further shipments for fear of losing their clients altogether; besides, breaking the tacit rule, "If you can't pay, don't claim payments from others," might backfire with similar sanctions from the angry community of other nonpayers. The coordination effect thereby fixed the mechanism of mutual arrears as a stable norm, which was further strengthened through linkage with barter and tax evasion.[12] As a result, application of the bankruptcy law was fully blocked by mutual arrears, which by then had become a universal practice.[13]

Tax Evasion

For an economic agent, the strategic choice between the payment and nonpayment of taxes is determined by a number of fundamental and organizational factors. The first group includes taxation policy and government expenditure policy.

To avoid nonpayment, citizens need to be assured that the money they pay will help improve their well-being (in a broad sense) and be spent with due efficiency. Lack of such assurances puts an edge on the free-rider problem. With the state performing inefficiently, tax evasion may prove to be the most clever behavioral option, not only for each individual free-rider, but also for society as a whole. Nonpayment of taxes becomes morally justified. Public confidence decreases especially rapidly if the government imposes higher tax rates and slashes social expenditures at the same time, as the Russian government has done since 1992, because people fail to see any positive effect from the growing tax burden.

For anyone making a strategic choice in the tax sphere, it is perhaps more important to consider the organizational factor, i.e., the system of enforcement causing a person to expect tax evasion to be dangerous. When sweeping reforms were launched in Russia, its tax-collecting service was still rudimentary, its enforcement machinery was very weak, and its tax police would not be formed until 1997.

Where tax rates are too high and the enforcement mechanisms are inefficient, tax evasion looks attractive to many economic agents. The individual's chance of being caught is small. The more widespread the nonpaying practice, the less tangible the damage one can expect to incur as a result of refusing to pay. This coordination effect gives an additional incentive for still bolder tax evasion.

Mass tax evasion leads to the emergence of an appropriate service system involving numerous mediators, creators of one-day firms, and designers of new tax evasion schemes (Dolgopyatova 1998). As usual, the learning effect is accompanied by the linkage effect: special organizational forms of production appear; false accounting and reporting becomes widespread; tax evasion conjoins with barter, arrears, and corruption. A firm wishing to quit the shadow sector would be exposed to high transformation costs; besides, having paid once, it would remain under the tax collectors' scrutiny for the rest of its days. Therefore, small-scale financial injections into the tax-collecting system can only lead to a further swelling of costs in the tax evasion system, thus adding to the overall exhaustion of the economy. Modest tax rate reductions cannot help either: the nonpayers will continue to evade taxation, and the law-abiding taxpayers will pay less. This is a striking illustration of the hysteresis effect.

Corruption

Every potential bribe-taker makes decisions comparing his/her gains from bribes and from honest behavior. In Russia, income inequality jumped sharply during transition because of uneven transitional rent expropriation (see next section). The state was not able to adjust properly the salaries of bureaucrats, which turned out to be insignificant in comparison to bribes from the newly rich. It was a base for an increase in corruption activity. Inefficient government policy, inadequate legislation, unclear norms for new market behavior, and weak mechanisms of government control contributed to a rise in corruption.

The larger the scale of corruption, the smaller the chances that a bribe-taker will be caught. This external dependence underlies the coordination effect, adding stability to a corrupt system. With time, it tends to perfect itself by building an internal hierarchy and linking with other shadow economy mechanisms.[14]

Foreign Trade-Related Economic Stagnation

Extreme trends in foreign trade policy can lead a country into an institutional trap. Over the past 20 years, much criticism has been voiced in the scientific community with regard to protectionist, import-substitution strategies of economic development. Barring domestic producers from competition with peers in the world market distorts the price structure of protected industries and gives them no incentive to work better. Unlike the case studies described above, there is no coordination effect here. The cumulative impact of macroeconomic policy is based on the learning and linkage effects: protectionist attitude to one industry affects—via prices—the production structure and consumer stereotypes throughout the economy. Attempts to change protectionist policies can be blocked by resistance from lobbyists, leading to the institutional trap's perpetuation.

However, a premature, ill-prepared attempt to liberalize foreign trade also leads to an institutional trap. This problem arises in technologically lagging countries like Russia, rich in raw materials. These resources are processed into consumer goods of such poor quality that they cannot be sold on the world market. For such countries, the best short-term strategy would be to invigorate exports of raw materials, curtail domestic production, and spend the bulk of export revenues on internal consumption. That, however, would inevitably lead to the closure of manufacturing enterprises and mass unemployment, which would have a destructive cumulative effect: declining labor skills, a wider gap in incomes, higher social tensions, rising crime, and social apathy. Such a policy would result in the national economy's collapse once the raw material sources were exhausted, or even sooner, in the event of a change for the worse on the world market for raw materials. Hence the best long-term strategy is to aid domestic production with subsidies that are gradually removed as modern technology is purchased with the help of export revenues.

A country with an unstable political system would be more likely to choose the short-term option. The longer the period during which the food-for-raw-materials policy is pursued, the higher the transformation costs, and the greater the difficulty such a country faces shifting toward a better behavioral norm. Thus the system would find itself in an institutional trap.

The cumulative effects of mass unemployment due to interaction with a more advanced economy have been especially pronounced as far as the ethnic groups inhabiting Russia's northern regions are concerned. A rapid economic degradation over the past few decades has occurred despite considerable financial assistance intended to integrate these nationalities into European civilization. This should serve as a serious warning to the proponents of shock therapy. The recently discovered negative correlation between rich natural resources and economic growth in developing countries demonstrates that it is vital to resist the temptation of choosing the short-term strategy option (see references in Rodrik 1996b).

Institutional Conflict

History knows many futile attempts to transfer institutions from one cultural environment to another. It is not accidental that economic mechanisms in once backward, but now rapidly progressing countries, such as Japan, South Korea or China, are strikingly different from their American or European prototypes. It is all the more surprising that at the outset of Russian reforms no one at the government level had actually raised the issue of how much the U.S. institutions (which were chosen for replication in this country) were compatible with Russia's cultural tradition. Meanwhile, cultural inertia could not fail to exert its influence on the forcibly imposed institutional innovations.

Conflict between established and newly introduced norms sometimes gives birth to nonviable institutions (such as Russia's Bankruptcy Law, passed at the peak of the mutual arrears crisis), although occasionally it generates some stable but inefficient mutant structures which essentially constitute a kind of institutional trap.

A good example of such a mutant structure is the open joint-stock company controlled by its workers, a new type of enterprise that emerged during Russia's privatization campaign.[15] Seeking to avoid the formation of collective enterprises (that are difficult to restructure) and to breed a

Western-style corporate system on Russian soil, the government produced a hybrid utterly unprepared for efficient development. If the majority of such a company's shares are distributed among its management and personnel, the managers cannot afford mass layoffs because, if the fired workers sell their shares to external investors, the old management is likely to leave. For similar reasons, the staff should be very careful about dismissing its managers, because if the latter sell their stock, the company might change hands, and unemployment could loom large over the workers. Many Russian firms have redundant staffs and suffer from manager incompetence; their paradoxical organizational structure, however, prevents them from cutting labor costs or inviting new managers.

Reform Process and the State

Since reforms are implemented by government, the state inevitably plays a decisive role during a period of major reforms. This holds true even when reforms are aimed at decreasing the role of the state. When launching a reform campaign, the government influences the future of citizens and manipulates assets far more than under normal circumstances.

The role of government is often measured by the share of expenditure in GDP. This indicator reflects the state's ability to redistribute resources within systems with established institutions, but is absolutely irrelevant, for instance, at a time of mass privatization when the value of the flow of redistributed assets increases many times over. It is this circumstance that makes market reforms possible: a government pursuing the reforms weakens the positions of its future successors, rather than its own position.

Large-scale economic reform is not a sudden act of creation. Rather, it is a process that requires preparation of the economy for transformation, effective provisional institutions to guide the reforms, proper rate and sequencing of the reforms, and consistent discretionary economic policy. Avoidance of institutional traps is one of the important tasks of the reformative state.

Transitional Rent and Reform Failures

Any limitation imposed on the free flow of resources or the level of prices is equivalent to a privilege-generating rental income (income that would not be present under competitive equilibrium). A major source of such income in the Soviet-style economies was the margin between wholesale and retail, as well as domestic and world prices. The bulk of the rent went into the state budget to be redistributed, and the rest was stolen by high-ranking officials and shadow dealers. The freeing of prices was expected to eliminate the rental income together with the opportunities for abuses associated with it. Comparison of the prevailing regime with competitive equilibrium was fully in favor of the latter; hence the conclusion that lifting the limitations and ending government interference would be sufficient to raise efficiency quickly. The problem was rooted in disregard for transitional period difficulties. It had less dramatic consequences for smaller countries with more advanced economic mechanisms, more efficient banking systems, and prices approaching world prices. Russia's losses, however, have been tremendous.

At a time of economic liberalization, some economic agents are able to derive additional income—transitional rent—exclusively from their prominent positions. Price liberalization gives the advantage to suppliers of goods in high demand. Foreign trade liberalization allows importers and exporters to profit from differences in domestic and world prices. The emergence of new stock exchanges and securities markets creates ample arbitrage opportunities for banks.

Until 1992, because of the foreign trade monopoly, all rental income derived from the low prices of raw materials in Russia was collected by the state. Some of it was lost because government officials were inefficient and corrupt, and the rest went into the state budget. The obvious deficiencies of this mechanism served as an argument for a shock liberalization of prices and foreign trade. The underlying rationale was that once domestic prices balanced out with world prices, the rent income would be eliminated, exporters would be given the necessary market incentives, government would no longer need to regulate economic performance, and there would be no losses at all.

This logic is faulty, apart from the impact of liberalized foreign trade on domestic production. In a country like Russia, with its vast territory and weak interregional ties, it takes years to attain a postliberalization equilibrium. During the transitional period, private firms continued to earn the rental income which the state rejected. Although this income tends to diminish gradually, it is so high at the initial stage that those finding themselves in the right place at the right time can get fantastically rich overnight. Since income reinvestment mechanisms are yet to be created, the income is spent on consumption by a small group of individuals, while the majority of the population falls into poverty.[16]

Price liberalization results in both redistribution of rental income abandoned by the state and—during the transition period—partial dissipation of rental income, because resources are spent on the search for an equilibrium. Specifically, losses occur because the economic agents' activities lack coordination. Firms try to use new opportunities and break long chains of traditional connections. This leads to disorganization (Blanchard and Kremer 1997). In the course of the search process, some production capacities stay idle because of a lack of raw material, supplies, or demand for the final products, and some of the products already manufactured cannot be sold. Losses of this kind are included in transformation costs. They are a major cause for what is referred to as "transformational recession."

The appropriation of transitional rent causes jumps of income inequality and crime rate, which are both observed in many economies in transition. As a result the system may fall into a corruption trap. Lack of coordination and the dissipation of rental income entail insolvency of many enterprises and contribute to the forming of the mechanisms of arrears and tax evasion. Reforms should be well prepared to diminish the transitional rent and to have most of it collected by the state.

Rate, Preparedness, and Sequence of Reforms

One of the important parameters of the reform process is the rate of reforms.[17] Proponents of shock therapy argue that reforms are similar to a surgery that has to be done as quickly as possible to minimize suffering. They also point out that reforms will be irreversible if their opponents do not have enough time to consolidate. Neither argument permits any doubt as to the expediency of the reforms. A more subtle and perhaps more valid point made by the supporters of shock therapy is that reforms can be launched only if the threshold values of certain parameters have been exceeded. For example, it would be silly to privatize just one enterprise; privatization can be efficient only when there is a sufficient number of privatized firms with a market infrastructure of their own.

An alternative, gradualist viewpoint is based on three key arguments. First, conducting reforms and creating new institutions require the availability of funds to finance the relevant transformation costs. If we look at the proposed plan of reforms in a package with other potential investment options, the overall target being to optimize consumption for a certain period, we will be able to design a well-balanced strategy that, typically, should provide for the gradual nature of any transformations.

Second, one can never be sure that the original plan of reforms will not have to be amended. No one can guarantee that the proposed changes will not lead the country into institutional difficulties. When reforms are too rapid, it is extremely difficult or impossible to make interim assessments or correct mistakes.

Third, reforms should be thoroughly prepared[18] and duly sequenced. As discussed above, shock liberalization of prices inevitably leads to barter and arrears traps if there is no efficient banking system to avoid inordinate transaction costs during the period of soaring prices. Similarly, foreign trade liberalization should not occur before the domestic market has been sufficiently liberalized and a system of (temporary) export tariffs introduced for purposes of collecting the transitional rent. In an economy with inflexible and unbalanced prices, the positive effects of market expansion and import growth can be reduced to naught because of the outflow of resources, high rates of unemployment, or considerable differentiation of income caused by the lifting of controls over exports and imports. A gradual approach does not necessarily delay positive transformation. On the contrary, good preparation and sequencing accelerate the success of reforms.

Experience of large-scale transformations reveals an important specific aspect of macroeconomic policy in economies in transition. If market mechanisms are well developed, macroeconomic policy will influence mostly economic indicators such as exchange rate, inflation, or GDP. However, in a country with an unstable institutional structure, macro-economic policies may easily alter that structure. In Russia, the standard recipe for fighting inflation—tough monetary policy—promoted formation of institutional traps. The government had abandoned seigniorage without having first established a reliable tax-collecting system. When the tax-collection level was low, stabilization was attained through external loans, mutual arrears, and barter, which contributed to the confidence crisis in August 1998.

Industrial Policy

Industrial policy is important for economies lacking well-formed market institutions. The "economic miracles" of South Korea and Taiwan began not with privatization but with the creation of state-owned enterprises in promising industries. These countries liberalized foreign trade on a step-by-step basis over a 30-year period, and have continued to maintain significant control over foreign investments almost to the present day. Rodrik (1995, 1996a) points out that Mexico, Bolivia, and Argentina, which have moved much faster in privatization and foreign trade/finance liberalization, have been far less successful than the Southeast Asian economies that made ample use of instruments of industrial policy such as credit benefits and protectionism.[19]

Where reforms are pursued in a system with an unstable institutional structure and strong fluctuations of macroeconomic variables, the position of enterprises may be more dependent on chance circumstances than on quality management. In such a context, industrial policy acquires added importance. It should be aimed at protecting selected companies from bankruptcy and even entire industries of national significance that may be in dire straits at the moment. It is no less important for the state to initiate and support economic growth, encourage competition, and regulate exports and imports by setting appropriate customs tariffs and quotas.

Indicative planning has been a useful instrument of government policy in a number of countries, especially in Japan and France during their transitional period after the Second World War (Cazes 1990; Sato 1990). Planning provides for a possibility to integrate different sides of the government's interference in the economic sphere, and to coordinate decisions of economic agents through a system of incentives and through a dialogue involving representatives of various social, economic, and political groups. It can be useful for modern transitional economies as well.

Reforms became necessary in Russia and Eastern Europe because the system of total government control over the economy had demonstrated its inefficiency. However, if the government cannot make efficient long-term decisions, reforms may fail. Neither managers nor private entrepreneurs have the necessary planning horizon. Feeling uncertain about their future, economic agents set short-term targets, while the invisible hand of the budding market is still unable to transform egoistic strategies into socially relevant behavior. Indicative planning is expected to mitigate this inevitable deficiency of the transitional regime.

A typical and important process for a transitional period is the emergence of large corporations (Dementjev 1998). This has been evident in virtually all economies undergoing successful transition, including postwar Japan and South Korea (see Chapter 8 by Irma Adelman). A large corporation has the necessary planning horizon and resources to make major investments. Also, the growth of corporations reduces market transactions, taking the edge off the problems of barter and criminalization. Assuming honest government administration, large corporations facilitate tax-collection. A long-term industrial policy providing support for large producers (such as financial-industrial groups), if combined with anti-monopoly measures and safeguards to ensure proper corporate governance, could help overcome institutional traps.

Conclusion

Every reform leaves space for unexpected forms of institutional development, and should be preceded by efforts to forecast and forestall possible institutional traps.

Preparedness of a system for institutional transformations is imperative for their success. Transformation costs should be taken into account. Proper choice of the rate and sequence of the reforms, and prudent industrial policy, are prerequisites for avoiding institutional traps. At the initial stage of reforms, an important task of the state is to collect most of the transitional rent, which would diminish production losses, minimize unfair income differentiation, and hold corruption and rent seeking activity in check.

Sometimes institutional targets of a reform conflict with macroeconomic goals. Routine manipulations of short-term macroeconomic policy instruments may lead to transformation of unstable institutional structures in harmful directions. Once an institutional trap is formed, the task of breaking out of it is very difficult. A standard approach is the imposition of harsher sanctions for deviation from socially efficient norms. Such a strategy may imply considerable expenditures and could generate even worse institutional traps. The history of Russia's struggle against arrears and tax evasion shows how difficult it is for a country to solve the problem solely in this manner.

There are reasons to believe that an economy could gradually develop mechanisms conducive to its exit from institutional traps. For example, after property is divided and transitional rent is exhausted, the winners (recent rent seekers) begin to be interested in stability and law enforcement. The institution of reputation starts to play a greater role in creating incentives for ethical personal behavior (Tirole 1993; Bicchierri and Rovelli 1996). These tendencies facilitate exit from corruption and tax evasion traps.

However, it is quite possible that new reforms will be necessary to get out of institutional traps. The measures should be directed to weaken the stabilizing mechanisms that support the traps (coordination, linkage, and inertia effects); to increase transaction costs of socially inefficient norms; to reduce transaction costs of socially efficient behavior; and to lower transformation costs of the transition process.

Transition policies would be more effective if greater attention were given to the role of government in the shaping of new institutions. No single agent other than the government is capable of making long-term decisions in situations characterized by fundamental institutional change. If the government is weak or passive, reforms are doomed to failure.

One should not think that a market institution could be effective regardless of culture and history. Naïve attempts to imitate economic organizations of more developed countries result in institutional conflicts. Wise reform strategies would help economies find their own forms of the invisible hand.

Notes

1. The exposition follows Polterovich (1999).

2. The first of these notions is widely known. According to Eggertsson (1990), transaction costs include: (1) search for information on a product/service and search for a prospective transaction partner; (2) bargaining, and the preparation and signing of an agreement; (3) control over, and enforcement of, compliance with a transaction agreement; (4) settlements under, and formalization of, the agreement in the process of its implementation; (5) the agreement's protection from third parties (e.g., from the tax-collecting authorities in the event of an illegal agreement).

3. Some authors use the term "transformation costs" in a different sense, meaning the costs of resource utilization. In this paper, it always refers to the costs of institutional transformation.

4. Rodrik (1996a) discusses the reform difficulty indicator as the ratio of income redistributed in the reform process to gains from increased system efficiency. In certain cases this indicator, referred to as the political cost-benefit ratio, can be effectively assessed.

5. Arthur considers the learning effect for technical changes. He argues that as certain products hit the market, their quality improves or their production

becomes less costly, which essentially implies some perfection (Arthur 1988). Learning models are dealt with in Arthur (1994, chapter 8).

6. Arthur and North use the term "lock-in."

7. The term has been borrowed from physics. In certain cases the state of a system is dependent not only on the value of an exogenous parameter but also on whether that value results from the parameter's decrease or increase. That is what is called hysteresis. If we have changed the state of a system by increasing the parameter (in our example, the transaction costs of monetary exchange), then, considering the hysteretic lag in the system's returning to its original state, we need to decrease the parameter to a value below the original one. Hysteresis is a form of a system's dependence on its path of development (path dependence).

8. For a detailed description of the barter exchange mechanism see Kleiner and Makarov (1996). By various estimates, between 50 and 80 percent of all exchanges among the producer companies were barter based in 1997. It should be noted that Russian Federation Pension Fund officials actively helped enterprises to organize barter chains in order to increase cash flows into the fund's budget. Fund head V. Barchuk recalls that the would-be premier, S. Kirienko, who still worked in Nizhny Novgorod at the time, succeeded in seeing through one of the most elaborate schemes of barter exchanges (Rubchenko 1998).

9. Hence V. Barchuk's observation that you cannot do away with barter overnight (Rubchenko 1998).

10. Of course, it is a very stylized description of the events. Two norms, barter and arrears, are caused by expensive real money and are substitutes in a sense: an agent can choose between two possibilities to avoid payments. Sometimes arrears are an implicit form of barter (see below). One can note also that the high price of real money was supported by a very high rate of return of government bonds in 1997–98.

11. The mechanism of arrears was studied in a number of papers (Polterovich 1993, Calvo and Coricelli 1995, and Gomulka 1994).

12. A company is not motivated to claim payments from its consumers if all funds credited to its account are automatically transferred to the state budget, as was the case with the blacklisted nonpayers in Russia in 1995–97.

13. It should be noted that many enterprises did their best to balance out their payables and receivables. If such a balance were kept up by each company, the

mechanism of arrears could have developed into a form of barter exchange which, however, would have been marked by a high degree of uncertainty and, consequently, by still higher transaction costs. Let me also point out that the government's own systematic nonfulfillment of obligations notably strengthened the mechanism of mutual arrears.

14. In fact corruption traps were studied in many papers. See Lui (1986), Tirole (1993), Polterovich (1998), and references in Bardhan (1997).

15. One sees similar mutants in other countries, but this form rarely dominates.

16. The notion of transitional rent is introduced in Polterovich (1998); similar ideas can be found in Gelb, Hillman, and Ursprung (1996).

17. The rates of reforms have been discussed in the scientific community largely in conjunction with privatization. See Blanchard (1997) and Polterovich (1996) for a review of opinions and references.

18. Reform preparedness (measured by the initial liberalization index) has been shown to be of primary importance to the success of reform programs in the East European economies (De Melo, Denizer, Gelb, and Tenev 1997; Volyansky 1997). A similar conclusion was drawn from the experience of Southeast Asian countries. Variations of their rates of growth between 1960 and 1994 can be largely explained by institution quality indexes (Rodrik 1996b). The absence among the independent variables of macroeconomic regulation characteristics leads one to believe that macroeconomic policy impacts the long-term growth inasmuch as it impacts the formation of economic institutions.

19. Joseph Stiglitz proposes a Post–Washington Consensus (Preface, Stiglitz 1998a and 1998b) that takes into account the role of government in promoting economic development. Stiglitz emphasizes government support for human capital development, financing of investment, and the dissemination of technology. Both factors have played a decisive role in economic growth in Asia.

References

Arthur, W. Brian. 1988. "Self-Reinforcing Mechanisms in Economics," in Philip W. Anderson, Kenneth J. Arrow, and D. Pines, eds., *The Economy as an Evolving Complex System*. Pp. 9–31. Santa Fe, NM: Addison-Wesley Publishing Company.

————— 1994. *Increasing Returns and Path Dependence in the Economy.* Ann Arbor, MI: The University of Michigan Press.

Bardhan, Pranab. 1997. "Corruption and Development: A Review of Issues." *Journal of Economic Literature* 35(3): 1320–1346.

Bicchierri, C., and C. Rovelli. 1996. "Evolution and Revolution: The Dynamics of Corruption." *Rationality and Society* 7(2).

Blanchard, Olivier, and M. Kremer. 1997. "Disorganization." *Quarterly Journal of Economics* 112(4): 1091–1126.

Blanchard, Olivier. 1997. *The Economics of Post-Communist Transition.* Oxford: Clarendon Press.

Calvo, Guillermo A., and F. Coricelli. 1995. "Interenterprise Arrears in Economies in Transition," in Robert Holzmann, J. Gacs and G. Winckler, eds., *Output Decline in Eastern Europe: Unavoidable, External Influence or Homemade?* Pp. 193–212. Boston and London: Kluwer Academic.

Cazes, Bernard. 1990. "Indicative Planning in France." *Journal of Comparative Economics* 14(4): 607–620.

De Melo, Martha, C. Denizer, Alan Gelb, and S. Tenev. 1997. *Circumstance and Choice: The Role of Initial Conditions and Policies in Transition Economies.* Washington, DC: World Bank.

Dementjev, V. 1998. "Integratsiia predpriiatii i ekonomicheskoe razvitie." Working Paper No. 38. Moscow: CEMI-RAS.

Dolgopyatova, Tatiana, ed. 1998. *Neformalnyi sektor v rossiiskoi ekonomike.* Moscow: ISARP.

Eggertsson, Thrainn. 1990. *Economic Behavior and Institutions.* New York: Cambridge University Press.

Gelb, Alan, A. Hillman, and H. Ursprung. 1996. "Rents and the Transition." Background Paper, World Bank Development Report.

Gomulka, Stanislaw. 1994. "The Financial Situation of Enterprises and Its Impact on Monetary and Fiscal Policies, Poland 1992–93." *Economics of Transition* 2(2): 189–208.

Kleiner, George B., and V. L. Makarov. 1996. *Barter v Rossiiskoi ekonomike.* Moscow: CEMI-RAS.

Lui, Francis T. 1986. "A Dynamic Model of Corruption Deterrence." *Journal of Public Economics* 31(2): 215–236.

North, Douglass. 1990. *Institutions, Institutional Change and Economic Performance.* New York: Cambridge University Press.

Polterovich, Victor M. 1993. "Ekonomicheskaia reforma v Rossii v 1992: Bitva pravitelstva s trudovymi kollektivami." *Ekonomika i matematicheskie metody* 29(4): 265–287.

————. 1996. "Towards the Theory of Privatization." Central Economic-Mathematical Institute, Russian Academy of Sciences. Working Paper No. 1.

————. 1998. "Faktory korruptsii." *Ekonomika i matematicheskie metody* 34(3).

————. 1999. "Institutsionalnie lovushki i ekonomicheskie reformy." *Ekonomika i matematicheskie metody* 35(2).

Rodrik, Dani. 1995. "Getting Intervention Right: How South Korea and Taiwan Grew Rich." *Economic Policy: A European Forum* 0(20): 53–97.

————. 1996a. "Institutions and Economic Performance in East and Southeast Asia," in Round Table Conference, The Institutional Foundation of Economic Development in East Asia. Pp. 391–429. Tokyo, December 16–19.

————. 1996b. "Understanding Economic Policy Reform." *Journal of Economic Literature* 34(1): 9–41.

Rubchenko, M. 1998. "Borba za spokoinaia starost." Interview with Russian Pension Fund Chairman V. Barchuk. *Ekspert* 11(17): 134.

Sato, Kazuo. 1990. "Indicative Planning in Japan." *Journal of Comparative Economics* 14(4): 625–647.

Stiglitz, Joseph E. 1998a. "More Instruments and Broader Goals: Moving toward the Post–Washington Consensus." Wider Annual Lectures 2. The United Nations University, May.

————. 1998b. "Towards a New Paradigm for Development: Strategies, Policies and Processes." 1998 Prebisch Lecture, Geneva, UNCTAD

Tirole, Jean A. 1993. *Theory of Collective Reputations with Applications to the Persistence of Corruption and to Firm Quality.* Paris: Institut d'Economie Industrielle, Toulouse, MIT, and Ceras.

Volyansky, D. 1997. "Infliatsiia, retsessiia i podgotovlenost reform v stranakh s perekhodnoi ekonomikoi." M.S. thesis, Moscow State University.

8

Lessons from Korea

Irma Adelman

No observer can fail to be deeply impressed by the economic development of South Korea. In the aftermath of the Japanese occupation and the Korean War, most of the population lived at subsistence levels. Since then, Korea has become a thriving OECD country with an even distribution of income and a per capita income over $10,000. Even the financial debacle of the late 1990s, which revealed serious policy flaws, does not disprove the fundamental effectiveness of the Korean strategy of government-led development.

The Korean experience contradicts the Washington Consensus, which is opposed to government-led development and has tied the hands of Russian policy makers. Korean development was led by an activist government. Mobilizing private entrepreneurs, the bureaucracy, and the general public, the government pushed its plan for economic growth and gave continual detailed attention to economic matters. Policies were developed and modified, and excesses corrected, in a deliberate and pragmatic fashion. Had the neoliberal prescriptions forced on Russia been adopted in Korea during the 1960s and 1970s, there would not have been a Korean economic miracle.[1]

This chapter describes two five-year plans implemented under President Park, who not only provided inspiration but also personally guided investment, trade, and financial policies. The first plan, 1962–66, focused on infrastructure development and import substitution. The second, 1967–72, emphasized export-oriented industrialization. After examining the critical role of these two plans in the rapid economic progress of Korea, this chapter discusses how mismanaged financial liberalization led to severe economic troubles in the late 1990s.

First Five-Year Plan (1962–66)

The turning point was the ascension to the presidency in 1961 of Major General Park Chung Hee. Before President Park took office, massive unemployment had provoked demonstrations by students and the unemployed. Foreign aid and government loans to an impoverished Korea were financing more than half of imports and over 80 percent of investment. Park quickly transformed the country from a passive *soft state* to an activist *hard state* with a banner slogan of "eradicating poverty through rapid economic growth." Economic development was an integral part of a nationalistic vision of a strong, independent Korea.

Upon coming to power, President Park quickly made his intentions clear and credible. He sacked 10 percent of the top bureaucracy and sent the rest to two-week retraining courses that stressed both management techniques and commitment. The president devoted three to four hours a day to the economy, and kept abreast of both general developments and specific issues (Jones and Sakong 1980).

Strategy

The basic strategy for increasing employment was to apply labor-intensive methods to construction of new infrastructure, including roads, dams, irrigation, and other transport and energy projects. Import substitution, a complementary means to increase employment, was adopted primarily to improve the balance of payments. Policies were targeted toward expanding industries that produce inputs for other industries—cement, chemical fertilizer, refined petroleum, iron and steel, and synthetic fibers. Another goal was self-sufficiency in food grains within five years.

Import substitution was pursued by implementing measures to reduce the inflow of foreign goods. The main mechanisms used to protect the domestic market were import controls, tariffs, a severely undervalued currency, and multiple exchange rates. The rate of protection was highest for consumer goods and lowest on intermediates. According to Westphal (1978), the effective exchange rate for exports was 10 percent above that for imports. Exchange premiums and cash subsidies, rather than indirect taxes and tariffs, were the main sources of this differential. Quantitative import controls were more important than the biased trade incentives. The list of prohibited imports exceeded 600 in 1965, and a third of actual imports were on the restricted list (Westphal 1978).

The government set low prices for staple foods to allow industrialization to take place at low wages. Lacking the stimulus of high prices, agricultural investment was low and farm productivity improved only slowly. Not surprisingly, Korea fell short of its announced goal of self-sufficiency in grains. Subsidized imports of grain from the United States (PL480) and rice rationing compensated for deficient agricultural development.[2]

Macroeconomic Management

The overall macroeconomic management of the economy was anything but conservative. In the face of a low domestic savings rate, the rapid industrialization generated inflation, which averaged 16 percent and exceeded 20 percent in two out of five years.[3] Some price controls were used prior to 1964 to stabilize prices, though with only limited success.

The financing of investment required foreign exchange and domestic savings. In 1962 the national savings rate was just over 3 percent with both personal and government savings negative. The national savings rate rose over the period to an average of 8 percent of GNP, but the gross domestic investment ratio exceeded the national savings rate by an average of 8.4 percentage points per year. The bulk of investment was financed by U.S. aid, which had started to decline in 1957, and foreign private loans, which previously had been negligible.

The mobilization of domestic savings was facilitated by two important policy changes in 1965. First, tax reform increased government revenue by 50 percent. Second, there was a doubling of real interest rates on bank deposits. The increase in real interest rates, which previously had been negative, raised the share of bank loans from less than one-fifth of loanable funds to over half.

Results

Contrary to present conventional wisdom on economic development, import substitution in Korea was successful and accounted for most of the economic growth during this period (Kim and Roemer 1979). Manufacturing production rose by almost 50 percent. GDP grew an average of 8 percent per year, almost double the annual growth rate from 1953 to 1962. Growth of per capita income averaged 7 percent, leading to an increase in GNP per capita of 40 percent. Labor absorption was significant with a 10 percent increase in employment. However, due to growth in the labor force, unemployment plus underemployment declined only moderately to 15.5 percent. Nevertheless, the trade deficit remained quite large as the industrialization effort forced a 75 percent increase in industrial imports.

There was substantial investment in education. Between 1961 and 1966, both primary and secondary enrollment rose by about a third, while university enrollment doubled. By 1966, Korea had achieved universal primary education and the rate of university enrollment was greater than in Great Britain. The health of the population improved, with infant mortality declining over 10 percent and life expectancy rising almost 6 years (National Statistical Office 1994). New social welfare measures were introduced, including government and military pensions. Poverty assistance and disaster relief policies were also initiated (Kwon 1993a and 1993b).

Poverty remained substantial with two-fifths of all households in 1965 falling below the absolute poverty line (55 percent of urban and 36 percent of rural households) (Suh 1985). However, Korea's income distribution in 1965 was one of the most even in the world. Egalitarian asset redistributions had been undertaken by the government after the liberation from Japan (Čhoo 1977 and 1985). During the 1962–66 period, there was rapid absorption of labor from a relatively low productivity sector, agriculture, to a high productivity sector, manufacturing. The technology used to construct infrastructure was labor-intensive, and the capital/output ratios were very low by international standards.

In sum, this short period of classical, import-substitute industrialization emphasized infrastructure development. The industrialization benefited from the protection afforded by strict and pervasive restrictions on imports, including tariffs and significantly undervalued exchange rates. Industrialization was further promoted by subsidized credit and by foreign exchange licensing and allocations. The strategy was successful from both a growth and social development perspective. However, the newly produced industrial output was not competitive in world markets and, by the end of the period, the opportunities for further industrial output expansion afforded by increases in domestic demand had been exhausted.

Second Five-Year Plan (1967–72)

The period of the second five-year plan was the golden age for Korean economic development. The emphasis shifted from import substitution in producer inputs to the exporting of labor-intensive consumer goods.[4] This yielded rapid industrialization and a surge in growth with equity. Starting the period with substantial unemployment, Korea virtually exhausted its supply of surplus labor. The export orientation of the second five-year plan was innovative, for at the time most developing countries were focused on import substitution.

Several factors motivated the reorientation toward exports. First, the size of the domestic economy was woefully small. The total Korean GDP generated the equivalent domestic purchasing power of a typical American city of about two-thirds of a million. This was hardly sufficient to support significant industrialization.

Second, the economy was poor in natural resources and, despite success with import substitution, still had few intermediate industries. Thus, the import content of gross output was large: 0.6 units in imports were required to generate 1 unit of additional domestic production. As foreign aid was expected to be phased out in about a decade, this meant that export capability would have to be built up to support domestic production. Of course, elevated import-output coefficients were used in other countries to argue for deepening import substitution into intermediates and machinery. But not only are the early years of import substitution in intermediates necessarily more import-intensive than existing production, they are also more capital-intensive. The deepening of import substitution into intermediates would therefore have caused a further widening of the trade gap and would have been unable to generate sufficient employment to absorb the unemployed labor force.

A third factor was that abundant human resources were available at low wages. Korea could capitalize on this comparative advantage by producing goods for export. Fourth, President Park, committed to economic independence, recognized that exports were necessary to reduce dependence on foreign aid. Finally, there were the examples of Japan and Taiwan, which were already successfully pursuing export-oriented strategies.

Strategy

The government aggressively sought to expand exports. The actions ranged from nondiscretionary market-oriented measures to presidential pressure on individual firms.

Measures to promote import substitution remained in place, strengthening the position of manufacturers with export potential. Foreign competition was restricted by tariffs, import licensing, foreign exchange controls, and prohibitions on imports of some commodities and quotas on others. Tariff rates varied from 13.5 percent on mining and energy to 106 percent on beverages and tobacco (Koo 1977). Keeping the exchange rate low not only restrained imports but also stimulated exports.[5]

New initiatives to expand exports included long-term low-interest government subsidized loans and price controls on critical inputs and wages (Song 1996). On a selective basis, and especially to favor new industries, manufacturers of exports were granted income tax reductions, loan guarantees to stimulate loans from abroad, and the right to purchase needed machinery and equipment free of import duties. Raw materials needed to manufacture exports could be imported duty free, and a "wastage allowance system" permitted the domestic resale of some portion of the raw materials ostensibly imported for the manufacturing of exports. Even though it was not the intention to discriminate among exporters, the incentive system resulted in commodity-specific effective exchange rates. The effective subsidy rate varied widely, ranging from 125 won per dollar for exported nylon fabrics to 5 won per dollar for fresh fish (Koo 1977).

Was this complex policy preferable to an outright devaluation? Second-best trade theory suggests that unified exchange rate systems are suboptimal in the presence of factor-market imperfections, externalities, monopoly, and "infant industries" (Little et al. 1970; Srinivasan and Bhagwati 1978; Mitra 1992a and 1992b; and Devarajan et al. 1990). Coordinated tax or tariff cum subsidy policies are needed to overcome these distortions and move the economy toward optimality.[6] Finally, in the presence of market imperfections and externalities, an exchange rate which is favorable to exports may delay capital deepening and the expansion of the domestic market for exportables. The last effect is especially important; even in export industries the contribution of domestic demand is likely to exceed that of exports.[7]

The analysis of market incentives does not tell the whole story of how the export drive was accomplished. The government established a variety of export-promotion organizations, including the Korea Trade Association, the Korea Trade Promotion Corporation, and government-financed research institutes. Discretionary command (nonmarket) methods were vigorously applied, including presidential jawboning. The Ministry of Commerce established ever rising export targets and monitored the performance of individual firms. Firms exceeding their quotas were rewarded by subsidized credit and import licenses. Firms that fell short were liable to lose their foreign trade licenses and occasionally were subject to rash measures such as tax audits and the shutoff of utilities.

The president himself kept close track of enterprise export performance and worked tirelessly to stimulate exports. Monthly meetings were held between the president and large exporters in which those who did best were honored. At such meetings and by other channels, the president was kept informed of specific bureaucratic and factor supply bottlenecks to export expansion, which he directed his staff to clear.

Macroeconomic Management

Macroeconomic management continued to be oriented toward growth rather than stability. The gross domestic investment rate averaged 22 percent of GNP, which exceeded the gross domestic savings rate by about a third. A large shortfall in savings occurred despite a doubling of the savings rate from its value in the previous period.[8] The ratio of credit to GNP more than doubled. Inflation, although moderate, exceeded 10 percent every year.

Almost two-fifths of the aggressive investment program was financed by foreign loans. The main instrument to promote this inflow was a system of guarantees by Korean banks for the repayment of loans.

Results

The economy grew very rapidly. GNP expanded on average 9.6 percent per year, and structural change accelerated as the share of manufacturing in GNP increased by 50 percent while that of agriculture dropped by a third. Per capita GNP increased by a factor of more than two and a half.

The annual increase of exports averaged a phenomenal 46 percent, leading to a tenfold increase in exports over the period.[9] Manufacturing led the way as its share of exports increased from 60 to 70 percent. In 1973 export-manufacturing industries accounted for 50 percent of the capital stock and 33 percent of employment.[10] However, since imports had been so much larger than exports, trade deficits continued to be substantial (Hong 1979, 361).[11]

The labor market became tight, with employment rising by 25 percent, and unemployment cut in half. The average wage of unskilled workers tripled. The distribution of income became even more level than it had been in 1965, with a doubling of the income share of the poorest decile. School enrollments increased by 28 percent, primarily due to expansion in secondary education.[12] Infant mortality dropped by 30 percent, and life expectancy rose by five years (National Statistical Office 1994).

The Planning Process

The planning process was integral to the Korean development strategy. A year and a half before the second five-year plan went into effect, well-publicized lengthy meetings began. Attending the meetings were the top staff of the Economic Planning Board and the economic ministers of the cabinet.[13]

The meetings were chaired by the deputy prime minister and began with the Economic Planning Board briefing the ministers on various features of the plan.[14] Each minister raised questions about the assumptions and implications relating to his or her own bailiwick: employment (Minister of Labor), agriculture (Minister of Agriculture), exports (Minister of Commerce and Industry), foreign exchange requirements and inflation (Minister of Finance). Thus, the planners were forced to consider the implications of their plan from a broad national perspective. The ministers and their staffs, whose efforts would be critical to plan implementation, were mobilized in support of the plan. Everyone was sensitized to interconnections among sectors and issues.

A press conference was held after each meeting to ensure that the public was also kept informed. When the plan was finally adopted, it contained no surprises. It was apparent that the content had been considered carefully and was based on nonpartisan analysis. This perception aided in the general acceptance of the plan and promoted adherence to its provisions.

Two linked quantitative models underlay the plan. A macroeconometric model forecast the growth of aggregate demand, inflation, and foreign exchange needs (Adelman and Kim 1969). A dynamic input-output model helped in determining the amount of investment in each sector (Adelman et al. 1969).

The macroeconometric model incorporated three gaps: a current balance gap, a savings-investment gap, and the government deficit. Various scenarios were run to predict the effects of policy choices on these gaps as well as the consequences for growth and consumption. Based in part on these calculations, but also on consultant reports[15] that were part of the preparation for the export drive, the currency was sharply devalued, interest rates on bank deposits were doubled, and selective trade liberalization was implemented (Adelman and Kim 1969).

The input-output model of sectoral investment requirements was also critical. Using the income, consumption, export, and government expenditure growth results of the macroeconometric model, the sectoral levels of final demand and the required levels of imports were forecast. These were then used as inputs to the input-output model. The input-output model predicted output and employment by sector, as well as the investment and import requirements for each sector (Adelman et al. 1969).

Investment requirements were calculated in an iterative fashion. Capital-output ratios were applied to the forecasts of sectoral outputs in order to determine capacity requirements for the sectors. Investment requirements were then calculated as the differences between capacity requirements and current capacity. Investment matrices, both by sector of destination and by sector of origin, were then incorporated into the final demand vector and the whole exercise was repeated until the initial and final investment levels converged.

Industry committees modeled on the French indicative planning process were formed for each of ten industrial sectors. These committees brought bureaucrats from the Ministry of Commerce and the Economic Planning Board together with each other and with entrepreneurs. Since there were investments on the drawing board which were not captured by the existing surveys, they recast the forecasts of changes in their sectors. The work was iterative, as changes forecast by industry committees for other sectors were fed into the work of each sector. Technological and market information was thereby imparted to entrepreneurs and bureaucrats alike as the planning proceeded.[16]

The next step was perhaps the most important. To make the investment plan "real," the government ensured that the appropriate investments would be made. Firms submitted investment applications to the Ministry of Finance. In most sectors, the ratio of proposed investments to investment requirements was above 500 to 1; in other sectors the industry committees had to solicit additional applications. Projects were evaluated on the basis of economic feasibility, financial rate of return, net foreign exchange generation, and calculations of social rates of return. The projects in each sector were ranked, and the highest ranking ones were selected until the requirements of the plan were attained.

The planning process and the very existence of a plan were essential. The building of the plan generated a national consensus in support of economic development. The presence of the plan afforded a rational, nonpartisan mechanism for government to promote private investment.

Financial Liberalization

Financial liberalization did not begin in Korea until 1981. Banks were gradually privatized, but the government continued to mandate loans in support of its agenda. It established a system in which specific banks were designated to finance particular corporations for specified activities.

Korea's capital market was closed to foreigners until after the two five-year plans discussed above were completed. Beginning in 1972, foreign banks were allowed to open branches in Korea. Portfolio investment by foreigners was not allowed until 1982. In 1985, Korean firms were permitted to raise capital abroad by issuing convertible bonds, but direct foreign investment in the Korean stock market was not permitted until 1992. Restrictions on the convertibility of the won in trade-related transactions were not lifted until 1988. In 1990, a managed float exchange rate system was adopted.[17] Capital account convertibility for capital inflows was started in 1991 with substantial restrictions. After 1994, under pressure from the

United States and the IMF, steps were taken to liberalize both the inflow and outflow of capital. Banks began to borrow abroad without significant oversight. Together with the high interest rates, this led to a rapid increase in foreign liabilities of banks.

As of 1996, the financial system of Korea was in a precarious transition from a completely nationalized to a fully developed market-based system. Bank regulation and supervision were not adequate. Initially, gradual financial liberalization was important to maintain the thrust of the government-led development strategy. However, government-mandated loans implied that banks wound up with unsound loan portfolios.

Elevated interest rates encouraged borrowing abroad, especially after world interest rates started declining during the 1990s. Naturally, the foreign borrowing was denominated in dollars, exposing banks to exchange rate risk. About 80 percent of loans were short-term, making the solvency of banks and *chaebols* (multinational conglomerates) sensitive to fluctuations in foreign confidence in Korea's economic prospects. Since Korea was committed to maintaining a stable exchange rate, the short-term debt was unhedged.

Between 1995 and 1997 international claims on banks had risen by 30 percent, from $77 billion to $103 billion. International banks enjoyed implicit government guarantees against the insolvency of Korean banks and could thus take excessive risks when lending to Korean banks.[18] An exogenously induced decline in exports and reduced profits deteriorated corporate balance sheets and put the private banking sector at risk. The banks responded to these developments with a mix of increased interest rates on loans and curtailment of credit, which in turn further hurt balance sheets, reduced their ability to service debt, and curtailed the growth of exports and domestic sales. Since banks were allowed to invest in stocks and real assets, they were also directly vulnerable to asset price fluctuations.

The government adopted a high interest rate, tight money policy, which set domestic real interest rates way above world markets. By 1997 the Korean stock market fell to below half its value in 1991. Unable to raise new equity capital on the stock market, firms had to resort to borrowing. The huge interest rate differential between domestic and foreign loans, in turn, accelerated foreign borrowing, thus deteriorating the soundness of bank balance sheets further and endangering macroeconomic stability.

Worsening Korean economic vulnerability was the government policy of supporting an unsustainably rapid rise in real wages. The motivation was political: to preempt the opposition parties, which represent labor interests, from gaining popular support. By 1994 the index of real wages stood about 11 percentage points above that of labor productivity. Just before the financial crisis, the average wage level in Korea was about 30 percent above that in the United Kingdom.[19]

Financial Debacle

The strategy of export-led growth made the economy sensitive to external price shocks (e.g., oil) and the pace of international trade. Ironically, the impressive economic progress contributed to Korea's vulnerability once overly optimistic evaluation of Korea's prospects turned excessively pessimistic. Most devastatingly, financial crisis elsewhere in Southeast Asia caused a reevaluation of Korea's creditworthiness.

In the crisis of 1997–98, the specific exogenous shocks to Korea were a lengthy recession in Japan and a worldwide decline in demand for computer chips, ships, automobiles, and garments. Simultaneously, the contagion from the financial crisis in Southeast Asia manifested itself in a decrease in exports to other Southeast Asian countries, and more importantly, increased export competition due to the precipitous fall in the value of the currencies of its competitors.

In late 1997, Korea experienced a huge swing in foreign capital flows. As a result, there was a $20 billion outflow for the year, compared with a $100 billion inflow the previous year. The ill-timed liberalization of capital flows was largely a consequence of President Kim's decision to join the OECD, apparently to increase his legitimacy and popular support. Joining the OECD required, as a precondition, free capital markets. (In this context, it is indicative that the Mexican crisis of 1994–95 occurred only six months after Mexico became a member of the OECD.)

Without premature capital-market liberalization, other policy mistakes and institutional inadequacies would merely have resulted in a recession, as they did in 1972, 1980–81, and 1992. The debacle would not have taken place if Korea had waited five to seven years before joining the OECD and used the interim period to: (1) strengthen the balance sheets of banks and the corporate sector; (2) grant greater independence to banks in making loans; (3) increase the capacity of banks to evaluate the financial soundness of proposed projects and the solvency of corporations; and (4) raise the transparency of corporate accounting practices.

Lessons for Russia

The growth of a developing economy cannot be adequately engineered through macroeconomic variables. In Korea, a multitude of "carrots and sticks"—market and nonmarket, discretionary and nondiscretionary—were used to achieve both general and specific goals. Government intervention thereby provided the dynamic behind growth. While some mistakes were made, interventions were market conforming or remedied market failures, if not in the short term, at least in the medium and long terms.

A "big bang" is to be avoided. All elements of liberalization should be phased in carefully: domestic markets, trade, financial system, macroeconomic management, and foreign capital inflows. Korea decontrolled trade only gradually and selectively. It used imports as a source of competition and exports as a test of competitiveness, while at the same time it provided sheltered markets for new industries during their "infant" phase. Korea paid dearly when, in violation of the strategy of gradualism, it prematurely opened domestic capital markets before its financial system was fully developed. The Asian financial contagion demonstrated the importance of a mix of regulation, disincentives, or other impediments to short-term capital flows is indispensable.

Nor should a puritanical approach be taken toward inflation. Korea pursued a moderately loose, though not profligate, macroeconomic policy in support of development. It worried relatively little over macroeconomic stability during its first 20 years. Nevertheless, during this loose-money period, budget deficits never exceeded 2 percent of GNP and the annual rate of inflation 30 percent. A facilitating factor was strict control over foreign capital markets.

A sound state is the sine qua non of a sound economy. With leadership committed to development, it is possible to turn a corrupt, soft state into a hard, developmental state. When the South Korean state was first created, the economy was considered a sinkhole for foreign assistance. It was only with the birth of the strong developmental state and the adoption of a coherent development program that the Korean economic miracle was born.

Notes

1. This conclusion is based not only on the Korean record but also on the experience of Taiwan and Japan and the late European industrializers. Scitovsky (1985) and Adelman (1997) show that Korean development policy was similar to that of Taiwan, and Song (1996) shows it was comparable to that of Japan. Morris and Adelman (1988) describe the activist development policy of the late industrializers.

2. Hardly a case of simply "getting prices right," economic policies violated neoliberal precepts. Prices that were temporarily distorted (combined with a suitable mix of subsidies and controls) had positive effects (Amsden 1989).

3. Between 1960 and 1981, Korea had the highest inflation rate among the Asian newly industrializing countries (Song 1996).

4. The design of the second five-year plan is described in detail in Adelman (1969).

5. The effective exchange rate for exports relative to imports was increased by about 20 percent and kept relatively stable thereafter (Westphal 1978). This figure does not take into account either the benefits from the protection of the domestic market or the reduction in incentives to producers of non-exportables. These factors increased prices and profits for domestic sales of exportables.

6. It is difficult to make the estimates of imperfections and externalities needed to optimize subsidies, and the discretionary nature of subsidies invariably leads

to some corruption and rent seeking. Nevertheless, Korea's success makes it hard to dispute that the positive effects outweighed the negative effects.

7. For example, expansion of domestic demand from 1968 to 1973 accounted for 63 percent of the total growth of light manufacturing, while growth in exports accounted for only 34 percent (Suh 1985).

8. High savings were not characteristic of Korea's economic development until after the mid-1980s. Prior to 1971, the savings rate fell far short of the Rostow minimum of 15 percent of GNP. Low savings meant that inflationary finance and high rates of foreign capital inflows were required to achieve growth. The recent shift to a high savings rate has enabled the continuation of growth while pursuing anti-inflationary policies.

9. The contribution of exports to GNP growth rose from 9.4 percent in 1966–68 to 23.6 percent during 1970–73 (Suk 1977, 401–403). One can question whether the growth in exports was dynamically efficient. The labor intensity of exportables decreased by one-third (Hong 1979, 370) while the import content of exportables increased (Suk 1977, 412). This reflects the use of import incentives, such as duty-free imports and "wastage allowances," which allowed the import of duty-free intermediate goods in excess of what was needed for production.

10. In 1968 manufacturing export industries accounted for only 14 percent of the capital stock and 20 percent of employment (directly and indirectly). Estimates are from Hong (1979, 363).

11. Substantial imports of intermediate goods and machinery were required to implement the export-led industrialization drive. The overall import coefficient for exported goods was 40 percent (Suk 1977). Thus, despite continued protectionist policies, the economy became considerably more open with the sum of imports plus exports almost doubling as a share of GNP.

12. The educational strategy was to expand primary schooling first, and then secondary schooling, and to delay expansion at the college level. This had an egalitarian effect. It contrasts with the Brazilian strategy, for example, in which secondary education was just sufficient to feed college enrollments (Adelman and Robinson 1978).

13. For a description of the planning effort, see Cole and Young (1969).

14. Discussions about the planning model posed difficulties. For example, the head of the Economic Planning Board asked how to explain a three-gap model to the ministers. Adelman suggested constructing a Calder-type mobile with

metal rods linking the savings-investment, import-export, and government revenue-and-expenditure functions.

15. The primary advisers were Bela Balassa and Margaret Musgrave on trade reform; Richard Musgrave on tax reform; Edward Shaw, John Gurley, and Hugh Patrick on monetary policy; and Irma Adelman on planning techniques.

16. Interestingly enough, the committees tended to overestimate the effects of planning changes on their sectors, and a postmortem comparison of the planned and actual changes revealed that the input-output coefficients could have been left unchanged.

17. In this system the Ministry of Finance and the Bank of Korea were no longer directly involved in setting exchange rates. But the bands imposed on the daily fluctuations of the won-dollar exchange rate were narrow, and the government continued to exercise indirect influence on the exchange rate through its foreign exchange transactions. In 1992, the exchange rate band was widened to 0.8 percent.

18. Krugman (1998) attributes the crisis to this factor.

19. Another policy error was to peg the exchange rate to the dollar. The result was to reduce export competitiveness, increase the trade deficit, and lower the growth rate of the economy. Japan's declining exchange rate meant an automatic currency appreciation of the won, some 12 percent between 1990 and 1996 (Radelet and Sachs 1998).

References

Adelman, Irma, ed. 1969. *Practical Approaches to Development Planning: Korea's Second Five-Year Plan.* Baltimore: Johns Hopkins University Press.

―――. 1997. "Fifty Years of Economic Development: Korea and Taiwan Compared." *Pacific Economic Journal.*

Adelman, Irma, David Cole, Roger Norton, and Lee Kee Jung. 1969. "The Korean Sectoral Model," in Irma Adelman, ed., *Practical Approaches to Development Planning: Korea's Second Five-Year Plan.* Baltimore: Johns Hopkins University Press.

Adelman, Irma, and Kim Mahn Je. 1969. "An Econometric Model of the Korean Economy (1956–66)," in Irma Adelman, ed., *Practical Approaches to Development Planning: Korea's Second Five-Year Plan.* Pp. 77–109. Baltimore: Johns Hopkins University Press.

Adelman, Irma, and Sherman Robinson. 1978. *Income Distribution Policies in Developing Countries: The Case of Korea.* Stanford: Stanford University Press.

Amsden, Alice. 1989. *Asia's Next Giant.* New York: Oxford University Press.

Čhoo, Hakchung. 1977. "Some Sources of Relative Equity in Income Distribution: A Historical Perspective," in Chuk Kyo Kim, ed., *Industrial and Social Development in Korea.* Pp. 303–330. Seoul: Korean Development Institute.

———— 1985. "Estimation of Size Distribution of Income and Its Sources of Change in Korea, 1982." Working Paper No. 8515. Seoul: Korean Development Institute.

Cole, David, and Young Woo Nam. 1969. "The Pattern and Significance of Economic Planning in Korea," in Irma Adelman, ed., *Practical Approaches to Development Planning: Korea's Second Five-Year Plan.* Pp. 11–37. Baltimore: Johns Hopkins University Press.

Devarajan, Shantayana, Jeffrey D. Lewis, and Sherman Robinson. 1990. "Policy Lessons from Trade Focused Two Sector Models." *Journal of Policy Modelling,* 625–658.

Hong, Wontack. 1979. *Trade, Distortions and Employment Growth in Korea.* Seoul: Korean Development Institute.

Jones, Leroy P., and Il Sakong. 1980. *Government, Business and Entrepreneurship in Economic Development: The Korean Case.* Cambridge: Harvard University Press.

Kim, Chuk Kyo, ed. 1977. *Industrial and Social Development in Korea.* Seoul: Korean Development Institute.

Kim, Kwang Suk, and Michael Roemer. 1979. *Studies in the Modernization of the Republic of Korea 1945–1975.* Cambridge: Harvard University Press.

Koo, Bon Ho. 1977. "Foreign Exchange Policies: An Evaluation and Proposals," in Chuk Kyo Kim, ed., *Industrial and Social Development in Korea.* Pp. 449–479. Seoul: Korean Development Institute.

Krugman, Paul. 1998. "What Happened to Asia." Conference paper delivered in Japan, January.

Kwon, Soonwon. 1993a. *Social Policy in Korea: Challenges and Responses.* Seoul: Korean Development Institute.

———— 1993b. *Improvement in Antipoverty Programs.* Seoul: Korean Development Institute.

Little, Ian, Tibor Scitovsky, and Maurice Scott. 1970. *Industry and Trade in Some Developing Countries.* New York: Oxford University Press.

Mitra, Pradeep. 1992a. "The Coordinated Reform of Tariffs and Indirect Taxes." *World Bank Research Observer* 7(2): 195–220.

———. 1992b. "Tariff Design and Reform in a Revenue-Constrained Economy: Theory and an Illustration from India." *Journal of Public Economics* 47(2): 227–251.

Morris, Cynthia Taft, and Irma Adelman. 1988. *Patterns of Economic Growth, 1850–1914*. Baltimore: Johns Hopkins University Press.

National Statistical Office. 1994. *Social Indicators in Korea*. Seoul: National Statistics Office.

Radelet, Steven, and Jeffrey Sachs. 1998. "Onset of the Financial Crisis." Mimeo.

Scitovsky, Tibor. 1985. "Economic Development in Taiwan and South Korea, 1965–1981." *Food Research Institute Studies* 19(3): 214–264.

Song, Byung Nak. 1996. *The Rise of the Korean Economy,* 2nd ed. New York: Oxford University Press.

Srinivasan, T. N., and Jagdish Bhagwati. 1978. "Shadow Prices for Project Selection in the Presence of Distortions: Effective Rates of Protection and Domestic Resource Costs." *Journal of Political Economy,* 86: 97–116.

Suh, Sang Mok. 1985. "Economic Growth and Change in Income Distribution: The Korean Case."Working Paper No. 8508. Seoul: Korean Development Institute.

Suk, Tai Suh. 1977. "Growth Contribution of Trade and Incentive System," in Chuk Kyo Kim, ed., *Industrial and Social Development in Korea*. Seoul: Korean Development Institute.

Westphal, Larry E. 1978. "The Republic of Korea's Experience with Export Led Development." *World Development* 6: 347–382.

PART TWO

Economic Crisis

9

Demise of the Command Economy

Marshall Pomer

When Mikhail Gorbachev became head of state in 1985, the Soviet Union was still a superpower. It had at its disposal abundant resources, both human and mineral, but industry had fallen behind Western standards. The party-state elite were afraid that centralized command had reached the point of diminishing returns. Top Soviet economists, hoping to achieve the best of both worlds, urged that markets and decentralization be combined with socialist principles. Even the military, alarmed over technological obsolescence, accepted the need for radical change.

Amidst lofty expectations, economic transformation was poorly conceived, hastily executed, and corruptly managed. Part Two of this book describes the disappointing results. Offering historical perspective on the Soviet command economy, this chapter tells the story of the cataclysmic change from one economic system to another.

The Classical Soviet Economic System

The "classical" Soviet economic system was Stalin's handiwork. After he ruthlessly acquired dictatorial power in 1927, Stalin banished private enterprise and imposed strict authoritarian control over the economy.[1] Combining communist ideology and Russian nationalism, the ostensible goal of the economic system was to "build socialism" and thereby create the basis for an eventual collective Utopia. Comprehensive social services were provided, but the main priority was to build military strength through rapid industrialization.

Large, strictly hierarchical enterprises were the units of the Soviet economic system.[2] Having a relatively small number of monopolistic enterprises not only simplified centralized control but also followed the Marxian tenet that large production units are the most efficient. Enterprises provided health care, education, childcare, and recreation. Many enterprises, especially remote ones, were virtually self-sufficient communities.

Enterprises were subordinate to "branch" ministries, with a separate ministry for each branch (or major sector) of the economy. The branch ministries were themselves subordinate to Gosplan, which in turn followed the dictates of top party leaders who comprised the Council of Ministers. In accord with a five-year plan, Gosplan issued detailed annual plans that established production quotas. Planners sluggishly adjusted production targets in response to surpluses and shortages. Managers not only were told what to produce but also were allocated the inputs deemed necessary. The involvement of other state agencies varied over time. Among the important participants were the state banking system; ministries of finance and foreign trade; and committees of labor, prices, and science and technology.

Each enterprise was headed by a general director drawn from party ranks and accountable to party superiors. To enhance party oversight, there was a separate department of the Central Committee corresponding to each branch ministry, and a party representative was assigned full-time to each enterprise. Party leaders at the levels of republic, province, and municipality also oversaw the enterprises within their areas. In addition, a trade union head was appointed for each enterprise.

Despite the Marxian aversion to markets, elements of a market system were present. Households received income in rubles, including wages, pensions, child allowances, and education stipends. They spent their incomes as they saw fit, and they put their savings in the state bank, though the interest rate was minimal and borrowing was seldom possible. Except for free services such as health care and education, each commodity had a price that was set by central authority. To further egalitarian goals, the prices of social necessities (e.g., housing, basic foods, transportation) were set below production costs, which meant that the state paid producers more than it charged consumers.

The use of prices allowed for the calculation of enterprise profits, a consideration that was far secondary to production quotas in evaluating managerial performance. In intermittent and largely unsuccessful attempts to simulate a market system, enterprises were allowed to retain a portion of their profits (Bornstein 1991). These funds were used for bonuses, small-scale investments, and a broad range of employee benefits (housing, childcare, health care, cultural activities, recreation, and even food).

Although the price structure was less meaningful than in a market system, it did provide the basis for indirect collection of mineral rents. Energy inputs were priced extremely low, while manufactured goods were priced high. As a result, industrial enterprises turned over substantial profits to the government, which was essential for macroeconomic balance.

The Soviet economic system did produce rapid industrialization.[3] Up until the mid-1970s, rates of economic growth were high by Western standards (Kotz 1997, chapter 3). After rapid recovery from enormous devastation during World War II, the Soviet Union by 1975 surpassed the United States in production of many industrial products (e.g., steel, cement, and tractors) and farm products (e.g., cotton, wheat, and milk). In 1989 it was the world's largest producer of a wide range of basic commodities, including oil, natural gas, mineral fertilizers, cement, and sulfuric acid (Goskomstat 1990, 692–693). Between 1950 and 1970, real per capita consumption increased 150 percent. While in 1960 only 1 in 10 households had a television and 1 in 25 a refrigerator, by 1985 most families had both. Necessities from bread to subway transportation were easily affordable. The literacy rate was high and health care was universally available.[4] The absence of unemployment—as well as achievements in science, arts, and athletics—was regarded as an indication of a high level of civilization. Although quality of construction was not high, housing was guaranteed and minimally priced.

Systemic Problems

Centralized control worked well in marshaling material resources and human talent for major military and industrial projects, including the space program. It also avoided the business cycles that afflicted market economies, in particular the Great Depression in the thirties. The steeply hierarchical command system, however, required forceful leadership and was vulnerable to bureaucratic incompetence and corruption. Reflecting the inherent limitations of centralization, the Soviet economic system was not efficient and was not conducive to technological progress and product innovation.

The annual plans were hamstrung by their own complexity. Obtaining unbiased information on an enormous number of details was a daunting problem, especially after economic development led to a proliferation in product variety (Shmelev and Popov 1989). Shortcomings in planning invariably resulted in shortages that disrupted production and frustrated consumers. The focus on production targets was associated with a lack of opportunity or incentives for managers to be innovative (Berliner 1976).

Soviet prices poorly reflected costs or demand, and they were rarely changed. It was an enormous undertaking to specify all prices, and any changes complicated the calculations for the central plan. In addition, prices were set to ensure that necessities were affordable. Since prices did not reflect marginal costs and benefits, strict budget constraints would not have been efficient. In the absence of such constraints, and lacking a profit motive, there was no automatic pressure to cut costs or to make product improvements that would attract buyers. Thus prices did not play their potential role of stimulating efficiency and prompting response to consumer preferences.[5]

Unpressured by competition, enterprises tended to be coddled. If revenues fell short of expenses, enterprises could expect minimal-interest loans, outright subsidies, or higher prices for their outputs. Thus budget constraints were "soft" and bankruptcy unknown (Kornai 1981). Much of industrial production was actually value-subtracting: if priced at world levels, output would have been worth less than its inputs.

The primacy of quotas led to the operating principle that producing more output was always for the good. As a result, except in military production, low product quality was endemic.[6] Consider, for example, the lack of incentives to produce high-quality tractors. If a tractor manufacturer is evaluated solely on the basis of quantity produced, why should it bother to check that all bolts are in place and fully tightened? Furthermore, low quality was self-perpetuating as farms, faced with frequent breakdowns and an inability to acquire spare parts, accumulated redundant tractors. Resistance to technological change was a consequence: Why risk dependence on a new product without having the spare parts that are likely to be needed? Thus, while the Soviet Union was by far the world's largest producer of tractors, technological obsolescence laid the basis for the virtual cessation in production today.

Oppression of the Soviet people[7] and profligate use of natural resources, rather than technological progress, were the bases for Soviet growth. Collectivization of agriculture reduced rural incomes and urban wages were kept low, which made it possible to channel resources into capital formation. Abundant natural resources were exploited with little concern for wastage, depletion, or environmental degradation. Physical infrastructure was designed without regard for squandering underpriced energy. For example, to save on construction costs housing was built without insulation. Much of growth was simply a reflection of a massive shift of population from low-productivity agriculture to capital-intensive industry.

Apart from the consequences of underinvestment in the consumer sector, the command system itself was ill-suited to handle the variability of con-

Figure 9.1. Leaders of the Soviet Union

Vladimir Lenin	1917–1924
Josef Stalin	1927–1953
Nikita Khrushchev	1956–1964
Leonid Brezhnev	1964–1982
Yuri Andropov	1982–1984
Konstantin Chernenko	1984–1985
Mikhail Gorbachev	1985–1991

Source: Nove (1992).

sumer preferences. Efficiently producing millions of shoes of the same style is no way to cater to consumers. Shortages were common, goods were occasionally rationed, and tedious searches and long lines were typical. With connections more important than ability to pay, the party elite shopped in special stores with better selection that included imports.

Liberalization and Stagnation

After Stalin's death and the execution of the head of the secret police (Beria), Khrushchev curbed the totalitarian character of the Soviet Union and provided basic legal protections to its citizens. (Figure 9.1 provides a chronology of Soviet leaders.) However, the Communist Party maintained its absolute hegemony,[8] religion was harshly suppressed, and freedom of speech was absent. The command economy implemented under Stalin remained largely intact.

Under Khrushchev's liberalization program, major strides were made in housing, education, and health care. More attention was given to consumer goods, and income inequality was reduced. The reorientation toward the needs and wants of the populace necessarily reduced the rate of investment, which contributed to a slowing of economic growth.

Khrushchev's successor, Leonid Brezhnev, was a passive figurehead apparently favored because he did not threaten the prerogatives of other top party officials (Dowlah and Elliott 1997, 160–166). Amidst the relaxation of the police state and the decline in Communist Party discipline, the black market flourished. On the one hand, the black market was tolerated because it helped alleviate production bottlenecks. On the other hand, it engendered criminal organizations and contributed to the corruption of party and government officials (Grossman 1993 and 1994). As the aging Brezhnev increasingly lost touch, incompetence and corruption worsened.

By 1970, economic growth was probably below levels typical in the West (Dowlah and Elliott 1997, 121–144).[9] Social liberalization led to increased exposure to the West that raised awareness of the relative inferiority of Soviet goods. In an attempt to create more opportunity for innovation, the 1976–1980 five-year plan deliberately set quotas based on a lower growth rate. This strategy backfired as unanticipated bottlenecks retarded both growth and product quality (Schroeder 1985).

During the last years of the Brezhnev era, growth may have ceased altogether (Kurtzweg 1987). The stagnation was especially ominous since it occurred despite surging oil revenues following the success of OPEC. After 1980, oil output began to falter due to lack of investment (Gustafson 1985). The transportation system, based primarily on railways, was neglected and lacked capacity to support further growth (Kontorovich 1992a). Managerial and worker discipline declined with the rise in corruption and the lack of incentives to motivate a socially protected workforce (Zaslavskaia 1990, 49).

Despite economic stagnation, the average Russian was not immediately disturbed.[10] Indeed, many Russians now look back fondly to the Brezhnev years as a kind of golden era. Unemployment was nonexistent, and the standard of living was higher than ever. Health care and education were universally free, and housing was very inexpensive. Russians generally faced rather lax demands at the workplace. Holidays were frequent, and vacations long. Modest country dachas were common for residents of Moscow and Leningrad, as were vacations at mountain and seaside retreats. Most urban children enjoyed summer camp in the country. As for the lack of political freedoms, most citizens were content to pass along jokes about their apathetic general secretary.

The party-state elite, who were acutely aware of the economic stagnation, were increasingly disaffected with the Soviet economic system. Many were impressed by the economies of Western Europe, where dynamic market-driven postwar recoveries accompanied the extension of comprehensive social welfare measures. High-level officials questioned why, as representatives of a superpower, they could not enjoy a standard of living comparable to that of their peers abroad. Military leaders were alarmed by the failure to keep abreast in electronics and computer technology. This spreading dissatisfaction provided the impetus for *perestroika*.

Perestroika

Brezhnev's elderly successors, first Yuri Andropov and then Konstantin Chernenko, each died after a little more than a year in office, paving the way for a dynamic young leader. Elected general secretary of the Communist Party on March 11, 1985, Mikhail Gorbachev proved to be a tragic hero. While courageous in ending the Cold War and creating a free and open society, he fell short as an economic reformer.[11]

One month after taking office, Gorbachev presented his program of *perestroika* ("restructuring")—his vision for building a new socialism, one that would be both prosperous and democratic. In earlier times citizens were asked to endure poor material conditions for the sake of a utopian future. Gorbachev instead promised immediate improvements in living conditions, claiming that national income would double by the year 2000.

The refurbished socialism was to be a beacon for all humankind. The Soviet Union was to surpass the West on its own terms: high quality consumer goods would be plentiful. There would be no unemployment, and no extremes of inequality. Everyone would be guaranteed health care, education, and housing. Democracy, the newly promised foundation for the political system, would be introduced in the workplace as well.

As formulated by Gorbachev's principal economic adviser Abel Aganbegyan, and reiterated by Gorbachev, the *perestroika* program consisted of "three closely intertwined directions fit together into a vague concept of *uskorenie* (acceleration)."[12] The three directions, discussed below, were technological progress, "democratization" of the economy, and social orientation of production. *Uskorenie* symbolized boldness of purpose in breaking out of the economic stagnation that characterized the Brezhnev years. It entailed commitment to a high rate of economic growth, which had once been the basis for claiming the superiority of Soviet socialism and was recognized as the foundation for improving the lagging standard of living. The goal was to accelerate growth at once and eventually achieve growth rates "two to three times faster than those in Western countries" (Aganbegyan 1988, 40).

Technological progress, the first objective of *perestroika*, was key. As discussed earlier, the Soviet Union had relied on an "extensive" development strategy—accumulation of physical capital, increased supplies of energy and raw materials, and a growing labor force. This was an unsustainable approach that was stymied by inefficiency, resource depletion, and falling returns on capital investment. It was necessary to switch to an "intensive" strategy whereby technological progress would spur growth. While perhaps exaggerating past Soviet performance, Gorbachev pointedly acknowledged the problem of slow technological advance:

> [the Soviet Union] was once quickly closing on the world's advanced nations [but] the gap in the efficiency of production, quality of products, scientific and technological development, the production of advanced technology and the use of advanced techniques began to widen, and not to our advantage. (Gorbachev 1987, 19)

If the capital goods produced in Russia were state-of-the-art, then workers would be better able to manufacture high-quality consumer goods. Such changes were needed not only to increase efficiency and win the approval of Russian consumers, but also to reduce economic dependence on exports of raw materials and energy. Transforming the economy into a major exporter of manufactured goods had long been a Soviet goal (Hewett 1988, 366).

Regarding the objective to "democratize" the economy, Gorbachev saw himself as the bearer of the progressive socialist torch that he believed

Lenin had lit. Sensitive to the pernicious effects of authoritarianism, he blamed Soviet failings on the absence of democracy:

> We know today that we would have been able to avoid many of these [political and economic] difficulties if the democratic process had developed normally in our country. (Gorbachev 1987, 31–32)

Economic democratization entailed greater enterprise autonomy, less ministerial control, and the expansion of worker responsibility. It also encompassed what Gorbachev referred to as the "human factor," which included competence and commitment:

> The very nature of restructuring implies that it must go on at every workplace, in every work collective, in the entire management system. . . . [E]veryone must work honestly and conscientiously, sparing no efforts and abilities. (Gorbachev 1987, 56)

The third objective, to enhance the social orientation of the economy, was the *"raison d' être of perestroika"* (Aganbegyan 1987, 278). Rather than continue the tradition of "residual allocation" of resources to social needs after first meeting demands for rapid industrialization and military might, the state was immediately to become more generous. With housing identified as the most acute social need, a major increase in construction of apartment buildings was planned. Also promised were a more abundant food supply, especially more meat and dairy, improvements in health care and education, and higher pension benefits.

Initial Reforms

Due to political and ideological constraints, and perhaps reflecting lack of background in non-Marxian economics, Gorbachev paid little attention to the potential role of the market.[13] Recognizing that initiative was stifled on both the individual and the enterprise levels, he believed that the system could be adjusted to stimulate innovation and technological progress.

Gorbachev rejuvenated the incentive system that Alexei Kosygin implemented unsuccessfully in 1965. Intended to increase enterprise autonomy without sacrificing centralized coordination, the Kosygin reforms were resisted by the ministries and not actively supported by General Secretary Brezhnev. Under Andropov, with Gorbachev playing a major role, the incentive system was revived on an experimental basis in two all-union ministries (transportation equipment and electronics) and three republican ministries (food processing in Ukraine, textiles in Belarus, and small-scale manufacturing in Latvia). The revised incentive system, which had mixed results after being in effect for about a year, was not carefully evaluated or refined. Nevertheless, just three months after taking office, Gorbachev mandated that it be adopted by all Soviet industry by the end of 1986.

The incentive system relied on success indicators (including sales revenue, profit, and measures of product quality) that complemented the mandated output targets. High scores boosted both worker bonuses and enterprise-provided social benefits.[14] A key feature of the new system was reduction in oversight by the branch ministries. They could request that improvements be made in the indicators but were now prohibited from interfering in the day-to-day operations of enterprises.

In addition to instituting a new incentive system, Gorbachev sought other more direct ways to address the "human factor." Intent on energizing a bureaucracy that had grown inert during the Brezhnev era, he summarily dismissed recalcitrant or incompetent officials and quickly promoted others, including Boris Yeltsin. In 1985 alone, 14 of 49 branch ministers were replaced.[15] Gorbachev also launched an aggressive, albeit naïve, campaign to curb alcohol consumption. Two months after taking office, he cut production and sales of alcohol, while imposing harsh penalties for public drunkenness.

To complement efforts to improve the human factor, an ambitious investment campaign was launched (Aganbegyan 1988, 99–108). The emphasis was on the machine-building industry, which supplied most of the capital equipment for the economy. In accordance with the eleventh five-year plan, only 5 percent of capital investment had gone into this industry during the 1981–1985 period. The five-year plan for 1986–1990, which planners had reluctantly reconfigured in accordance with Gorbachev's demands, called for nearly doubling investment in this sector. The rate of replacement of capital stock was to be pushed up to 8 or 9 percent a year, compared with a past annual level of 2 percent. It was envisioned that by the end of 1990, for example, 40 percent of all metalworking equipment would be replaced with state-of-the-art "computers, processing centers and modern automatic production lines" (105).

While Western observers criticized Gorbachev for making adjustments rather than fundamental changes (Schroeder 1991a), his initial early reforms can also be faulted for being hasty and unrealistic. The new incentive system, coupled with personnel cuts,[16] eroded the power of the branch ministries. Since the ministries had developed the required expertise for investment analysis, reduction in their authority degraded investment decisions. Moreover the ministries had long functioned to curb managerial corruption and incompetence.

Gorbachev promised to deliver more of everything: Housing construction and other social spending rose in accordance with the social orientation objective of *perestroika*; investment was dramatically increased; and there was a covert arms buildup (Noren and Kurtzweg 1993, 19–20). Producing and importing more capital goods and military equipment reduced the supply of consumer goods, causing shortages that belied the promise of consumer abundance.[17]

Gorbachev did not acknowledge the short-run tradeoff between modernization and higher production; having both "better and more" was not feasible. To produce high-quality modern consumer goods it was necessary to retool the consumer goods industry, and this in turn required retooling the capital goods industry. Faced with higher output quotas, enterprises did not replace equipment or retool obsolete production lines. Instead of investing in new technology, they merely expanded their facilities. Also, a zealous new quality-control program resulted in a high rejection rate that reduced supplies, including the availability of new capital equipment.[18] Thus, despite higher investment, neither productivity nor product quality showed improvement (Kontorovich 1992b).

Emblematic of unrealistic reform was the campaign to curb alcohol consumption. A groundswell of opposition forced its cancellation in 1988 and eroded popular support for *perestroika* (White 1996). Gorbachev's weakened credibility, further undermined by the consumer shortages and the bureaucratic disarray, made it all the more difficult to confront macroeconomic and institutional problems.

Toward Market Socialism and a Mixed Economy

In the face of worsening shortages, Aganbegyan regarded private enterprise as a quick fix that would increase the supply of goods and services that state-owned enterprises were neglecting.[19] Gorbachev supported the creation of a mixed economy, though his intention was for state ownership and collective employee ownership to dominate. Private enterprise was consistent with Gorbachev's intent to establish incentives that fostered initiative and productivity. It was also consonant with expansion of personal freedoms supported by *glasnost* ("openness") (Hauslohner 1987, 67).

In late 1986 and early 1987, steps were taken to increase the scope for privately owned businesses. The Law on Individual Labor Activity formalized the right of the self-employed, mostly in crafts and services, to hire immediate family members. It also was made legal for foreigners to become private partners in joint ventures with Soviet enterprises. Most important was the Decree on Cooperatives, which legalized virtually any enterprise as long as it had at least three owners. This produced a surge in retail trade, small-scale construction, and services (Hughes and Butler 1993, 277; Jones and Moskoff 1991).

The pivotal and hastily conceived Law on State Enterprises was implemented in half of the economy in 1988 and half in 1989. Disempowering the ministries, it moved the Soviet system toward market socialism. Output quotas from the annual central plans were no longer obligatory, and workers were given the authority to select managers. Enterprises were to be autonomous and self-financing, but in practice much of the economy continued to operate as before. The state remained the primary buyer of output and continued to distribute goods to the retail sector. The self-financing objective was partially undone by mounting arrears and by state assistance in the form of favorable purchases. Nevertheless, enterprises felt increased pressure to be responsive to prices.

Insulated from the rest of the world, the Soviet economy had a distorted price structure radically different from the price structure outside its borders. Prices for raw materials and food were set extremely low, while manufactured products were expensive. Since prices did not reliably provide meaningful measures of marginal costs, cost minimization did not ensure efficiency. To the extent that trade was possible, legal or illegal, there was a compelling incentive to shunt abroad inputs previously earmarked for domestic production.

The incentive system instituted in 1986 and 1987 sought to make prices a significant influence on state-owned enterprises. More important, however, was the pressure on state enterprises to become self-financing. The price structure became critical after 1988 with the spread of private enterprise. Since inflexible state-dictated prices remained in place, introduction of the market and the dismantling of central planning meant endemic shortages.

Apart from the errors of commission in economic policy, price reform was a fatal omission.[21] When the Law on State Enterprises was implemented, Aganbegyan announced that it would take two or three more years to prepare a comprehensive price reform program.[20] While such a delay was unwise, worse still was that meaningful reform never came. The rigid and distorted price structure, in combination with severe inflationary pressure and the precipitous dismantling of central control, made acute economic crisis inevitable.

There was negligible institutional development to support change in the governance and financing of enterprises. Workers were ill prepared for their unfamiliar role in management. Able but demanding managers were subject to dismissal, while shop-floor resistance to technological change stiffened. Compensation rose and investment fell. Subsequently, worker control was reduced, and the net effect of the Law on State Enterprises was to entrench managers regardless of competence.

Thus, while the economy had performed well in 1986 relative to the previous ten years, in the next three years growth fell back to pre-1985 levels.[22] Changes in the economic system, including both the weakening and the removal of institutions of central control, made prices increasingly consequential in the functioning of the economy. Without a flexible price system, the economy moved toward an unstable and incompatible mix of centrally controlled enterprises, private enterprises, and market socialism. Furthermore, sudden removal of outside scrutiny and growth of the black market widened opportunities for organized as well as casual criminality. In the final Gorbachev period, economic contraction accelerated amidst suppressed inflation.

Final Crisis

Suppressed inflation meant acute, widespread shortages. One shortage bred another as a hoarding mentality took hold. The reduction in centralized coordination of product flows caused input shortages that forced factories to cut back. Monopolistic enterprises occasionally restricted output to force black-market prices upward. The supply interruptions, aggravated by criminal interference with transport and marketing, worsened the suppressed inflation. With relaxation of government supervision and the legacy of an active underground economy, shortages provoked an explosive growth in the black market. Looting by managers and workers diverted output to the black market, while Russian mafia conspired in this process or instigated shortages on their own.

Ultimately, the inflation can be traced to government finance. Government spending rose to fulfill quixotic promises to restructure the economy, boost investment, and increase social services. The government took a smaller share of enterprise profits, while expanding illegal activity meant that much of these profits went unreported. Also, the anti-alcohol campaign had lowered tax receipts from sales of domestic wine and vodka and had cut gains from government resale of imported liquor. Concurrently, external shocks depleted government resources: a steep fall in the world price of oil, the Chernobyl disaster, the earthquake in Armenia, and the continuing war in Afghanistan. Insubstantial when Gorbachev took office in 1985, the deficit rose to about 10 percent of GDP in 1988, and it exceeded 20 percent in 1991.[23] The deficit was all the more inflationary because it was covered not by financing but, in effect, by the printing of money (Ellman 1992). Moreover, the Law on State Enterprises and the growth of the private sector permitted previously stable wage rates to climb.[24]

Government decree held some prices rigid, but market-determined prices skyrocketed (Åslund 1995, 42). Some goods were available at less than 1 percent of prices outside of Russia. At one point, a well-connected entrepreneur could sell one pack of Marlboros and use the proceeds to purchase three tons of crude oil. Low prices for oil and other raw materials led to enormous illicit outflows. This process enriched corrupt managers in league with crooked officials and criminal organizations. Honest managers who dared to stand in the way were vulnerable to political and criminal retribution.

While recessions and depressions in mature market economies are demand driven, the Soviet slowdown beginning in 1989 and the contraction that followed are best understood as supply-side phenomena. Compounding the disruptive factors already mentioned, the breakup of the Soviet trading bloc destroyed supply channels.[25] Between 1990 and 1991, the dollar value of both imports and exports between the Russian Republic and the former Soviet satellites fell by about two-thirds (Christensen 1993, 38). Also, governmental bodies within the Soviet Union, attempting to avoid local scarcities, erected barriers to the flow of goods (Schroeder 1991b).

The ruble began to be discredited as a medium of exchange and a store of value since it was often not possible to make purchases using rubles. No longer required to sell their food to the state for rubles, farms began selling their produce for hard currency (e.g., dollars) or fuel for farm machinery. The use of barter and supply interruptions, aggravated by criminal interference with transport and marketing, were repeated in many other sectors. For the first time during peacetime, GNP fell in 1990, and in 1991 the contraction reached severe proportions.[26] Bare store shelves, time spent searching for goods, long waiting lines, and the surge of the black market all incited popular discontent. As shortages became more acute, disillusionment and desperation spread.

In response to the crisis, Soviet economists debated various reform plans. Most significant were the proposals of Leonid Abalkin, Stanislav Shatalin, and Grigori Yavlinsky (Brown 1996, chapter 5), which set three priorities: improving government finance, remedying the enormous buildup in private savings (the "ruble overhang"), and enlarging the domain for private enterprise. Abalkin favored gradual and limited privatization with strong government oversight. Shatalin and Yavlinsky advocated more rapid change and a greater degree of private ownership.

Faced with resistance in the Soviet parliament, Gorbachev hesitated. Rather than move forward with either of these plans or other suggested compromises, he postponed price reform. If he had introduced market-determined prices, his gradualist approach might have been successful.

Geopolitical problems magnified the economic crisis. Amidst worsening economic conditions in 1990, all Soviet republics formally claimed the primacy of their own laws over Soviet laws. The fateful rivalry between Gorbachev and Boris Yeltsin, who was elected president of the Russian Republic in June 1991, led to the formal dissolution of the Soviet Union before the end of the year.[27] Yeltsin refused to turn over tax revenues to the Union, and other republics followed suit. Preceded by loss of the Soviet satellites, these actions accelerated the final collapse of the once powerful empire. By late 1991, reserves of foreign exchange were depleted and the authority of the Soviet state to implement economic policy had disappeared. After the failed *putsch* of August 1991, Russian President Yeltsin in effect seized the reins of power from Soviet President Gorbachev.[28]

Aftermath

Russian President Yeltsin championed immediate capitalist transformation of Russia. On January 2, 1992, one week after the formal dissolution of the Soviet Union, he boldly implemented the shock therapy program advocated by Western advisers.[29] The goal was not to balance government and the market, but rather to complete the transition from one polar extreme to the other (see Chapter 10 and Bergson 1995).

The ruble overhang fueled intense inflation as soon as price controls were lifted. The jump in prices was magnified because advance announcement of removal of price controls had precipitated severe shortages.[30] Inflation fed on itself as households and enterprises feverishly converted their rubles, which were rapidly losing value, into commodities and foreign currencies. The flight to dollars caused the exchange rate to plummet, generating further inflation as the ruble price of imports escalated.[31] Moreover, with monopoly positions to exploit, enterprises favored price increases over output increases. By the end of 1992, one ruble was worth less than one twenty-fifth of its value at the start of the year. Most Russians, deeply embittered, lost nearly all their savings.

Lower government spending and an influx of foreign goods sapped demand for domestic output.[32] Faced with a radically changed price structure that dramatically raised input costs, many enterprises quickly became insolvent. Unable to make payments, enterprises resorted to offering one another credit, which resulted in a huge accumulation of interenterprise debt. Since industry was monopolistically organized, the collapse of one enterprise sometimes meant another lost its only customer or its sole supplier of a needed input. Severed trade ties with suppliers in the former Soviet bloc and mafia interference with deliveries also interrupted production.

Responding to widespread impoverishment and the fear of total collapse, the Russian parliament, which originally gave Yeltsin carte blanche, became recalcitrant. Despite falling tax revenues, the Yeltsin administration, with the cooperation of the central bank, began to cushion the blow of shock therapy with subsidies and credits. Given the administration's ideological opposition to government intervention, the subsidies were determined by partisan pressures and insider influences rather than by a coherent long-term plan for restructuring the economy.[33] Local governments, lobbying for federal support and mandating that local utilities offer unlimited credit or accept payment in kind, were consistently aggressive in shielding major employers from market forces.

The pace of privatization was without historical precedent (Peck 1995). Closures of large plants impoverished entire communities while insiders and their collaborators benefitted from liquidation of assets. For some well-connected enterprises, privatization was nominal in that they remained afloat thanks to continued subsidies, including offsets whereby goods were provided at inflated prices in lieu of tax payments. Rarely did subsidies fund long-term investment in new equipment and technology (Spechler 1996).

Other enterprises, utilizing ties from Soviet times, evaded market discipline via mutual nonpayments and barter (Linz and Krueger 1998).

Corruption and criminality escalated, as wealth was transferred to an unprincipled few who shunned long-term investment. Complicity with private banks diverted much of the subsidies to capital flight. Some funds, left on deposit at very high interest rates, financed resale of imported goods and investment in high-yield government debt available only to banks. Private banks that funneled subsidies often collected excessive fees and made improper and imprudent loans to insiders. Contributing to corruption, the same person or group often controlled an enterprise as well as the associated bank (see Chapters 14 and 15).

The post-Soviet economy was saddled with technology and a capital stock ill-suited for international competition (Rosefielde 1998). In the consumer goods sector, few enterprises could produce goods of the kind and quality demanded in the world economy (Belousov 1996). Technological progress suffered as the economy was reoriented toward supplying energy and raw materials to the West (Chapter 11). Investment collapsed in the face of slack demand for Russian products, lack of government or financial institutions to support investment, and short-term time horizons of the new capitalist class (see Chapter 13 and Blasi et al. 1997).

In the first three years following the initiation of shock therapy, real GDP fell 33 percent, industrial production 44 percent, and investment 60 percent. Over the next four years, albeit at a slower rate and with a slight uptick in 1997, economic decline continued as economic policy focused on rapid disinflation and real appreciation of the ruble (Chapter 12). Compared with 1990, employment in 1998 was off by 11 million workers, poverty had become endemic, and social services were decimated (Chapter 16). Finally, the August 1998 ruble devaluation provided a foundation for the economic recovery that got underway in 1999, seven years after shock therapy was administered. [See the Statistical Appendix for historical data on the course of the economy from 1990 through 1999.]

Reform Challenge

Both Gorbachev and Yeltsin inspired the Russian people with the possibility and necessity of positive change. Neither leader, however, had a realistic transition program. Thus Russia continued on its historic path, lurching from one utopian fantasy to another—from communism to *perestroika* to laissez-faire capitalism.

Politically constrained, Gorbachev was ensnared by his own promise that economic democratization would quickly invigorate the economy. He delayed action on reforming the price system and badly mismanaged government finances. At the same time, he prematurely disempowered institutions that curbed corruption and malfeasance.

Yeltsin was heroic to cut military spending sharply, and he was right to decontrol prices, though a more measured approach might have been better. Adhering to a narrow view of the role of government, he failed to provide competent administration and oversaw a botched privatization program. The macroeconomic problem of maintaining demand for Russian output was ignored. Rather, it was vainly hoped that quick privatization and inflow of foreign capital would provide the basis for industrial modernization. Instead, investment collapsed while transfer of control over natural resources sapped government revenues and entrenched an unscrupulous elite.

More impulsive than deliberate, both Gorbachev and Yeltsin gave undue priority to speed, in one case "acceleration" and in the other "shock therapy." They did not proceed in a pragmatic, measured fashion: one sector and geographical area at a time—monitoring results to establish a basis for extending what worked and eliminating what did not. More ideological than realistic, they brought to an end a draconian system of centralized control without providing a viable mix of market and government.

Notes

1. Lenin had introduced in 1921 the "New Economic Policy" (NEP), which established a somewhat successful mixed economy (Dowlah and Elliott 1997, chapter 3). Centralized control had failed to revive the Russian economy after the Bolsheviks fully consolidated their power by 1920. Under the NEP, private business and market activity were encouraged in all sectors except heavy industry and basic infrastructure, and investment by foreigners was welcomed. The NEP ran afoul of anticapitalist sentiment, impatience for more rapid industrialization, and Stalin's appetite for power (Farber 1990).

2. See Nove (1986 and 1992) and Gregory and Stuart (1990) for thorough descriptions of the Soviet economic system.

3. There were numerous superficial modifications and constant tinkering. The most significant, though temporary, change occurred under Khrushchev (Schroeder 1982). In the second half of 1957 and the first half of 1958, the responsibilities of the branch ministries were transferred to regional and local bodies. The disappointing economic results led to Khrushchev's dismissal and the complete restoration of the ministerial system. According to President Bush's director of Soviet affairs, Khrushchev was responding to "enduring weaknesses" in the Soviet economic system but "surely went too far too quickly" (Hewett 1988, 227). As discussed later, Russian economic reform in the twentieth century was characterized by alternating periods of paralysis and precipitous leaps.

4. In 1980 on a per capita basis, Russia had twice as many physicians and hospital beds as the United States (Kotz 1997, 248). The literacy rate was, and still is, substantially higher in Russia than in the United States.

5. In Part One, Arrow and Klein discuss the potential role of a price system and markets for guiding and disciplining state-owned enterprises. See Temkin (1996) for a skeptical analysis of the possibilities of market socialism.

6. In the absence of consumer influence, elaborate but ultimately ineffectual administrative-command methods were introduced to discourage compromise of quality for the sake of quantity (Hewett 1988, 205–207).

7. Western scholars attribute as many as 20 million deaths to forced collectivization and Stalin's murderous political purges (Cohen 1985, 95).

8. Authoritarianism may or may not have been necessary to implement the Soviet command system, but it surely has served to discredit it and its socialist ideals. Lavigne (1995) discusses how Stalin's legacy undermined the prospects

for reform of socialism in Russia. Authoritarian features and other distortions instituted under Stalin proved tenacious, and at the same time there developed a reactionary antipathy to government planning and control.

9. Influenced by Russian economists Khanin and Seliunin (1987), many Sovietologists revised their previous judgments and concluded that Soviet growth was modest by the 1960s. Kotz (1997, 170–186) criticizes Khanin's methodology and argues that growth was rapid through 1975.

10. This paragraph is based on interviews conducted by the author during numerous visits to Russia. See also Bova (1988), Kotz (1997), and Remnick (1997).

11. Political factors were critical. Hewett (1991, 4) alleges that, at least during the initial years, Gorbachev appeared "to have been driven primarily by a desire to score quick political gains, even at the expense of implementing a coherent reform." Berliner (1993), who compares Gorbachev's policies with the more successful gradualist program implemented in China, maintains that Gorbachev was thwarted by political obstacles. Goldman (1991 and 1994) is more critical. He argues that, constrained by both ideology and a desire to be popular, Gorbachev wavered indecisively.

12. Aganbegyan (1987, 277). Aganbegyan served as Gorbachev's principal economic adviser until early 1988. Before Gorbachev came to power, Aganbegyan had captured the attention of the Soviet leadership with evidence of an ominous slowdown in productivity growth.

13. See "Perestroika: Origins, Essence, Revolutionary Character" (Gorbachev 1987, chapter 1) for evidence of Gorbachev's ideological orientation. Gorbachev never mentions the word "market," though he cites Lenin on the utility of accounting methods developed under capitalism (25–26). He rebukes the West for portraying Lenin as "an advocate of authoritarian methods of administration:"

> This is a sign of total ignorance of Lenin's ideas and, not infrequently, of their deliberate distortion. In effect, according to Lenin, socialism and democracy are indivisible. (32)

Invoking the "true Leninist revolutionary spirit," Gorbachev states:

> There is only one criterion here: we will listen to and take into consideration everything that strengthens socialism, whereas the trends alien to socialism we will combat, but, I repeat, within the framework of the democratic process. (57)

14. The success indicators affected funding for bonuses, social benefits, and capital improvements (Hewett 1988, 260–263). The bonuses were paid to both managers and workers. Social benefits included services ranging from housing to childcare. The payments for capital improvements could not be utilized until projects were accepted by Gosplan. Each type of reward was calculated by a different complicated function of the success indicators.

15. Hewett (1988, 312). Hanson (1991, 25) documents improvements in industrial growth after Stalin (1953–1958), Khrushchev (1966–1970), and Brezhnev (1983–1985). Hanson attributes this pattern to the salutary effects of extensive changes in personnel, as well as to increased attention to neglected bottlenecks in the production system. See Arbatov (1992) for criticism of the Brezhnev bureaucracy.

16. Between 1986 and 1989, the staff of the branch ministries was cut by a third (Goskomstat 1990, 50).

17. Shmelev (1987) warned that the credibility of reforms required a prompt and large expansion in the supply of consumer goods, if necessary with higher consumer imports. Instead, in 1986 and 1987 production of consumer goods lagged well behind other industry (Noren and Kurtzweg 1993, 15). Of the ten major industrial categories, two represent consumer goods: light industry and food industry. In 1986, these two categories significantly underperformed all others. In 1987, only one category performed worse than light industry, while food industry had yet to reattain the production level achieved two years earlier.

18. Aganbegyan (1987, 281). In fall 1986 a new agency, Gospriemka, was created to strengthen the monitoring of product quality (IMF et al. 1991, 20–22). One aim was to ensure that at least 95 percent of Soviet machines met "highest world standards" by 1991–1993. However, the program caused major disruptions in supply, and after March 1987 quality controls were largely vitiated.

19. While Gorbachev had initially stressed the traditional socialist aim of workers' control in the workplace, the goal of democratization was used to justify private enterprise, which Gorbachev's top economic adviser termed part of the "new economic mechanism" (Aganbegyan 1987, 281). The following remarks suggest absorption with ideological concerns rather than economic issues:

> The aim of socialist development in the final analysis lies in meeting the needs of all members of society more fully. Cooperatives and self-

employment contribute to this end and therefore reinforce our socialist principles. They completely correspond to Gorbachev's slogan for *perestroika*, "Give us more socialism!" (Aganbegyan 1988, 30)

20. Aganbegyan (1987) presented his plans for delayed price reform to a group of American economists visiting Moscow in December 1987.

21. Åslund (1995), who describes the pivotal role of distorted prices, claims that "Gorbachev made almost every conceivable mistake" (51). This assertion would seem to open the possibility that Gorbachev's gradualist approach might have succeeded had he not made so many blunders.

22. According to CIA estimates, GNP grew at a healthy, though not exceptional, rate of 4.1 percent in 1986. The growth rates for GNP in the next three years were 1.3 percent, 2.1 percent, and 1.5 percent, respectively. The 1.5 percent figure for 1989 is deceptive, for a 6.1 percent jump in agricultural output, largely due to favorable weather, helped to offset a 0.6 percent decline in industrial output (Noren and Kurtzweg 1993, 14).

23. Adjusting for subsidized imports and off-the-books government credits, Åslund (1995) estimates that the 1991 Soviet deficit was on the order of 30 percent of GDP (47–49).

24. According to official Soviet estimates, the average wage rose 14 percent in 1990 and 70 percent in 1991, while goods production declined by 4 percent and 15 percent, respectively (Goskomstat 1991, 7, 36; UN 1992, 105).

25. Poland, Czechoslovakia, East Germany, Hungary, Bulgaria, and Romania accounted for more than half of Soviet imports in 1988 (IMF 1992, 78). During 1989 and 1990 pro-Western leadership displaced pro-Soviet communist parties in all of these countries and immediately realigned trade toward the West.

26. For all ten industrial sectors, output growth was lower in 1989 than in 1988, and in 1990 and 1991 output performance progressively worsened. Based on CIA statistics, for only food and light industry was the growth rate in 1989 as much as half its value for 1988. In 1990, electric power was the only one of the ten industrial sectors with positive growth. Overall, industrial output had grown by about 2.5 percent each year from 1981 to 1985, and by 2.4 to 3 percent each year from 1986 to 1988. From 1989 to 1991, the growth rates in total industrial output were –0.6 percent, –2.8 percent, and –10.5 percent, respectively. GNP, after posting a modest 1.5 percent increase in

1989, fell 2.4 percent in 1990 and 8.5 percent in 1991 (Noren and Kurtzweg 1993, 14–15).

27. Gorbachev brought Yeltsin to Moscow in March 1985 to head the Moscow City Communist Party. Two years later at a closed meeting of the Central Committee, Yeltsin, originally a pro-Gorbachev reformer, criticized the "tendency in the leadership to create a 'cult' around Gorbachev" (Remnick 1997, 19). Yeltsin was soon removed from his post in Moscow and from membership in the Politburo. But the next month, in March 1989, he was elected in the first free Soviet elections to serve in the Congress of People's Deputies of the Soviet Union. In May, over Gorbachev's virulent opposition, Yeltsin achieved membership in the USSR Supreme Soviet when another deputy yielded his seat. The next year, 1990, after being elected to Russia's Congress of People's Deputies, he became head of the Republic of Russia. Shortly after Yeltsin was elected chairman, Russia's Supreme Soviet declared its sovereignty and the precedence of its laws over those of the Soviet Union. In July 1990 Yeltsin quit the Communist Party following Gorbachev's reelection as party head. The following February in a nationally televised address, Yeltsin called for Gorbachev's resignation.

28. President Yeltsin and the heads of Belarus and Ukraine had a secretive meeting December 7–8, 1991, at a forest dacha in Minsk. Without any parliamentary support or grounds in the Soviet constitution, they issued a declaration of dissolution of the Soviet Union. Yeltsin personally contacted President Bush by phone before he had the president of Belarus announce the surprise declaration to Gorbachev (Remnick 1997, 28). On December 25, Gorbachev formally resigned and the Russian flag replaced the Soviet flag over the Kremlin.

29. The Introduction to this book cites the most noted Western proponents of shock therapy. In 1990 John Kenneth Galbraith (1990, 51) wryly forewarned that "arch exponents of free enterprise" were counseling "the replacement of a poorly functioning economic system with none at all." Two other early attacks against shock therapy are Kregel et al. (1992) and Pomer (1993). Other forceful critiques include Abalkin (1995), Amsden et al. (1994), Cohen (2000), Goldman (1994), Millar (1995), Murrell (1995), and Yaryomenko (1995).

30. Cochrane and Ickes (1995) provide a useful description of the 1992 inflation. Their explanation, which attributes the inflation mostly to the ruble overhang, is not tenable, however. The ruble overhang evaporated rapidly with

prices quadrupling within about a month, causing the real value of savings deposits and the real value of the money supply to plummet. Thus, while inflation would have been less explosive if there had not been a ruble over-hang, it still would have been severe for the reasons mentioned in the text.

31. McKinnon (1995), reviewing the cases of Chile and China, shows how government finance and monetary equilibrium (low inflation and a stable exchange rate) are jeopardized by abrupt liberalization of prices and foreign trade.

32. De Melo and Gelb (1997) contrast the decline in domestic demand under Russian shock therapy with the growth of domestic demand under Chinese gradualism. (See discussion of macroeconomic conditions in Chapter 1.)

33. The most favored sectors were coal mining and agriculture, reflecting the strength of the coal miners' unions and the agrarian political parties. As discussed by Nekipelov and Grinberg (1994), their complete elimination would not only have created political problems but also would have intensified social distress and further undermined faltering Russian production. Ad hoc rather than carefully designed subventions are less likely to lead to productive investment (Sychev 1994).

References

Abalkin, Leonid I. 1995. "The Economic Situation in Russia." *Problems of Post Communism*, July/August: 53–57.

Aganbegyan, Abel G. 1987. "Basic Directions of Perestroika." *Soviet Economy* 3(4): 277–297.

———. 1988. *The Economic Challenge of Perestroika*. Bloomington, IN: Indiana University Press.

Amsden, Alice H., Jacek Kochanowicz, and Lance Taylor. 1994. *The Market Meets Its Match: Restructuring the Economies of Eastern Europe*. Cambridge, Ma: Harvard.

Arbatov, Georgi. 1992. *The System: An Insider's Life in Soviet Politics*. New York: Times Books.

Åslund, Anders. 1995. *How Russia Became a Market Economy.* Washington, DC: Brookings Institution.

Belousov, Andrei R. 1996. "The Russian Economy in a System Crisis: Current State and Prospects for Development." *Studies on Russian Economic Development* 7(2): 87–100.

Bergson, Abram. 1995. "The Big Bang in Russia: An Overview." *Proceedings of the American Philosophical Society* 139(4): 335–349.

Berliner, Joseph. 1976. *The Innovation Decision in Soviet Industry.* Cambridge, MA: MIT Press.

———. 1993. "Perestroika and the Chinese Model," in Robert W. Campbell, ed., *The Postcommunist Economic Transformation: Essays in Honor of Gregory Grossman.* Boulder, CO: Westview Press.

Blasi, Joseph, Maya Kroumova, and Douglas Kruse. 1997. *Kremlin Capitalism: The Privatization of the Russian Economy.* Ithaca, NY: Cornell University Press.

Bornstein, Morris. 1991. "Price Policies and Comment on Shmelev," in Ed A. Hewett and Victor H. Winston, eds., *Milestones in Glasnost and Perestroika: The Economy.* Pp. 167–203. Washington, DC: Brookings Institution.

Bova, Russell. 1988. "The Soviet Military and Economic Reform." *Soviet Studies* 40(3): 385–405.

Brown, Archie. 1996. *The Gorbachev Factor.* New York: Oxford University Press.

Christensen, Benedicte Vibe. 1993. *The Russian Federation in Transition: External Developments.* International Monetary Fund Working Paper: WP/93/74. Washington, DC: IMF.

Cochrane, John H., and Barry W. Ickes. 1995. "Macroeconomics in Russia," in Edward R. Lazear, ed., *Economic Transition in Russia: Realities of Reform.* Pp. 65–106. Stanford, CA: Hoover Institution Press.

Cohen, Stephen F. 1985. *Rethinking the Soviet Experience: Politics and History since 1917.* New York: Oxford University Press.

———. 2000. Failed Crusade: *America and the Tragedy of Post-Communist Russia.* New York: W. W. Norton.

De Melo, Martha, and Alan Gelb. 1997. "Transition to Date: A Comparative Overview." Paper presented at the annual meeting of the American Economic Association, New Orleans, January 5.

Dowlah, Alex F., and John E. Elliott. 1997. *The Life and Times of Soviet Socialism.* Westport, CT: Praeger.

Ellman, Michael. 1992. "Money in the 1980s: From Disequilibrium to Collapse," in Michael Ellman and Vladimir Kontorovich, eds., *The Disintegration of the Soviet Economic System.* Pp. 106–133. London and New York: Routledge.

Farber, Samuel. 1990. *Before Stalinism: The Rise and Fall of Soviet Democracy.* Cambridge, UK: Polity Press.

Galbraith, John Kenneth. 1990. "The Rush to Capitalism." *New York Review of Books* 37(16): 51–52.

Goldman, Marshall I. 1991. *What Went Wrong with Perestroika.* New York: W. W. Norton.

———. 1994. *Lost Opportunity: Why Economic Reforms in Russia Have Not Worked.* New York: W. W. Norton.

Gorbachev, Mikhail. 1987. *Perestroika: New Thinking for Our Country and the World.* New York: Harper and Row.

Goskomstat SSSR. 1990. *Narodnoe khoziaistvo SSSR v 1989 gody.* Moscow: Finansy i statistika.

———. 1991. *Narodnoe khoziaistvo SSSR v 1990 gody.* Moscow: Finansy i statistika.

Gregory, Paul R., and Robert C. Stuart. 1990. *Soviet Economic Structure and Performance,* 4th ed. New York: Harper and Row.

Grossman, Gregory. 1993. "The Underground Economy in Russia." *International Economic Insights* 4(6): 14–17.

———. 1994. "What Was—Is, Will Be—the Command Economy." *MOCT-MOST* 4(1): 5–22.

Gustafson, Thane. 1985. "The Origins of the Soviet Oil Crisis, 1970–1985." *Soviet Economy* 1(2): 103–35.

Hanson, Philip. 1991. "Gorbachev's Economic Strategy: A Comment," in Ed A. Hewett and Victor H. Winston, eds., *Milestones in Glasnost and Perestroika: The Economy.* Pp. 23–29. Washington, DC: Brookings Institution.

Hauslohner, Peter. 1987. "Gorbachev's Social Contract." *Soviet Economy* 3(1): 54–89.

Hewett, Ed A. 1988. *Reforming the Soviet Economy: Equality versus Efficiency.* Washington, DC: Brookings Institution.

Hewett, Ed A., and Victor H. Winston, eds. 1991. *Milestones in Glasnost and Perestroika: The Economy.* Washington, DC: Brookings Institution.

Hughes, Sandra, and Scot Butler. 1993. "Measuring the 'Private Sector' in Russia," in Richard F. Kaufman and John P. Hardt, U.S. Congress, Joint Economic Committee, *The Former Soviet Union in Transition.* Pp. 273–289. Armonk, NY: M. E. Sharpe.

IMF, IBRD, OECD and EBRD. 1991. *A Study of the Soviet Economy, Volume 1.* Paris: OECD.

International Monetary Fund (IMF). 1992. *Economic Review: The Economy of the Former USSR in 1991.* Washington, DC: The Fund.

Jones, Anthony, and William Moskoff. 1991. *Ko-ops: The Rebirth of Entrepreneurship in the Soviet Union.* Bloomington, IN: Indiana University Press.

Khanin, Gregory I., and Vladimir Seliunin. 1987. "Lukavaia tsifra." *Novyi mir* 2.

Kontorovich, Vladimir. 1992a. "The Railroads," in Michael Ellman and Vladimir Kontorovich, eds., *The Disintegration of the Soviet Economic System.* Pp. 174–192. London and New York: Routledge.

———. 1992b. "Technological Progress and Research and Development," in Michael Ellman, and Vladimir Kontorovich, eds., *The Disintegration of the Soviet Economic System.* Pp. 217–238. London and New York: Routledge.

Kornai, Janos. 1981. *Growth, Shortage, and Efficiency: A Macrodynamic Model of the Socialist Economy.* Oxford: Basil Blackwell.

Kotz, David M. (with Fred Weir). 1997. *Revolution from Above: The Demise of the Soviet System.* London and New York: Routledge.

Kregel, Jan, Egon Matzner, and Gernot Grabher. 1992. *The Market Shock: An Agenda for the Economic and Social Reconstruction of Central and Eastern Europe.* Ann Arbor, MI: University of Michigan Press.

Kurtzweg, Laurie. 1987. "Trends in Soviet Gross National Product," in U.S. Congress, Joint Economic Committee, *Gorbachev's Economic Plans.* Pp. 126–165. Washington, DC: United States Government Printing Office.

Lavigne, Marie. 1995. *The Economics of Transition: From Socialist Economy to Market Economy.* New York: St. Martin's Press.

Linz, Susan J., and Gary Krueger. 1998. "Enterprise Restructuring in Russia's Transition Economy: Formal and Informal Mechanisms." *Comparative Economic Studies* 40(2): 5–52.

McKinnon, Ronald I. 1995. "Gradual versus Rapid Liberalization in Socialist Foreign Trade," in Edward R. Lazear, ed., *Economic Transition in Russia: Realities of Reform.* Pp. 276–287. Stanford: Hoover Institution Press.

Millar, James R. 1995. "From Utopian Socialism to Utopian Capitalism: The Failure of Revolution and Reform in Post-Soviet Russia." *Problems of Post-Communism* 42(3): 7–14.

Murrell, Peter. 1995. "The Transition According to Cambridge, Mass." *Journal of Economic Literature* 33(1): 164–178.

Nekipelov, Alexander D., and Ruslan Grinberg. 1994. "Economic Reform and Structural Policy in Russia." *Berichte des Bundesinstituts der Wissenschaftlichen und Internationalen Studien, Köln Institut für Ost Europa* 19: 33–36.

Noren, James, and Laurie Kurtzweg. 1993. "The Soviet Economy Unravels: 1985–1991," in Richard F. Kaufman and John P. Hardt, U.S. Congress,

Joint Economic Committee, *The Former Soviet Union in Transition.* Pp. 8–33. Armonk, NY: M. E. Sharpe.

Nove, Alec. 1986. *The Soviet Economic System,* 3rd ed. Boston: Allen and Unwin.

———. 1992. *An Economic History of the USSR, 1917–1991,* 3rd ed. New York: Penguin Books.

Peck, Merton J. 1995. "Russian Privatization: What Basis Does It Provide for a Market Economy?" *Transnational Law and Contemporary Problems* 5(1): 21–38.

Pomer, Marshall. 1993. "Pir sred gniiushchikh ostankov imperii." *Nezavisimaya gazeta* 70, June 16.

Remnick, David. 1997. *Resurrection: The Struggle for a New Russia.* New York: Random House Inc.

Rosefielde, Steven, ed. 1998. *Efficiency and Russia's Economic Recovery Potential to the Year 2000 and Beyond.* Brookfield, VT: Ashgate.

Schroeder, Gertrude E. 1982. "Soviet Economic 'Reform' Decrees: More Steps on the Treadmill," in U.S. Congress, Joint Economic Committee, *Soviet Economy in the 1980's: Problems and Prospects.* Pp. 65–88. Washington, DC: United States Government Printing Office.

———. 1985. "The Slowdown in Soviet Industry, 1976–1982." *Soviet Economy* 1(1): 42–74.

———. 1991a. "Gorbachev: 'Radically' Implementing Brezhnev's Reforms," in Ed A. Hewett and Victor H. Winston, eds., *Milestones in Glasnost and Perestroika: The Economy.* Pp. 36–46. Washington, DC: Brookings Institution.

———. 1991b. *"Perestroika in the Aftermath of 1990,"* in Ed A. Hewett, and Victor H. Winston, eds., *Milestones in Glasnost and Perestroika: The Economy.* Pp. 459–469. Washington, DC: Brookings Institution.

Shmelev, Nikolai. 1987. "Avansy idologi." *Novyi mir,* June.

Shmelev, Nikolai, and Vladimir Popov. 1989. *The Turning Point: Revitalizing the Soviet Economy.* New York: Doubleday.

Spechler, Martin C. 1996. "Privatization Is Not the Key to Successful Transition." *Challenge* 39(1): 48–51.

Sychev, V. A. 1994. "Strategy for Survival." Interview by Yuri V. Kuznetsov, *Studies in Russian Economic Development* 5(6): 540–544.

Temkin, Gabriel. 1996. "The New Market Socialism: A Critical Review." *Communist and Post-Communist Studies* 29(4): 467–478.

UN Economic Commission for Europe. 1992. *Economic Surveys of Europe in 1991–1992.* United Nations.

White, Stephen. 1996. *Russia Goes Dry: Alcohol, State and Society.* Cambridge, England: Cambridge University Press.

Yaryomenko, Yuri V. 1995. "The Priority: Structural-Technological Renewal of the National Economy." *Problems of Economic Transition* 37(12): 28–34.

Zaslavskaia, Tatiana. 1990. *The Second Socialist Revolution: An Alternative Soviet Strategy.* Translated by S. M. Davies. Bloomington and Indianapolis, IN: Indiana University Press.

10

Origins and Consequences
of "Shock Therapy"

Georgi Arbatov

The economic system created by the Soviet Union, and inherited by Russia, was inefficient and wasteful. It was unable to provide proper economic development of the country and a decent standard of living for its citizens. By the time Boris Yeltsin took charge, the problems with the "administrative-command" system were quite obvious and the main subject of political debate.

Different groups of economists prepared possible programs that were openly debated. But the country was taken by surprise by the "Chicago School" program prepared by Yegor Gaidar, and approved in haste by President Yeltsin. On January 2, 1992, Gaidar launched the shock therapy program to inject laissez-faire capitalism immediately into the Russian economy. The West cheered, perhaps for ideological reasons. Influential Western experts, including Jeffrey Sachs and Anders Åslund, the International Monetary Fund (IMF), the World Bank, and the leaders of the G7 all gave their blessings.

The Gaidar program rejected the need for government to guide the economic transition. It ignored the requirements for Russian enterprises to make the adjustment to a market system. Little attention was paid to the immediate needs of the people. Education, health, science, and culture all fell victim to fiscal austerity, which included long delays in payment of salaries and nonpayment of government contracts.

Paradoxically, inflation was stimulated by the Gaidar program. A primary cause of this was the sudden removal of price controls in January 1992. The most beneficial way to restrain inflation would have been to foster increased production of goods and services by fighting against monopolistic and criminal restraints on supply from domestic sources. Attempts to curb inflation through macroeconomic means (fiscal austerity and constraints on the money supply) would have been more feasible and effective if markets and market competition were more developed. But the market had been ruthlessly eroded by more than 70 years of clearing the ground for a communist-run, militarist economy.

Even in long-standing market systems, it is unwise to assume that markets alone can produce robust economic development, or timely recovery from either recession or depression. Clearly, the market does not guarantee that basic human needs are met and that there is a humane distribution of social and economic benefits. It cannot provide sufficient education, science, health, and even public safety. Industrial and agricultural infrastructure—roads and bridges, most means of transportation, energy supplies, and communications—are established and managed either by the government or by giant monopolies, which hardly differ from government agencies.

In an effort to force Third World countries to honor debts to the West, the IMF has had, since the antigovernment Reagan era, a stringent policy of demanding a laissez-faire environment and austerity. Reflecting perhaps intent to please the IMF and gain its favor, the Gaidar program turned out to be essentially a carbon copy of the IMF's reform model, despite totally different economic and social challenges from those prevailing in Third World countries.

To ensure "truth in pricing," for example, IMF policy requires abolishing subsidies on basic necessities. Serious anti-austerity uprisings, often called "IMF riots" by those involved, have resulted in the loss of lives and civil freedom in over two dozen countries. Economist Susan George's account, written before shock therapy in Russia, aptly foreshadowed events:

> Prices for food, water, transport, and energy skyrocket at the very time people can least afford to pay. Imports are "liberalized" and the shops are full of goods which practically nobody can afford. State social budgets are slashed: education, housing, transport, health and the environment are usual victims. The conditions of women and children deteriorate sharply while hunger, illiteracy and disease rates increase. (6)[1]

Socioeconomic Consequences

The poorly conceived transition program resulted in an unprecedented decline of the national economy. By 1998 Russian GDP was only about one-half its 1990 level, with the crisis spread to virtually all areas of production.[2] Russian industry found itself unable to compete even in its own domestic markets. All of this was accompanied by a sharp reduction in investment and a disintegration of scientific and technological potential. We are now witnessing processes of pauperization and de-intellectualization, accompanied by criminalization, as Russia increasingly takes on the appearance of a Third World republic.

The standard of living of most Russians has decreased dramatically.[3] Rampant inflation has eliminated the savings of much of the population, while the increase of salaries and pensions has lagged far behind the price rises. The mortality rate has grown, and the birthrate has plummeted. As a result, Russia has been losing more than one-half million in population each year.

The sharp decline in the standard of living of the overwhelming majority is not only expressed in the obvious fact that diet, health, and elementary conditions of life have become worse for millions of people, but also in the loss of social benefits. The customary summer camp for all children has now become an unusual luxury. Few can still afford to vacation at a resort, be it a most modest one. Such previously expected amenities have become unaffordable because of large increases in railway and airplane ticket prices, making it hardly feasible to visit relatives. People who settled in the Far North or Far East have become "hostages" of these distant places. Because of high tariffs on long-distance telephone calls, for many the usual means of communication with relatives and friends has become a rare luxury.

Life has become especially hard for the millions of people who are dependent on pensions, many of whom now live in impoverished conditions. Their savings were practically eliminated by inflation, and the level of pensions is below the minimum necessary, even by the official calculations, for bare survival. Their situation is aggravated by the tremendous increase in the prices of medicines and the lower quality and reduced availability of subsidized health care. In addition, there is a traditionally Russian concern: when you die who will bury you and with what money?

Though the sheer fact of being young makes life look not so hopeless, the situation of Russian youth is also very difficult. Education has deteriorated drastically. Higher education is not free anymore and is unaffordable for many. Even more serious are the problems of unemployment and the financial difficulty that a young family has in getting a house and raising children.

Russians now have less access to culture—books and magazines, museums, libraries, arts, theaters, and music. During the past five years, the overall number of published books fell by 65 percent, circulation of newspapers by 80 percent, and the number of copies of published magazines by over 90 percent. Theater tickets, music concerts, CDs, and traditional records have also become unavailable for the majority. The futures of many theaters, music schools, and the large national libraries are in question.[4]

Faced with overwhelming difficulties and misfortunes, ordinary people have become helpless. Government agencies, which in the past cared about them, at least to a minimal degree, disappeared or continued in name only with the decline of the state and its power. The old pseudo trade unions, which represented the state, also disappeared. New ones have just started to be organized. As a result, only spontaneous protests are possible against extreme circumstances such as long overdue payment of salaries.

The way of life for ordinary Russians has deteriorated remarkably. The majority are fully immersed in the day-to-day fight for survival. This is now the major subject that people think and talk about. Friends and colleagues meet each other less frequently and rarely travel. Staying at home is also encouraged by the unprecedented rise in crime, which has made big cities and many of the smaller towns dangerous places.

It is very difficult for me—a nonspecialist—to analyze the impact of all of this on the psyche, on the minds and emotions of the people. It is obvious, however, that it could not have a positive effect, the more so because any feeling of tomorrow's security has been grossly undermined. This does not mean that the future seemed cloudless and happy to everybody before transition, but at least it was perceived without fear. Today most people have little hope for improvement.

The Russian population is now sharply polarized. In 1991, the ratio between the income of the most affluent 10 percent and the poorest 10 percent was 4:1. The ratio has increased since then by 600 percent, taking into account estimates for illegal incomes.[5] Another study found that only 15 percent of Russians have been "successful" during the past five years, while 25 percent are now in a "desperate situation."[6]

In a time span of five years, especially during a period of sharp economic decline, it is difficult for a person to prosper in an honest way. There is a practically unanimous belief, to a large degree correct, that the country is being robbed of its wealth. The increasingly obvious growth of crime and corruption have been practically accepted as an inevitable fact of life by the government, which appears to do little to fight back.

Political Implications

The socioeconomic circumstances that are developing in Russia today are surprisingly similar to those that developed just prior to the Bolshevik Revolution, when there was widespread corruption and a vast difference between the wealthy elite and the majority of the population. One might conclude that shock therapy has put Russia on the historically familiar path to further upheaval.

In 1991, after the failure of the *coup d'état*, the communists were completely discredited in Russia, but the disastrous economic events of the past five years have led to their revival. Although they lost the presidential elections in 1996, they were a strong second, leaving other contenders far behind. The Communist Party has reemerged as the biggest faction in the parliament, though luckily not yet the majority.

Shock therapy adherents like to point to Poland as a favorable example for their policies, but Poland is different from Russia. Poland is much smaller and far more connected to the West. The Poles had not lost practical knowledge of how to live and work in a free-market economy. Polish agriculture was privatized long ago and has become more or less modernized. In addition, Poland has a large emigrant population in the West ("Polonia"), which renders substantial financial help. The leadership that started shock therapy in Poland—Solidarity and Lech Walesa—enjoyed enviable support of the population. But even the Poles have had problems with laissez-faire economic policy and have sent the proponents of this approach, including Balcerowicz and Walesa, into retirement. In other Eastern European countries where shock therapy was implemented, it ended with a return to power of the left-wing parties and leaders. Prime Minister Klaus of the Czech Republic was acclaimed in the West as a strong proponent of shock therapy, but in practical policy he behaved with extraordinary caution.

The secret of the success of the communists is quite obvious—nostalgia about the past. Despite all the difficulties and misgivings, people remember living better and more safely. This shift to the left in Russia differs from the changes in Eastern Europe. There, most of the former communists have really become Social Democrats. In my country the communist leaders, at least the majority of them, as well as a big part of their electorate, have resisted such a political evolution.

In 1996 we managed to escape a return to dictatorship. Gaidar's "reform" had nothing to do with democracy or democratic changes. Quite the contrary. Policy that breeds poverty and crime, that promotes irresponsible behavior by the government at the expense of citizens, can survive only if democracy is suppressed. Such an approach needs a dictator, and it is not by chance that many supporters of Gaidar openly say that Russia can now be saved only by authoritarian rule, by "a new Pinochet." Indeed, steps toward such a political order were visible in the constitution adopted under Yeltsin.

I do not believe that, to improve the state of the economy, we had first to destroy it and make beggars of our people. A change in economic policy is needed to build effectively and humanely a modern market economy. We should reject not only the laissez-faire policy but also conservative programs which could lead us back to the centralized and militarized command system. We should take international experience into account, especially the experiences of those who did not follow blindly the directives of the IMF and have achieved success—several countries of the Pacific region, postwar Japan, and China.

A market system, no doubt, is necessary for an effective economy, but laissez-faire has never dominated the actual economic policies of developed countries, and no modern developed country would now agree to establish an absolutely pure capitalist market economy. It is vital that government policy represent the interests of society as a whole and supplement the "invisible hand" of the market. This is actually the basis for all the great reforms in capitalism since the times of Smith and Marx.

What I Would Like to Tell the West

How could it happen that the shock therapy approach was so easily accepted, without any attempt even to discuss it? The leadership, which included (as often happens after a revolution) many inexperienced people, permitted itself to be persuaded that this economic concept represented the highest achievement of economic thought and reflected the experience of the most successful and prosperous nations. Western governments and their leaders were perceived in Moscow as having unconditional confidence in shock therapy. In addition, Russia was told that if it followed this approach, it would receive massive help from the West.

Most Western statesmen simply had no comprehension of the economic situation in Russia. And, I suspect, the fate of Russia was not their primary concern. They were—which is natural—overwhelmed primarily by the concerns of their own countries. They saw shock therapy as the most dependable instrument for putting a quick end to everything that remained from the communist system. Many of my countrymen now understand shock therapy as a conscious design to undermine Russia completely as a great power and transform her into a kind of Third World country. The actual results of economic shock therapy have not been far from this goal.

Notes

1. Taken from a 1991 report on the IMF by Susan George to the Ninetieth Nobel Jubilee Symposium. George uses OECD data to document the frequent failure of IMF policies to achieve even the narrow goals of "reducing the debt burden and promoting prosperity" (12).

2. The official Russian GDP in 1995 was only 50.6 percent of its value in 1990. With "corrections" made by the State Committee on Statistics to include illegal economic activity, the GDP in 1995 was 60 percent of 1990 (*Statistical Yearbook of Russia*, Moscow, 1995).

3. It is estimated that 80 percent of Russians have experienced a substantial decline in real income (*Vlast,* November 11, 1995, 42).

4. See section 3.5 of Goskomstat of Russia, *Russia in Figures,* Moscow, 1996.

5. The ratio is 13.5:1 excluding illegal income, and 25:1 if illegal income is included (*Izvestiia*, February 14, 1996; *Vlast*, November 11, 1995, 42). See *Nezavisimaya gazeta,* June 7, 1996, for comparable data.

6. *Passport to the World*, March/April 1996, 61.

11

Economic Subordination to the West

Sergei Glaziev

Rapid liberalization of foreign trade is a basic component of shock therapy, along with fiscal austerity and swift privatization. According to the orthodox economic theory of comparative advantage, throwing the domestic market wide open to foreign competition leads to greater efficiency of production and a higher standard of living. Notwithstanding the theoretical appeal of the laissez-faire doctrine, most countries shelter their domestic producers from foreign competition. Furthermore, many countries have achieved spectacular economic success with intensely protectionist policies, including Japan and China.

When Gaidar's shock therapy program was implemented in January 1992, Russian enterprises were ill-equipped for the market economy. There were, and still are, severe organizational and financial problems, as well as a lack of experience and connections in marketing. Also, production technologies were based on a suddenly outdated price structure and yielded low-quality products with little market appeal. It was wholly predictable that rapid liberalization would cause the destruction of a large part of industry and agriculture at the hands of more effective foreign enterprises. Moreover, gradual liberalization would have mitigated the negative repercussions, first from the dissolution of the Soviet trading bloc (CMEA), second from the breakup of the Soviet Union, and finally from the "shock" experiments of the Gaidar program.[1]

Cognizant of Russia's circumstances and international experience, the government and the parliament resisted IMF pressure and took steps to liberalize trade gradually. But after the storming of the parliament by President Yeltsin in 1993, foreign trade was radically liberalized. De-industrialization accelerated as imports continued to push out domestic products, transforming Russia into a kind of massive colonial appendage supplying gas and other raw materials to Europe.

Before 1992

Foreign trade in the Soviet command economy, as in any economy, fulfilled a compensatory function by augmenting scarce or inferior goods with imported ones. To pay for these imports, the Soviet Union was obligated to sell to the West. And yet, the history of Soviet industry can be characterized as industrialization in an attempt to reduce imports.

In the 1930s, the Soviet Union relied on agricultural exports to provide the foreign exchange needed to pay for imported capital equipment. Priority was given to building up the production of steel and heavy machinery, including both military and agricultural vehicles. During the 1950s and 1960s, proceeds from energy exports were used to buy equipment to expand domestic production of chemicals, nonferrous metals, oil synthetics, and processed food.

Export revenues grew rapidly in the 1970s due to higher energy prices and better equipment for extracting oil and gas. Rising export proceeds allowed increased imports of consumer goods as well as equipment to build up the electronics industry. After the 1970s, the export base stagnated, while imports continued to rise.

In the early 1980s, a program was initiated to increase the production of consumer goods, including processed food. The flawed plans to accelerate economic growth and reorient the economy toward consumers entailed large expenditures for imported capital goods. This program was severely undermined by shortfalls in export revenues. To help fill the gap, foreign indebtedness and state currency reserves were drawn upon in the second half of the 1980s in the face of falling energy prices.

The last Soviet government borrowed more than $50 billion from foreign sources during its five years in power, as it simultaneously depleted the nation's gold reserves. Although this temporarily mitigated the structural crisis, it only made it deeper in the long run. By 1990, expenditures for servicing the foreign debt reached close to one-third of export revenues.

The fossilized structures of the national economy implied an absence of flexible mechanisms for adapting to new limits and opportunities. As a consequence, the distorting influence of oil dollars practically blocked all stimuli for economic growth, once the flow of easy money from oil revenues began to run dry.

With the dissolution of the Soviet trading bloc and subsequently the Soviet Union itself, the economy faltered badly. Trade volumes with CMEA countries fell by two-thirds from 1989 to 1991, in part due to an ill-considered and hurried transition to accounting in hard currency. Production began to decline in 1990 and 1991 in practically every sector. Led by a 50 percent drop in oil revenues, exports fell by more than a third and returned to 1981 levels. Imports were cut by 43 percent, which, in turn, negatively affected the dynamics of domestic production and export.

1992

When shock therapy was initiated in January 1992, circumstances were inhospitable for sudden liberalization of foreign trade. Enterprises, for decades walled off from the world market, reacted indecisively in the crisis environment. Government credits to producers and customers, which previously supported exports of manufactured goods, were unavailable under the new laissez-faire policies. A radical orientation toward the industrially developed countries ensued as raw materials assumed a substantially larger role in exports.

The crisis was aggravated by several factors. During the years of the oil-dollar boom, industry developed dependence on imported inputs and increased its output capacity, largely for the production of goods not meeting Western standards. Half of the Russian border was left unprotected by the breakup of the Soviet Union. The collapse of the state banking system, coupled with lack of regulation of private banks, made it impossible to implement currency controls. In addition, the attempt to establish a "ruble zone" within the Commonwealth of Independent States caused a complete loss of control over the money supply since each country independently issued rubles.

Control over foreign trade was effectively surrendered with the collapse of the Soviet administrative-regulatory system. The volume of licenses for exporting energy resources and other strategically important raw materials became practically equal to their very levels of production. Massive amounts of contraband crossed Russia's western and southern borders. In several categories, the export of Russian goods from the Baltic states exceeded legal volumes transferred from Russia itself.

Concurrently with the laissez-faire Gaidar program, the government took steps to impose order and to institute a program of gradual liberalization of foreign trade. The primary policy instruments were tariffs on both imports and exports, combined with requirements that exporters sell a share of their hard currency revenues to the government. Previous regulatory structures were streamlined. The system of export quotas, unwieldy and ineffectual, had encompassed more than one hundred categories of goods and involved fifteen ministries and departments, as well as ministerial councils of the Commonwealth of Independent States. The scope for export licenses and quotas was restricted to a list of strategically important raw materials. The previous requirement that exporters sell a portion of their hard currency revenues entailed differential exchange coefficients. The whole system was irrationally implemented, prone to corruption, and the source of costly hidden subsidies.

Although export tariffs provided needed revenue for the government, their primary purpose was to slow changes in the domestic price structure, especially the steep upward climb in prices for energy and raw materials. Projections indicated that an immediate shift to world prices would have suddenly bankrupted much of manufacturing and agriculture. In many cases, the value of materials in world prices exceeded the market price of finished goods. Under these conditions, the gradual reduction of export tariffs was an important means to help producers adjust to the market economy. In addition, these export tariffs combated collapsing prices due to market gluts, for they restrained the tendency to flood foreign markets with raw materials, though often not sufficiently. The trade policies were tailored to stimulate the export of manufactured goods. To this end, manufacturers of consumer products neither paid export tariffs nor were required to sell a portion of their hard currency receipts to the government.

Many enterprises, involved in foreign trade for the first time, exported their products as quickly as possible. This caused an avalanche-like fall of world prices for traditional Russian exports, especially nonferrous metals and chemical products. In 1992 alone, world prices for aluminum fell almost 30 percent, copper 20 percent, nickel and tin 15 percent, and oxygenized fertilizer and basic petroleum products from 20 to 60 percent. European countries responded with antidumping duties or volume quotas on Russian goods.

In an attempt to evade taxes, hard currency proceeds were frequently hoarded abroad. This was facilitated by failure to monitor hard currency bank accounts where exporters accumulated proceeds, rarely with the intention to use the funds for productive investment. At the same time, there was extensive capital flight abroad, much of it in the form of smuggled exports.

Attempts at currency control, initiated in 1992, included the following measures: government seizure of funds hoarded abroad that were not repatriated within the required time period, a procedure for recording receipts in conjunction with customs declarations, and the founding of a government agency to oversee currency control. To improve compliance, a protocol was instituted to register and monitor major exporters of strategically important raw materials.

In the middle of 1992, an import tariff was implemented. It was initially levied at one rate, but differential rates were soon established. The base rate was 15 percent of full value, and other rates varied from 20 to 50 percent (earlier in 1992, there had been less need for an import tariff because a severely depressed exchange rate afforded protection of the domestic market. Another factor was the organizational unpreparedness of Russian customs to control imports.) The import tariff served to compensate for the absence of excise and value-added taxes in the period before the passage of corresponding legislation.

The introduction of external convertibility for the ruble was planned, since limits on currency conversion hampered foreign trade, especially with those countries of Eastern Europe and Central Asia whose currencies were not convertible. External convertibility could have enabled the ruble to serve as a reserve currency for the Commonwealth of Independent States and Eastern Europe. It would have considerably simplified foreign trade calculations for Russian enterprises, and it would have reduced the tendency for Russians to put their savings into holdings of foreign currency. At the same time, other measures were planned in order to push foreign currencies out of domestic circulation. These included comprehensive sales of currency proceeds to the government and restrictions on enterprises' foreign currency accounts. The intention was to restrain capital flight and raise investment activity in the country.

Retreat into the Abyss

Government policies to liberalize foreign trade gradually and bolster the competitiveness of Russian enterprises were abandoned in mid-1993. Blackmailed by the IMF's threat to withhold deferments on servicing foreign debt, the government removed most export tariffs. It also unilaterally committed itself to neither increase import tariffs nor apply import quotas.

These policy changes were implemented despite the fact that a steep climb in the real value of the ruble had already strengthened demand for imports. To the further delight of importers, the government continued to buttress the ruble in an apparent effort to demonstrate stabilization amidst inflation of from 5 to 7 percent per month. As a consequence, the competitiveness of Russian goods fell by two-thirds from spring 1993 to summer 1994. (That is, the relative real value of the dollar fell by two-thirds: the dollar's value in rubles doubled from the end of May 1993 to the end of May 1994, while the composite index of consumer prices rose by a factor of about six.) The following year, competitiveness fell by another fifth. Despite this tremendous blow to producers of manufactured goods, no compensatory measures were taken to protect the domestic market.

It is not surprising, therefore, that the steepest cuts in production took place, not in 1992, but in the second half of 1993 and the first half of 1994. In comparison with roughly 20 percent several years earlier, imports grew sharply to 54 percent of domestic trade in 1995, and they continue to grow. Consumer goods (including processed foods), transportation equipment, and capital goods have been especially vulnerable.

Under pressure from the IMF, Russian authorities continued to both abstain from protective measures and support a high exchange rate for the ruble. There were two main props for the ruble: foreign purchases of large quantities of short-term government bonds that offered very high yields, and financial support from the IMF. In effect, Russian economic policy was hostage to foreign interests, for at any time Western disapproval could have toppled these props, causing a destabilizing collapse of the ruble.[2]

The government made no effort to help raise the competitiveness of Russian goods. On the contrary, it is suggested that budgetary losses from the elimination of export tariffs on oil and gas should be compensated with an increase in excise taxes on their use, which would raise the cost of energy inputs and further reduce the competitiveness of Russian industry.

The main long-term result of radical liberalization of foreign trade is the bifurcation of the Russian economy into two weakly linked realms. On the one hand, extraction of raw materials has linked up with global economic networks and is now oriented toward export (from 30 to 80 percent of each major category). On the other hand, there have been drastic cuts in production for the domestic market. The declines range from 50 to over 95 percent in end-use goods. As a rule, the higher the level of manufacturing and the greater its complexity, the more severe is the decline.

Opportunities for Revival

Despite its dramatic deterioration over the past five years, the Russian economy still has enormous potential: natural resources are abundant, the labor force is well educated and highly skilled, and there is extensive technological and scientific expertise in a variety of fields. Much needs to be done by the government if existing enterprises and new ones are to benefit from these advantages.

The climate for economic activity must be improved, and the entire institutional and physical infrastructure needs revamping. Consider, for example, transporting goods within Russia. To address this universal problem, it is necessary to improve transportation infrastructure, regulate railway and other freight charges, and curb mafia interception of transported goods. Responsibility to maintain the overall economic environment is unavoidable for any government.

But there is much else to be done by an activist government to guide economic transition, to facilitate economic restructuring, and to build the competitiveness of Russian industry. Support can come from temporary tariff protection, government purchases of output, subsidized loans, tax incentives for investment in equipment and technological advance, and marketing assistance. There should be government-sponsored institutes for crediting and ensuring export operations, infrastructure for certification and quality control, and an extensive system for providing information to participants in foreign trade.[3]

The experience of successful, newly developed countries demonstrates the benefits of government support for particular sectors that can compete internationally and become agents for economic growth. The most promising sectors for Russia are those where it has comparative advantages.

Especially important are sectors involving advanced technology, for development here would have substantial spillover benefits.

In addition to its oil and gas resources, Russia has extensive mineral resources for production of ferrous and nonferrous metals. With the decline in the national economy, domestic purchases of metals have dropped precipitously while exports have grown. A promising focus of industrial development is manufacturing that requires extensive inputs of energy and metals, including technical alloys and precision components for machinery.

In many scientific fields, Russia possesses highly qualified teams of specialists with considerable accomplishments that have achieved international recognition. Thus there is promise in the areas of applied scientific research and experimentation, engineering, and computer software.

A number of Russian industries are characterized by high levels of technology, including aviation and aeronautics, lasers, nuclear industry, and shipbuilding. Given the steep decline in domestic demand, tapping into export markets is essential. Also, strengthening technology-intensive industries that are responsive to international competition would stimulate improvements of allied industries, giving impetus to their technological and organizational modernization. Technological sectors could thereby become locomotives for progressive structural change.

As a result of Russia's abundant material resources, the availability of skilled workers at relatively low wages, and an untapped manufacturing capacity, there is considerable potential in areas other than high technology. In addition, the Russian market itself has great potential, especially once the economy begins to revive. For the domestic market, Russian producers would have an advantage over foreign producers because of lower transport costs. Three lines of development are particularly important: (1) mastering the production of goods that are typically manufactured in highly developed countries, including autos and capital equipment; (2) final assembly in Russia using imported components; and (3) creation of manufacturing joint ventures with foreign partners, with an emphasis on commercial assimilation of untapped scientific and technological potential.

Russia's prospects for integrating into the world economy depend on the resolution of two complex problems. First, products must be upgraded to the standards of the world market. In particular, there is extensive technological obsolescence due to the high energy consumption in the production and use of Russian products. Adaptation therefore requires revamping technology. Second, Russian comparative advantages are generally focused on markets where opposition from Western governments, tied to geopolitical interest, is especially fierce (aviation and aeronautics, armaments, and energy production). This opposition takes the form of product requirements, import tariffs, and quotas. The lowering of such barriers to Russian products requires concerted action by the Russian government.

Government involvement must be combined with market mechanisms, neither intentionally substituting for nor suppressing their activity. Such a combination is wholly distinct from the vulgarly simple ideological opposition between market and plan. In a transition economy, government must not shirk its leading role in organizing transitional processes, both in transforming property relations and establishing appropriate market infrastructure. Under current circumstances, multifaceted government activism is essential in order for Russia to realize its technological potential and to be successful as an exporter of more than natural resources.

Notes

1. Ronald I. McKinnon, "Macroeconomics in Russia," in Edward R. Lazear, ed., *Economic Transition in Russia: Realities of Reform* (Stanford, CA: Hoover Institution Press, 1995).

2. With its extremely formal positions on questions of macroeconomic policy, the IMF has given Russia much bad advice. It has considered Russia's economic system as a collection of financial markets and ignored the processes going on in the real sector. It effectively gave the green light to the policy of building financial pyramids. If it were not for the IMF's authority, the policy of self-destruction of the economic system could have been stopped much earlier. Nevertheless, it is incumbent on Russia to carry out negotiations with the IMF.

3. Sergei Glaziev, *Economics and Politics: Episodes in the Struggle* (Moscow: Gnozis, 1994).

12

Sham Stabilization

Yevgeny Gavrilenkov

The Russian experience in the 1990s is an instructive example of macro-economic mismanagement. Most dramatic was the shattering in 1998 of the myth of stabilization with the default on government debt, the collapse of financial markets, and the devaluation of the national currency. Government economists pointed to external factors, namely falling energy prices and shifting investor attitudes toward emerging markets. The real causes, however, were short-sighted policies and failure to address distortions in the transition process.

In 1997, an illusion of macroeconomic stability appeared. Inflation was substantially reduced, there were slight improvements in the real sector, the exchange rate was stable, and small gains were made in real incomes and consumption. Optimism that economic growth would soon accelerate was reflected in government documents and public statements by top officials. But mishandling of the transformation of the Russian economy continued. This chapter reviews the false stabilization and examines several fundamental imbalances thwarting Russia's transformation, including capital flight, weak tax-collection, demonetization, and low investment.

Macroeconomic Performance

A two-year period of seeming improvement began with the reelection of Boris Yeltsin in mid-1996. The price level and the exchange rate were stabilized with the introduction of an exchange rate corridor and the issuing of government securities to cover fully the government deficit. Foreign investors not only rushed in to buy government debt but also propelled the inchoate Russian stock market. By 1997 inflation was running at only about 10 percent. (See the Appendix for basic data on economic performance.)

The real economy showed modest gains. In the second half of 1996, for the first time since the dissolution of the Soviet Union, production rose, though only slightly. During the next year, industrial output grew almost 2 percent. While GDP continued its downward descent in 1996, the decline was a relatively moderate 3.5 percent, and in 1997 GDP rose 0.8 percent, the first annual increase in the 1990s. In the second half of 1997, there were also the first signs that fixed investment was beginning to recover. This could be attributed in part to a fall in lending rates to below 30 percent.

Equally important, social inequality, which had worsened dramatically after 1992, began to ameliorate after the presidential election. Real incomes started to grow in the second half of 1996, contributing to an increase in retail sales and private consumption in 1997. Thus, the improved macroeconomic performance in 1997 reflected rising domestic demand. In contrast, the few positive developments in the real sector from 1992 to 1996 were due to expanding exports.

The fiscal deficit, though it decreased somewhat in 1997, remained substantial.[1] Offsetting the impact of the deficit and supporting the exchange rate were the positive account balance and the inflow of foreign capital, largely borrowing by the government. The overvalued ruble and high interest rates artificially restrained inflation, which was the primary focus of policy. Moreover, the massive inflow of foreign capital that penetrated financial markets did not reach the real sector.

The Descent

While the appreciation of the ruble in real terms lowered inflation, it simultaneously led to an ultimately destabilizing growth in imports. Imports in 1997 and the first half of 1998 averaged $6 billion per month, up 50 percent from 1994. At the same time, primarily due to falling energy prices, the value of exports shrunk. In 1998 monthly exports averaged only about $6 billion, compared with a $7.5 billion monthly average during the two previous years. At the same time, interest payments to foreign investors rose sharply with the rise in borrowing from abroad. Thus the current account of the balance of payments shifted from substantial positive values ($3 billion to $13 billion in 1993–1997) to large negative values (-$6 billion in the first half of 1998).

In the fall of 1997 foreign investors, alarmed by the devaluations in Southeast Asia,[2] began to withdraw from Russian markets. After October, international reserves started to fall as the central bank attempted to support the ruble. By December 1997 the stock of GKOs (short-term government debt) in circulation was twice as high as international reserves (excluding gold), a clear signal for investors to continue to withdraw their assets from the country. In the meantime, the fiscal deficit forced the government to continue to borrow, while rising interest rates drove up the amount that had to be borrowed.

The real sector was negatively affected by developments on the financial markets, and GDP began to fall. With the corporate sector as the major taxpayer, contraction negatively affected tax-collection. The stock of inter-enterprise arrears grew as concern increased that there would be a liquidity crisis.

After Prime Minister Viktor Chernomyrdin was dismissed in March 1998, the economic situation further worsened. Economic policies of the new government were unclear. In the face of deteriorating financial conditions, declarations of intentions to cut the deficit, rather than the implementation of specific measures, only caused further loss in confidence. Interest rates surged in April, eventually exceeding 100 percent in real terms by summer.

Looking to improve the economic situation, the government drafted decrees calling for cuts of over 50 percent in the prices of transportation, electricity, and gas (natural monopolies subject to administrative prices). Since these price reductions would have undermined tax revenues, their mere discussion aroused concern over the solvency of the government and provoked outflows of foreign capital. When finally issued, the price reductions were softened to allay these concerns.

As the year progressed, the cost of servicing government debt increased rapidly due to the dependence on short-term borrowing. Debt service went from 16 percent of federal revenues in February to over 50 percent in August. At the same time, fiscal revenues as a percentage of GDP fell substantially, from 13 percent in January to 10.7 percent in July. This forced cuts in other areas and increased wage arrears, exacerbating social instability.

Default or devaluation, or both, were virtually unavoidable with more than half of revenues being spent on debt service. Unable to garner another massive international bailout, the government stopped borrowing on the domestic market, but it was too late. Expecting devaluation, foreign lenders withdrew. The Russian population started taking their money out of banks and converting it into dollars. The country soon faced a banking crisis that spread throughout the economy. Tax-collection fell further and interest rates kept rising. On August 17, 1998, the government defaulted on domestic debt and devalued the ruble.[3]

The situation in Russia continued to deteriorate. The outflow of mobile foreign capital destabilized not only financial markets but the entire economy as well. Due to the low levels of monetization and liquid international reserves (reserves excluding gold reached their top level of $20.4 billion in mid-1997), the outflow of $10 to $20 billion of foreign capital harmed the entire financial system.[4]

Russia was scheduled to pay $17 billion to foreign creditors in 1999, a sum equivalent to the entire federal budget. Negotiations with Russia's major creditor, the International Monetary Fund, will influence Russia's ability to attract foreign assistance and private investors in the future

(EBRD 1998, IMF 1998, and UN-ECE 1998). More fundamental though are structural reforms that limit capital flight and improve capacity to collect taxes.

Fundamental Imbalances

Capital Flight

The full extent of Russian capital exported to the rest of the world is not completely known. Statistics on capital flight derived from the quarterly balances of payments reveal three major types of capital outflow. (We do not make a distinction here whether these are legal or illegal.) First, there are so-called "net errors and omissions," which can scarcely be treated as such. Most likely these are unrecorded outflows of capital. Every year they are negative, and are too large to dismiss at approximately $8 billion each year.[5] Second, there are nonreturned export earnings and import advances, the sum of which varied from about $4 billion in 1994 to over $10 billion in 1997 and 1998. Finally, the credits which the Russian commercial sector gives to the rest of the world, often without repayment, should also be considered capital flight.

Capital flight has certainly exceeded the current account surplus. This suggests that export revenues, or more generally the trade surplus, was the main source of capital flight until 1996. Since 1996, and especially since 1997, capital flight has also been financed through government foreign borrowing. According to the balance of payments statistics, change in liabilities of the public sector increased in 1995 by almost $9 billion, and rose to $14.8 billion in 1996 and $21.9 billion in 1997. So there was a vicious cycle: firms did not pay taxes, the government borrowed abroad to cover the fiscal deficit, more money left Russia, and the government was forced to borrow again.

Tax-Collection

Tax-collection has been a key problem. Introducing tougher tax discipline among corporate taxpayers should not only boost fiscal revenues but also stem capital flight. There is also an obvious case for collecting more personal income taxes from wealthy individuals. The personal income tax is a primary source of fiscal revenues in all developed market economies. In Russia it has varied between only 2 and 3 percent of GDP.[6] Tax evasion is especially common among the wealthy.

Profitable firms in Russia are generally not willing to pay taxes, while unprofitable firms cannot pay at all. Improvement of tax-collection from the corporate sector depends on improvement in the legal environment. It also will require remonetization of transactions, which is discussed below, and growth in the money supply.[7]

Accumulated tax arrears are enormous. In mid-1998, tax arrears including nonpaid social security contributions and penalties on unpaid taxes were two and a half times the country's ruble money supply. In principle, one should distinguish between stocks and flows of arrears. It is more important to normalize regular tax flows, and then begin considering what can be done with stocks.

The backfiring of initiatives has long been a problem. For example, in early 1998 the government initiated discussion on restructuring of tax arrears, and immediately tax-collection fell as firms expected future amnesty. Quoting former Prime Minister Chernomyrdin, "we wanted to make the situation better, but it turned out as usual." Moreover, severe penalties have created a self-perpetuating mechanism of arrears. If a firm did not pay its taxes on time it was charged penalties that were very high in real terms, because they were introduced during a period of high inflation and were not changed after inflation went down. By mid-1998 accumulated penalties substantially exceeded tax arrears. Since a firm's bank account could be unconditionally transferred to the state budget if the firm owed taxes, firms became reluctant to put money into Russian banks.

Demonetization

Two key steps in the transformation of the Russian economy were the ending of direct central bank credits to enterprises and the expanded issuance of government securities. Although these changes reduced inflation, they greatly diminished money flows between enterprises and banks. In such an environment, banks were mostly serving the government and not the real sector, and interenterprise arrears and the use of barter increased rapidly. In turn, demonetization of the real economy undermined tax-collection.

Russia has returned to a dual monetary system somewhat reminiscent of Soviet times. In transactions among enterprises, rubles have largely been replaced by barter, arrears, and foreign currency. When not relying on barter or build up of arrears, firms prefer to pay each other in U.S. dollars circulating in Russia, or by making payments to each other abroad through foreign banks. Existing regulations, in effect, encourage firms to put money in offshore accounts rather than in Russian banks, and to engage in illegal transactions hidden from the Russian tax authorities (Gavrilenkov 1998).

Barter and the dollarization of the Russian economy facilitate economic activity, and the government should be cautious in attempting to break these mechanisms, which, though imperfect, are at least functioning. There is no guarantee that better mechanisms can be created overnight. In the short run, such transactions are an important part of economic behavior, though ultimately they impede growth.

Investment

Real investment has contracted by a startling 80 percent since 1992.[8] Absent a solid rebound, economic growth cannot resume and remain sustainable (Gavrilenkov and Kuboniwa 1997). Manufacturers of finished goods are especially dependent on new investment to replace machinery and technology designed to make products that are obsolete. As of 1997, the average age of industrial equipment exceeded 15 years, while the portion under five years of age dropped to under 10 percent (compared with 40 percent in 1970).

A major obstacle to investment is the peculiar Russian banking sector, which has largely stayed apart from the real economy and has failed to operate as an intermediary between savings and fixed investment.[9] Even before the weak banking system collapsed with the domestic default in 1998, banks lacked the liquidity to finance large investment projects. High interest rates are a critical deterrent. Even if Russian banks functioned properly, they would remain disinclined to lend to the real sector as long as government securities offered very high rates of return. Also, firms are discouraged from borrowing by high interest rates. One of the solutions is to encourage foreign banks to operate in Russia, though with restrictions to ensure that they don't simply expedite the export of capital (Gavrilenkov and Sundstrom 1998).

Conclusion

The collapse of the "bubble economy" in 1998 is instructive. The economic stabilization was narrowly conceived and superficially implemented. Instead of structural reforms and fiscal adjustment, the government chose the seemingly less painful strategy—namely foreign borrowing and a propped-up exchange rate. Quite simply, Russia was living beyond its means while fundamental problems went unaddressed.

Fiscal adjustment is key to sustainable growth. Achievement of fiscal balance requires not only budgetary discipline but also strengthening of controls related to capital flight and taxation. Otherwise foreign debt service, capital flight, and high interest rates will continue to stifle investment needed for restructuring and growth.

Notes

1. In economies with a low real money supply, a high fiscal deficit pushes interest rates up and makes domestic borrowing extremely expensive. With the ratio of the money supply (M2) to GDP varying around 15 percent, a fiscal deficit of about 5 percent of GDP, if covered by domestic credit, increases the money supply by about one-third, which is likely to be strongly inflationary. See Heymann and Leijonhufvud (1995) for discussion of the relationship between inflation and public finances in transitional economies.

2. By fall 1997, Russia was near the top of the list of emerging markets with high ratios of short-term foreign debt to international reserves.

3. If there had not been anticipatory loss of confidence, the government could have managed debt service until October 1998, at which time 35 billion rubles was due to creditors. This amount was much greater than total monthly federal revenue.

4. Before the August crisis, the money supply was equal to some 370 billion rubles, or approximately U.S.$60 billion.

5. "Net errors and omissions" is negatively correlated with changes in the stock of interenterprise arrears. Thus arrears grew much less rapidly when capital was flowing back to Russia.

6. Household incomes in 1997 reached 1,619.4 trillion rubles or 62 percent of GDP. After subtracting social transfers received, which are not subjected to taxation, taxable household incomes accounted for some 53.2 percent of GDP. During this period the government collected only 75 trillion rubles of personal income tax, which is equal to 5.4 percent of taxable household income. This figure is much smaller than the legal rate in the lowest tax bracket.

7. The ratio between monthly tax revenues and firms' bank accounts is quite stable (apart from some seasonal peaks). The account balances constitute approximately 20 to 25 percent of the entire money supply (M2), which in late 1998 was only about 70 billion rubles or about U.S.$3 billion.

8. A substantial part of the decline can be justified on the grounds of previous overinvestment. In the Soviet era, investment rates were higher than growth rates, for the efficiency of investment was low.

9. Gavrilenkov (1997 and 1998) discusses implications of banks shunting household savings to the government via purchases of government securities.

References

Bureau of Economic Analysis (BEA). 1998. *Analytical Bulletin*, No. 5. Moscow: BEA.

European Bank for Reconstruction and Development (EBRD). 1998. *Transition Report*. London: EBRD.

Gavrilenkov, Yevgeny. 1997. "Banking, Privatization and Economic Growth in Russia," in Paul J. Welfens, and H. C. Wolf, eds., *Banking, International Capital Flows and Growth in Europe: Financial Markets, Savings, Monetary Integration in a World with Uncertain Convergence*. Heidelberg and New York: Springer.

———. 1998. "Enterprise and Bank Restructuring in Russia." *UN-ECE Economic Survey of Europe* 2: 87–99.

Gavrilenkov, Yevgeny, and Masaaki Kuboniwa. 1997. *Development of Capitalism in Russia: The Second Challenge*. Tokyo: Maruzen.

Gavrilenkov, Yevgeny, and Niclaus Sundstrom. 1998. " Other Option." *The Wall Street Journal Europe,* September 29.

Heymann, Daniel, and Axel Leijonhufvud. 1995. *High Inflation*. Oxford: Clarendon Press.

International Monetary Fund (IMF). 1998. *World Economic Outlook*, October. Washington, DC: The Fund.

United Nations Economic Commission for Europe (UN-ECE). 1998. *Transition Report*, No. 3.

13

Macroeconomic Disorder:
A Comparison with China

Andrei Belousov and Lance Taylor
with
Elena Abramova, Dongyi Liu,
Alexander Vorobyov, and Stanislav Zhukov

Growth rates and distributional trends diverged strongly in the early 1990s in the two major postsocialist economies—Russia and China. Russia has had strongly negative growth and increasing inequality. In contrast, China has enjoyed economic growth averaging close to 10% annually with a stable, or at least not rapidly deteriorating, personal income distribution.[1]

Why have the two economies behaved so differently over the past ten to fifteen years? A fully reasoned answer to such a world historical question cannot be attempted here. Rather, what we can do is demonstrate the countries' macroeconomic similarities and differences[2] using simple social accounting matrixes (SAMs) for China in 1992 and for Russia from 1989 to 1990 and 1992 to 1995. (See tables at the end of the chapter.) Besides production, the SAM contains: income and current expenditure statements for households, firms, government, and the rest of the world (foreign);

accumulation accounts; and flows of funds for the aforementioned aggregates as well as for the financial system (mostly made up of the central and commercial banks for the two economies at hand). (Available data for 1991—the year of the political collapse of the USSR—are too inconsistent to be used.) These accounting systems were put together using publicly available sources, and involve a degree of data interpolation and smoothing.

The main results from comparison of SAMs are striking enough to merit serious consideration. Highlighted is the dissimilarity in the interface between the enterprise and the financial sector. Also discussed are the differences in investment rates, export performance, and management of effective demand.

China

A snapshot view of China's macroeconomy provides a natural background to analyze Russia's tumultuous changes since the mid-1980s. Table 13.1 presents the aggregate SAM for the year 1992.[3] Several points about distributional and spending patterns stand out: First, in comparison to capitalist industrialized economies (and even some developing ones), the share of GDP paid to households was fairly small at 52.5% (cell B-1).[4] Firms got the complement of 47.7%, and intermediate imports amounted to 8.2% of GDP.

Second, there were substantial transactions between firms and the (fiscal) government, an important aspect of socialist production systems. In total, firms transferred 31% of GDP as taxes and profit remittances to government, and got almost 24% as transfers in return. At the sectoral level, a complex system of cross-subsidization was involved, partly in support of the system of multiple prices for the same or similar commodities that the Chinese have practiced for many years.

Third, for a subcontinental nation, China's economy was quite open, with foreign income (imports plus household remittances to abroad) amounting to 16.8% of GDP. This number increased substantially over the 1980s.

Finally, accumulation, measured in terms of both saving and investment flows, was high. Household saving was 10.4% of GDP (18% of household income) and firms saved 37.5% (53% of income). By contrast, in 1992 there was a current account surplus or negative foreign saving of 1.5% of GDP, and the fisc had a deficit or public sector borrowing requirement of nearly 3%. Total accumulation, or the sum of gross capital formation and inventory changes in columns (6) and (7), was 43.5% of GDP. This is an extremely high number by international standards, consistent with the argument of Akyuz and Gore (1996) that capital accumulation plays an essential role in East Asia's recent economic success. However, the massive increase in stocks (11.3% of GDP) suggests that the process does not run without hitches.

Flows of Funds and Accumulation

Households saved 10.4% of GDP, which they used to increase their holdings of financial system liabilities (money, essentially).[5] Financial system liabilities went up by 17.4%, as households and firms increased their money holdings by 10.2% and 8.6% respectively while the government reduced its deposits by 1.3%.

Firms themselves financed the bulk of capital accumulation, again consistent with Akyuz and Gore (1996). Their financial deficit—or investment minus saving—of 6.0% of GDP has interesting implications. It was more than covered by an increase of net credits from the financial system (new assets minus new liabilities to firms of 8.7%). What did firms do with the extra 2.8% of funds? Mostly, they placed them abroad, building up new external assets of 2.1% and paying back debt by 0.5%. To what extent these transactions represented capital flight or else "round-tripping" of funds by state enterprises (putting resources abroad, later to bring them back in disguised fashion to invest in the special trading zones) are hotly debated questions.

The main liability counterpart to credit creation for the uses of firms was an increase in household deposits of 10.2%, exhausting virtually all their savings flow of 10.4%. Between them, households and firms raised their holdings of financial system liabilities by 18.7% of GDP (F-9 and G-9)—an extremely large increase in the amount of broad money in the hands of the public.

Why did not such a large increase in money supply trigger hyper-inflation? The monetarist "story" for China would be that high money supply growth did not cause hyperinflation because of increased transactions demands due to rapid output expansion and (as in India) ongoing monetization of rural economic activity. To what extent such money sinks can absorb aggressive credit expansion in the future is an open question.[6] So far, expansionist policy has been effective: "China's monetary policy, then and now, has only a single goal and that is 'economic develop-ment'" (Li 1991).

To summarize, China is an economy with a large state presence and large-scale transactions between the government and productive sectors. It has a fast pace of accumulation, mostly financed by earnings of enterprises supplemented by credit creation with a money counterpart absorbed by household saving. There is apparent capital flight (or round-tripping) and a high rate of money creation. Many of these same observations apply to poorly performing Russia—but with key differences as discussed in the following section.

Russia

Russia's 1992 global shock via incomplete liberalization was only the culmination of a long-running crisis. The Soviet economy had already passed through severe shocks—the disintegration of CMEA trade, sharp drops in hard currency earnings, rising inter-republic tensions, and inept macroeconomic management.

Many features of the Soviet accounts resemble those of China.[7] At around 30 percent of GDP, the rate of gross capital formation in the USSR exceeded that in China (although much "investment" under Gorbachev took the form of unfinished projects). As in China, most of this activity was financed by retained earnings of the enterprise sector, with the authorities mandating financial flows among specific firms.[8] The Soviet economy appeared to be more closed to foreign trade than China's, with both imports and exports amounting to only 6.7% of GDP. To a large extent, however, these low Soviet trade shares were the consequence of an extremely strong ruble (a symptom of the extreme form of "Dutch disease" which helped doom the economic system). As will be seen, when the ruble collapsed in 1992–93, import and export shares of GDP jumped by factors ranging between five and ten.

Households received about the same proportion of GDP from participation in production as did their Chinese counterparts. The GDP share of their transfers from the government was higher, so that the overall household income share exceeded 60% of GDP. Like the Chinese, Soviet households saved a lot—nearly 10% of GDP. The bulk of this saving was directed to liabilities of the financial system (roughly in proportions of 1/3 and 2/3 for cash and deposits). The corresponding increases in system assets took the form of credits to firms and the government.

New deposits of enterprises with the financial system were small in comparison to their investment outlays, and basically went into "settlement accounts" which could only be accessed with permission of the planning authorities—in effect, the monetary economy of the USSR (as until very recently in China) rested almost exclusively on transactions of households. As in China, there were large payments flows both ways between government and firms. Despite a distorted economy, state-to-enterprise transfers in the USSR were 15% less than in China as a share of GDP (compare values in C-4 across Tables 13.1–13.3).

Transition Disequilibria in 1992

In January 1992, subsequent to the collapse of the USSR, the Russian economy was subjected to a "global shock" involving a massive exchange rate devaluation, widespread liberalization of controlled prices, and promises of fiscal and monetary restraint. Prices that month jumped by a factor of about 3.5 and 7.7 over the rest of the year (Braguinsky 1996). Effects on the macroeconomy were far-reaching, as one can see by comparing the Russian SAM for 1992 in Table 13.4 with Tables 13.2 and 13.3.[9]

The first point to note is that the price jumps fed into a massive shift of the primary income distribution—compared to 1990, the household share fell by 19% of GDP and the enterprise share rose by 18% (C-1). Household consumption dropped by 17% of GDP as "forced saving" due to reduced real income made households cut their purchases. Together with a reduction in real investment of 39.5% in 1992 as compared to 1991, the consumption drop provoked a big decrease in effective demand—the decline in real GDP in 1992 was on the order of 14.5%.

Given the big increase in their share of income from production as well as capital gains on inventories, enterprises' retained earnings net of capital gains on inventories reached over 50% of GDP. (Estimate is subject to a discrepancy between row and column sums of 8.6%, which reflects the approximate cell values for 1992.) This savings flow vastly exceeded firms' investments of 17% of GDP. What happened to their financial surplus?[10]

Tracing the flows is complicated by another important disequilibrium phenomenon. Although enterprises benefited from the price jumps for their products, they lost as purchasers of intermediate inputs. Because the old system of noncash ruble payments among firms via settlement accounts had been curtailed, they hit on the expedient of creating "credits" for one another by running up mutual arrears. The volume of such interfirm lending skyrocketed, from about 39 billion rubles in January 1992 to 3,900 billion in July. During the second half of the year, this bad debt was refinanced, with the central bank channeling credits via commercial banks to firms which summed to 22.6% of GDP over the year. The liability counterpart was an increase of 23.8% in enterprise deposits, still largely blocked (if only by the snail's pace of commercial bank clearing operations at the time).

The net outcome was that transactions between the firms and banks, although very large, roughly balanced. The only other place the saving surplus of enterprises could go was abroad—they built up foreign assets to the tune of 18.5% of GDP. Large transactions of the financial system with the rest of the world helped underwrite this capital flight. Its current account counterpart was a trade surplus of 14% of GDP. The Russian economy suddenly became very "open" to foreign trade (with a reduced import level due to the output collapse), largely due to real depreciation of the ruble in the wake of the global policy shock.

Overall money creation in (G-90) and (H-9) summed to 30.5% of GDP, about 60% greater than China's rate of emission. In China, large-scale money creation was associated with inflation of 25% per year and in Russia with 25% *per month*. This observation supports the arguments of many Russian (as opposed to Western) economists that their inflation process was not solely driven by "excess" monetary emission. More details are given below.

According to the national accounts estimates which underlie Table 13.4, while all this action was going on the government sector remained in general balance, saving 5.1% of GDP and investing 6.5%, broadly consistent with a Ministry of Finance estimate that the fiscal deficit was 3.4% of GDP (Braguinsky 1996). More detailed data show that central bank credits to the government went up by 5.2% of GDP, while its "rediscount" to commercial banks was 13.1%. The bank ran a deficit of 8.8% on foreign operations, so that most creation of high-powered money took place through the liquidation of enterprise arrears.[11] The government also ran up deposits with the financial system of 4.3% of GDP. To a large extent, these balances were subsequently turned over to households as pensions (B-4). Slowing down these disbursements became an important anti-inflationary tactic from 1994 to 1995.

Developments in Russia from 1993 to 1995

After the cataclysm of 1992, the economy continued to slump, with GDP falling to 62% of its 1990 level by 1995. Real capital formation stayed in the range of 20+% of GDP, dropping steadily in real terms. After a massive upsurge in 1992, stock changes settled down to more "normal" GDP shares.

As shown in Tables 13.5–13.7 for the years 1993 through 1995, household and enterprise shares of income from production moved back toward the proportions observed in the Soviet Union during the late 1980s, but not completely. Nor did household consumption return to the (roughly) 50% share of GDP that it represented in the Soviet period.

There were also changes in the sources of household income. On the basis of income-expenditure surveys, Braguinsky (1996) reports the following breakdown (as percentages of GDP):

	Wages and Salaries	Social Payments	Distributed Profits
1992	26	5	6
1993	27	8	12
1994	28	10	22

The emergence of an affluent class of "new Russians" is reflected in the rising share of profit income, or monetized transfers from firms to households as opposed to Soviet-style payments in-kind. This tendency has been associated with rapidly increasing income concentration overall. Vorobyov and Zhukov (1996) report an increase in the Gini coefficient for household income from 0.256 in 1991 to 0.390 in 1994.

In line with these regressive distributional trends, the household saving share of GDP rose steadily from 7.4% in 1992 to 15.5% in 1994, and then dropped back to a Soviet-style level of 9.2% in 1995. Much of the savings increase in 1994 can perhaps be attributed to the expansion of pyramid schemes in the first half of the year ("MMM" was the best known). When they crashed, there was a rush toward foreign currency, leading to a 30% exchange rate devaluation on "Black Tuesday" in October. In the Table 13.6 SAM, this shift is reflected in a 14.9% increase in financial system liabilities to households, which include both ruble and hard currency deposits.

Foreign trade and government operations—two other major components of GDP—also showed declining trends from 1993 to 1995. The latter reduction was real and the former mostly nominal, but with potentially important consequences for the financial and production sides of the system. With regard to government, total tax shares of GDP over the period are: 1989, 38.8%; 1990, 40.2%; 1992, 32.8%; 1993, 34.5%; 1994, 29.0%; and 1995, 25.5%. Initial reports for 1996 suggest that tax receipts may have fallen below 20% of GDP. The implications of this massive contraction of the state for future economic management (not to mention maintenance of a semblance of a welfare state in the face of increasing income concentration) may not be reassuring.

With regard to foreign transactions, the most striking development is consistent strengthening of the ruble. After the nominal devaluation and price jumps of January 1992, the internal inflation rate has consistently outpaced nominal exchange devaluation (isolated episodes such as "Black Tuesday" aside). Using somewhat different estimation methods, Braguinsky (1996) and Vorobyov and Zhukov (1996) report "real" ruble/dollar exchange rates from 1994 to 1995 at less that 10% of their levels in early 1992. This appreciation of the ruble is reflected in the falling export and import shares of GDP.[12]

A strong ruble poses a number of problems for economic policy; we can mention three. The first is that macroeconomic management becomes very difficult when Russian economic actors hold massive assets abroad (adding up the flows in cells H-7 in the SAMs for 1992 through 1995, while deflating by the strengthening exchange rate, suggests a cumulative outflow of funds on the order of $80 billion). Further capital flight in anticipation of devaluation of an "excessively" strong ruble is always a risk—a risk heightened by the absence of controls on capital movements. The authorities are forced to play a complex game of interest and exchange rate adjustments to maintain external balance, with consequent downward pressure on investment demand due to a high internal cost of funds which goes hand-in-hand with a strong exchange rate.

Second, the "fundamentals" underlying the strong ruble are a low-level of economic activity (reducing imports) and a phenomenal natural resource base that permits exports of fuels, metals, and forest products to continue almost regardless of the exchange rate. Machinery exports, meanwhile, dropped by 50% between 1991 and 1994 (Vorobyov and Zhukov 1996). Maintaining Russia's industrial base in the face of the present relative price structure will be challenging. Although it runs counter to contemporary opinion, sensible trade protection may be required.

In 1994 the current account surplus fell to 2% of GDP. At the same time, enterprises continued to build up foreign assets at about double the level of the current account. Foreign transfers entering the economy, in other words, continued to be diverted abroad. The underlying cause was the continuing financial surpluses of enterprises, as reflected in the numbers that follow:

	Enterprise saving net of capital gains (H-3 – C-7)	Capital formation + inventory changes (A-7 + H-6)	Enterprise financial surplus
1992	51.7	30.8	20.9
1993	27.3	21.8	5.5
1994	22.6	20.3	2.3
1995	23.0	20.1	0.9

The usual pattern of investment by firms exceeding their savings flows continues to be conspicuous by its absence.

A few words should be added about inflation. The shift in the functional income distribution against firms already suggests that inflationary super-profits—the basic driving force behind the price escalation of 1992—could not be sustained. On the monetary side, there was a gradual reduction in the share of new money creation in GDP, but the relationship with a falling inflation rate was not close, as the following figures demonstrate:

	Price ratio (end to beginning of year)	Ratio of new money creation to GDP (%)
1992 (Feb–Dec)	7.7	30.5
1993	9.9	19.9
1994	3.2	19.1
1995	2.3	10.3

At least from such summary data, it is not obvious that lower money creation in the last column "caused" inflation to go down. The reduction in money supply growth was in turn related to reduction in the growth of central bank assets, but again the relationship is not strict:

	New Central Bank Credits (% of GDP)			
	Government	Net Foreign	Banks/Firms	Total
1992	5.2	-8.6	13.1	9.7
1993	5.8	2.3	0.8	11.9
1994	9.0	0.0	1.2	10.2
1995	1.6	2.9	1.5	6.0

By 1994 new advances to commercial banks and/or firms had been drastically reduced, with credits to the government following in 1995. Comparing the expansion of central bank assets to the money supply numbers above suggests a credit multiplier of a bit less than two, but the relationship between growth of central bank assets and inflation is not tight. Nevertheless, its credit restriction along with a proliferation of "nominal anchors" (notably a strong real exchange rate and high real interest rates, as noted above) were ultimately correlated with slower inflation. The social processes underlying this change and likely adverse effects on accumulation over a longer period of time remain to be explored.

Conclusion

The aggregate actors in the Russian and Chinese dramas are households, enterprises, the fiscal side of government, the local financial sector, and the rest of the world. Which of the five were mainly responsible for the divergent economic experiences of the two countries?

The SAMs suggest that the main difference lay in the interface between the enterprise and the financial sectors, which reflected differences in state intervention. Households saved at an impressive rate in both countries, and put their money in bank deposits or cash (plus more foreign currency in Russia than China). Neither government's fiscal accounts were wildly out of line (although the steady decline in Russia's tax receipts is troubling), and it would be difficult to argue that either economy has been seriously constrained by lack of foreign exchange, at least in the first half of the 1990s.

As pointed out for industrialized economies by Pollin (1997) and for semi-industrialized ones by Akyuz and Gore (1996), the key to accumulation lies in interactions among enterprises' saving and investment and in intermediation by the financial sector. Under postsocialism these linkages have been restructured in China and largely sundered in Russia. Therein lies one major macroeconomic difference between the two economies.

China has managed to sustain a high rate of accumulation, in an economic system which is still largely planned. Potential saving has been absorbed by investment as the economy expanded despite a high incremental capital-output ratio of about four (40% of GDP is invested and there is 10% growth). In contrast, Russian accumulation has dropped off, with increasing financial imbalances between enterprise saving and investment as discussed above. The plan whip once cracked by Gosplan and Gossnab has not been replaced by effective investment planning and finance at the enterprise level.

There are substantial differences, moreover, in trade performance. Led by low-wage manufactured goods, Chinese exports in dollar terms grew at an average annual rate of 14.6% between 1980 and 1993 (Amsden, Liu, and Zhang 1996). The "real" exchange rate (defined in terms of both the GDP deflator and the consumer price index) has been stable. Russia, with its strongly appreciating real exchange rate, relies increasingly on exports of raw materials. In terms of long-term productivity growth and penetration of world markets, it is hard to argue that China is on an inferior path. Moreover, large investment outlays will be needed to keep Russia's production of oil and gas at current levels; if this capital replenishment does not occur, an increasingly binding foreign exchange constraint cannot be ruled out.

Finally, an important difference centers on effective demand. It is maintained at a high level in China by the export push and expansionary monetary policy. With its shrinking government and stagnant real exports, such options may not be open for Russia. Its economy may very well be wage-led, so that a reversal of the regressive trends in the functional income distribution reported above could stimulate demand for industrial products, e.g., textiles (which suffered an output decline of 80% in the 1990s) and other consumer-related products. There is also room for selective public investment in infrastructure. Such demand-reactivation programs may provide the only viable means for reactivating the economy.[13]

Table 13.1. Social Accounting Matrix for the China, 1992 (percentages of GDP)

	Output cost (1)	Current expenditures House-holds (2)	Firms (3)	Gov. (4)	Foreign (5)	Capital form. (6)	Chg. in stocks (7)	Financial system Chg. in assets (8)	Chg. in liab. (9)	Foreign claims Chg. in nat'l liab. (10)	Chg. in nat'l ass. (11)	Chg. in firms' arrears (12)	Total (13)
(A) Output use	147.7	44.8		8.3	18.2	25.7	11.3						255.9
Incomes													
(B) Households	52.5		2.7	2.7	0.1								58.0
(C) Firms	47.7			23.9									71.3
(D) Government		2.4	31.1		0.1								33.5
(E) Foreign	8.2	0.4		1.6		6.6							16.8
Flow of Funds													
(F) Households		10.4							-10.2			-0.3	0.0
(G) Firms			37.5			-32.2	-11.3	17.3	-8.6	-0.5	-2.1	-0.2	0.0
(H) Government				-3.0				0.7	1.3	0.5		0.5	0.0
(I) Foreign					-1.5					-0.1	1.6		0.1
(J) Financial system								-17.9	17.4		0.6		0.0
(K) **Total**	255.9	58.0	71.3	33.5	16.8	0.0	0.0	0.0	0.0	0.0	0.0	0.0	

Table 13.2. Social Accounting Matrix for the USSR, 1989 (percentages of GDP)

| | Output cost (1) | Current expenditures | | | | Capital form. (6) | Chg. in stocks (7) | Financial system | | Foreign claims | | Chg. in firms' arrears (12) | Total (13) |
		Households (2)	Firms (3)	Gov. (4)	Foreign (5)			Chg. in assets (8)	Chg. in liab. (9)	Chg. in nat'l liab. (10)	Chg. in nat'l ass. (11)		
(A) Output use	102.8	47.5	3.0	15.3	7.5	32.2	1.5						209.8
Incomes													
(B) Households	49.3		1.2	8.1				2.2					60.8
(C) Firms	40.1			7.0			2.7					0.3	50.1
(D) Government	10.6	5.7	14.9	0.6								-0.3	30.9
(E) Foreign	7.4												8.0
(F) Financial system						-1.2		2.3	-4.2				-0.8
Flow of Funds													
(G) Households		7.6		-0.2		-0.9	-0.1		-6.3				0.1
(H) Firms			26.8			-20.4	-4.1	-1.6	-0.7				0.0
(I) Government				0.1		-9.7		8.4	0.1	1.1			0.0
(J) Foreign					1.2					-1.1			0.1
(K) Financial system								-11.2	11.2				0.0
(L) **Total**	210.2	60.8	45.9	30.9	8.7	0.0	0.1	0.1	0.1	0.0	0.0	0.0	

Table 13.3. Social Accounting Matrix for the USSR, 1990 (percentages of GDP)

	Output cost (1)	Current expenditures — House-holds (2)	Firms (3)	Gov. (4)	Foreign (5)	Capital form. (6)	Chg. in stocks (7)	Financial system — Chg. in assets (8)	Chg. in liab. (9)	Foreign claims — Chg. in nat'l liab. (10)	Chg. in nat'l ass. (11)	Chg. in firms' arrears (12)	Total (13)
(A) Output use	99.5	50.8	2.6	15.3	6.3	30.8	1.9						207.2
Incomes													
(B) Households	53.9		1.4	8.9				1.6					65.8
(C) Firms	35.1			8.2			3.3	-1.6				0.2	45.2
(D) Government	11.0	5.6	18.2									-0.2	34.6
(E) Foreign	6.9			0.6									7.5
(F) Financial system						-2.2		2.2	-0.8				-0.8
Flow of Funds													
(G) Households		9.4		-0.6		-1.2	-0.3		-7.2				0.1
(H) Firms			22.3	-0.3		-20.1	-4.8	5.7	-2.7				0.1
(I) Government				2.7		-7.2		3.8		0.8			0.1
(J) Foreign					1.7			-0.8	-0.2	-0.8			-0.1
(K) Financial system								-11.0	11.0				0.0
(L) **Total**	206.4	65.8	44.3	34.8	8.0	0.1	0.1	-0.1	0.1	0.0	0.0	0.1	

Table 13.4. Social Accounting Matrix for Russia, 1992 (percentages of GDP)

	Output cost (1)	Current expenditures						Financial system		Foreign claims		Chg. in firms' arrears (12)	Total (13)
		House-holds (2)	Firms (3)	Gov. (4)	Foreign (5)	Capital form. (6)	Chg. in stocks (7)	Chg. in assets (8)	Chg. in liab. (9)	Chg. in nat'l liab. (10)	Chg. in nat'l ass. (11)		
(A) Output use	107.4	33.5	1.8	13.0	62.3	23.9	13.7						255.6
Incomes													
(B) Households	35.2		1.1	5.5	3.6			1.4				-0.1	46.7
(C) Firms	52.9			3.2			22.8	1.2				5.4	85.5
(D) Government	12.0	2.3	16.7									-5.3	25.7
(E) Foreign	48.3			0.4				5.0					1.9
(F) Financial system								11.2	-9.3				1.9
Flow of Funds													
(G) Households		7.4		-0.3		-0.3			-6.7				0.1
(H) Firms			74.5	-1.2		-17.1	-36.5	22.6	-23.8		-18.5		0.0
(I) Government				5.1		-6.5		5.2	-4.3	0.5			0.0
(J) Foreign					-15.5			13.0	-15.5	-0.5	18.5		0.0
(K) Financial system								-59.6	59.6				0.0
(L) Total	255.8	43.2	94.1	25.7	50.4	0.0	0.1	0.0	0.0	0.0	0.0	0.1	

Table 13.5. Social Accounting Matrix for Russia, 1993 (percentages of GDP)

	Output cost (1)	Current expenditures						Financial system		Foreign claims		Chg. in firms' arrears (12)	Total (13)
		House-holds (2)	Firms (3)	Gov. (4)	Foreign (5)	Capital form. (6)	Chg. in stocks (7)	Chg. in assets (8)	Chg. in liab. (9)	Chg. in nat'l liab. (10)	Chg. in nat'l ass. (11)		
(A) Output use	74.5	38.9	6.3	15.1	38.2	22.5	8.5						204.0
Incomes													
(B) Households	38.3		4.2	7.3	1.4			3.3				-0.4	54.1
(C) Firms	43.7			5.2			15.8	0.4				8.3	73.4
(D) Government	18.0	2.7	20.0		0.2							-7.8	33.1
(E) Foreign	30.5			2.3				3.0					35.8
(F) Financial system								2.2	-6.2				-4.0
Flow of Funds													
(G) Households		10.9	-0.4	-0.4		-0.7			-9.4				0.0
(H) Firms			43.1	-1.2		-13.3	-24.3	13.7	-10.5		-7.5		0.0
(I) Government				4.9		-8.2		5.9	-5.3	2.7			0.0
(J) Foreign					-7.5	-0.4		4.2	-1.1	-2.7	7.5		0.0
(K) Financial system						-0.1	0.1	-32.6	32.6			0.1	0.0
(L) **Total**	205.0	52.5	73.2	33.2	32.3		0.1	0.1	0.1	0.0	0.0	0.1	

Table 13.6. Social Accounting Matrix for Russia, 1994 (percentages of GDP)

	Output cost (1)	Current expenditures				Capital form. (6)	Chg. in stocks (7)	Financial system		Foreign claims		Chg. in firms' arrears (12)	Total (13)
		House-holds (2)	Firms (3)	Gov. (4)	Foreign (5)			Chg. in assets (8)	Chg. in liab. (9)	Chg. in nat'l liab. (10)	Chg. in nat'l ass. (11)		
(A) Output use	81.5	41.3	6.2	20.9	27.7	25.1	3.8						206.5
Incomes													
(B) Households	45.5		4.2	8.1				3.1				-0.6	60.3
(C) Firms	35.2			12.5			11.2	0.5				3.3	62.7
(D) Government	19.3	3.2	17.3		2.2							-2.7	39.3
(E) Foreign	23.2			1.7				1.1					26.0
(F) Financial system									-1.4				-1.4
Flow of Funds													
(G) Households		15.5				-0.7			-14.9				-0.1
(H) Firms			33.8	-2.3		-16.5	-15.0	8.0	-4.2		-3.7		0.1
(I) Government				-1.8		-7.6		10.5	-3.1	2.1			0.1
(J) Foreign					-1.7	-0.3		0.8	-0.5	-2.1	3.7		-0.1
(K) Financial system								-24.0	24.0				0.0
(L) Total	204.7	60.0	61.5	39.1	28.2	0.0	0.1	0.0	-0.1	0.0	0.0	0.0	

Table 13.7. Social Accounting Matrix for Russia, 1995 (percentages of GDP)

	Current expenditures						Chg. in stocks (7)	Financial system		Foreign claims		Chg. in firms' arrears (12)	Total (13)
	Output cost (1)	House-holds (2)	Firms (3)	Gov. (4)	Foreign (5)	Capital form. (6)		Chg. in assets (8)	Chg. in liab. (9)	Chg. in nat'l liab. (10)	Chg. in nat'l ass. (11)		
(A) Output use	95.3	41.8	6.3	16.5	27.1	21.9	6.2						215.1
Incomes													
(B) Households	39.5		4.9	8.1	0.1			2.4				-0.6	54.4
(C) Firms	43.0			3.7			4.4	0.8				2.9	54.8
(D) Government	17.5	3.3	12.1		1.2							-2.4	31.7
(E) Foreign	21.6							0.8					23.9
(F) Financial system				1.5		-0.2		1.5	-1.0				0.5
Flow of Funds													
(G) Households		9.2		-0.2		-0.8			-8.3				-0.1
(H) Firms			27.4	-2.1		-13.9	-9.6	4.0	-2.0		-3.7		0.1
(I) Government				4.4		-6.6		4.0	-2.9	2.2			0.2
(J) Foreign					-1.8	-0.4		1.9	-1.1	-2.2	3.7		0.1
(K) Financial system								-15.2	15.2				0.0
(L) **Total**	216.9	54.3	50.7	31.9	26.6	0.0	0.1	0.2	-0.1	0.0	0.0	-0.1	

Notes

1. See Singh (1993) and Amsden, Liu, and Wang (1996) for reviews of China's experience; and Braguinsky (1996), Braguinsky and Yavlinsky (1996), and Vorobyov and Zhukov (1996) for Russia's.

2. Deep institutional differences also separate the two nations. Russia, for example, eliminated "petty bourgeois" grassroots agriculture and small-scale industry decades ago. Today, such structures propel the Chinese miracle, perhaps suggesting à la Gerschenkron (1992) that a more "backward version of socialism" can ultimately provide a base for rapid growth.

3. The entries are scaled by "GDP," i.e., the sum of payments from the production account to households, firms, and government (the last payment is recorded at zero in the Chinese, but not the Russian, accounts). Row (A) summarizes demand-side uses of total output, and column (1) shows its costs of production. As a principle of SAM balancing, the two totals must be the same. The incomes statements appear in rows (B) to (E) and the expenditures statements in columns (2) to (5). The flows of funds, describing the accumulation of financial assets and the financing of investment, appear in rows (F) to (K).

4. The income breakdown between urban and rural households was roughly 45/55.

5. The flows of funds in rows (F) to (J) summarize how the accumulation process was financed. The sign convention is that "sources" of funds (savings and increases in liabilities) are positive while "uses" (investment and increases in assets) are negative. Columns (6) to (12) give the balances of investment flows and changes in financial claims. (Rounding errors explain the differences in the sums.)

6. In the presence of price controls and multiple pricing systems, Chinese inflation indexes are subject to a great deal of interpretation. However, recorded annual growth rates of prices in the range of 25 percent in the early 1990s probably were at the limits of social acceptability.

7. Tables 13.2 and 13.3 are SAMs for the USSR for 1989 and 1990. They are set up in the same way as Table 13.1, except that column (12) now summarizes changes in "arrears" of firms, as opposed to government liabilities. The SAMs also do not fully balance (as shown in row (M) for "discrepancies") and include a number of small financial transactions (in cells B-8, F-6, F-8, F-9, G-4, I-4) which were difficult to consolidate into the flows of funds. Cell C-7

shows within-year capital gains on existing inventories, which were quite substantial in Russia's years of high inflation; firms' purchases of goods and services in cell A-3 were ultimately passed along to their employees. As discussed below, over the years the export estimates in cell A-5 appear to be valued at external prices times the ruble/dollar exchange rate.

8. Specifically, enterprises' wage arrears to workers and tax arrears to the government are included in the SAMs for the USSR and Russia, but *not* the interenterprise arrears underlying the "payments crisis" discussed later in the text.

9. Two sets of social accounts have been constructed for Russia in the 1990s, Braguinsky's (1996) and those presented here. The pictures they paint are broadly similar, with the main difference being that Braguinsky attributes more responsibility for the financial disequilibria about to be described in the text to the government as opposed to the enterprise sector.

10. In "normally" functioning economies the productive sector always invests more than it saves, with the balance covered by net savings flows coming from other sources and channeled through the financial system. Russia, South Africa since the mid-1980s, and perhaps a few other stagnant systems are the only exceptions.

11. Braguinsky (1996) agrees with the present analysis that "the real culprit" for the inflation of 1992 was the behavior of state-owned enterprises (112). However, he prefers to attribute the bulk of money creation to a "broad fiscal deficit," which includes the loans that the central bank channeled to firms as well as credits to other member countries of the CIS. His interpretation and the one presented here perhaps boil down to complementary views of the complex interactions between the new Russian state and its inherited public enterprises.

12. Available data for Russia did not permit imports to be disaggregated by destination, as in row (E) for China.

13. Braguinsky and Yavlinsky (1996) provide detailed suggestions for demand reactivation programs.

References

Akyuz, Yilmaz, and Charles Gore. 1996. "The Investment-Profits Nexus in East Asian Industrialization." *World Development* 24(3): 461–470.

Amsden, Alice H., Dongyi Liu, and Xiaoming Zhang. 1996. "China's Macro-economy, Environment, and Alternative Transaction Model." *World Development* 24(2): 273–286.

Braguinsky, Serguey. 1996. "Transaction Economics—A Microeconomic Approach (with Application to the Russian Economy)." Yokohama: Faculty of Economics and Business Administration, Yokohama City University.

Braguinsky, Serguey, and Grigori Yavlinsky. 1996. "A Positive Approach to the Design of Russian Transition." Moscow: EPICenter; Yokohama: Faculty of Economics and Business Administration, Yokohama City University.

Gerschenkron, Alexander. 1992. "Economic Backwardness in Historical Perspective," in Mark Granovetter, and R. Swedberg, eds., *The Sociology of Economic Life*. Pp. 111–130. Boulder and Oxford: Westview Press. Previously published 1952.

Li, Yunqi. 1991. "Changes in China's Monetary Policy." *Asian Survey* 31(5).

Pollin, Robert, ed. 1997. *The Macroeconomics of Saving, Finance, and Investment*. Ann Arbor, MI: University of Michigan Press.

Singh, Ajit. 1993. "The Plan, the Market and Evolutionary Economic Reform in China." UNCTAD Discussion Paper No. 76, December.

Vorobyov, Alexander Y., and Stanislav V. Zhukov. 1996. "Russian Economic Growth: Lessons from Liberalization, Medium-Term Constraints, and Ecological Challenges." *World Development* 24(2): 359–371.

14

Ersatz Banks

Michael S. Bernstam and Andrei Sitnikov

Russian banks are ersatz banks not much engaged in normal banking practices. For the most part, they do not make loans on the basis of commercial criteria, nor do they accept deposits paying a market rate of interest. Their focus has been on garnering subsidies, holding government debt, acquiring assets via insider privatization, and abetting capital flight. As a consequence, productive firms have been deprived of needed credit and investment.

Diversion of Resources

Private banks were not established in Russia until after the collapse of the Soviet Union in late 1991. Concurrently, the main state bank, Gosbank, was dismantled, but three other state-owned giants remained: State Savings Bank (Sberbank), the Bank for Foreign Economic Relations (Vneshekonombank), and the Bank for Foreign Trade (Vneshtorgbank). Three types of private banks were formed: "wildcat" banks, domestic banks, and joint-venture banks. Banks of all three types were created by large enterprises in pursuit of special benefits.

Wildcat banks were formed not only by enterprises but also by local governments and by ministries overseeing particular industrial sectors. They grew rapidly to constitute the majority of all banks (in number, not assets). Capital requirements were low and regulation, initially nonexistent, remained lax. Their main activity was to borrow from the central bank at subsidized rates and lend the proceeds to designated enterprises, which were the legal or de facto owners of the banks.

Most of the assets of the Russian banking system are held by the large domestic banks (e.g., Inkombank, Uneximbank). While they provide some short-term credit to enterprises, they derive the bulk of their income from foreign currency trading, dealing in government bonds, and other nonlending activities. Joint venture banks, due to official hostility, have had only a limited presence.

On January 1, 1996, Russia had 2,598 banks with 5,580 branch offices.[1] Most of these banks were undercapitalized and had incentives to misallocate and loot deposits (Akerlof and Romer 1993). By January 1999, the number of banks had dropped to 1,852 with 4,453 branch offices. Although most are registered as private corporations, the federal government and the Moscow city government hold stakes in major Moscow banks (e.g., Menatep, National Credit), while regional and municipal governments frequently own stakes in the leading banks in their cities.

Taking the German model to an extreme, many banks hold controlling stakes in leading firms and are the sole lenders to those firms. At the same time, many Russian firms own banks outright and are the principal borrowers of funds from those banks. These circumstances give new meaning to the concept of "insider" lending. Borrowers' ownership, which has been underwritten by government bailouts and subsidies, creates a double moral hazard: banks are more vulnerable to insolvency because they lack the independence to reject unsound loans, which in turn puts depositors at greater risk. Also, government is vulnerable because of pressure to protect depositors and prevent a damaging financial collapse. As concluded at a bankers' conference in Moscow, "Russia formed a banking system unfit for survival" (Makarevich 1995).

The most important sources of support were central bank credits to the banks' own captive, and often money-losing, enterprises. Acting as redistributive agencies of the state, banks received cheap credits from the central bank to support the enterprises, shunting off much of the funds in the process. Moreover, firms would transfer funds to banks rather than use their own or borrowed funds to invest and restructure. The banks also gained substantial profit from operating the government payments system and customs accounts. Although the government removed both flows from the banks and placed them directly with the treasury at the end of 1997, it returned the customs accounts to the banks a year later. Banks did engage in foreign exchange transactions, some servicing of foreign trade, and a modest amount of real estate investing.

Government Finance

In the early 1990s the central bank granted huge amounts of credits to the government to offset shortfalls in revenue. In 1994, for example, almost all of the budget deficit (10.4 percent of GDP) was financed in this manner, fueling rapid inflation and eroding the exchange rate. This led to legislation that sharply limited direct central bank financing of the budget. In response, the government financed its deficit through a new means: government bonds. In June 1994 it began selling three-month treasury bills (GKOs in Russian). In 1995, 70 percent of the deficit was financed in this way. The growing stock of short-term debt drove up interest rates on new and refinanced issues to over 60 percent per annum. The explosion in GKOs carried over into 1996, a second year of exceptionally high yields on government debt.

The change in government finance focused banks on highly profitable operations in government securities. As interest rates of government bills rose (amounting to annualized rates of 163.7 percent in 1994 and 159.3 percent in 1995), the share of GKOs in the total assets of the banking system rose from 8.5 percent at the end of 1994 to 31 percent at the end of 1997.[2]

It is interesting to compare 1993 and 1994 with 1995 through 1997. During the first period, interest on short-term debt was zero and 0.7 percent of GDP respectively, while the total deficit came to 10.4 and 11.4 percent. Interest payments as a percentage of GDP rose to 1.8 percent in 1995, 3 percent in 1996, and 4 percent in 1997, while the total deficit ranged from 4.8 to 7.6 percent over the three years. In 1996, the banking system as a whole derived about 70 percent of its income from government securities. Thus the banks were effectively recapitalized to the tune of several percentage points of GDP between 1995 and 1997.

Yields on GKOs, along with yields on subsequently issued longer-term bonds (OFZs), began to decline in mid-1996. This decline created severe problems for banks. For almost all banks, there was no new source of funds emanating from household deposits. A total of 370 banks were liquidated by the central bank, and many small banks were merged with one another or into larger institutions. At the end of June 1997, 742 banks had their operating licenses withdrawn by the central bank and were awaiting liquidation.

As yields on government debt declined, the stock market rescued the banks. From President Yeltsin's reelection in mid-1996 through the third quarter of 1997, the Russian stock market was the best-performing market in the world in percentage terms. Banks stocked up on equities, which allowed them to show profits and improve their balance sheets.

After April 1995, direct central bank credits to banks were stopped. In their place, the Ministry of Finance provided subsidies through the rollover of high-yield bonds (Perotti 1994). This subsidy was especially generous for large, government-connected banks in which the government held its deposits and through which it conducted its foreign exchange and debt service operations.

Banks used government deposits to buy government bonds and kept the difference in interest—a huge sum. Then, selected banks used their growing accumulation of capital to purchase shares of the best energy and other enterprises at rigged government auctions—the "loans-for-shares" privatization phase of 1995.

Loans for Shares

A spin-off from the Russian office of CS First Boston, composed of Western investment bankers of Russian descent and their Russian partners from Uneximbank, developed an imaginative scheme. Ostensibly, the goal was to help the government finance the deficit with low-interest loans. The scheme, an obvious abuse, worked as follows:

The government consolidated its considerable but dispersed demand deposits in a small number of banks that had been politically loyal. The banks then loaned these same funds (the government's own deposits) back to the government. In return, the banks received options to purchase at very low prices stock in valuable, state-owned, natural resource enterprises. The fact that these options were to be exercised only in the event of default diverted attention from the low prices specified. The government listed these loans as additional budget revenues, thereby appearing to reduce its budget deficit and thus qualifying for the receipt of further foreign currency credits from the IMF.

This scheme, called "loans-for-shares" in the Western press, actually went into effect amidst a liquidity crisis in August 1995. The government was running a larger-than-reported budget deficit, while the banking system was largely insolvent. The loans-for-shares scheme operated until September 1996 and raised five times more revenue in 1995 and 1996 than all other forms of privatization. Predictably, the government never repaid the "loans," and the banks acquired the shares and took resources off the government's hands at bargain-basement prices. The government also sold to the banks, through closed auctions, large portfolios of shares in the remaining natural resource state-owned enterprises, instead of offering shares to the public.

The significance of this development went beyond deficit finance and bank recapitalization. With few restrictions, the ruble was made convertible into foreign currency on the capital account. The government bond market was partially open to foreigners, who were permitted to purchase up to 30 percent of all ruble-denominated government debt. Equity markets were fully open to all potential purchasers. After the equity and bond markets were thereby broadly opened to foreigners in 1996 and 1997, a steep rise in share values helped sustain the banks. The resale of shares and bonds to foreigners became the principal source of money creation instead of the purchase of government debt by the central bank.

The banks began to resell their assets in equity on the stock market to foreign investors and used the proceeds to purchase government bonds. The government also sold debt to foreigners and entered the dollar-denominated foreign bond market, issuing Eurobonds. Those efforts enabled the government to finance its debt and recapitalize the banks. Access to foreign funds throughout 1997 provided operational liquidity that sustained an otherwise unsustainable monetary regime.

Financial-Industrial Groups

The Russian voucher process of privatization gave control of enterprises to hold-over managers and, in some cases, to workers and outsiders. Often those who gained control, given the insecurity of property in Russia, liquidated valuable assets for short-term gains. Too little attention was given to reforming the enterprises into profitable, value-adding businesses.

Ostensibly as a solution to the problem of restructuring, the Yeltsin administration supported the creation of bank-led financial-industrial groups (FIGs). Originally, the enterprises owned the banks. The FIG model encouraged banks to obtain controlling stakes in the firms in their groups. FIGS were intended to acquire, restructure, and sell profitable enterprises. They were also expected to overcome the lack of financing for needed investment.

The government supposedly expected the FIGs to restructure energy and resource production and other industrial sectors. It was hoped that the banks would drag enterprises forcibly into the market economy. Purportedly, this arrangement also held out the promise of converting the financing of business itself into a commercial enterprise. However, the end result was that politically connected banks were once again appointed as the middlemen between the government and firms, funneling subsidies and state loans from the government to enterprises.

The underlying assumption (perhaps hope is the better word) of the FIG model was that selling controlling stakes in companies to banks would put the firms in the hands of the few people qualified to restructure them financially. Another common assumption was that the FIGs would hire Western managers to run them efficiently. However, for the most part FIGs were unable to manage their companies efficiently and steadfastly resisted the participation of Western partners. A handful of dominant FIGs simply built up monopoly positions.[3]

Any financial gains of the banks were primarily diverted to their owners, and there were not sufficient funds available to finance the modernization of industry. In rare cases, the FIGs gained access to Western capital. For example, in 1997, Uneximbank attracted more than $500 million in capital from BP in the sale of 10 percent of its oil-related firm, Sidanco.

Banks that gained control of valuable industrial assets have not made the necessary investments in capital and management to accomplish serious restructuring. Moreover, in the rush to gain control of as many assets as possible, many banks overextended themselves.[4] Finally, the banks' dominant position in both finance and industry gave them easy access to political influence and government favors. The bank-led FIGs have become the new powerful redistributors of resources in the Russian economy.

Secret Swaps

The Ministry of Privatization conducted a series of secret swaps of the holdings of insolvent banks (an effective partial nationalization) for government equity in oil corporations. These covert actions were especially important in late 1995 when, after the rise of interest rates and the liquidity crisis, major banks lacked funds to purchase enterprise shares even at a great discount.

One of the most prominent Russian banks, Menatep, was saved by a secret swap (Pisotsky 1996; Proskurnina 1996). The switch from recycling government debt to recycling shares in mineral rights could continue while the supply of shares in natural resources lasted. But this means of enriching banks was undermined by the Asian debt crisis as foreign investors fled emerging markets in late 1997. Russia was hit particularly hard: net foreign assets of the monetary authorities and banks collapsed from nearly $15 billion in mid-1997 to $1.2 billion in January 1998 and then turned negative, falling to more than minus $2 billion in March.

Bank activity in the real economy actually declined during the stabilization period following the mid-1996 reelection of President Yeltsin. Performing loans, adjusting for inflation, fell by more than 20 percent from the beginning of 1996 to the end of 1997 as the share of performing loans in bank assets fell in half. The share of government debt in bank assets more than tripled.

Credit Collapse

Banks neither mobilized the savings of the population nor created additional deposits. They simply automatically multiplied central bank additions to the monetary base. This led to a collapse of credit in Russia that is almost unparalleled in modern history.[5]

Between 1991 and 1995, credit resources to the Russian economy contracted by almost 80 percent. Real credit declined from 439 billion rubles at the end of 1991 to 104 billion (December 1991 prices) at the end of 1995. The index of real credit declined by over 75 percent. Total credit contracted from 31 percent of GDP to 11 percent from 1991 to 1995, while ruble credit contracted to 8.1 percent of GDP and total loanable funds contracted from 68 percent of GDP to 17 percent of GDP.

Savings deposits of households were destroyed by the extreme inflation of the early 1990s. In 1992 and 1993, real interest rates on deposits were negative 93 percent; and in 1994 and early 1995 they were negative 40 percent. In the aggregate, the banking system literally stole its liabilities—depositors' real funds. (Interest rates did not turn positive for savings deposits until mid-1995.)

The ratio of money supply to cash in circulation is an indicator of the degree of financial and economic development in a country. The decline in real credit went hand in hand with the sharp decline in the ratio of money supply (M2) to cash. This ratio dropped from a low 5:1 in 1991 to only 2.7:1 in 1995, which compares to about 12:1 in a typical modern economy.

Russian banks entered the reform process without a debt burden inherited from the past (the debt burden was the government's foreign debt). Unfortunately, the high levels of inflation and highly negative interest rates of 1992 financed a rapid growth in nonperforming debt, up to a third of all loans. As nonperforming assets constituted an ever larger share of banks' balance sheets, they reduced the banks' ability to make new loans. The balance sheets of enterprises became endowed with negative collateral as paper liabilities exceeded paper assets.

Household deposits, equal to 34 percent of GDP in 1990, fell to 27 percent in 1991, and then dropped precipitously to 3 percent in 1993, and settled at 4.3 percent at the end of 1995. Reflecting the increasing irrelevance of banks as a source of finance for businesses, their credits to enterprises fell from 31 percent of GDP in late 1991 to 8 percent of GDP at the end of 1995. Russian banks (apart from Sberbank) were largely irrelevant to the household sector, holding household deposits equivalent to about 1 to 1.5 percent of GDP.

In Russia there is little retail banking. Ordinary Russians do not use checking accounts or credit cards. Home mortgage credit is minuscule. As of January 1, 1996, total household debt equaled only under 1 percent of GDP.[6] Russia is thus deprived of mortgages, consumer credit, and other household credit that function as engines of growth in other modern economies.

Veksels

In a problematic reaction to the credit collapse, Russian banks have issued a growing stock of private bills of exchange, or promissory notes, called "veksels." Veksels complicate the task of building a real monetary system by adding liabilities to the country's financial system and making the banks more vulnerable to insolvency.

Veksels, named after the German bills of exchange of the nineteenth century, work as follows: Russian banks extend loans to enterprises in the form of veksel banknotes that resemble checks. They are redeemable in cash at the issuing bank on a particular date. In the meantime, the veksels circulate like regular money, being endorsed and passed along from one holder to another. Veksels are generally used only among enterprises and other businesses, not by individuals. Their credibility is not backed by hard assets and rests on the public's willingness to accept them as a means of payment.[7]

Banks began to issue veksels in substantial amounts after the fixed exchange-rate regime was put into place, which reduced the issue of central bank credit and created a liquidity squeeze. In effect, veksels replaced the central bank supply of liquidity with self-liquidity. Veksels constitute a largely uncontrolled form of quasi–central bank credit. Banks do not place reserves with the central bank for the right to issue veksels. However, the central bank limits the total amount of veksels that can be issued and selects which banks can issue them. In those regulations, the central bank implicitly ensures the convertibility of veksels into real credit, the equivalent of real money.

The quantity of veksels more than doubled during 1996 and 1997, amounting to about 6 percent of bank liabilities. That sum, by itself, slightly exceeded the value of bank reserves held with the central bank, aggravating the illiquidity of the banking system. The interest rate of veksels at the end of 1997 was in the neighborhood of 40 percent.

Corporations have also issued veksels, which trade at a much higher discount than bank-issued veksels. One reason is that corporate veksels are not necessarily redeemable in cash, but rather in-kind. Also, corporate finances are even shakier than those of the banks. In addition to bank and corporate-issued veksels, cities and regional governments have issued veksels that amounted to 350 trillion rubles by the end of 1997.

Conclusion

The banking system is a winding maze of borrower ownership, insider lending, rollover of bad loans, and misallocation of a limited amount of credit. Banks have been the instruments for transferring public assets to private hands and for redistributing public funds to the favored few. A vicious cycle has developed, reinforcing financial repression and depressing the real sector. What has been good for those who control the banks has been punishing for the broader economy.

Russian banks have not fulfilled the role of intermediating between saving and investment. Lack of credit has impeded the development of the new private sector and the restructuring of potentially viable enterprises. Emerging private firms have been forced to self-finance or to organize informal arrangements, all too often with criminal structures.

It does not make economic sense for firms owned by banks to be their chief clients. The incentives are wrong. The development of normal banks in Russia is going to require that FIGs be scuttled or reconfigured.

Notes

1. These data and related statistics may be found on the Web site of the Central Bank of the Russian Federation (www.cbr.ru).

2. Statistics on government finance are taken from releases of Goskomstat (Russian Statistics Committee) and the central bank.

3. Three prototypical FIGs are: Interros, closely linked to Uneximbank; the Alfa Group, a private partnership developed by a group of domestic entrepreneurs linked to Alfa Bank; and Menatep, linked to Menatep Bank. Uneximbank (or United Export-Import Bank) acquired Norilsk Nickel and Sidanco, while Menatep got Yukos, a large oil company. Gazprom and Lukoil, which own their own banks, constitute the dominant FIGs in the gas and oil industries.

4. Recent problems with the *keiretsu* in Japan and *chaebols* in Korea raise doubts with regard to concentrating financial and industrial assets in huge multinational corporations. *Keiretsu* and *chaebols* did not initially have a common budget with the government, but they grew to acquire one (Aoki

1990; Berglof and Perotti 1994; Perotti 1992). In the Czech Republic FIG model, the government owned the banks, which owned the investment privatization funds, which owned the companies. Failure of Czech microeconomic restructuring prompted the Czech government to retreat from the FIG model and sell its shares in the banks to foreign banks.

5. For extensive statistical detail, see Bernstam and Rabushka (1998).

6. See *Biznes-Segodnia*, January 23, 1996, p. 8.

7. Adam Smith wrote about the "fictitious bills of exchange" drawn and redrawn between banks and enterprises in larger and larger amounts. Since there were no real "debtors" behind these bills, they were eventually redeemed by the Bank of England. This "artful contrivance" ruins "public credit" and endangers the monetary system (Smith 1895).

References

Akerlof, George A., and Paul M. Romer. 1993. "Looting: The Economic Underworld of Bankruptcy for Profit." *Brookings Papers on Economic Activity* 0(2): 1–60.

Aoki, Masahiko. 1990. "Toward an Economic Model of the Japanese Firm." *Journal of Economic Literature* 28(1): 1–27.

Bernstam, Michael, and Alvin Rabushka. 1998. *Fixing Russia's Banks.* Stanford, CA: Hoover Institution Press.

Makarevich, Lev. 1995. "Conclusions of the Conference of Russian Banks for Industry and Construction." *Finansovie izvestiia* 4: 102.

Perotti, Enrico C. 1992. "Cross-Ownership as a Hostage to Support Collaboration." *Managerial and Decision Economics* 13(1): 45–54.

———.1994. "A Taxonomy of Postsocialist Financial Systems: Decentralized Enforcement and the Creation of Inside Money." *Economics of Transition* 2(1): 74.

Perotti, Enrico C., and Erik Berglof. 1994. "The Governance Structure of the Japanese Financial Keiretsu." *Journal of Financial Economics* 36(2): 259–284.

Pisotsky, Gennady. 1996. "The Bank Is Authorized to Roll." *Finansovie izvestiia* 10: 3.

Proskurnina, Olga. 1996. "Menatep Will Receive the Stock of Five Oil Companies in Exchange for 15 Percent of Its Shares." *Segodnia,* February 3.

Smith, Adam. 1895. *An Inquiry into the Nature and Causes of the Wealth of Nations.* London: T. Nelson and Sons.

15

Crime and Corruption

Svetlana P. Glinkina, Andrei Grigoriev, and Vakhtang Yakobidze

The Russian economy has been transformed into a highly corrupt and criminalized economic system. Rampant crime and corruption have degraded everyday life, obstructed legitimate business activity, and impaired the functioning of government. The most valuable of state assets have been transferred to a small number of "oligarchs," who compose a politically connected business elite largely oriented toward plunder. Though the proclivity for corruption and illegality predates the economic transition, primary blame resides with the reform strategy.

Soviet Roots

The economic transition in the 1990s may be seen as a continuation of long-established trends. Beginning in the 1950s, loosening of state control spawned tainted activity. There developed a substantial degree of illegal and quasi-legal interplay among high party officials (nomenclatura), enterprise managers, top regional bureaucrats, and black market entrepreneurs.[1]

As the centralized Soviet economy expanded beyond military demands and basic consumer needs, it became increasingly difficult for the center to monitor all economic activity. Beginning with Khrushchev, limited autonomy was granted to local officials and managers. Plans were individually adjusted on the basis of negotiations that included occasional bribing.[2] For several years, centralized ministries were actually abolished, placing managers and local bureaucrats in a more powerful position.

Central "branch ministries" were reestablished by Kosygin in 1965, but managers and local bureaucrats still retained considerable authority. Of greater consequence, profitability became a consideration for the first time. Previously money had played a minimal role in the operation of enterprises, which were allocated inputs and obligated to meet output quotas. The shift to planning in terms of money gave management the opportunity to include as costs many expenses that were unrelated to production. In this new dynamic, enterprises accumulated their own funds for social welfare expenditures. The power to use these funds was shared by management and the supervising nomenclatura.

The more cunning managers quickly discovered the black market, which offered greater opportunity for profit than producing officially planned output. A network of entrepreneurs servicing black market operations emerged, making "connections" the foremost asset of any manager or entrepreneur.[3]

Collusion between managers and government officials escalated under Brezhnev. Even the General Prosecutor's Office acknowledged that conditions had developed to the point where "it became unrewarding to live and work honestly" (Gdlyan and Ivanov 1988). In Uzbekistan, for example, cotton producers and nomenclatura for several years obtained payments for output that was never produced.

Inadvertently, *perestroika* fueled corruption. Denationalization and liberalization of the Soviet economy may be viewed as the conversion of Soviet "wealth" into something more tangible: many within the ruling elite traded in power for money and property.[4] State resources, in the form of property, low-interest credits, and profitable contracts, started to flow over to semi-state and later to private entities.

Toward the end of the Gorbachev period, the Soviet state lost authority as the constituent republics claimed supremacy. Under siege from Gorbachev, the very head of the party, the Communist Party ceased to exercise its previous role in strengthening the authority of the state. Spontaneous "unofficial privatization" occurred on a wide scale. Assets, including whole enterprises, were transferred to party officials and enterprise managers.

Money was also found in subsidized imports. To avoid famine during the winter of 1991–92, the government sold dollars earmarked for imported food at 1 percent of their real value. The difference was subsidized with the help of Western commodity credits. Selling the products at a normal market rate, the country's food scare enriched a small number of Moscow traders.[5]

Komsomol, the communist youth organization, was pivotal in giving young communists a rapid start in accumulating wealth. Under its aegis, they were given special privileges to start private businesses and were excused from taxes for five years. Particularly lucrative was the importing of foreign goods that were otherwise unavailable due to the prior state monopoly on foreign trade.

Shock Therapy

The Gaidar reforms, which quickly lifted most government controls, gave government officials and top managers even more opportunities for unofficial and other forms of self-dealing.[6] A company created by a minister differed only in scale from an enterprise taken over by its former director. These illegal seizures were passed off as economically essential acts (Kryshtanovskaia 1997). Responding to criticism of the unfair and uneven distribution of state property, the reformers said that their actions would liberate market forces; should new owners prove unable to manage property effectively, they would lose it through bankruptcy.[7]

Unregulated banks and investment funds were important avenues for gaining wealth. While spiraling inflation made ordinary citizens desperate to conserve their savings, the investment funds and many banks launched advertising campaigns promising rates of return over 1,000 percent. Virtually all of the funds and many of the banks were pyramid schemes. More than 20 million people put their savings or privatization vouchers in investment funds that collapsed. In most cases, the victims had no knowledge of financial markets.[8]

Unlike in the West, there were no reporting requirements regarding sources of large deposits. Banks engaged in extensive money laundering and embezzlement on the part of insiders. They also played an important role in the allocation of central bank credits to mismanaged enterprises. These credits were forthcoming after the first few months of government austerity threatened to cause a shutdown of all industrial activity.

The exporting of raw materials was another mechanism used by insiders to gain quick wealth. With the abandonment of the government monopoly on foreign trade, securing export licenses created opportunities for enormous personal gains. Raw materials would typically be purchased with rubles at internal prices and then sold abroad for dollars. In Moscow, licenses were issued by the Ministry of Foreign Economic Relations in return for bribes that dwarfed the license fee itself. Licenses for iron, steel, and nonferrous metals were usually given at the oblast level, where officials charged with regulating enterprises became de facto business partners.

The reforms permitted many other ways of acquiring unearned wealth. Among them was the "milking of the credit cow." The central bank would extend a special, low-interest loan to an enterprise, perhaps for wages or supplies in arrears. Instead of using the credit for these purposes, however, much of the money would be immediately reinvested in a bank at a higher market rate of interest. The bank would, of course, maintain special relations with the enterprise in question, and the gain from the interest rate differential would be shared among the insiders who arranged the deal, including bank officials and enterprise managers.

After political conflict escalated to the point of bloodshed, parliament was formally disbanded on October 3, 1993, leaving the presidency as the only center of power. Members of the Yeltsin administration, convinced of their impunity after this victory, became more susceptible to bribery.

Control over tax revenue was placed with the president shortly thereafter. Concurrently, certain banks which had supported Yeltsin during the crisis were rewarded with deposits of government funds. Not surprisingly, by delaying payments on government obligations and giving short-term interbank credits at outrageous interest rates, the bankers were able to amass substantial fortunes. Regional banks and enterprise directors soon joined the rush to lend the government's money by acquiring their own share of budgetary funds from the Kremlin. At the same time, federal and local governments routinely reneged on paying salaries.

Organized Crime

Taking advantage of weak law enforcement, mafia influences have become prominent in all facets of Russian life.[9] An estimated 200,000 active criminal groups existed in Russia by the mid-1990s, including 5,500 large organizations.[10] In addition to extortion, their activities included burglary, embezzlement, and criminal misappropriation of both public and business funds.

Retail markets in every Russian city are controlled by gangsters who collect a share of the revenues of each vendor. This system is so well established that payments are calculated on the basis of records that the vendor is required to maintain. Gangsters may even agree to defer payments in light of special circumstances, creating, through force of habit, the impression that they are reasonable partners performing a needed security function.

Cities are divided into spheres of influence. For example, rival mafia groups divided the northern city of Arkhangelsk into two parts. It was not possible to start a business in that city without permission from the criminal group in control of the particular locale.[11]

Organized crime has also been active in theft and exportation of fuels and metals. It is estimated that from 1992 to 1994, over 20 percent of the petroleum output and one-third of metals production were smuggled out of the country. So much of this contraband passed through Estonia that this resource-scarce country became a major exporter of natural resources.[12] At one point, 70 percent of the raw materials shipped from Russia by rail through Lithuania never reached their legal destination, the Russian city of Kaliningrad. Disappearance of trainloads of oil was a daily occurrence. Railway personnel and customs officials conspired in these operations.[13]

Apart from corruption in the primary export industries, nearly every small business or street kiosk had felt the mafia presence by the first year of the transition period. Nevertheless, opportunity for embezzlement from these small businesses could in no way compare with the wealth that could be taken from the state budget. The vast sums of money appropriated by opportunistic Soviet officials attracted the attention of these gangsters, who quickly terrorized them and took over their enterprises. Government information indicates that roughly 70 to 80 percent of banks, as well as state and private companies, make payments to racketeers and corrupt officials.[14] Other data show three-quarters of businessmen routinely make payoffs, and ordinary citizens are also frequently forced to give bribes.[15]

The gangsters did end their terror campaigns against those businessmen who were the most well connected in government. Criminals depended on businessmen to invest their wealth. Businessmen, in turn, made use of gangsters in forcing clientele to honor their obligations. All the while, corrupt officials approved their projects in return for hefty bribes.

Their alliance, of course, soon grew to envelop more than debt collection services. The potential to eliminate unwanted competitors and coerce business partners to soften their terms was a fact that was not lost on the gangsters. Indeed, the large number of murders of businessmen and bankers reflects a general moral breakdown (Glinkina 1998a). Due to the availability of former KGB operatives and the fact that law enforcement is lax, the cost of a professional murder in Russia is low.[16]

Privatization

The privatization process was key to the transfer of the nation's wealth to a tainted minority.[17] Most enterprises were privatized by the mid-1990s, with employees and managers holding more than 50 percent of all shares of privatized firms (Radygin 1996, EBRD 1996). However, employee shares were mostly locked in trusts controlled by management, effectively giving ownership to managers.[18]

The first phase of "official" privatization entitled individual Russians to vouchers that were redeemable for cash or a share of industry. Conversion of vouchers into shares was of little consequence, since dividends were rarely paid and investors had little say in the decision-making process. For those who were able to obtain a large quantity, however, the vouchers were extremely useful. Quick to see the rewards of such a program, criminal and commercial elements soon began to collect vouchers from transients, alcoholics, and gullible citizens who were promised high dividends in television advertisements. With the vast amounts they collected, these groups bought up the most desirable enterprises at giveaway prices (Medvedev 1998, 170–91). Often the enterprises were quickly shut down as the new owners made gains by simply selling off real estate.

The first step in money privatization was determining a selling price for a particular enterprise. Using an estimate of building and equipment costs, price was determined by the factory director and officials of the relevant ministry. To ensure enterprises would go to intended buyers and to discourage others from bidding, the figures could be artificially lowered using outdated prices, or artificially raised. An established price would then go through an approval process via the local state property committee, which usually offered little objection.

Corrupt privatization aggravated Russia's financial woes.[19] as the state disposed of valuable assets at extremely low prices. Uralmash, the giant machine-building plant in Sverdlovsk, and the Cheliabinsk Metallurgical Combine went for around $4 million each. The Kovrovsky Mechanical Factory, which supplied the Russian military with firearms, sold for under $3 million (Lunev 1997). Telephone companies were sold for $100 per line compared to about $650 in North America. The power company United Energy Systems was sold for $200 million, whereas a company with similar kilowatt production would be worth $50 billion in the United States (Glinkina 1998a).

Under pressure from the IMF to create a balanced budget and reduce inflation, the Russian government in late 1994 halted the printing of money to meet current expenses. Ostensibly to offset the shortfall in revenue, the "loans-for-shares" program was established, in which shares of desirable, nonprivatized industries were used as collateral in exchange for bank credits. The program was corruptly administered and, in effect, the collateral was surrendered to further enrich wealthy insiders.

The Oligarchs

A young, unscrupulous economic elite known as the "oligarchs" now controls much of the Russian economy, including the nation's natural wealth. They also control banks that operate in a pathological fashion, industries that owe billions in unpaid taxes, and media empires. Through their use of money and media to sway elections, as well as by provision of bribes and sinecures, they have influenced all branches and levels of government. While they certainly have influence on government rules, their primary mode of operation is to circumvent them. Overseeing the tainted transfer of government assets and the corrupt allocation of government funds, the oligarchs have been integral to the creation of Russian-style kleptocracy (Glinkina 1998b). (The Appendix at the end of this chapter identifies the more prominent of the oligarchs.)

It was opportune for them that President Yeltsin lacked support of a serious political party. In early 1996, he was given virtually no chance of reelection. During the World Economic Forum in Davos, Switzerland, a prestigious annual gathering of prominent Western corporate leaders and policy makers, members of the new Russian economic elite agreed to combine efforts to prevent restoration of socialism. The "oligarchization" of modern Russia was signaled soon after by the "letter of thirteen." It suggested a cancellation of the presidential election, warning that election of a socialist as president would cause blood to flow in the streets.

The oligarchs used the media they controlled and large sums from their own gains to support a lavish reelection campaign. There is also evidence that they were direct recipients of state money, which they "washed" clean and funneled into Yeltsin's campaign. While the legal spending limit for the election campaign was $3 million, there are estimates that the oligarchs mobilized well over $100 million (Bernstein 1996).

From the outset, the oligarchs have been reluctant to invest to modernize production. Little has been accomplished in the way of upgrading the plants, oil companies, banks, and steamship lines that they acquired so cheaply. In some cases, new owners simply failed to comprehend the enormity of the problems that had to be solved in order to reform production. For example, while taking control of Norilsk Nickel, Oneksimbank was completely unaware of the vast number of social issues involved, and the extent of the related costs.[20] Moreover, it diverted revenues to pay for bank speculation in securities, in the process accumulating large wage arrears (Politkovskaia 1997).

Profiting from the weakness of the legal system and corrupt officials, the oligarchs even acquired state property on deferred payment conditions and then paid nothing. There was sometimes a requirement that the new owner implement an investment program in order to renovate production. For example, the purchase by Mikhail Khodorkovsky of a controlling interest in the Volzhsk Pipe Plant was predicated on the condition that 146 billion rubles (about U.S.$70 million) would be invested in the enterprise within three years.[21] But these investments were never made. After numerous legal proceedings, the Federal Arbitration Court ruled to cancel the contract. However, by that time, the shares had already been resold several times. The court is still trying to determine the owner. Khodorkovsky made similar transactions with shares of Novokuznetsk Aluminum Plant, Moscow Cotton-Printing Factory, Stavropolpolimer Concern, and Cheliabinsk Zinc Plant.

In addition to bribery, the oligarchs have employed blackmail in order to influence government appointments. For example, the security company Atoll has conducted extensive investigations to collect discrediting material on decision makers. According to the newspaper *Moskovskii Komsomolets* (January 20, 1999), Atoll's staffers were spying on top state officials, including Yeltsin's immediate entourage and family members, using the most up-to-date equipment. Boris Berezovsky, for whom Atoll worked, invested over $3 million in its technical resources.[22]

The oligarchs not only used state funds for their own ends by utilizing and often embezzling money through their own banks, but, as it became clear after the crisis of August 1998, these leaders of Russian business also cheated a great number of their compatriots who entrusted their savings to the banks. Each of the five largest private banks—Inkombank (Vinogradov), SBS-Agro (Smolensky and Berezovsky), Most-Bank (Gusinsky), Menatep (Khodorkovsky), and Rossiiskii Kredit (Malkin)—granted loans to their affiliated companies for amounts greater than those of their debts to private depositors (Grigoriev and Yakobidze 1998). They then engineered a partially successful propaganda campaign in the press to pressure authorities to make the central bank settle their debts. The Bank of Russia proposed that clients of these banks transfer their deposits to Sberbank (on very unfavorable terms), while SBS-Agro and Most-Bank received stabilization loans at a preferential rate.[23]

The oligarchs hardly qualify as the Russian version of the "robber barons" who helped to industrialize the United States. Instead of creating and building new industries, they have shunted the wealth of Russia abroad. Rather than transform their profits into domestic investment, they have expatriated them. Illegal capital flight has also helped them shield their gains from taxation, undermining the capacity of government to finance itself adequately.

Conclusion

Corruption and criminalization in Russia have created a corrosive economic environment. Productive economic activity is inhibited while the siphoning off of the nation's resources continues. Potential investors are fearful that criminals and corrupt officials will impose unforeseen costs and even expropriate their investments. Forced or enticed to join forces with criminal structures, managers are not inclined toward company strategies that are optimal for the long run. A plundering oligarchic elite, with strong influence over the media and politicians, has had a noxious influence on government.

To put the problem of crime and corruption in perspective, it is helpful to consider how economic transition was approached. Young reformers, trained to serve communist organs like the newspaper *Pravda* and the journal *Kommunist*, "became radical free-marketeers without abandoning either their Marxist faith in the primacy of economic relations or their disrespect for the rule of law" (Satter 1999).[24] Once they had power, their primary goal was to replace public ownership with private ownership. Their haste, and lack of concern for legality and fairness,[25] apparently led them to accept unscrupulous entrepreneurs as allies, creating opportunities for criminals to take control of the economy.

Russian reality—not only the lack of rule of law but also weak economic policy—may well continue to provide opportunities for the parasitic existence of criminal structures. In the final analysis, the future of any country is jeopardized by swindling of the state and criminal interference with market competition. So long as such activity is not only possible, but acceptable, Russia's prospects will be dim.

Appendix

Who Are the Oligarchs?

Following is a list of the most well known of the Russian oligarchs, all of whom rose to power at a relatively young age:[26]

Roman Abramovich, a latecomer to the ranks of the oligarchs, became head of oil company Sibneft, and owner of 36 percent of its stock, with the support of oligarch Boris Berezovsky. According to the former chief of staff of the Yeltsin administration, Aleksander Korzhakov, Abramovich was the "wallet of the Yeltsin family." Widely regarded as the patron of Nikolai Aksenenko, he was instrumental in Aksenenko's elevation to first deputy prime minister following the dismissals of Yevgeny Primakov and Yuri Maslyukov (*Kommersant*, May 27, 1999). One of the first acts of Aksenenko was to increase Sibneft's quota for oil imports (*Interfax*, May 27, 1999).

Vagit Alekperov is president of Lukoil, which was rated the world's number one oil company by its oil reserves (prior to the Mobil-Exxon merger). As head of the Soviet Oil Industry Ministry, he oversaw privatization of the Soviet oil and energy complex.

Boris Berezovsky has extensive holdings in the oil sector. He owns Russian Public Television, the daily *Nezavisimaya gazeta*, and several banks. He initially gained wealth by controlling the sale of autos in Moscow with the LogoVAZ imported cars dealership and a policy of ruthlessly eliminating competitors. He served President Yeltsin first as head of the Security Council and later as secretary of the Commonwealth of Independent States. He may face prosecution for arranging that all revenues of Aeroflot, Russia's largest airline, be accumulated in accounts of the Swiss company Andava, which he controlled. He had close ties with Yeltsin's daughter and son-in-law.

Vladimir Bogdanov is president of Surgutneftegaz, a major company in the oil and energy sector. He obtained state-owned Surgutneftegaz shares via the loans-for-shares scheme.

Mikhail Fridman is head of Alfa Bank. In 1998 this bank purchased Tiumen Oil Company.

Vladimir Gusinsky is president of Media-Most, which owns the television network NTV and 7 Days publishing company. He started publishing the daily *Segodnia* in 1993 and was the first Russian businessman to pay serious attention to mass media. Like Berezovsky, he uses a mass media empire to influence public opinion to support the government in return for government largesse.

Mikhail Khodorkovsky established the bank Menatep and is head of YUKOS oil company. He was a well-known businessmen in *Komsomol.*

Vitaly Malkin is president of Bank Rossiiskii Kredit and has interests in nonferrous metallurgy. He is a noted backer of General Alexander Lebed, who won the gubernatorial election in Krasnoiarskii Krai with funding from Rossiiskii Kredit.

Vladimir Potanin is head of Interros holding, which includes such enterprises as Norilsk Nickel, Sidanco, and Oneksimbank. He started his business career at the Ministry of Foreign Economic Relations, where he founded Oneksimbank.

Alexander Smolensky is head of the banking group SBS-Agro. Smolensky has lobbied for and benefited from government subsidies for agriculture, which have been funneled through his bank. He is closely tied to First Deputy Premier Gennady Kulik, whose son became deputy chairman of SBS-Agro in October 1998.

Vladimir Vinogradov is founder and head of Inkombank.

Rem Vyakhirev is chairman of the board of RAO Gazprom. This is the world's largest gas concern and Russia's largest corporation, and it provides over 10 percent of its revenues to the Russian budget. In January 1999, his son Yuri was appointed head of the gas export monopoly Gazexport, which is a subsidiary of Gazprom.

Two other figures, more noted for their governmental roles, could be added to the list: Moscow Mayor Yuri Luzhkov and former deputy prime minister Anatoly Chubais. Luzhkov, a popular mayor, is widely alleged to have criminal ties and to have acquired extensive real estate holdings while in office. Chubais, the primary figure in Russian privatization and a darling of the West, is head of RAO EES Rossii (Integrated Power Grid of Russia).

Notes

1. The interpretation below of changes prior to Gorbachev borrows from Braguinsky and Yavlinsky (1999).

2. Berliner (1957), who examines the Stalin era, reports that even then there were various methods of cheating the planning authorities.

3. For details, see Gdlyan and Ivanov (1988).

4. The description of abuses during the Gorbachev and Yeltsin eras draws heavily on Satter (1999).

5. See Åslund (1996), who reports severe abuses yet supported a strategy of rapid privatization that lacked safeguards against wrongdoing.

6. Yavlinsky and Braguinsky (1994) and Kotz (1997) argue that the Gaidar reforms were partly motivated by the drive of the nomenclatura and managers to garner property rights. For further perspective, see Kleiner (1996).

7. Intricate and undeveloped bankruptcy procedures gave insolvent companies the power to block actions by creditors.

8. See Glinkina (1997). Many people turned over their privatization vouchers to investment funds that simply disappeared (*Extra M,* 1994, No. 38, 1).

9. Handelman (1995) provides a graphic description. See also Hendley et al. (1999), who conclude from interviews with directors and managers of manufacturing firms that mafia intrusion is less pervasive than generally thought. However, one can assume it would endanger those being interviewed if they were entirely truthful.

10. Estimates of the Ministry of Interior (*Rossiiskii vesti*, 1994, 173). See also RIA, *Goriachaia liniia–1*, March 23, 1994.

11. Information on the partition of Arkhangelsk by two mafia groups was reported in news accounts when the 33-year-old crime boss named Privalov was killed in September 1996 by a bomb blast. Braguinsky and Yavlinsky (1999) refer to this incident to illustrate barriers to new entry. They also discuss more benign illegal activity, such as the common practice of workers conducting business activities using firm resources.

12. *Novaia ezhednevnaia gazeta* (New daily newspaper), March 30, 1994.

13. *Global Finance*, January 1994, 34–38.

14. *Rossiiskii vesti* (Russian news), 1994, No. 56.

15. *Argumenty i fakty* (Arguments and facts), 1994, No. 48.

16. Alexander Lebed proposed the creation of a "Russian Legion" to fight criminals "with their own methods" (Maksimov 1997, 108). However, a police force not subjected to legal constraints would itself pose a major danger and could be a prelude to the return of authoritarian terror.

17. See Shleifer and Vishny (1995) for a theoretical analysis that concludes that privatization is irrelevant if corruption is severe.

18. See Aukutsionek et al. (1995) for evidence.

19. On September 9, 1994, the investor bulletin *Independent Strategy* stated: "The greater part of basic productive funds of Russia are being sold for somewhere around $5 billion. Even if one considers that in Russia, the price of the basic means of production is equal to her gross domestic product [in the West, it is usually at least 2.6 times higher] . . . in effect, 300 to 400 billion dollars; the sum realized in privatization is minimal. For this reason, the agency recommends English investors not to miss the chance to take part in the purchase of Russian enterprises."

20. The nickel industrial complex is the only large enterprise in the city of Norilsk; the whole municipal infrastructure is funded at its expense. Vladimir Potanin is now considering selling the complex to a foreign company.

21. Sergei Baburin, first vice-speaker of the State Duma, submitted these data in spring 1998, based on information from the Russian Federal Property Fund.

22. Former Central Bank Chairman Sergei Dubinin objected to the granting of unjustified advantages to SBS-Agro, a bank in which Berezovsky had a direct interest. According to an account in *Kommersant* (January 19, 1999), former Prime Minister Sergei Kirienko alleged that this conflict was instrumental in Yeltsin's decision to dismiss Dubinin.

23. For other examples of oligarch machinations, see Grigoriev (1998), Grigoriev and Yakobidze (1998), Yakobidze and Grigoriev (1998), and Boutrin and Yakobidze (1998).

24. Satter (1999) also alleges: "[M]any of the reformers took it for granted that they were morally superior, not because of their fidelity to transcendent values, but because they favored private ownership over socialism. The need to provide a legal and ethical framework for the reform process was ignored. . . . The speed of the reform process and its criminalization totally subverted the purpose of democracy." For further insight into the perspective of the reformers see Dolgova (1994) and the unguarded remarks in a notorious radio interview of former privatization chief Alfred Kokh (Minkin 1998).

25. Confronted with the fact that parliament had previously voted to index the savings of Russian citizens in the event of price liberalization, Gaidar's position was that the loss of savings due to hyperinflation was the fault of the previous regime (Shmeliov 1997, 22; Medvedev 1998).

26. Following are the years of birth of the oligarchs: Roman Abramovich 1966, Vagit Alekperov 1951, Boris Berezovsky 1946, Vladimir Bogdanov 1951,

Mikhail Fridman 1965, Vladimir Gusinsky 1953, Mikhail Khodorkovsky 1964, Vitaly Malkin 1952, Vladimir Potanin 1961, Alexander Smolensky 1954, Vladimir Vinogradov 1955, and Rem Vyakhirev 1944.

References

Åslund, Anders. 1996. "The Three Basic Sources of the New Russian's Wealth." *Izvestiia*, June.

Aukutsionek, Sergei, L. Ivanova, and E. Zhuravskaia. 1995. *Privatization in Theory and Practice: Analysis Based on Russian Industrial Enterprises Surveys.* Paper presented at the twenty-second CIRET conference, Singapore.

Berliner, Joseph S. 1957. *Factory and Manager in the USSR.* Cambridge: Harvard University Press.

Bernstein, Jonas. 1996. "Watergate: Day at the Beach." *Moscow Times,* November 22.

Boutrin, Dmitri, and Vakhtang Yakobidze. 1998. "Grandson of Austrian Citizen and His Bank." *Kompaniya*, October 27: 39.

Braguinsky, Serguey, and Grigori Yavlinsky. 1999. *Incentives and Institutions in the Transition to a Market Economy in Russia.* Princeton: Princeton University Press.

Dolgova, Azalia. 1994. "Strengthening of Respect for Law." *Trud,* December 10.

European Bank for Reconstruction and Development (EBRD). 1996. *Transition Report for 1996.* London: EBRD.

Gdlyan, Telman, and Nikolai Ivanov. 1988. *Confrontation* 26.

Glinkina, Svetlana. 1997. "The Criminal Components of the Russian Economy. " Working Paper No. 29, *Berichte des Bundesinstituts der Wissenschaftlichen und Internationalen Studien, Köln Institut für Ost Europa.*

———. 1998a. "Characteristics of the Shadow Economy in Russia." *Nezavisimaya gazeta*, March 5.

———. 1998b. "The Ominous Landscape of Russian Corruption." *Transitions*, March: 20.

Grigoriev, Andrei. 1998. "Oligarchs for Sale." *Kompaniya*, June 9: 20.

Grigoriev, Andrei, and Vakhtang Yakobidze. 1998. "Tell Me Who Is Your Client . . ." *Kompaniya*, December 8: 45.

Handelman, Stephen. 1995. *Comrade Criminal: Russia's New Mafia*. New Haven: Yale University Press.

Hendley, Kathryn, Peter Murrell, and Randi Ryterman. 1999. "Law, Relationships and Private Enforcement: Transactional Strategies of Russian Enterprises." Mimeo, University of Maryland.

Kleiner, G. 1996. "Russia's Economy of Today as the Economy of Physical Entities." *Voprosy Ekonomiki* 4.

Kotz, David M. (with Fred Weir). 1997. *Revolution from Above: The Demise of the Soviet System*. London and New York: Routledge.

Kryshtanovskaia, Olga. 1997. "In Whose Hands Is Property?" *Argumenty y fakty* 15.

Lunev, Stanislav.1997. "Russian Organized Crime," *Prism* 10, May 30. Jamestown Foundation.

Maksimov, Alexander. 1997. *Russian Crime: Who Is Who*. Moscow: EKSMO.

Medvedev, Roy. 1998. *Capitalism in Russia?* Moscow: Prav Cheloveka.

Minkin, Alexander, Jr. 1998. "Confessions of Former Vice–Prime Minister of Russia." *Novaia gazeta*, November 2.

Politkovskaia, Anna. 1997. "Norilsk Is Ready to Break the Bank." *Obshchaia gazeta:*12, March 6.

Radygin, A. 1996. "Privatization Process in Russia in 1995." *Voprosy Ekonomiki* 4.

Satter, David. 1999. "The Rise of the Russian Criminal State." *Nezavisimaya gazeta*, January 19.

Shleifer, Andrei, and Robert Vishny. 1995. "Politicians and Firms." *Quarterly Journal of Economics* 109(4): 995–1025.

Shmeliov, Nikolai. 1997. "Plokhaia moral–plokhaia ekonomika." *Politekonom* 1.

Yakobidze, Vakhtang, and Andrei Grigoriev. 1998. "Alexander Smolensky's New Ideas." *Kompaniya*, November 17: 42.

Yavlinsky, Grigori, and Sergei Braguinsky. 1994. "The Inefficiency of Laissez-Faire in Russia: Hysteresis Effects and the Need for Policy-Led Transformation." *The Journal of Comparative Economics* 19(1): 88–116.

16

Poverty and Social Assistance

Vladimir Mikhalev

In the Soviet era, notwithstanding the well-known deficiencies of the economic system, virtually all Russians had sufficient income for an adequate diet and a socially respectable standard of living, albeit below Western standards. Employment was guaranteed, and housing was universally provided at a nominal price. Health care and education were free, and the elderly and infirm received decent pensions.

The transition brought immediate impoverishment to many. With the sudden liberalization of prices in January 1992, almost at once the average wage lost half its purchasing power. There was some recovery later in 1992 and in 1993, but in 1995 real wages declined by another quarter. By the beginning of 1998, the average real wage was only about 40 percent of its pre-reform level.[1] The sharp devaluation of the ruble during August and September 1998 brought a further drop in real wages.

Wages actually paid are lower still, since about 60 percent of workers are not paid on time. The total amount of wages paid each month is about a third less than the amount of wages earned. Wage arrears typically vary in duration from two to six months. They are not indexed for inflation, which often attained a rate of 20 percent per month from 1992 to 1994 and again spurted to 40 percent in the month of September 1998.

Depressed wages and large wage arrears, as well as rising unemployment, have increased dependence on other sources of income. Thus wages now account for only 40 percent of total personal income, compared with a pre-reform level of over 80 percent. Roughly 45 percent of total personal income is derived from entrepreneurial profits, dividends, and interest. About 15 percent is from pensions, stipends, and other social benefits, which for the most part do not apply to the employed (Goskomstat 1997, 73).

Inequality

Sources differ, but all indicate a marked increase in income inequality, especially during the first year that shock therapy was launched. Based on government statistics for total money income, the share of the richest fifth grew steadily in the 1990s. The lower three quintiles, which used to receive close to half, now receive only about 30 percent of a greatly shrunken total. Data for decile shares indicate that the income ratio of the richest tenth to the poorest tenth jumped from 3.4 in 1991 to 13.3 in 1998 (Goskomstat 1998, 213).

The income share of the lowest quintile was cut in half in 1992. Due to the decline of income to be distributed, the total income of the poorest group is now only about a quarter of what it was in 1991.[2]

Incomplete coverage of illegal and other informal sources of income in the Goskomstat data is likely to cause an underestimate of the extent of inequality (Mikhalev 1996b). The Russian Longitudinal Monitoring Survey (RLMS) and surveys by the Russian Center for Public Opinion Research (VCIOM) show higher income inequality than shown by the Goskomstat statistics. While the Gini inequality coefficient calculated from Goskomstat data is 0.409 for 1994 and 0.375 for 1996, a dramatic increase from 0.26 for 1990, the RLMS data for the end of 1993 yield a Gini coefficient of 0.49, and the VCIOM data for March 1994 yield a value of 0.46. These statistics are within the range of countries characterized by highly unequal income, such as Argentina or the Philippines, and are much higher than levels in Western Europe.[3]

Poverty

Poverty measurements are complicated by definitional problems, rapid social change, income instability, and difficulties in monitoring incomes. The official government (Goskomstat) statistics on variation in poverty can be questioned because of inflation and changing definitions.[4] Nevertheless, the drop in personal income in combination with its more uneven distribution has clearly resulted in a massive increase in poverty.

The Goskomstat measure of the poverty rate more than doubled in 1992. The trend in poverty from 1992 to 1998 is difficult to ascertain in part because of fluctuations in the monthly rate of inflation. Quarterly poverty rates reported by Goskomstat from 1993 through 1998 range from 34 percent in the third quarter of 1993 to 21 percent in the first quarter of 1998. Mozhina and Ovcharova (1996), after making adjustments for increases in the cost of public transport and other services, find instead that the poverty rate continued to rise after 1993.

An alternative way to assess poverty is to survey people's opinions about their own standards of living. The results of such surveys are influenced by the specific situation of Russia. In their perceptions, people naturally refer to standards typical of their previous circumstances as well as to the living standards of the new elites. In a 1995 VCIOM survey, 80 percent of respondents reported living in conditions of poverty.[5]

There is a small amount of evidence on the prevalence of extreme deprivation. The regional surveys discussed below provide scattered evidence of the high proportion who cannot afford the subsistence minimum food basket and are therefore vulnerable to famine (the "very poor"). The incidence rate is 5 percent for the richest region and 44 percent for the poorest.[6]

Poverty is now pervasive among social groups which once were economically secure. This is largely attributable to low wage levels. Based on the poverty line used by Goskomstat, about three-quarters of poor households include an adult worker with a permanent, full-time job.

Wage levels differ markedly by sector and occupation (Mikhalev and Bjorksten 1995). Employment in the public sector and agriculture are both likely to be associated with poverty. In industry, although low-skilled industrial workers are more likely to be poor than professionals, poverty has also widely affected engineers and other highly educated workers.

The highest wages are in the oil, gas, coal, and energy supply industries. For example, the average pay for employees of the gas monopoly (Gazprom) is 7.5 times the economy-wide average. Earnings in the expanding banking sector before the 1998 crisis were twice the average. Workers in the transport and communications sector are also relatively well-off. Wage levels in the budgetary sector, agriculture, light manufacturing, and textile industries are only about half the average. The new private businesses, which are primarily in the trade sector, generally pay relatively high wages, but many such jobs are not stable.

Regional Differences

Economic inequality has a significant regional dimension. Mining of valuable mineral resources is characterized by high earnings and supports the economies of some regions. Most other regions are severely depressed by industrial decline, including much of Central Russia and the republics in the Volga region. Predominantly agricultural areas, such as the republics of the Northern Caucasus, are among the poorest. In addition, local price levels vary and sometimes accentuate differences in regional per capita incomes.

Disparity in regional economic and social conditions has increased rapidly in the course of transition. For example, Siberia and the Russian Far East used to have high nominal incomes because regional wage coefficients were applied to compensate for their harsh climatic conditions, but now they show a significant diversity in real income levels. The ratio of real per capita income between the richest and the poorest region increased five fold from 1992 to 1994 (World Bank 1995, 31).

Table 16.1. Incidence of Poverty in Selected Regions

	Percent Poor	Percent Very Poor
Rich in Mineral Resources		
Magnitogorsk City	17.0	4.8
Iakutiia Republic (Sakha)	28.8	5.8
Khanty Mansiyski District	28.8	13.2
Agriculture and Food Processing		
Astrakhan Oblast	72.4	44.3
Orel Oblast	58.7	32.6
Adygeia Republic	51.9	19.4
Industrial or Mixed		
Chuvash Republic	42.5	22.7
Khanty–Mansiiskii District	28.8	13.2
Krasnoiarskii Krai	43.5	20.1
Moscow Oblast	41.0	19.7
Tver Oblast	39.1	18.1
Voronezh Oblast	20.4	10.2

Note: The "poor" do not have enough income to purchase the subsistence minimum consumer basket as defined in Goskomstat poverty measures; the "very poor" are unable to afford even the food component of the subsistence minimum. Moscow Oblast excludes the city of Moscow.

Data are not available to compare income levels and poverty across all 89 regions of the Russian Federation. However, there are two comprehensive, recent regional surveys of the incidence of poverty. The Ministry of Social Protection (MOSP) surveyed nine regions between October 1994 and February 1995. The other survey, covering two other regions, was conducted in February and March 1994 by the Center for the Study of Living Standards for the Ministry of Labor (Mikhalev 1996b). In both surveys, the national poverty line calculated according to Goskomstat methodology was adjusted to local price levels, thus defining regionally specific poverty lines. Here the "very poor" (extreme poverty) were identified as those whose income was less than the cost of the food component of the subsistence minimum. Table 16.1 displays the results for each region. The incidence of poverty is high in all regions, ranging from 17 to 72 percent. The rate of extreme poverty is typically 20 percent, and ranges as high as 44 percent.

The two most favored regions have economies that are built around mining of valuable minerals. The primary economic base of Magnitogorsk City is the mining of iron ore, and Iakutiia Republic contains the largest gold and diamond mines in Russia. In both regions, the incidence of extreme poverty is about 5 percent, a substantially lower incidence rate than in any other region. Regarding the standard poverty rate, Magnitogorsk has the lowest rate at 17 percent, and Iakutiia is tied for third lowest at 28.8 percent

The majority of the population in Astrakhan and Orel are in poverty, with rates of extreme poverty reaching 33 and 44 percent, respectively. These two regions, which have the highest poverty rates in the sample, specialize in intensive agriculture and food processing. The other regions have economies that do not depend exclusively on either mineral resources or agriculture. Of these, Voronezh has the lowest rates of poverty and extreme poverty (20 percent and 10 percent). This poverty rate is unexpectedly low, given that Voronezh is largely agricultural with a concentration of machine building in the oblast center. Poverty may have been moderated by local government policy of subsidizing prices for basic foodstuffs.

Sharp contrasts in living standards and poverty rates are also associated with types of community (i.e., large cities, small towns, or rural areas). According to the MOSP survey, in five of nine regions the incidence of poverty was higher in smaller towns than in the regional centers. High incomes are concentrated in the large urban commercial and banking centers, especially Moscow. The transformation of the economies elsewhere is impeded by lack of transport and other infrastructure. Smaller cities and towns suffer more from the decline of local industrial enterprises, and there are very few opportunities in rural labor markets. In the small town of Viazniki, for example, 5 percent of workers secured a second job compared with 20 percent in St. Petersburg (Mozhina et al. 1995). Adjustment to opportunity differences via labor mobility is hindered by many economic and social factors, not least by the lack of available housing in the relatively prosperous urban areas.

Rural poverty is especially serious in areas where subsistence agriculture is not feasible. In some fertile regions intensive household farming allows for provision of adequate food. Such activity produces virtually no cash income; the livelihood of households in some regions consists entirely of consumption of the harvests collected from private plots. For example, in the Orel oblast, which is located in the "black soil" area, the incidence of poverty in rural areas is less than half the rate in the capital city.

Policy

Erosion of incomes and rising inequality have been aggravated by the failure to maintain either the pay levels of public employees or the level of cash transfers. These changes resulted from a decline in the real level of the official minimum wage, which serves as a benchmark for computation of cash transfers including child allowances and unemployment benefits. Changes in the minimum wage also determine wage movements of public employees, including teachers and medical personnel.

The minimum wage, and therefore government wages and social benefits, have lagged far behind inflation. During the high inflation of 1992 and 1993, the minimum wage was adjusted every three or four months. Since then it has been adjusted typically once every seven months. By 1998, the real minimum wage amounted to only 20 percent of its 1991 level and was equal to 8 percent of the average wage.

Unlike other sources of income, government-paid pensions, which are received by about 25 percent of the population (almost 38 million pensioners), have become more equal. The difference between the minimum and maximum pension has diminished, while the proportion of pensioners on a higher pension decreased. In 1994, 80 percent of pensioners received pensions which were between 1.0 and 1.5 times the minimum pension (Mikhalev 1996b).

During the first reform years, most pensioners experienced a clear deterioration of their relative position. Between 1992 and 1994, the average pension fell from 40 percent to 25 percent of the average wage. However, the reindexation in 1995 increased pensions significantly to approximately their prior relation to the average wage.[7] This relative pension level has been maintained through 1998.

It was assumed during the Soviet era that virtually all working-age citizens could provide for themselves. Accordingly, the core of the post-Soviet safety net is pensions for retirees. Yet most of the poor are in families with one or more adults who work full time but receive very low wages.

All workers are legally entitled to sick pay, maternity benefits, child allowances, and unemployment benefits. The child allowances previously were important in reducing the adverse effects of income inequality. However, at the end of 1994, the level of child allowance was equal to only 18 percent of the minimum subsistence for a child, contributing no more than 8 percent to the budget of an average poor household (Mozhina et al. 1995, 95). Unemployment benefits are likewise meager, averaging in 1994 only one-tenth of the average wage and one-third of the subsistence minimum (OECD 1995, 197).

A national system of means-tested benefits has never existed in Russia. One approach to alleviating poverty is to move toward the West European model and introduce a benefit to those whose incomes fall below the poverty line (and who have less than a certain level of assets). At present, no country in Eastern Europe has such a system, although the Czech system is closest (Milanovic 1998, 115). The concept of a universal poverty benefit, however, has been considered by the Russian Duma. One proposal is to guarantee all citizens an income level equal to at least 50 percent of the subsistence minimum.

A universal poverty benefit, however, poses numerous problems. First, there is no administrative framework for incomes testing, so its introduction would be costly and problematic. Second, widespread informal (and illegal) activities make it impossible to monitor household incomes. Third, social security budgets are unable to provide adequate funding to fill the poverty gap. Guaranteeing half the subsistence minimum would be far more attainable, but this would leave many in dire circumstances. Fourth, as the experiences of Poland and other countries show, benefits are also likely to be claimed by persons somewhat above the adopted poverty line; social assistance programs may be overwhelmed by the number of claimants. Given these problems, a strong system for targeting social assistance is important.

Programs of poverty relief and other social assistance are the responsibility of regional authorities, although the federal government provides guidelines. Funding is provided mainly by regional and local budgets. (The Appendix provides a case study of Krasnoiarsk.)

Cash support is relatively minor. In 1993, for example, cash support accounted for a trivial share of the assistance to poor families with children (Mozhina et al. 1995). Vouchers and subsidies are provided for purchases of food and medicine. Discounts for housing, utilities, and transportation are arranged. Transportation subsidies are provided to all pensioners and school children. Discounts of 50 percent on utility and telephone bills are automatic for war veterans, the disabled, and single pensioners.

Some localities provide subsidies for housing rent and utilities. However, housing is an acute social problem for young adults now that privatization has virtually eliminated the practice of getting housing from one's employer. Fifteen percent of families live in acutely overcrowded conditions with under eleven square meters of space per capita. Four percent reside in substandard *communalki* (common flats) with other families with whom they have no family ties and about a quarter of all dwellings lack some basic amenities such as water, sewers, telephone, or central heating.[8] The waiting list for public housing numbered ten million families in 1991. Housing prices in the emerging private market are far beyond the reach of the average citizen.

Although increased cash support is needed to reduce poverty, a suggestion by the World Bank (1995) to shift toward cash benefits and reduce in-kind assistance does not seem fully justified. Pharmaceutical subsidies are vital for the survival of many of the poor. In-kind support can be better directed to the real needs of the family in the not uncommon case of a household head with a drinking problem. Also, cash support cannot replace discounts for transport and other essential services.

Existing local social protection departments have the potential to alleviate poverty significantly. However, the poor financial conditions of most regions render the majority of such programs ineffective. According to a Ministry of Social Protection survey in 1995, only 10 to 15 percent of households with incomes below the subsistence minimum received social assistance. Disparities in social assistance, moreover, contribute to the high degree of interregional inequality.

Conclusion

It has been said that the major hardships of the transition were placed on the shoulders of the working population, while privatization removed what used to be at their disposal (Gordon 1995). In the Russian context, such a development was favored by the weakness of the new democratic institutions and the virtual absence of a union movement. For example, adjustment of the benchmark minimum wage has been regularly postponed, and it has long been customary for government to delay payment of wages.

A shocking phenomenon is the appearance of great numbers of highly educated, well-trained working poor. Over time these newly destitute will lose much of their human capital and may become socially isolated, making their path out of poverty ever more difficult. The likelihood of such a prospect makes an adequate response to the social welfare crisis all the more urgent.

Assistance to the poor can be only marginally effective in the absence of an expanding economy. Once growth resumes, economic prosperity will not "trickle down" on its own accord to benefit all the needy. Appropriate income distribution policies and a viable social safety net will continue to be critical. Moreover, government support for improvements in housing, education, and health care is important.

Despite frequent declarations of its importance, social welfare policy has been neglected. Further deterioration in living conditions and worsening inequality could undermine economic reforms and the process of democratization. The threat is exacerbated by the size of the country and the diversity of regional conditions, with especially dire situations in large rural territories.

Appendix
A Case Study of Krasnoiarsk

Information on social assistance programs is scarce; statistics or published surveys are nearly nonexistent. For this reason, the author carried out field research in Krasnoiarsk. This central Siberian city of about one million is the administrative center of the largest region in the Russian Federation, Krasnoiarskii Krai.[9] In May 1995 extensive interviews were held with officials at the city and krai departments of social protection. Valuable documentation was obtained, including annual departmental reports and social monitoring data.[10]

In Krasnoiarsk, living standards are lower than average for Russia, and poverty rates higher. The economy is heavily dependent on machine-building and military-related production, both of which are suffering deep decline. While the average wage is about 50 percent above the Russian average, the cost of living more than makes up for the difference. As elsewhere in Siberia, the prices for goods and other expenses are elevated because of the frigid cold and high transportation costs.

At the same time, production of exportable resources, in particular aluminum and other nonferrous metals, is active. Workers at the aluminum and metallurgy plants are paid well. As a result, income inequality is high. This situation is repeated in other large Russian industrial cities where remnants of the military-industrial complex coexist with natural resource-based industries, namely mining and metallurgy.

While the federal Ministry of Labor and Social Development provides oversight,[11] programs of social assistance are locally designed and implemented. According to the Standard Regional Program for Social Protection, the primary goal is to mitigate the effects of transition on those living below regional subsistence levels.

Each program includes both cash and in-kind benefits as well as services that are delivered to individual recipients. The scope and magnitude of assistance depend on assessed needs and available resources. There are three major features common to these programs: First, support is subject to income tests or other obvious criteria such as being a single pensioner. Second, in-kind support is more prevalent than direct monetary assistance. Third, funding is mainly from local resources, although there are also limited central government transfers.

The system of social protection, largely inherited from the Soviet past, includes: keeping records on pensioners, calculating pension entitlements, and paying pensions; and keeping records on the disabled, defining disability categories, and making disability payments. Expenditures are financed from the pension fund, so are not part of the budget of the krai department of social protection. Child (family) allowances (paid universally to every child) were added to the responsibility of regional departments of social protection when they were introduced in 1990. These are paid from the state budget (mainly regional with federal transfers for in-deficit regions). The actual disbursement of child allowances for workers is done at places of employment. Social security offices are responsible for paying family allowances to the nonworking population. Holes in coverage are widespread due to poor administration.

The krai (and oblast) departments of social protection are subordinate to the federal Ministry of Labor and Social Development. The krai department supervises the work of the city department and offices in rural districts (raion). Krasnoiarsk is also divided into districts, each with an office subordinate to the city department. The actual implementation and distribution of pensions and social services is at the district level. The city department is an intermediate agency which is nonexistent in rural areas or small towns where district offices are subordinate directly to krai (oblast) departments of social protection. Thus the city department is not working with pensions at all. Those are administered through the krai department working directly with the city districts. The city department concentrates its activity on new forms of social protection and services, including cash and in-kind support for the poor. In this particular area it supervises the work of district offices as well and is subordinate to the krai administration, the latter also located in Krasnoiarsk. Funding comes mainly from the krai level, though some resources are provided by the federal and city governments.

Delivery of assistance and services in Krasnoiarsk has become increasingly decentralized. In a decree of the mayor of 25 June 1992, six centers of "sotsialnoe zdorovie" (social well-being) were established with a total staff of about 200. The staff includes sociologists, teachers, psychologists, lawyers, and medical specialists. An investment of about $300,000 from 1992 to 1994 was made to equip these centers.

As acknowledged in a report by the krai department of social protection, the existing infrastructure for social assistance is still very inadequate. The funding, equipment, and the number and skill level of the personnel are insufficient to meet the acute demand. The judicial and methodological base for the operation of district centers for social assistance is also underdeveloped. In some areas of the krai, no services are available at all.

Throughout Russia, departments of social protection maintain complete records for retired pensioners and the disabled. Such data have recently been extended to include large and single-parent families. This information, however, provides only incomplete data on incomes, assets, and housing conditions and is generally inadequate to evaluate the extent of poverty and particular needs of various social groups. With the assistance of the government statistical office and academic institutions located in Krasnoiarsk, the social protection department has conducted its own surveys. The results indicate that 80 percent of families need some form of assistance or services from the department of social protection. The district centers have been equipped with computer facilities allowing a local database to be developed containing the so-called "passports" of families in need. These passports, however, are compiled only on individuals and families that have already been clients of these services. Despite all these efforts, reliable information on household incomes is still lacking.

In addition to monitoring these needs, the dissemination of information to potential recipients on assistance and services available is no less important. Among others, the purpose of such information is to address the stigma associated with becoming a client of welfare services, and to help people overcome psychological barriers to applying for aid. This problem is dealt with by publicity in the local press, distribution of booklets and leaflets, and the display of posters in the streets and on local transport.

Targeting is key to efficient delivery of social assistance. It should be clear from the above analysis that establishing criteria for needs determination in Russia presents major problems. A monitoring of incomes that would extend to an actual individual or household is inadequate, while certain readily observed attributes, such as demographic indicators and family composition, do not show significant correlation with poverty status. For example, single-parent households constitute less than 8 percent of the poor, while families with three or more children account for only 9 percent of the poor (World Bank 1995, 59). With regard to housing conditions and asset ownership there is little distinction made between the poor and the nonpoor, for rising poverty is only slowly affecting the long-standing asset holding of the population. Dwellings and most consumer durables were acquired by households, including those currently poor, during Soviet times when income disparity was much less.

To cope with these difficulties, local centers for social assistance try to rely on three major principles: (1) self-targeting, or granting assistance by application; (2) declaration, and in some cases verification, of income details; (3) use of other criteria, such as a limited earning capacity (three or more children, single parent, the presence of disabled or elderly family members, and/or alcoholism of a family member). This arrangement of social assistance involves a considerable amount of administrative work, including individual interviews and home visits both to check the details of the needs as well as to deliver assistance. The approach is highly personalized with the risk of subjectivity and arbitrariness. Assistance is awarded on an occasional rather than ongoing basis, which multiplies routine administrative work.

Further administrative complications arise from the multiple types of assistance provided, of which cash support is not the most important. For example, cash support formed only 4 percent in the total countrywide amount of transfers available to poor families with children in 1992, and cash support decreased to 1 percent in 1993 (Mozhina et al. 1995, 95). Almost half of respondents of the 1995 MOSP survey indicated a preference for in-kind assistance, in part because high inflation quickly erodes the value of cash, especially when payment is delayed. The total amount of cash relief provided by the Krasnoiarsk City Department of Social Protection in 1994 totaled only 356 million rubles ($161,661) and covered 27,720 people. This represents only 27 percent of needy families with three or more children and only 6.5 percent of single mothers in need. The amount of monthly support for an individual was thus a symbolic sum of 12,300 rubles ($6), roughly equal to 14 percent of the monthly average and 1 percent of the annual subsistence minimum. Cash relief averaged slightly more for single pensioners. Special treatment was afforded a small group of 81 orphans, who received cash relief at five times the average level for single pensioners.

Local departments of social protection accord a higher priority to in-kind subsidies and services, since in-kind support is considered to be better targeted, especially in light of the prevalence of alcoholism and its related abuse. Compensation for housing, utility, and transportation costs is larger in scope and coverage compared to direct cash assistance. Such subsidies rose due to the significant rise in rent, utility prices, and transportation fares. Local transportation subsidies are offered to all pensioners and school-children. Housing, utility, and telephone discounts at the rate of 50 percent are automatically provided to all war veterans, the disabled, and single pensioners. For households with per capita incomes below the subsistence minimum, such support can be granted by application.

The market price of a two-room apartment of 50 square meters in Krasnoiarsk is about $30,000, far beyond the means of most citizens. Most families cannot afford to rent an apartment from other than a municipality or from an employer. A privately paid monthly rent may be as high as $100, close to an average salary (although much lower than in Moscow or St. Petersburg). Meanwhile, no subsidies are provided to those who have to rent housing privately, which becomes the only available option to young families, migrants, and refugees.

Access to telephones, which are costly and present in only 40 percent of homes, is an issue for single elderly pensioners and the disabled, who may need to call for medical assistance. In response, the department of social protection provided 200 private telephones in 1994. It might be noted that in some rural areas of Krasnoiarskii Krai there may be neither a telephone available nor an ambulance to call.

Much of in-kind support goes to children. This includes subsidized kindergartens, school uniforms, school meals, and child recreation. Large and single-parent families have priority access. School meals, which are provided to almost 40 percent of children in school, represent the largest form of support. Discounts for kindergartens were available to less than 10 percent of children and school clothes to less than 5 percent, meaning that a large number of the poor were excluded. Purchase of a school uniform can be an even more serious problem than obtaining food since many rely on food they grow themselves.

Special attention is also paid to summer camps for children, in particular those who are orphans, disabled, or from large and single-parent families. These camps are especially in high demand given the long severe winters in these regions, including Krasnoiarsk. Summer holidays at "pioneer" country camps were traditionally the most common form of recreation available to practically all schoolchildren. Most of these camps were arranged by enterprises. However, since 1992 it has become rare for firms and governmental institutions to provide such services. In 1994, only 35 percent out of 200,000 schoolchildren had a chance to spend their holidays in summer camps.

In 1995, Krasnoiarskii Krai allocated 12.3 billion rubles ($2.7 million) from the regional budget to subsidize child recreation. A similar amount was also contributed to the program by the regional branch of the Social Insurance Fund, and another 800 million rubles by the branch of the Medical Insurance Fund. In addition, the krai Employment Fund provided 3 billion rubles for children of the unemployed, including summer jobs for schoolchildren. In 1995, a total of 80,000 schoolchildren in the krai participated in organized recreation.[12]

Other forms of in-kind assistance are scarce. In Krasnoiarsk in 1994, fewer than one in five below the poverty line received food vouchers, at an average cost of 9,000 rubles, barely enough for a kilo of meat. Less than 3 percent received pharmaceutical subsidies, with an average cost of about 14,000 rubles. Vouchers for clothing and other goods were provided to under 10 percent of the poverty population, at an average cost of about 11,000 rubles.

Notes

1. *Russian Economic Trends, Monthly Update*, various dates, London: London School of Economics, Center for Economic Performance.

2. Estimate obtained by applying quintile percentages discussed in the text to data on total real disposable money income of households (Goskomstat 1997, 79–81).

3. See World Bank (1995, 30). The Russian Longitudinal Monitoring Survey, which was undertaken by the World Bank in collaboration with Goskomstat, is based on a nationally representative sample of approximately 17,000 individuals in 6,500 households. The VCIOM data are based on a detailed survey of about 3,000 respondents.

4. Mikhalev (1996b) discusses the methodological issues in poverty measurement and presents numerous statistics.

5. *Izvestiia*, 14 February 1996.

6. Volkova and Migranova (1994) provide further evidence on extreme economic deprivation. For example, they report that average real consumption for the "very poor" in Iakutiia is only 36 percent of the subsistence minimum food basket (32).

7. Goskomstat 1997, 98 and 101.

8. Ibid., p. 227.

9. Krasnoiarskii Krai is the largest by area of the 89 constituent regions of the Russian Federation. It covers much of Siberia, extending 2,000 miles from the far north to the southern edge of Central and Eastern Siberia. About three million people live in Krasnoiarskii Krai. This study focuses on the city of Krasnoiarsk, for which the data are more complete, although occasional reference is made to krai data.

10. The author is grateful for the cooperation and assistance of Igor L. Pokrovsky, head of the Krasnoiarsk City Department of Social Protection, and Alexander D. Tugaev, head of the Krasnoiarskii Krai Department of Social Protection.

11. In 1997 the Ministry of Labor and Social Development was formed by the merger of the Ministry of Labor with the Ministry of Social Protection.

12. To a Western observer, in the face of massive poverty and breakdowns in education and health care, spending on child recreation may seem frivolous. However, most Russians live in cramped apartment complexes, and wholesome recreation continues to be regarded as essential to children's health and development. It was part of the package of basic benefits provided by the Soviet state, usually through industrial enterprises.

References

Gordon, Leonid. 1995. *Oblast vozmozhnogo, varianty sotsiialno-economicheskogo razvitiia Rossii i sposobnost rossiiskogo obshestva perenosit tiagotu perekhodnogo vremeni.* Moscow: The Russian-American Foundation for Trade Union Research and Education and the Institute of World Economy and International Relations.

Goskomstat. 1997. *Uroven zhizni naseleniia Rossii, 1997.* Moscow: State Committee of the Russian Federation on Statistics.

———. 1998. *Economic and Social Situation of Russia,* January-April 1998. Moscow: State Committee of the Russian Federation on Statistics.

Mikhalev, Vladimir. 1996a. "Social Security in Russia under Economic Transformation." *Europe-Asia Studies* 46(1): 5–25.

————. 1996b. *Poverty Alleviation in the Course of Transition: Policy Options for Russia*. Florence, Italy: European University Institute.

Mikhalev, Vladimir, and Nils Bjorksten. 1995. *Wage Formation During the Period of Economic Restructuring in the Russian Federation*. Paris: OECD.

Milanovic, Branko. 1998. *Income, Inequality and Poverty: Social Policy During the Transition from Planned to Market Economies*. Washington, DC: World Bank.

Mozhina, Marina A., and L. Ovcharova. 1994. *Izmeneniia v urovne zhizni i sotsiialnye problemy adaptatsii naseleniia k rinku*. Moscow: Institute for the Economic and Social Studies of the Population.

————. 1996. *New Factors of Poverty and Inequality in Russia*. Moscow: Institute for the Economic and Social Studies of the Population.

Mozhina, Marina A., et al. 1995. *Uroven zhizni gorodskogo naseleniia Rossii i sotsiialnye problemy reform*. Moscow: Institute for the Economic and Social Studies of the Population.

OECD. 1995. *Rossiiskaia Federatsiia, 1995*. Paris: OECD.

The Russian Centre for Public Opinion Research (VCIOM). Various dates. *Economicheskie i sotsiialnyie peremeny: Monitoring obshestvennogo mnenia*. Moscow: VCIOM.

Volkova, G. N., and L. A. Migranova. 1994. "Nekotorie problemy bednykh semei i putiikh sotsiialnoi zashiti. Po materialam sotsiiologicheskikh obsledovanii." *Uroven zhizni naseleniia regionov Rossii*, Bulletin No. 12. Moscow: The Russian Center for Living Standards Studies, Ministry of Labor.

World Bank. 1995. *Poverty in Russia: An Assessment*. Washington, DC.

PART THREE

Policy Agenda

17

Government Leadership

Marshall Pomer

As documented in Part Two, the failures of hasty liberalization-privatization-stabilization are all too evident. Western advisers are wont to put the blame on government interference in the economy. Part One argues that this diagnosis reflects the biases and limitations of the orthodox economic paradigm. The thrust of market reform is rightfully to replace government control with competition, but government leadership is indispensable.

Part Three of this volume recommends needed government actions. Government has broad responsibility to shape market institutions (e.g., rules of corporate governance, supervision of banks), regulate essential services when competition does not suffice (e.g., utilities), and meet social needs (e.g., health, education, and a social safety net). National and local governments remain the sole, or partial, owner of major enterprises. New institutions are proposed to oversee timely reorganization or liquidation of bankrupt enterprises, to manage government holdings appropriately, and to remedy deficiencies in corporate governance. Temporary renationalization may be necessary in the case of illegal or quasi-legal transfers of natural resources to owners oriented toward asset stripping. The chapters focus on aircraft and auto manufacturing, agriculture, the coal industry, real estate markets, energy use, and human capital.

Standing in the way of vigorous government leadership are two concerns that have dominated Western counsel. First is the need for fiscal responsibility. Second is the belief that industrial policy will invariably lead to kleptocracy. Both of these issues are addressed in this chapter.

The first section presents a model of aggregate demand that explores the affects of government policy on demand for Russian production. The model focuses on the openness of the economy and its criminalized character. Complementing Menshikov's analysis in Chapter 19, simulation results suggest that economic recovery would have been more prompt if government policy had put less emphasis on fiscal austerity.

The second section of the chapter considers the benefits and risks of industrial policy. Without benefit of a coherent industrial policy, Russian manufacturing has had to reorient itself away from military production and toward a depressed, consumer-driven economy. Properly conceived and executed, industrial policy would complement macroeconomic efforts to ensure adequate demand.

The potential benefits from activist government depend on the quality of government. Clarity of direction would help bolster competence and integrity. Accordingly, the final section proposes the creation of a development council to spearhead and coordinate economic reform.

Macroeconomics of an Open Criminalized Economy

The transitioning Russian economy has been characterized by a high degree of openness combined with pervasive criminality and corruption. While the severing of ties with the other republics of the Soviet Union meant loss of markets,[1] even more important has been the onrush of imports. At the same time GDP fell by 35 percent from 1991 to 1995, imports climbed 37 percent.[2] By 1996 more than half the goods sold in Russia were imported as manufacturing of consumer goods fell to less than half the 1990 level.

Pervasive criminality and corruption, combined with pathological features of the export sector, fostered unequal income distribution and capital flight, which in turn constricted demand. Exports of raw materials and minimally processed natural resources involving little labor input have grown rapidly but much of the export revenues have been transferred abroad as illegal capital flight.

Cuts in government spending, high real interest rates, and real appreciation of the exchange rate also depressed demand. Starting in 1995, the primary federal deficit was only about 1 or 2 percent of GDP, and the total deficit for regional and local government about 1 percent of GDP. By 1997 a large share of the interest payments went to foreign creditors.

While a higher degree of government austerity would have lowered inflation, the presence of inflation does not prove that demand was excessive. Inertial and cost-push components of inflation are especially important in transition economies (Cottarelli and Szapary 1998). Since inflationary expectations are themselves a cause of rising prices, the extreme inflation of 2,500 percent in 1992 ensured subsequent high inflation. Substantial disinflation did occur each year thereafter, which can be interpreted as evidence of weak aggregate demand. Moreover, in a period of massive reallocation of labor and other resources, the stickiness (rigidity) of prices and the occurrence of supply bottlenecks justify some inflation to facilitate realignment of relative prices.

The 1998 devaluation provides evidence that the highly depressed demand for Russian production was an avoidable concomitant of the transition process. Despite its crippling effects on the banking system and a surge in inflation, the devaluation boosted demand for Russian goods, thereby providing a basis for sustained advances in production.[3]

A Heuristic Model

We now consider a heuristic model that clarifies the macroeconomic consequences of an open criminalized economy. The model shows that criminal gains distort an income distribution that is already highly unequal due to a low wage share. The distribution of income affects aggregate demand because of differing propensities to consume, invest, import, and send funds abroad in the form of illegal capital flight. Inflation is endogenous (determined by the model) while other monetary factors, namely the real exchange rate and the real interest rate, are exogenous (determined outside the model). Parameters are specified not only for tax rates and government spending but also for the criminal diversion of government funds. For convenience, the equations in the appendix are linear so that the demand multiplier can be derived analytically.[4]

A criminal elite is distinguished as one of three basic "classes" of income recipients. The other two classes are ordinary households and legitimate businesses. Payments are routinely made by businesses to criminal organizations for a "roof" to shield them from further extortion. Bribery of government officials, the police, and even the courts is also prevalent.

National income is subdivided into three shares: criminal gains; wages and salaries; and profits, rents, and interest income. For simplicity, cyclical variation is ignored, and the income shares are proportional to national income net of indirect taxes. Net interest is assumed to be zero, and depreciation is exogenous. The income shares are determined separately for the export sector to reflect a lower wage share and a higher rate of capital flight.

Government spending has five exogenous components: purchases of goods and services, transfers to businesses, transfers to households, interest payments to Russians, and interest payments to foreigners. The criminal elite receives government funds by embezzlement, which is assumed proportional to government purchases and transfer payments.[5] Taxation rates are defined for wages, profits, indirect sales and value-added taxes, and import and export duties. To specify compliance for each tax, the model includes parameters for the rates at which different types of income are reported.[6]

Capital flight is defined here as acquisition of foreign financial assets by Russian citizens and firms.[7] The rates of capital flight are highest for criminal gains and unreported profits. Underinvoicing of exports to hide profits from the export of Russian mineral wealth is a major problem. For ordinary households, capital flight is low.[8]

The income distribution is affected by extortion, bribery, and criminal diversion of government funds. Criminal diversion of government funds intended for pensions and poverty relief lowers the income share of ordinary households, while diversion of subsidies reduces business income. Extortion and bribery reduce the income shares of both households and businesses.

"Spendable income" consists of income remaining after subtracting taxes, transfer payments, and capital flight. The propensity to consume is highest for spendable income of ordinary households. Investment is a function of business income (including depreciation) and, to a lesser degree, criminal gains. The real interest rate also has an influence. Imports are affected by each category of spendable income as well as by import tariffs and world prices on imports. Exports are treated as exogenous.

Compared with government spending and other exogenous expenditures, increases in exports have a relatively weak effect on aggregate demand. This is due to a low income share for wages and salaries and a high rate of capital flight for unreported business income. Thus exports have a separate multiplier (equation 32).[9]

The inflation equation determines the division of demand increases between higher output and higher prices. The model recognizes three factors. First is the degree of slack in the economy as indicated by the gap between actual and potential GDP measured in real terms. Potential GDP is conceived of as the noninflationary, full-employment level of output.[10] The second factor is change in the real exchange rate, a critical cost-push factor given the high dependence on imports.[11] The third factor is inflationary inertia.

In the specification of the inflation equation, it is assumed that there is substantial unused productive capacity. The capital stock, however, was primarily formed in the Soviet era and reflects an orientation toward the military rather than consumers, a price structure that drastically undervalued energy inputs, and out-of-date technology. Many proponents of shock therapy (e.g., Pekka 1998) and some advocates of gradualism (e.g., Wasow

1996) claim that the capital stock is largely "worthless." The positive effects of the 1998 devaluation show that this view is exaggerated. Moreover, expansion of aggregate demand spurs investment. In any case, the need for investment to modernize and increase productive capacity is a major rationale for industrial policy, which is discussed below.

Simulation Analysis

Following is a summary of simulation results using the model presented in the appendix. The model was calibrated to conditions present in Russia in 1997 (Pomer 2000).[12] The simulations provide a basis for analyzing the macroeconomic consequences of critical features of the Russian economy: pervasive criminal activity, openness to trade and capital flows, and cost-push inflation. Though they should not be regarded as a basis for precise predictions, the simulation results suggest that performance of the economy in 1997 would have been even less favorable if tax rates had been raised and more favorable if a moderate devaluation had been implemented.

In 1993, exports of goods, primarily raw materials, equaled about one-third of GDP. The dollar value of these exports climbed almost 50 percent over the next three years, while real GDP over this period contracted about 20 percent. As a consequence of the low export multiplier, real growth declined by one-quarter of 1 percent for each percentage point increase in exports accompanied by a comparable cut in government purchases.

Between 1993 and 1997, the dollar value of imported goods rose by two thirds. Accordingly, both multipliers (for exports and for government or other exogenous spending) were depressed due to high import propensities. A one-fifth reduction in the import propensities elevates the export multiplier from 1.20 to 1.28 and the other multiplier from 1.55 to 1.69.

The simulations also show that criminal activity undermines aggregate demand. With a decline in criminal gains, capital flight is reduced and the increase in spendable income for businesses is double that of households. In the simulations, the percentage increase in criminal gains approximately equals the percentage decrease in nominal demand.

Tax evasion, an important factor in capital flight, has a small positive effect on the multipliers. Under the assumption that all income, excluding criminal gains, is reported, the export multiplier is virtually unchanged at 1.19 and the other multiplier is reduced to 1.49 (versus 1.20 and 1.55). A reduction in tax evasion of 10 percent, which lowers nominal demand only about 1 percent, reduces the budget deficit by 1 percentage point.

The model of inflation recognizes cost-push factors and inflationary inertia. As a result, the simulations support the thesis that increased nominal demand will result in higher output even if there is substantial inflation. Thus, though helpful in attracting foreign investment in government debt, the policy of guaranteeing a high exchange rate for the ruble, coupled with high interest rates, can be faulted for suppressing aggregate demand.

A simulation was run to assess what might have happened in 1997 if there had been a 35-percent nominal devaluation accompanied by a 10-percent cut in interest rates.[13] Rather than the actual sharp drop in inflation from 44 percent to 14 percent, inflation declined to 38 percent, implying real devaluation of 10 percent. The simulation projected a 5-percent real increase in GDP rather than the less than 1-percent growth that actually occurred.

Industrial Policy: Potential and Pitfalls

While the adequacy of aggregate demand is a macroeconomic issue, lack of demand is experienced on a sector-by-sector basis. Since support for a faltering sector may be critical for maintaining demand in other sectors, recovery and growth may require targeted efforts to promote demand.

Pressure for government support for sectors that are deemed to have particular social or strategic significance—industrial policy—is strong in any country and has been especially intense in transitioning Russia.[14] The closings of large Soviet- era enterprises has meant the loss of the economic bases of entire communities, making government support a political imperative. The demand shocks from a collapsed enterprise, moreover, go beyond the community immediately affected due to cancelled input purchases and the loss of employment income. Idle human and physical capital not only implies loss of potential output but also causes deterioration of productive capability. A more affirmative rationale for industrial policy is that accumulation of capital and technological progress are concentrated in particular sectors, and these sectors are unlikely to develop rapidly without government encouragement (Chenery et al. 1986).

Japan and Southeast Asia relied on comprehensive industrial policy to achieve rapid, egalitarian growth (see Chapter 8).[15] Their development programs included protection of domestic markets and investment subsidies.[16] In general, government support has been conditional on export performance and has been tapered over time. Orientation toward exports ensured competitive exposure to the latest technology and forced attention to product quality.[17, 18]

After first discussing the applicability of tariff protection and development loans to Russia, this section examines two pivotal industries, aircraft and automobile manufacturing, which could provide well-paid jobs for many of the unemployed and underemployed skilled workers and engineers. Revival of these industries would stimulate the rest of the economy because of both specific linkages with suppliers and general effects on domestic purchasing power (Auty 1994).[19]

No less important than industry-specific support is government action to create a favorable economic context for industry in general.[20] The importance of physical infrastructure is most obvious. For example, since natural resources and many large plants are in remote locations, an effective industrial policy will not be possible unless transport costs are stable and economical.

Tariffs

Protection from foreign competition has played a role in the development of virtually all economies. During transition in Russia, meaningful import protection on a selective and temporary basis would have facilitated adjustment of domestic industry[21] while encouraging foreign multinationals to produce in Russia to gain access to protected markets.[22] In addition, tariffs bolster government finance. High taxes on imported luxuries would redistribute some of the disproportionate, often unlawful, gains of those able to indulge in lavish consumption.

Five months after the January 1992 removal of trade barriers, import tariffs were reintroduced. The degree of tariff protection, however, was modest. Official tariff rates averaged only about 15 percent. With compliance low, the average effective import duty on manufactured goods was merely 5 percent. Thus despite the high volume of imports, import duties were less than 1 percent of GDP.[23]

More significant in restraining foreign imports in the early 1990s was the drastic deterioration in the real exchange rate. This source of protection, however, dissipated by the mid-1990s when the real exchange rate appreciated as part of the aggressive program of high interest rates and government borrowing from abroad to eliminate inflation. As a consequence of the August 1998 financial collapse, the real value of the ruble fell approximately 50 percent. Equivalent to establishing a 100-percent tariff on all imports, the ruble devaluation substantially negates the case for import tariffs.

More recently, with tighter control over capital flight and a ballooning trade surplus, the nominal exchange rate has been stable despite moderately high inflation. If the real exchange rate continues to rise, tariffs will again be justified while industry struggles to become internationally competitive.

A rational program would have low tax rates on high-tech capital equipment and high rates on consumer luxuries.[24] Continued tariff protection for particular industries should be conditional on improvements in productivity, product quality, growth, profitability, and export performance. Sharp price rises or supply reductions would trigger tariff reductions.

Compliance is a major challenge. For example, it may be necessary to have a computerized registry of identification numbers for foreign cars to ensure that import duties are paid. Compliance requires not only adequate salaries for customs officials but also vigilance at the highest levels.

Tariff hikes could jeopardize Russia's efforts to join the World Trade Organization and even initiate a destructive cycle of retaliatory increases. If the real exchange rate appreciates, however, Russia should be able to increase tariffs without inciting retaliation. In justifying rate increases, Russia can point to the stunning rate of penetration of foreign imports, its own role as supplier of energy and raw materials, and Western barriers to Russian exports.

Development Loans

Government lending to Russian industry has been problematic. Much of the central bank's credits to industry from 1992 to 1995 was corruptly diverted, in part due to malfeasance of the private banks that distributed the funds (Granville 1995). Perhaps half of the subsidies to the coal industry were simply stolen (Chapter 22). Apart from corruption, government loans to business can forestall dismissal of surplus employees and closure of uneconomic enterprises. In lieu of assistance to faltering enterprises, government-sponsored severance packages, including retraining and relocation, do not interfere with market discipline. In addition, such aid lowers resistance to restructuring and facilitates labor mobility.

Notwithstanding the hazards, government-sponsored development loans can promote long-term investments in more efficient production and improved products.[25] Also important for economic growth are loans for marketing and export finance.[26]

Stringent criteria are needed to discourage support for nonviable enterprises. Obligation to repay, assuming it is enforced, would pressure enterprises to use funds responsibly. Following the East Asian model, government support should also be guided by a "strategic vision" that emphasizes technological development and support should be tapered over time so that maturing enterprises are exposed to international competition (Auty 1994, Lall 1997).

Rather than lending directly, a development bank could subsidize interest payments on qualifying loans made by private banks. An important advantage of interest subsidies is that loans would require approval of banks as independent third-parties. As stakeholders in the loans, banks would be motivated to select borrowers wisely. Government support would not eliminate the role of private banks in overseeing managerial performance (Aoki and Kim 1995).

To ensure cooperation of private banks, the central bank could make bank licenses contingent on participation in the program of development loans, with the required amount of loans increasing gradually. Also, full or partial deposit insurance could be instituted for banks that combine strong balance sheets with proven records as providers of development loans. The development loan program could thereby help the banking system evolve into a genuine intermediary between savings and real investment.

Aircraft Industry

The Russian aircraft industry well illustrates the potential of industrial policy. Once a leader in aviation technology, the Soviet Union was the first to use jet aircraft for passenger service. Soviet technology, however, was oriented toward the military, and fuel efficiency was not a real concern. Unable to meet the competition of the likes of Boeing and Airbus,[27] manufacturing has virtually collapsed. Civilian sales are minimal, and the Russian air force has ceased procurement, though some military planes are being manufactured for export.[28]

The aircraft industry could provide large numbers of well-paid jobs for skilled workers and engineers. Indeed, if productive capacity were fully utilized, Russia would have the largest aircraft industry in the world. Its recovery would stimulate the economy because of linkages with suppliers and the effects on domestic purchasing power. Failure to redevelop aircraft manufacturing would create a drain on foreign exchange due to the need to rely on imported aircraft.

Although air transport has dropped dramatically since 1992, the recent trend is upward.[29] Also, the aging of the fuel-inefficient fleet, the need to reduce maintenance costs, and the priority of flight safety will create demand for new planes. The nation's immense proportions, lack of highways, and single-hub railway system suggest strong demand in the long run (Nikoulichev 1997).

To overcome the obstacles of technology and finance, Ilyushin Aviation Complex designed a 350-seat, wide-body jetliner using engines made by United Technology (Il-96M/T). The U.S. Export–Import Bank agreed to lend $1 billion to finance an initial fleet of 20 of these planes. Faced with the possibility of losing customers not only in Russia but also worldwide, Boeing pressured the U.S. Congress and the Clinton administration to cancel the loan. A compromise was achieved whereby the Export–Import Bank agreed that this would be the last time it financed the use of American engines on Russian planes. Moreover, the Clinton administration forced the Russian government to suspend, at least temporarily, its 30-percent tariff on imported aircraft.[30]

The tariff suspension resulted in the sale of ten Boeing 737–400 twinjets to Aeroflot in April 1997. An American bank associated with Boeing provided financing. As one of the concessions previously agreed upon to secure the Export–Import loan discussed above, Russia guaranteed the Western lender that it would be able to repossess the Boeings if Aeroflot defaulted. Suggestive of a colonial role, in the same month Boeing signed a contract to purchase 2.4 thousand tons of Russian-produced titanium ingots for use in manufacturing American-made planes.[31]

To enable Russian airlines to finance the purchase of Russian-made planes, government could temporarily subsidize interest payments on leases of Russian aircraft. An appropriate legal framework is needed to establish leasing businesses, however. Export credits could be used to promote foreign sales of Russian aircraft, a mechanism widely used outside Russia. With emphasis on the transfer of technology to Russian soil, government should foster continued cooperation with foreign companies to develop better engines.

While government help could revive the aircraft industry, such assistance might cause the industry to delay change. For example, current airplane certification procedures allow design bureaus (e.g., Ilyushin, Tupolev, and Yakovlev) to obstruct modernization efforts of aircraft manufacturers (e.g.,

Voronezh, Samara, and Ulyanovsk).[32] Another legacy of the former system of state planning is the lack of multiple sources for aircraft components. For both reasons, "supplemental type certificates (STCs)," as used in the West, are needed to promote competition by allowing independent manufacturers to supply parts.

Automobile Industry

In countries with large automobile industries, industry success has not been the result of private initiative alone. The latecomers have depended on stiff protection from foreign competition. Japan and Korea virtually prohibited purchases of foreign-made autos (Wade 1990). Brazil allowed its citizenry to buy cars from foreign manufacturers only if they were produced in Brazilian plants (Shapiro 1991).[33] China has also been aggressive in requiring foreign automobile companies to introduce modern technology as a condition of selling in the Chinese market (Mann 1997).

Under current conditions in transitioning economies, major joint ventures will require government support and protection. Only time will tell whether the costs of intervention, including the risk of corruption and higher prices for imported goods, will be justified by higher economic growth.

Efforts to revive Ukraine's automobile industry provide cautionary lessons. With the bulk of its facilities in or near the central Ukrainian city of Zaporozhe, AvtoZAZ, the country's only auto producer, produced 150,000 cars in 1992. The breakup of the Soviet Union led to supply bottlenecks that interfered with production. In addition, the cars were low in quality and lost much of their demand once consumers were able to buy low-priced used cars from the West. By 1996 production dwindled to fewer than 6,000 cars.

Rather than let AvtoZAZ become defunct, the Ukrainian government conferred extraordinary privileges to entice South Korea's Daewoo Corporation to oversee and finance the restructuring of this giant enterprise. The intent was not only to rescue AvtoZAZ but also to stimulate other Ukrainian industries. The plan was eventually to build automobiles with 90-percent domestic content, compared with less than 50-percent during the Soviet era.

The joint venture agreement between Daewoo and AvtoZAZ originally anticipated annual production of 80,000 cars in 1997 and 230,000 within seven years. Daewoo committed to providing $1.3 billion in investment over seven or eight years, including an initial contribution of $250 million toward working capital. This commitment represents by far the largest foreign investment in Ukraine; total foreign direct investment from 1992 through 1997 totaled only $1.5 billion.

The Ukrainian government provided the joint venture both tax preferences and protective trade restrictions. For ten years, taxes on profits were to be reduced, and import tariffs on spare parts eliminated. Sharp restrictions were to be placed on imports of cars more than five years old. In addition to these favors, the government has forgiven AvtoZAZ an $80 million debt, and land owned by the joint venture has tax-free status.

The joint venture was assailed on many fronts. First, the 1998 economic crisis largely eliminated potential middle-class buyers. Second, an active shadow economy evaded restrictions on used cars. Also, amidst allegations of payoffs and a lack of transparency, it is not publicly known whether Daewoo lived up to its financial commitments.[34] In all of 1998, Daewoo produced only 24,000 cars and sold barely 11,000. Production was suspended altogether in February 1999.[35] Finally, the measures to support the auto industry alienated the IMF and the World Bank, and the European Union threatened to prevent Ukraine from joining the World Trade Organization.[36]

These results are sobering. It is in the self-interest of the foreign partner to use a joint venture agreement as a cover for expanding imports of its own products. The profits from sale of these imports, moreover, often go untaxed because of concessions or creative transfer pricing. Daewoo-AvtoZAZ, for example, assembled kits from Korea in a port near Odessa with minimal input of Ukrainian labor and then sold these vehicles at high margins in the protected Ukrainian market.

Foreign partners, as well as domestic manufacturers, that benefit from concessions must be held responsible to fulfill their commitments. Government should suspend concessions and exercise sanctions if commitments are not fulfilled, whether the beneficiaries are international multinationals or home-grown "crony capitalists." Also, government agreements with foreign entities to facilitate transfer of technology are important. To ensure that national interests are not compromised, transparency and government vigilance are crucial.

Quality of Government

If applied by an inept and corrupt government, industrial policy can lead to national insolvency and hyperinflation. Support for special interests erodes market discipline and undermines economic efficiency, especially if combined with irrational government controls.

In the 1990s the Russian government was co-opted by a corrupt elite (Chapters 14 and 15). Many government officials enriched themselves in alliance with organized crime and the Russian oligarchs. Concern persists over partisan forces in Putin's administration and the pressure to serve Western interests.

Transparency of government requires an active free press and democratic elections. Public understanding and discussion of the policy agenda are helpful in giving direction to and gaining support for needed reforms. Clear goals and objectives provide a basis for accountability and the assessment of competence and integrity. Without monitoring of costs and results there can be no accountability. Whenever government supports private interests, mechanisms are needed to determine whether continued assistance is justified. If there is evidence of abuse, appropriate sanctions should be imposed. In general, policies should promote competition and minimize bureaucratic discretion.

Other chapters of Part Three propose new government institutions to achieve these objectives, including restructuring agencies (Chapter 18) and government-managed public wealth funds (Chapter 25). Discussed next is the creation of a new government agency to expedite economic reform.

Development Council

The most successful modernizing economies have relied on some form of development council to fortify government leadership (Amsden et al. 1994, chapter 8; Wade 1990, chapter 7). Such an institution would enhance Russian capacity to design, implement, and monitor economic policies from the perspective of the national interest.[37] The council would have overall responsibility for improving the business environment in general and strengthening critical industries that require temporary government support to achieve their potential.

A development council would be a potent symbol of renewal, countering a defeatist presumption that the Russian government lacks direction and capability. The head of the council, if not the Russian president or prime minister, would be a top official charged with adding momentum to economic reform. Council members would include the heads of key economic ministries (Economy, Finance, Trade, and Industry), the chair of the central bank, and legislative leaders. A staff of well-paid professionals would support the council.

Biweekly meetings would ensure that bureaucratic impediments are removed and that abuses are addressed promptly. The full range of economic issues would be addressed, including institutions of corporate governance, availability of finance, the social safety net, and liquidation of unprofitable enterprises. Monitoring of industry, in conjunction with strict reporting requirements, is necessary to stem corruption and ensure that government support does not destroy market discipline and abet capital flight. Accelerating successful programs and terminating others, the development council would serve as a watchdog to eliminate waste and corruption.

Conclusion

Western counsel has emphasized deficit reduction and the ill effects of government assistance to faltering enterprises. While government has buttressed many enterprises that should be liquidated, preoccupation with government austerity is ill-advised. Prior to the August 1998 devaluation, the narrow focus on eliminating inflation, which included commitment to an overvalued ruble, undermined aggregate demand. Moreover, demand for Russian goods and the financing of real investment have been jeopardized by capital flight associated with criminalization and export of natural resources. The potential for Russian prosperity to reduce capital flight is moot if ongoing capital flight prevents such prosperity.

On the one hand, industrial policy can enhance the responsiveness of investment to increases in aggregate demand. On the other hand, government intervention may artificially prolong the life of politically protected enterprises. A well-designed program of development loans would speed reallocation of resources, reduce dependence on the export of natural resources, and establish the basis for a modern, high-tech economy.

There should be no question that government maintain an adequate level of aggregate demand for Russian products, though the choice of policy depends on analysis of inflation, a difficult task. It is less certain that government should try to spur growth and promote development of particular sectors. Whether such actions help or hinder the essential goal of economic transition—the introduction of market forces and market discipline—depends on government capability.

Appendix:

A Heuristic Macroeconomic Model
of a Criminalized Economy in Transition Shock

National Income Accounting with Illegal Income

National income, measured in current prices, is decomposed into three categories:

W = wages and salaries;

B = illegal income (extortion, bribery, and other forms of "payments for protection" incident to the production and sale of goods and services); and

P = profits and other income, including corporate and entrepreneurial net income and rents.

GDP (Y) is divided into domestic final sales (Y_D) and exports (X):

$$Y_D = Y - X. \tag{1}$$

The three income categories (W, B, and P) as well as depreciation (D) and indirect taxes (TI) are subdivided accordingly. Thus, in accordance with national income and product accounting,

$$
\begin{aligned}
NI &= Y - TI - D \\
&= Y_D + X - TI_D - TI_X - D_D - D_X \\
&= W + B + P \\
&= W_D + W_X + B_D + B_X + P_D + P_X.
\end{aligned}
\tag{2}
$$

The six income shares are assumed to be proportional to final expenditure net of indirect taxes. Profits and depreciation are combined.

$$W_D = s_{WD} (Y_D - TI_D) \tag{3}$$
$$W_X = s_{WX} (X - TI_X) \tag{4}$$
$$B_D = s_{BD} (Y_D - TI_D) \tag{5}$$
$$B_X = s_{BX} (X - TI_X) \tag{6}$$
$$P_D + D_D = (1 - s_{WD} - s_{BD}) (Y_D - TI_D) \tag{7}$$
$$P_X + D_X = (1 - s_{WX} - s_{BX}) (X - TI_X). \tag{8}$$

Government Finance, Tax Evasion, and Criminal Diversion

Government expenditures, G_T, are divided into five components, each of which is regarded as exogenous:

$$G_T = G + G_P + G_W + G_{IR} + G_{IF}, \tag{9}$$

where

G = funds allocated for goods and services (public investment in and maintenance of economic infrastructure; education, health care, environment, sanitation; government operations, including legislative expenses, foreign policy, military, police, courts, and regulation);

G_P = subsidies to business (whether to bailout the weak, to provide temporary support to the ailing, or to encourage investment by the strong);

G_W = funds allocated for pensions and poverty relief;

G_{IR} = government interest payments to Russians; and

G_{IF} = government interest payments to foreigners.

Each of these variables is regarded as exogenous. An endogenous variable G_B is defined to take into account criminal diversion of funds due to malfeasance.

$$G_B = s_{BG} G + s_{BGP} G_P + s_{BGW} G_W. \tag{10}$$

Tax rates are defined for wages (t_W), profits from exports (t_{PX}), other profits (t_{PD}), import revenues (t_M), export revenues (t_X), and other indirect taxes (t_D). The corresponding rates of tax compliance are: r_W, r_{PX}, r_{PD}, r_M, r_X, and r_D. (For simplicity, it is assumed that interest paid to Russians on the government debt is taxed at rate t_{PD} at full compliance.) Thus

$$
\begin{aligned}
T_W &= r_W t_W W & (11) \\
T_P &= t_{PD} (r_{PD} P_D + G_{IR}) + r_{PX} t_{PX} P_X & (12) \\
T_M &= r_M t_M M & (13) \\
TI_X &= r_X t_X X & (14) \\
TI_D &= r_D t_D Y_D . & (15)
\end{aligned}
$$

Capital Flight

Capital flight is high for unreported income and criminal gains. Accordingly, different rates of capital flight are specified for six income categories: (1) reported ordinary household income, including government transfers, net of taxes (q_W); (2) unreported ordinary household income (q_W'); (3) illegal income and criminally diverted government funds (q_B); (4) reported business profits and depreciation allowances, including government transfers, net of taxes (q_P); (5) unreported business profits (including estimated depreciation) for export sector (q_{PX}'); and (6) other unreported business profits (including estimated depreciation) (q_{PD}'). The corresponding amounts of capital flight are:

$$F_W = q_W [r_W(1 - t_W)W + (1-s_{BGW})G_W] \tag{16}$$

$$F_W' = q_W' (1 - r_W)W \tag{17}$$

$$F_B = q_B (B + G_B) \tag{18}$$

$$F_P = q_P \{ r_{PX} (1-t_{PX}) (P_X + D_X)$$
$$+ r_{PD} (1 - t_{PD}) [(P_D + D_D) + G_{IR}] \} \tag{19}$$

$$F_{PX}' = q_{PX}' (1 - r_{PX}) (P_X + D_X) \tag{20}$$

$$F_{PD}' = q_{PD}' (1 - r_{PD}) (P_D + D_D). \tag{21}$$

Spending Functions

For each of three categories of income recipients, a spendable income variable is defined. Spendable income includes depreciation and government transfers and is net of direct taxes and capital flight.

$$W^* = W + G_W (1-s_{BGW}) - T_W - F_W - F_W' \tag{22}$$

$$B^* = B + G_B - F_B \tag{23}$$

$$P^* = P + D + G_P(1-s_{BGP}) + G_{IR} - T_P - F_P - F_{PX}' - F_{PD}'. \tag{24}$$

With these three variables as arguments, spending functions are defined for consumption C, gross investment I, and imports M. Government spending G and exports X are exogenous.

$$Y = C + I + (1-s_{BG})G + X - M \tag{25}$$

$$C = a + bW^* + b'P^* + b''B^* \tag{26}$$

$$I = c + d'P^* + d''B^* - eR, \tag{27}$$

where R is the real interest rate.

$$M = g + mW^* + m'P^* + m''B^* + n E - n't_M - n''WP, \qquad (28)$$

where E (dollars/real ruble) is the real exchange rate, t_M is the average tax rate on imports, and WP is an index of world prices for Russian imports.

Multipliers

The multiplier for exogenous expenditure other than exports is

$$\text{mult}^{-1} = 1 - (1 - r_D t_D) [s_{WD} (b - m)(1 - Z_W)$$
$$+ s_{PD}(b' + d' - m')(1 - Z_{PD}) + s_{BD}(b'' + d'' - m'')(1 - q_B)] \qquad (29)$$

where

$$Z_W = r_W t_W + q_W rw (1 - t_W) + q_W'(1 - r_W) \qquad (30)$$
$$Z_{PD} = r_{PD} t_{PD} + q_P r_{PD} (1 - t_{PD}) + q_{PD}'(1 - r_{PD}). \qquad (31)$$

The export multiplier is

$$\text{mult}_X = 1 + \lambda \text{ mult} \qquad (32)$$

where

$$\lambda = (1 - r_X t_X) [s_{WX} (b-m) (1 - Z_W)$$
$$+ s_{PX} (b' + d' - m')(1 - Z_{PX}) + s_{BX} (b'' + d'' - m'')(1 - q_B)] \qquad (33)$$

and

$$Z_{PX} = r_{PX} t_{PX} + q_P r_{PX} (1 - t_{PX}) + q_{PX}' (1 - r_{PX}). \qquad (34)$$

Inflation

$$\text{INF} = f[\text{INF}_{-1}, (\text{Real } Y - Y^*) / Y^*, (E - E_{-1}) / E_{-1}] \qquad (35)$$

INF_{-1} is prior inflation. In the second argument, aggregate demand, measured by GDP in real terms, is compared with the noninflationary, full-employment level of real GDP. The derivative is positive with respect to the first two arguments and negative with respect to the third. The third argument embodies the importance of change in the exchange rate as a cost-push factor.

Notes

1. See Chapter 20 by Grinberg and the discussion of "Macroeconomic Conditions" in Chapter 1.

2. Unfortunately for economic growth, only one-quarter of imports in 1995 were for machinery and equipment, compared with almost half in 1990. These and other data given in this chapter may also be found in the Statistical Appendix.

3. Wellisz (1997) argues that a consistently undervalued zloty, while adding to inflation, was key to strong economic growth in Poland.

4. Given linear functional forms and nominal variables, when inflation is substantial it is necessary to rescale the constant terms.

5. The model could be expanded to address the related problem of wasteful and inefficient government spending.

6. Tax arrears, much of which are never paid, can be regarded as a mechanism of tax evasion.

7. No attempt is made to distinguish capital outflows attributable to normal diversification. It should be noted that capital flight associated with tax evasion causes loss of future taxation on the gains from the invested flight capital.

8. This does not apply when there is a run on the ruble, as in 1998.

9. The multipliers ignore the possibility that increased demand for money may elevate the real interest rate and thereby dampen investment. Such an effect, however, is likely to be weak in Russia because financial intermediation is underdeveloped. Moreover, the "acceleration effect," whereby economic growth shifts the investment function upward, is not embodied in the multipliers.

10. A more developed model would make potential output endogenous and relate demand and potential output on a disaggregated basis.

11. Increased monopolization and elimination of alternative sources of supply as a result of bankruptcies are cost-push factors not included in the model.

12. The baseline simulation for 1997 implies $33.2 billion of capital flight, which is in the upper range of conventional estimates. For example, the Bureau of Economic Analysis in Moscow has recommended summing three categories from the balance of payments data provided by the Central Bank of Russia: (1) change in the stock of non-repatriated export proceeds and non-repatriated

import advances; (2) commercial credits and advances extended (trade credits from the non-bank private sector); and (3) net errors and omissions. Using this method, capital flight for 1997 was about $27 billion.

13. The model could be extended to include two other important benefits from devaluation. First, devaluation is likely to reduce capital flight since it reduces the incentive to speculate against the domestic currency. Second, devaluation increases export demand for Russian manufacturing. Drawbacks include increased cost of debt payments denominated in hard currency and higher prices for intermediate and capital goods.

14. The discussion here focuses on the federal government. Some local governments restricted trade with other parts of Russia to shield local producers and to ensure agricultural supplies. Such actions threaten the national economy of Russia as a whole.

15. Vogel (1991) discusses the role of the Japanese model in providing inspiration to other East Asian economies. In a comprehensive report on East Asia, the World Bank (1993) acknowledged that industrial policy was key to the "East Asian Miracle." However, the report argued that macroeconomic stability and investment in human capital mattered more, and it warned that most countries lack governmental capacity to apply industrial policy.

16. In the details, each country went its own way, in particular with regard to selectivity in encouraging and limiting foreign direct investment (Aoki et al. 1998, Lall 1997). Typically on an industry-by-industry basis, each country had a well-defined, vigorously implemented, and consistent policy with regard to encouraging, screening, or rejecting foreign direct investment. But the degree and nature of openness to foreign investment differed radically.

17. China provides another contrasting model. Having had their self-contained civilization overwhelmed by Western intrusion culminating in the Opium Wars, the Chinese have been far less compliant than the Russians to external demands. Mann (1997), illustrating the aggressive industrial policies in China, provides a graphic account of conflict between the assertive Chinese government and the foreign partner in an automotive joint venture.

18. The Asian financial crisis of 1997–1998 underscores the need to strictly oversee banks that are conduits for foreign capital. Abrupt reversal of massive foreign capital inflows was compounded by austerity measures imposed by the IMF (Feldstein 1998; see also Chapter 8).

19. Economists in the Russian Academy of Sciences have long protested the lack of a well-developed industrial policy (RAS 1997).

20. Adams and Klein (1983) discuss the full spectrum of industrial policy, both general and industry-specific, including: programs to disseminate technology, government action to guarantee the prices and supplies of critical inputs, quality control inspection of standardized exports, export promotion fairs, and other assistance with international marketing. See also Pomer (1999, 1998).

21. See Ocampo and Taylor (1998) and Rodrik (1995) for theoretical analysis of the conflict between openness and economic development. McKinnon (1993) forcefully supports tariffs to ease integration of formerly socialist countries into the world economy.

22. This is well illustrated by the building of plants in the United States by Japanese and German auto companies to circumvent tariffs and import quotas (Gordon 1995).

23. This paragraph is based on Appendix 6, Effective and Nominal Tariffs, RECEP (1997). For imported manufactured goods in 1995, they determined that the average nominal duty was 12 percent and the average effective duty 4.2 percent. More recently, the State Customs Committee reported that the overall trade-weighted tariff, unadjusted for compliance, was 13.4 percent (John Helmer, *Journal of Commerce*, 6/29/98). Recent statistics on customs revenues indicate compliance is improving, and thus the effective duty may have risen.

24. Oreshkin et al. (1997) call for analysis of the effects of tariff policies on the domestic market as well as on the costs of modernization in Russian industry. Trade policy since 1992 has been preoccupied with exchange rates and taxation of exports. For discussion of trade policy in relation to the European Union, see Welfens (2000).

25. As discussed in Part One, the rudimentary theoretical model that helped rationalize shock therapy does not take account of external finance. Simple extensions assume perfect capital markets, whereby any firm with opportunity to make a productive investment is able to borrow from financial institutions or issue corporate securities. Trade credit is another external source of funds, though not a viable basis for investment. While it is normal to obtain some credit from suppliers and extend credit to customers, escalation of trade credit in Russia (the "arrears crisis") has eroded market discipline.

26. There has been a tendency to look to the West for finance. However, substantial Western investment is unlikely until there is evidence of stable growth. Encouraging Western investors to take full or partial ownership may be vital for transfer of technology and managerial expertise as well as for establishing an adequate distribution network.

27. Boeing, as well as Airbus, benefits from substantial state support (Krugman and Obstfeld 1997, 289–293).

28. According to data supplied by Interfax, 282 Russian aircraft were sold in 1992 and only 31 in 1995 and 12 in 1996. The Ministry of Economy has reported that the industry, with a capacity to produce 650 planes, in 1996 manufactured only five aircraft for Russian airlines (Nikoulichev 1997).

29. Data furnished by Henrik Konarkowski, Director of Konversult, a consulting firm that specializes in the Russian aviation market. (According to Konarkowski, deliveries of Russian planes to Russian airlines for the years 1992 to 1997 were 199, 119, 11, 9, 8 and 7, respectively.)

30. John Mintz's report in the *Washington Post* (February 2, 1996) provides details. The senior vice president for planning and international development at Boeing, Lawrence Clarkson, explained, "We obviously must be concerned over the long term that the Russian aircraft industry could become a competitor."

31. Boeing Press Release, Seattle, April 30, 1997.

32. In a comment appearing in "Johnson's Russia List" on the Internet (June 18, 1998), Jeffrey Barrie referred to this problem as the "supreme illogicality" in the Russian aviation industry. A senior consultant to the Price Waterhouse Aviation Group, Barrie has followed the Russian aviation industry for 14 years.

33. Brazil now produces about two million cars annually. Auto makers are expected to invest $20 billion in Brazil over the period 1996–2000 (*Wall Street Journal*, May 14, 1998, p. A18).

34. Based on interviews at the AvtoZAZ headquarters in Zaporozhe on April 24, 1998 with Nikolai Koval, Deputy General Director, and Alex Rizhenko, Department of Foreign Affairs; and the *Moscow Times* (3/28/98, 3/14/98, 3/13/98, 3/11/98, 2/17/98, 1/22/98, 9/4/97, 5/7/97, 4/25/97, 4/10/97, 1/9/97, 10/18/96, 7/31/96, 2/17/94).

35. Stefan Korshak (*RFE/RL*, May 5, 1998) examines constraints on Daewoo as a consequence of the Korean financial crisis.

36. Jaroslav Koshiw (*Kiev Post*, January 15, 1999, and March 4, 1999).

37. The Japanese Ministry of Industry and Trade (MITI) is the classic example of a powerful elite agency overseeing economic development (Johnson 1982). A better model for a Russian development council would be the Economic Planning Board that was established under Korean President Park (Chapter 8 and Song 1990). While MITI operated somewhat behind the scenes, the Economic Planning Board acted to build consensus and to mobilize the public support required to reconfigure the economy rapidly.

References

Adams, F. Gerard, and Lawrence R. Klein, eds. 1983. *Industrial Policies for Growth and Competitiveness: An Economic Perspective.* Lexington, MA: D.C. Heath.

Amsden, Alice H., Jacek Kochanowicz, and Lance Taylor. 1994. *The Market Meets Its Match: Restructuring the Economies of Eastern Europe.* Cambridge: Harvard University Press.

Aoki, Masahiko, and Hyung-Ki Kim, eds. 1995. *Corporate Governance in Transitional Economies: Insider Control and the Role of Banks.* EDI Development Series. Washington, DC: World Bank.

Aoki, Masahiko et al. 1998. *The Role of Government in East Asian Economic Development.* Oxford: Clarendon Press.

Auty, Richard M. 1994. *Economic Development and Industrial Policy: Korea, Brazil, Mexico, India and China.* New York: Mansell Publishing.

Chenery, H. B., S. Robinson, and M. Syrquin. 1986. *Industrialization and Growth: A Comparative Study.* New York: Oxford University Press.

Cottarelli, Carlo, and Gyorgy Szapary, eds. 1998. *Moderate Inflation: The Experience of Transition Economies.* Washington, DC: International Monetary Fund and National Bank of Hungary.

Feldstein, Martin. 1998. "Refocusing the IMF." *Foreign Affairs* 77(2): 20–33.

Gordon, Sara L. 1995. *The United States and Global Capital Shortages.* Westport, CT: Quorom Books.

Goskomstat. 2000. *Russia in Figures, 1999.* Moscow: State Committee of the Russian Federation on Statistics.

Granville, Brigitte. 1995. *The Success of Russian Economic Reforms.* Washington, DC: Brookings Institution.

Johnson, Chalmers. 1982. *MITI and the Japanese Miracle: The Growth of Industrial Policy.* Stanford, CA: Stanford University Press.

Krugman, Paul R., and Maurice Obstfeld. 1997. *International Economics: Theory and Practice*, 4th ed. Reading, MA: Addison-Wesley.

Lall, Sanjaya. 1997. *Learning from the Asian Tigers: Studies in Technology and Industrial Policy.* New York: St. Martin's Press.

Mann, Jim. 1997. *Beijing Jeep: A Case Study of Western Business in China.* Boulder, CO: Westview Press.

McKinnon, Ronald I. 1993. *The Order of Economic Liberalization: Financial Control in the Transition to a Market Economy.* Baltimore: Johns Hopkins University Press.

Nikoulichev, Michael. 1997. *Russian Aviation Industry.* Washington: U.S. and Foreign Commercial Service and U.S. Department of State.

Ocampo, Jose Antonio, and Lance Taylor. 1998. "Trade Liberalisation in Developing Economies: Modest Benefits but Problems with Productivity Growth, Macro Prices, and Income Distribution. *The Economic Journal* 108(450): 1523-46.

Oreshkin, V.A., A.N. Spartak, A.T. Nikonov, and E.I. Ishenko. 1997. *Russia's Trade and Foreign Exchange Policy in the Transition Period, 1992–1997.* Research Report Under the TACIS ACE Project. Moscow: TACIS.

Pomer, Marshall. 1998. "Neobkhodima ratsionalnaia promyshlennaia politika: Bez nee strana prevratitsia syrevoi pridatok Zapada." *Nezavisimaya gazeta,* December 17.

———. 1999. "Activist Government." *Studies on Russian Economic Development* 10(1): 66–70; "Ukreplenie roli gosudarstva v ekonomike Rossii v perehodnyi period." *Problemy prognozirovaniia* 10(1): 94-101.

———. "A Simulation Model for a Criminalized Economy in Transition Shock." Working Paper. Santa Cruz, CA: Macroeconomic Policy Institute.

Rodrik, Dani. 1995. "Trade and Industrial Policy Reform in Jere. R. Behrman and T. N. Srinivasan, eds., *Handbook of Development Economics*, Vol. 3B. Amsterdam: North-Holland.

Russian Academy of Sciences (RAS). 1997. *Guidelines of the Program for the Medium-Term Social and Economic Development of Russia.* Moscow: RAS.

Russian European Centre for Economic Policy (RECEP). 1997. "The Integration of Russia into the World Economy." Draft Paper Prepared for the Ministry of Foreign Economic Relations, October.

Shapiro, Helen. 1991. "Determinants of Firm Entry into the Brazilian Automobile Manufacturing Industry, 1956–1968." *Business History Review* 65(4): 876–947.

Song, Byung-Nag. 1990. *The Rise of the Korean Economy.* New York: Oxford University Press.

Sutela, Pekka. 1998. *The Road to the Russian Market Economy: Selected Essays, 1993–1998.* Helsinki: Kikimora Publications.

Vogel, Ezra F. 1991. *The Four Little Dragons: The Spread of Industrialization in East Asia.* Cambridge: Harvard University Press.

Wade, Robert. 1990. *Governing the Market: Economic Theory and the Role of Government in East Asian Industrialization.* Princeton, CA: Princeton University Press.

Wasow, Bernard. 1996. "The Soviet Block in Transition," in Leonard Silk and Mark Silk, *Making Capitalism Work.* Pp. 59–80. New York and London: New York University Press.

Welfens, Paul J. J. 2000. "The EU and Russia: Strategic Aspects of Transformation and Integration," in Paul J. J. Welfens and Evgeny Gavrilenkov, *Restructuring, Stabilizing and Modernizing the New Russia: Economic and Institutional Issues.* Berlin: Springer.

Wellisz, Stanislaw. 1997. "Inflation and Stabilization in Poland, 1990–95," in Mario I. Blejer and Marko Skreb, eds., *Macroeconomic Stabilization in Transition Economies.* Pp. 157–171. New York: Cambridge University Press.

World Bank. 1993. *The East Asian Miracle: Economic Growth and Public Policy.* New York: Oxford University Press.

18

Restructuring Agencies

David Ellerman, Dmitri Kuvalin, and Marshall Pomer

It was naïve to expect that privatization alone would modernize Russian industry. Rather than lead to revitalization, voucher privatization discouraged investment and left in place unprepared and often unscrupulous managers. As arrears continue to accumulate and enterprises slide toward bankruptcy, the state is acquiring new responsibility despite having ceded ownership.

There are three alternative responses: liquidation, renationalization, or reorganization cum restructuring. Severe political and social constraints oppose the first two alternatives, leaving the third as the most feasible. A new type of institution, the restructuring agency, is proposed here to facilitate reorganization and restructuring of troubled enterprises with potential.

The restructuring agency would have legislated powers to oversee the dismantling and revitalization of incompletely privatized, renationalized, or bankrupt enterprises. It would facilitate the birthing of new, vital daughter enterprises from ailing privatized industrial enterprises. The agency would be established on an experimental basis, and would be extended if it fostered dynamic daughter firms while eliminating nonviable entities.

This chapter has five main sections. The first discusses the merits of decentralization, and it characterizes profit centers and spin-offs as incomplete forms of decentralization. The second section introduces the strategy of enterprise decomposition. The third section describes the proposed restructuring agency. The fourth part focuses on upgrading management. The final section considers the limits to decentralization.

Decentralization

The industrial sector of the Russian economy, reflecting the exaggerated Soviet emphasis on returns to scale, is still characterized by enormous enterprises. In the fast-changing world economy, and especially during the transition period, innovation is critical. Rather than put one's hopes in the turnaround plans of entrenched managers of stagnant behemoths, it would be better to rely on creative adjustment of smaller, more dynamic firms.[1]

The case for further decentralization of Russian industry is strengthened if it is recognized that principal-agent relationships are problematic in any economy.[2] Institutional inadequacies regarding corporate governance are particularly severe in unsettled transitional environments. One solution is smaller firms where there is less distance between owners, managers, and workers.[3] In large organizations, the connection between efforts expended and the fruits of those efforts is less evident.

Organizational Reform

Firms can be vertically and/or horizontally divided into separate self-managing teams or profit centers, thereby creating a more direct connection between effort and success or failure. Full autonomy would permit direct exchange ties outside the enterprise. Units would be free to buy inputs and sell products independently of suppliers and customers internal to the enterprise. Decentralizing to profit centers would allow the units to spread their wings and respond individually to challenges and opportunities.

Unfortunately, significant organizational reform has been difficult to achieve in postsocialist countries. With top management intent on maintaining power, decentralization of an organization is invariably resisted. After decentralization, central management may hoard information in an effort to reassert its power over the decentralized units.[4] The strategy of enterprise decomposition, proposed below, may be thought of as turning profit centers into fully independent firms.

Spin-offs

It is common in modern capitalist countries to spin off profit centers or other valued components of a firm.[5] For example, a vertically integrated chemical firm might spin off the production of synthetic fibers. Thus one approach to further decentralizing Russian industry would be to carve out a unit, or several units, from the mother firm and have the mother firm continue to operate as before, though reduced in size.

Amidst initial optimism, there were modest successes with Russian spin-offs involving large industrial companies (Kuznetsov 1994), but subsequent results have not been encouraging outside of the wholesale and resale sectors (Kuznetsov 1997; Kotov 1997). The mother companies are too weak, and paternalistic expectations are too strong. Spinning off valued assets enfeebles the mother firm, aggravating the initial problem of a failing enterprise. The mother firm is neither closed down nor improved. Even worse, spinning off the most valuable parts is an invitation to plunder. A spin-off takes a bite out of the best part of the apple, and it is corrupt insiders who are likely to do the biting.

The Process of Enterprise Decomposition

The creation of profit centers and spin-offs constitutes a partial step toward decentralization. Enterprise decomposition takes these strategies to their logical conclusions: a firm is divided into profit centers, each of which is either spun off or shut down. The mother firm produces one or more daughter firms, with the remainder of the mother firm liquidated.

The decomposition process requires that a firm be conceptually divided into a set of units of production. Each unit encompasses assets, managers, workers, and some form of output. The reorganization and restructuring of the mother firm can then be conceptualized as having two main components: (1) liquidation of nonviable units, and (2) conversion of potentially viable units into new daughter firms.

The daughter firms should be reconstituted as newly formed entities. New, fresh organizations are more vital than old, stagnant ones. Old loyalties and alliances often obstruct rational change, especially when the change involves shutting down obsolete activities, discharging redundant workers, and requiring employees to work harder than before.

Rather than simply eliminate the original mother firm, a conglomerate structure could be devised. Under conglomerate decomposition, the mother company would be transformed into a holding company with ownership stakes in each of the daughter firms. The holding company would provide outside oversight of management and governance and could help coordinate production targets if the daughter firms were technologically related. It could retain responsibility for other functions to take advantage of economies of scale in marketing and finance. In transitional economies, credit may be especially subject to political directives, and a large enterprise would have more political clout than its separate parts.

Enterprise decomposition is invariably complex: Should a simple or conglomerate decomposition be implemented? How many daughter firms should be created? Which assets and liabilities should be assigned to each daughter firm? Who will be the new owners and the new managers? What governance rules and practices would effectively balance the powers of owners, managers, and potential outside investors?[6]

Ownership

Ownership of these new units is critical, and experimentation with different approaches is needed to determine optimal guidelines. The following simple prototype provides a starting point for further analysis:

The mother firm gives birth to three new firms and is then dissolved. Stockholders in the mother firm receive three options for each of their shares of stock. Each option is convertible into a share of stock in any one of the three daughters. Those stockholders who regarded a particular daughter as highly valuable could convert all of their options into shares of that daughter.[7] Others who had no reason to choose one daughter over another could evenly distribute their options. Strict disclosure would be required to allow stockholders to evaluate the daughters.

Under a conglomerate model, there would be shares of stock in both the holding company and the subsidiaries. The simplest ownership form would be for the holding company to be the sole owner of all the shares in each daughter, but it would be more desirable if the ownership stake were under 50 percent with further reductions scheduled. One possibility is for the holding company to receive a certain percentage of the shares of each of the new units and to distribute the remaining shares to the owners of the holding company, who would then be free to sell their shares on the secondary market.

Employees

Enterprise decomposition would break up paternalistic expectations that undermine efficiency, such as guaranteed lifetime employment. Since enterprises are generally overstaffed, many employees will be unable to obtain positions in one of the daughter firms. Dismissed employees would be offered a severance package, and those with stock holdings could be offered cash or notes receivable. To boost motivation of employees who find a position in a daughter firm, it could be mandated that rehired employees exchange their shares in the mother firm for shares in whatever daughter firms they join.

Creditors

As part of the process of enterprise decomposition, creditors would be asked to forgive a portion of the mother firm's liabilities. In exchange for other debt, they could be provided with equity shares. Any remaining liabilities could be reassigned to the daughter firms. If the mother firm continued as a holding company, then the mother company could continue to be responsible.[8]

The daughter firms are likely to be more creditworthy than the mother firm. The most obvious factor is their greater economic viability. Another factor is that the larger mother firm is more likely to be shielded from legal action on the part of unpaid creditors; courts would be less likely to order liquidation of assets since bankruptcy of a larger firm would have more substantial socioeconomic repercussions.

Outside Investors

Proponents of voucher privatization in Russia falsely predicted that the messy job of restructuring would be undertaken by foreigners. Strategic investors presumably would buy shares in privatized firms in the public secondary market, overcoming high transactions costs in order to amass a controlling share. Interest on the part of outside investors, including foreign investors, however, would be substantially improved as a result of enterprise decomposition. An investor would be better able to assess the potential of a particular daughter unit than of the mother firm. Also, decomposition would spare the potential investor from employee and governmental resistance to radical downsizing.

Proposed Restructuring Agency

The restructuring agency would expedite reorganization of large enterprises in serious default. Providing an alternative to bankruptcy proceedings and government-run asset management, it would foster creation of viable daughter firms. To ensure integrity and competence, the staff should consist of well-paid professionals. They would serve in many roles: consultants to managers, mediators among stakeholders, watchdogs for malfeasance, monitors of government assistance, and catalysts for change.

The restructuring agency would have legislated authority to decide which parts of the mother firm to revitalize and which parts to close down.

It would fashion corporate structures that would enable owners to press for improved management and permit subsequent takeovers by still more capable new owners.[9] The restructuring agency would also expedite the dismantling and downsizing processes by coordinating government social support, including job training and relocation assistance.

Given differences in local governments and other regional variation, the restructuring agency will need to tailor its operations on a regional basis. To speed action, branch offices should be given a large degree of autonomy. Their powers would be established by federal legislation, and their operating methods would be determined by the federal administration in conjunction with local governments. The branch offices would exercise the voting rights of any government-owned shares.

It is important to establish a "public space" for discussion of results. Staff could be rotated between the various branch offices to better absorb implicit information. International assistance, both funding and expertise, should be provided in a way that enhances transparency and communication. Foreign consultants (possibly from central-eastern Europe) could work with and train local counterparts, who would then continue the work. Knowledge would thus be horizontally transmitted to drive a process of continuous improvement.

Strategic Investors

A promising way to foster transfer of assets to investment-oriented owners is to seek strategic investors. By definition, they would take an active interest in the management or operation of the enterprise and would facilitate finance, technological advancement, marketing, or some other activity to strengthen the enterprise.

Various options are possible to encourage strategic investors. If a foreign investor were to pay cash, the proceeds could be divided among the stakeholders of the mother enterprise. The creditors could be paid a discounted amount in return for debt forgiveness. Dismissed employees could be awarded bonuses as part of their severance packages. Any remaining cash could be distributed among the other units or the holding company. The strategic investor could also finance the acquisition by offering common or preferred stock, as discussed below, or notes payable.

The restructuring agency could also negotiate commitments from strategic investors regarding investment and transfer of technology. Indeed, what the strategic investor pays for a controlling share could be set at a nominal level if the investor were committed to substantial investment. Mechanisms should be established so that if such commitments were not kept, then the investors would be required to forfeit their equity and perhaps pay penalties as well.

Evaluation

Since reformers overestimated what the market would solve on its own, there has been little experimentation with government-led reorganization and restructuring. Thus methods of operation should evolve on the basis of experience with what works and what does not. Some of the branch offices could be costly and ineffectual failures. Worse, they could turn out to be obstacles to market forces and a new opportunity for political abuse and corruption. At the same time, they can play a pivotal role in eliminating obstacles to market forces, such as criminal structures, informal rent-seeking cartels, and political machinations of the "oligarchs."

Funding and qualified personnel are limited resources. It is imperative to set forth a program that does not exceed what is possible. Nevertheless, doing too little is also an error. The program must focus on larger enterprises and those with technological potential. To control costs, quick liquidation is desirable when the restructuring prospects are not favorable. If management or owners fail to cooperate with the restructuring agency, the firm's assets should be sold promptly under liquidation bankruptcy to satisfy tax authorities and creditors.

Accountability is crucial. Independent auditing could be carried out by a team that included professionals from the Russian Academy of Sciences, the World Bank, foreign universities, international accounting firms, and international investment banks. The results, and the auditing process itself, should be reviewed by an independent group that might include internationally respected economists. The branch offices should be accountable to the federal administration and parliament, as well as to local government, and should operate in a transparent way so that they can be evaluated by researchers and journalists. On the basis of the results, individual branch offices would either be improved and expanded, or terminated.

Management

Critical to the prospects of the daughter firms is the installation of competent owners and managers with long-term time horizons. Since a daughter enterprise is not a continuation of an old corporate form with a transfer of old shares to new owners, as was the case in voucher privatization and in privatization auctions, managers would need to leave the old legal entity and be rehired by the new one. Thus enterprise decomposition creates opportunity for upgrading management. Unless new business units are established, there is likely to be internecine struggle to topple the center.

In order to overcome the problem of entrenched management, the restructuring agency would require that suitable governance procedures be followed regarding choice of management by owners. It would do its own review of qualifications and would disqualify managers on the basis of prior malfeasance and criminal ties. The goal of this process is to recruit experienced, law-abiding managers of the mother company as managers of each of the newly formed units, although it is important to allow for the recruitment of capable outsiders as well. If a conglomerate were created, some top managers would remain as officers of the holding company, supervising management of the individual subsidiaries.

Following is one possible tactic for developing a viable decomposition plan and assigning management teams to daughter firms: The restructuring agency could divide current managers, perhaps supplemented with new recruits, into a number of teams. Each management team would submit a plan for dividing the troubled enterprise into daughter firms. The agency would specify basic requirements, including governance standards and the handling of debts. The plans would specify asset and liability redistribution and would resolve ownership issues. The restructuring agency would rank the plans and be guided by them in creating a final decomposition plan. To reward the efforts of the contributing teams, the manager-owner team with the best plan would have first choice of daughter firm, and the team with the plan ranked second would have the second choice, and so on.

Managerial training would help foster managerial competence and integrity. Moldova has had success with a form of restructuring agency that mandated managerial training. After local preparation and selection, managers and consultants are sent for training and internships (6–12 weeks) in successful domestic or foreign firms.[10]

Management Buyouts

In the early conception of privatization in Russia, "private ownership" referred to active owners who would control and refashion privatized enterprises. But with the use of voucher-based mass privatization and employee-based privatization, many privatized enterprises do not have owners oriented toward restructuring.[11] Once again, there is a question of how to install owners who are able to act as a coherent unit.

One of the striking facts to emerge in the former Soviet satellite countries is the success of the de novo private sector as opposed to the privatized (or to-be privatized) sector. In Russia too there has been a massive flow of managerial and entrepreneurial talent to the new private sector. Thus one of the rationales for creation of daughter firms is to increase the opportunities and rewards to entrepreneurial activity in the privatized sector.

One strategy to attract managerial talent and forward-looking owners is to promote management buyouts (MBOs). Thus the process of going from state ownership to effective private ownership could be seen as a two-stage process: the first stage being voucher privatization, and the second stage an MBO program. It may be that an MBO would enable the managers to undertake enterprise decomposition on their own.

Bank or other third-party credit is not likely to be available to finance MBOs in transitional economies. However, an MBO could offer the previous owners a term note to be paid off over a period of years. A more flexible arrangement is to issue redeemable preferred stock divided into different issues to be redeemed at fixed time intervals. If a redemption payment is missed, then the issue of preferred stock converts into voting common stock. Thus if the MBO fails to keep up its payments, it becomes increasingly owned by the previous owners. Another possibility is a seller-financed transaction with ownership changing once all payments are made.

Limits to Decentralization

The creation of daughter firms should stimulate competition and open new possibilities for initiative and growth. But one must not be doctrinaire. Increased decentralization is not always the best route to efficiency.[12] Indeed, a number of hastily divided Russian enterprises have already been re-integrated (Krasnova 1999).[13] If government has fewer firms to monitor, then industrial policy, tax compliance, and control over capital flight may be more feasible.

For any particular market, competition among many Russian firms would not be feasible if the number of customers or the potential volume of sales were low. It could also play into the hands of a strong foreign producer intent on achieving a dominant position. Substantial size is required for many production processes to be efficient. Economies of scale are also important for marketing and finance. Larger enterprises may be better able to justify the salaries required to recruit the best managerial talent. They also may be better positioned to support their own legal staff and security force needed to defend against criminal harassment. More generally, it is often more efficient to have activities coordinated within an enterprise rather than via the market (Coase 1988).

Care also must be taken as to how an enterprise is unbundled. It is more hazardous to eliminate vertical integration than lateral integration. Breaking apart the components of a vertically integrated monopoly could rupture technological ties and yield several smaller monopolies in which each one is the sole source of supply of a needed input to another. This would replace internal transfers with bilateral monopolistic bargaining situations.[14] It is also critical to safeguard against malfeasance when an enterprise is divided. After the financial crisis of August 1998, managers of nearly bankrupt firms in many instances transferred all the valuable assets to spin-offs they owned themselves. The mother firms kept only liabilities and bad assets, and were more or less abandoned without settling debts.[15]

Thus, under some circumstances, the best strategy for restructuring is to merge enterprises. A prime example, discussed in the previous chapter, is the Russian aircraft industry, which is characterized by major economies of scale, a drastic shrinkage of the market, and powerful foreign competitors.

Conclusion

The market on its own is not bringing about the reorganization and restructuring needed to modernize the Soviet legacy of mammoth industrial enterprises. A properly designed and prudently run restructuring agency would provide the impetus needed to eliminate uneconomic activities and create viable new enterprises.

Gradual, step-by-step decentralization may be best. The first step, leaving the mother firm intact, would be to reorganize the enterprise into separate profit centers. The second step would entail shutting down those profit centers that do not prove themselves. The third step, which may not be necessary, would be to transform the profit into separate firms.

Economic transition from a command system to a market system is necessarily a decentralization process. But we must be realistic. While privatization did not result in an adequate degree of decentralization, enterprise decomposition could produce excessive decentralization. Effective restructuring does not always achieved by breaking large enterprises into smaller units.

The proposed program of government-led reorganization and restructuring of obsolete industrial enterprises will have to be carefully implemented. We must not create any illusions that there is a simple solution, a mistake already made during the voucher-privatization campaign.

Notes

1. Rosenberg and Birdzell (1986, 34) express in broader terms this problem of elites obstructing experimental evolution: "And *successful* change requires a large measure of freedom to experiment. A grant of that kind of freedom costs a society's rulers their feeling of control, as if they were conceding to others the power to determine the society's future. The great majority of societies, past and present, have not allowed it. Nor have they escaped from poverty."

2. Witness the separation between ownership and control in the large American corporations (most notably, Berle and Means 1968).

3. This is the Jeffersonian operating principle of the small farm or owner-operated shop, where the farmers or shopkeepers are working for themselves.

4. This is why "dis-integration" often takes place only in the context of bankruptcy, when much of the organizational capital, key people, and market opportunities have already vanished. Thus most reorganization bankruptcies end up as liquidation bankruptcies. The lesson is that when the reorganization has to be enforced by a bankruptcy court, then it is probably too late to save much of the business as a going concern. See Sabel's (1995) model of bootstrapping reforms for a sophisticated treatment of organizational change.

5. Regarding the restructuring of Russian industry, the tendency would be to spin off the best-performing parts of an enterprise. More typically in the United States, divesture of a business segment usually occurs when the segment is underperforming (Schnee et al. 1998).

6. Determination of ownership and assignment of debts to creditors could be done by adapting procedures used in the case of spin-offs. The mother firm could be compensated for asset transfers to the daughters and then liquidated to satisfy creditors. If the mother ended up with cash, it would use that cash to help finance the daughters. Apart from stock and payment in the form of notes and assumption of liabilities, there are numerous ways the mother firm could be rewarded: compensation for explicit release of rights to technology, right of first refusal for subsequent financing, and right of first refusal on licensed production (Bernstein 1995, 205).

7. Suppose that there are 1,000 shares of stock in the mother firm, implying a sum total of 3,000 shares for the three daughter firms. It might be that one daughter has only 300 shares, while the other two have 1,350. Someone with one share in the mother who converted that share into shares of the lower-

valued daughter would have exchanged an ownership stake of 0.001 in the mother firm for an ownership stake of 0.010 in the daughter.

8. It is essential to minimize the risk that certain creditors will influence the appointment of affiliated consultants, and then plunder the assets of the bankrupt firm at the expense of the other creditors. This happened in the case of a Moscow electromechanical factory in 1997. The newly appointed restructuring manager began delivering all production to a small new firm known as Luka. Employees were not paid their salaries unless they went to work at the new firm. Once all production had been diverted to Luka and all liquid assets had disappeared, the old enterprise was shut down ("Sanitators and Marauders," *Ekspert*, No. 8 March 1, 1999.)

9. To reduce transaction costs and bargaining stalemates, the restructuring agency should enforce standard procedures and terms. See the examples of Polish leasing and the Slovenian draft law on internal privatization (Ellerman 1993).

10. A strong business culture would allow managers to learn from their more successful brethren. This could be accomplished by supporting the formation of business clubs, the publication of business magazines that detail successes and analyze failures, and the clustering of related businesses in trade associations. Managers could tour successful companies in other parts of the country, and perhaps internships could be established. Strong companies could accept business-related but weaker companies as partners, to be tutored and guided to restore their strength. See, for example, Logue and Plekhanov (1995) or Logue and Klepikova (1998).

11. Voucher privatization leading to control by an investment fund was an often touted ideal. However, if the fund owns 20 percent of the firm and the fund management company's fee is 2 percent of the value of the assets under management, the amount of the ownership value that filters down is only 0.4 percent. $(0.02 * 0.20 = 0.004)$. Thus, if the fund management company is able to control a firm, it has a strong incentive to extract value out of the company.

12. The advantages of increased concentration constitute one of the rationales for deliberate efforts to foster financial-industrial groups (FIGs). The results have not been promising (Makrushenko 1998).

13. The experience of Angström is an interesting example (Krasnova 1999). Angström was the first microelectronics enterprise located near Moscow in Zelenograd, the Soviet "Silicon Valley." With the collapse in demand for high-tech Soviet military electronics, Angström shifted production in 1993 to

become a supplier for Chinese producers of calculators and electronic games. In 1994, it divided into four profit centers (instruments, microchips, calculators, and crystals). All of them were completely independent in marketing, planning, production process, labor and salary policy, and profit distribution. At the same time, some central functions were conserved, including finance, accounting, and R&D. In 1997, the four profit centers were reintegrated. Moreover, Angström decided to pursue integration at a higher level. A cartel with two neighboring electronics factories was arranged to unite technological, financial, and marketing potential. The main goal of this action is expansion within the Russian national market. (In 1998, Russian microelectronics producers controlled less than 10% of the Russian market.)

14. During the privatization campaign, the Raspadskaia coal enterprise split into three independent entities. Two of these emerged as micromonopolies that sharply raised their prices, while the third entity became insolvent (Kuvalin 1995).

15. For example, the Russian metallurgy company Norilsk Nickel was broken into manufacturing and trading companies. But most of the revenue was diverted abroad by the latter, leaving almost nothing (just 100 million out of 10.8 billion rubles in revenues in 1996) to the former to pay off its debts ("Who Will Stop Thefts at Norilsk Nickel?" *Profile*, No. 15, 1997).

References

Berle, Adolf A., and Gardiner C. Means. 1968. *The Modern Corporation and Private Property*, revised ed. New York: Harcourt, Brace & World.

Bernstein, David. 1995. "Spin-offs and Start-ups in Russia: A Key Element of Industrial Restructuring," in Michael McFaul and Tova Perlmutter, eds., *Privatization, Conversion, and Enterprise Reform in Russia*. Pp. 201–215. Boulder and Oxford: Westview Press.

Coase, Ronald H. 1988. *The Firm, the Market, and the Law.* Chicago: University of Chicago Press.

Ellerman, David. 1993. "Management and Employee Buy-Outs in Central and Eastern Europe," in David Ellerman, ed., *Management and Employee Buy-Outs as a Technique of Privatization*. Ljubljana: Central and Eastern European Privatization Network.

Kotov, A. P. 1997. "The Practices of Structural Transformation in the Defence Industries." *Studies on Russian Economic Development* 8(5): 467-470.

Krasnova, V. 1999. "Council at Angström." *Ekspert* 7: 28–31, February.

Kuvalin, Dmitri. 1995. "The Story of the Raspadskaia Mine." *Studies on Russian Economic Development* 6(1).

Kuznetsov, Yuri. 1994. "Strategy for Survival, An Interview with Deputy Manager of the Arsenal Manufacturing Association." *Studies on Russian Economic Development* 6.

———. 1997. "Organization Structures of Industry and Their Influence on Working Capital." *Studies on Russian Economic Development* 8(5): 461–466.

Logue, John, and Olga Klepikova. 1998. *Restructuring Elinar: A Case Study of Russian Management Reform, Decentralization and Diversification.* Case study prepared for World Bank (processed).

Logue, John, and S. Plekhanov, eds. 1995. *Transforming Russian Enterprises: From State Control to Employee Ownership.* Westport, CT: Greenwood Press.

Makrushenko, Vladimir. 1998. "Financial Industrial Groups: Development and Problems." *Problems of Economic Transition* 40(12): 62–79.

Rosenberg, N., and L. E. Birdzell. 1986. *How the West Grew Rich: The Economic Transformation of the Industrial World.* New York: Basic Books.

Sabel, Charles. 1995. "Bootstrapping Reform: Rebuilding Firms, the Welfare State, and Unions." *Politics and Society* 23(1): 5–48.

Schnee, Edward J., Lee G. Knight, and Ray A. Knight. 1998. "Corporate Spin-offs." *Journal of Accountancy* 185(6): 47–54.

19

Aggregate Demand

Stanislav Menshikov

The monetarist view that prevailed in Russia during the 1990s gave priority to deficit reduction. It was commonly expected that growth in Russia would resume automatically once annual inflation was reduced below 30 percent. That goal was achieved in both 1996 and 1997 (CPI rose respectively by 22 and 11 percent), but output continued to fall in 1996 and there was only marginal growth in 1997. Another explanation is that exorbitant interest rates, which were attributed to heavy government borrowing, stifled growth. This may have been true in 1996 when real lending rates approached 100 percent. But in 1997 real lending rates came down to about 30 percent, and in 1998 and early 1999 they were in the negative range.

An alternative view is defended here: the Russian economy since the mid-1990s suffered from inadequate aggregate demand. Austerity policies applied to an economy in recession create a vicious circle since less output means lower income, as well as less budget revenue and persistence of the budget deficit problem. This chapter provides perspective by addressing supply barriers and the collapse of investment. It then applies a simulation model to evaluate the macroeconomic effects of alternative fiscal policies.

Macroeconomic Issues

Supply barriers deserve mention, though they do not excuse ignoring the problem of inadequate demand. Frequently cited is lack of working capital, which is related to the prevalence of barter and the excessive cost of bank credit. Another supply bottleneck is inadequate transportation and other distribution infrastructure. Also, supply problems tend to emerge in the more highly monopolized industries where increasing demand gives rise to higher prices rather than to higher production.

Perhaps most critical in evaluating whether to boost aggregate demand is the apparent lack of inflationary potential from labor costs. Consider that between 1992 and 1998 real GDP declined about 30 percent while employment fell by 12 percent, indicating average productivity declined about 20 percent. In the same period the average real monthly wage rate fell by 21 percent, implying that unit labor costs had not changed. While wage rates vary widely between the various industries, direct wage costs in 1997 averaged only 12 percent of total costs of manufacturing and mining (17 percent including social taxes). The total direct wage bill for the 23 industries represented in the 1995 input-output table was only 10 percent of their combined gross outputs (13 percent including social taxes). After the financial crisis in August 1998, moreover, the real wage rate fell much further than industrial production (Table 19.1).

A related point is that a structural anomaly in the composition of national income seriously erodes aggregate demand. The share of wages and labor is very low compared to the industrial countries of the West, and the share of gross cash flow is high (depreciation plus profits and other entrepreneurial income). While total labor income is only about one-third of GDP (compared with 60 percent in the US), net cash flow runs as high as 40 percent (compared with 17 percent in the US) (Goskomstat 1998 and CEA 1998). Low wages explains low personal consumption while, as we shall see, high gross cash flow has not led to high domestic investment.

Table 19.1. Wages and Industrial Output, 1998–1999 (1997 = 100)

	Jan 1998	Sep 1998	Nov 1998	Jan 1999	July 1999	Dec 1999
Real wage rate	104.4	98.6	72.5	62.7	66.5	82.4
Industrial production	99.0	91.4	93.1	97.4	105.2	105.6
Ratio (%)	*105.0*	*107.9*	*77.9*	*64.1*	*63.2*	*78.0*

Source: RECEP (1994–2000).

Capital Investment

Since 1990, investment has been very low. In constant 1990 prices, the share of gross capital investment in GDP fell from 29 percent in 1990 to less than 10 percent by 1996. This downward trend continued in later years. Measured in 1995 prices, the share fell from 20 percent in 1995 to 17 percent in both 1997 and 1998 and to 15 percent in 1999.

More striking are the data on net capital investment, which is the difference between gross capital investment and capital consumption (depreciation). The measurement of capital consumption is controversial in Russian statistics (Goskomstat 1998). If official figures are to be believed, net investment has been *negative* starting in 1995: minus 5.5 percent of GDP in 1995, minus 8.8 percent in 1996, and minus 11.7 percent in 1998. By comparison, at the trough of the US Great Depression net investment bottomed out at minus 7.7 percent to GDP in 1933. Moreover, much of investment is for repairs and a relatively small share goes toward new equipment.

Russian National Accounts show the clearly depressive way in which cash flow resources are used (Goskomstat 1997 and 1998). When non-government investment is considered (80 percent of the total figure), only 15–17 percent of depreciation and 20–40 percent of after-tax profits were used for financing capital investment. A sum equivalent to 15 percent of total net cash flow was spent on financial investment. The use of the remaining half of the net cash flow is not disclosed in the data.

Unofficial estimates by the central bank and private estimates (Westin 2000) indicate that approximately 60 per cent of this remainder are transferred directly abroad (i.e. capital flight). Another third or more is channeled to commercial banks that buy foreign currency with their excess reserves or park their excess reserves in accounts at the central bank rather than lend to businesses. The paradox is that while Russia has abundant internal sources for investment, only a small part of them are actually used for modernizing the economy. This suggests government measures to reduce capital flight could stimulate capital investment.

Macroeconomic Simulation

The macroeconomic model applied here represents the marriage of the Leontief model with the Keynesian system (Menshikov 1976, 2000). It was fitted to national income account statistics for the period 1990–1998 (Goskomstat 1997 and 1998, BEA 1999, RECEP 1994–2000) and input-output tables calculated by Goskomstat and the Institute for Mathematical-Economic Research for a number of years inside the same period (Goskomstat 1998, IMR 1997). A system of simultaneous equations are solved to determine the components of gross domestic product and national income, as well as changes in the price level. Final demand is disaggregated into 23 different product groups. For each product group, the model calculates where these products originate and the cost structure, including intermediate material costs, primary incomes, and indirect taxes. The structure of final demand and income components is determined by coefficients derived from the input-output tables.

Labor income largely determines total personal income which, after deducting personal income taxes, determines aggregate personal consumption. Depreciation and profit are the basic determinants of gross fixed capital investment. These causal connections make possible the extension of the classic Leontief system where primary incomes (as part of gross output) are the result of exogenously determined final demand:

$$X = Y * (I - A)^{-1} \tag{1}$$
$$V, W, D, P, OI = f(X), \tag{2}$$

where:

X is the vector of gross output by industry;

Y is the vector of total final demand by product of the various industries;

A is the matrix of input-output coefficients;

I is the matrix in which the diagonal elements equal unity;

V is the vector of value added by industry; and

W (labor income), D (depreciation), P (profit), OI (other incomes) are the vectors for components of primary income disaggregated by industry.

This closed system is extended to include:

$$c = f(W, OI) \tag{3}$$
$$inv = f(D, P), \tag{4}$$

where c is household consumption and inv is gross fixed investment. Through structural coefficients c is transformed into C (vector of household consumption) and inv is transformed into INV (vector of gross investment). C and INV are used to determine total final demand via the identity

$$Y = C + INV + G + EX - IM, \tag{5}$$

where G is the vector of government consumption, EX is the vector of exports, and IM is the vector of imports. This extended Leontief system is solved iteratively by initially introducing all components of final demand as exogenous variables, but permitting C, INV, and consequently Y (total final demand) to be determined endogenously.

Consumption and investment are endogenously determined subject to changes in autonomous demand, equal to government consumption plus exports. Imports are determined by gross outputs and coefficients of import dependence (im): $IM = im*X$. Endogenizing gross outputs and the two basic components of final demand (personal consumption and investment)

Table 19.2. Inflation and Ruble Depreciation, 1998–1999

	July 1998	Sep 1998	Dec 1998	Mar 1999	July 1999	Dec 1999
Producer price index (PPI)	1.00	1.06	1.24	1.44	1.66	2.07
Consumer price index (CPI)	1.00	1.44	1.77	2.05	2.27	2.42
External producer parity (R/$)	11.8	12.5	14.6	17.1	19.3	24.4
External consumer parity (R/$)	9.00	12.9	15.9	18.5	20.4	21.7
Market exchange rate (R/$)	6.27	16.1	21.1	24.9	24.2	27.0
Producer parity/exchange rate	1.88	0.78	0.69	0.69	0.80	0.91
Consumer parity/exchange rate	1.44	0.80	0.75	0.74	0.84	0.80

Source: RECEP (1994–2000) and unofficial estimates of producer and consumer external parity provided by the Central Bank of Russia.

makes it possible to calculate the combined effect of Leontief's gross output multiplier dX/dY with Keynes's final demand multiplier $dY/d(G+EX)$. A submodel estimates retail and producer prices, money supply variables, and the ruble/dollar exchange rate. Income variables generated by the model determine all major components of government revenue (total of federal, provincial, and local revenue), including profit and income taxes, VAT and excise taxes, and revenue from foreign economic activity.

Factors of Recovery in 1999

In 1999, GDP and industrial production rebounded strongly for the first time since 1990. However, household consumption decreased and export revenues would have declined if oil prices had not increased. The principal contributor to growth was the fall in imports as a consequence of ruble devaluation (Table 19.2).

The domestic price/exchange rate relationship determines the relative competitive power of domestic versus imported products. Our estimates are that every tenth of a point change in the producer price/exchange rate parity yields a $1.8 billion change in merchandise imports. The ruble devaluation thereby accounted for more than $11.5 billion in lower imports, or more than 70 percent of the total change. Import substitution was strongest in consumer goods, which is where import dependence prior to the 1998 crisis was highest. This was particularly true of light industry, which produces most consumer nondurables except food, where 55 percent of total sales were imports.[1]

Future import substitution will depend on whether domestic prices rise in line with the dollar/ruble exchange rate. If producer prices continue to rise faster, as they did in 1999, there will be "counter-substitution." For instance, we estimate that a rise in the parity from an average 0.8 in 1999 to 1.0 in 2000 would lead to an estimated addition of $3.5 billion in merchandise imports, or roughly 5 percent on top of larger imports due to growth in real GDP.

The effects of devaluation were slower to materialize, and less consequential, for exports. Around 40 percent of merchandise exports are accounted for by crude oil, petroleum refinery products, and natural gas. In 1999 these exports increased in value due to a recovery in world prices, but not in volume. Exports of these items depend on output and transportation infrastructure. Expansion is limited by inadequate capital investment in exploration, drilling, production, and transportation. Other exports are mostly in intermediate products, such as metals, chemicals, and wood and pulp. Competitive pricing in these markets is important and has been a major factor in their 1999 recovery.

Fiscal Policy

The 1999 increase in GDP of about 3 percent was supported by a 6.4 percent increase in government purchases (in real terms). GDP continued to rise in 2000 at an even higher pace—growing by 7.3 percent in the first half compared to the same period the previous year. Unlike 1999, a major factor contributing to growth was private domestic demand: household consumption rose by 7.8 percent and capital investment by 14 percent, while government purchases of goods and services rose by 6.2 percent. These factors were more important than further growth in the external surplus which was more nominal (due to higher oil prices) than real. Despite expanding money supply, price inflation in 2000 was much smaller than in 1999 due to surging domestic output. Also strong growth helped turn a fiscal deficit into a substantial fiscal surplus. The welcomed expansion was supported by policies stimulating aggregate demand rather than by cutting government expenditure and raising taxes.

To examine what would have happened under greater austerity, we ran simulations for 1999. The results indicate that cutting government purchases by 7.6 percent would have totally eliminated growth in 1999. An indirect effect, of course, is a fall in government revenues, which would be about half as great as the cut in government spending.

Simulations show that similar negative effects would be produced by raising excise taxes. We introduced a threefold rise in the excise tax for gasoline by increasing the excise tax coefficient derived from the relevant column of the input-output table. The expected addition to government revenue would practically wipe out the overall budget deficit if macroeconomic effects were not taken into account. However, the excise tax increase would reduce real GDP by 0.6 percent, and the net addition to the government budget would be only half what is expected when macroeconomic effects are not counted.

An opposite, positive macroeconomic effect could be produced by setting the value-added tax (VAT) at 15 percent rather than 20 percent.[2] The final consumer pays the full VAT rate on the sales price and cannot normally claim a refund. Therefore, reducing the VAT rate would provide the consumer with a chance of getting at least a partial discount from the sales prices or would have, at least, the effect of reducing cost pressures on producers. These considerations make it possible to simulate macroeconomic effects of changes in VAT in our model.[3] Even with producers passing on to consumers most of the VAT reduction, they would still benefit from an increase in after-tax profits. The estimated loss of government revenue is nominal.

Conclusion

A general explanation for the prolonged economic stagnation is that Russia is not a real market economy; it is too corrupted and criminalized for businesses to react to market signals in the way they should. Further reforms to promote competition and create a true legal infrastructure are surely part of the solution. But this institutional recipe will take time to implement, and there are instances of corrupt and otherwise imperfect market economies that have grown quickly. Growth can be promoted by macroeconomic means even in today's imperfect environment.

Increased government purchases or reduced taxes will not suffice to create sustained growth. The key is growth in aggregate domestic demand supported by increasing supply. Capital investment is crucial. Its main limitation is not the inadequacy of national savings, which might actually be increased by lower taxes. On the contrary, gross cash flow is much larger than gross investment, an excess that is leading to large capital flight. One way to close the savings-investment gap is by centralizing government control over the use of the national cash flow in order to channel it into capital investment. More compatible with a decentralized market economy is to rely on macroeconomic policies to increase domestic investment. Our simulations suggest that making the tax structure less restrictive is a viable approach.

Notes

1. The 1999 leaders in import reduction were foodstuffs, cigarettes, alcohol, clothing, footwear, and machinery.

2. The VAT is difficult to avoid and easy to collect, and constitutes a large part of government revenue. VAT is paid as an addition to the company sales price, not from value added, as its name seems to indicate. The value-added nature of the tax is important only *post factum* when the company is able to claim a refund for the VAT it had paid to its suppliers.

3. Because figures for VAT appear in the value-added quadrant of the input-output table, average VAT rates for all industries are available for calculations. Data, derived from the 1995 input/output table, were adjusted for later years on the basis of actual data for VAT collection.

References

Bureau of Economic Analysis (BEA). 1999. *Review of Economic Policy in Russia in 1998*. Moscow: Bureau of Economic Analysis.

Council of Economic Advisers (CEA). 1998. *Economic Report of the President*. Washington, DC: GPO.

Goskomstat. 1997. *System of National Accounts*. Moscow: State Committee of the Russian Federation on Statistics.

———. 1998. *Methodological Guidelines to Statistics, Vol. II*. Moscow: State Committee of the Russian Federation on Statistics.

———. 1997 and 1998. *Statisticheskii ezhegodnik*. Moscow: State Committee of the Russian Federation on Statistics.

———. 1999. *Wages and Employment in the Economy, Monthly Data, 1992–1999*. Moscow: State Committee of the Russian Federation on Statistics.

Institute for Mathematical-Economic Research (IMR). 1997. *Input-Output Tables of the Russian Economy*. Moscow: Ministry of the Economy, Russian Federation.

Menshikov, Stanislav. 1976. "New Approaches to Dynamic Input-Output Models," in Lawrence Klein et al., eds., *The Brookings Model, Volume 2*. Washington, DC: The Brookings Institution.

———. 2000. "Macropolicies to Help Re-Start Economic Growth in Russia." Working Paper, Centre for Development, Aalborg University, Denmark.

Russian European Centre for Economic Policy in Cooperation with Working Centre for Economic Reform, Government of the Russian Federation (RECEP). 1993–1999. *Russian Economic Trends Quarterly, Vols. 2–8*.

———. 1994–2000. *Russian Economic Trends. Monthly Update*.

Westin, Peter. 2000. "Export Revenues: Repatriation or Expropriation?" *Russian Economic Trends, Monthly Update, February*.

20

Trade Within the Commonwealth of Independent States

Ruslan S. Grinberg

The breakup of the USSR, apart from its political and social benefits, undermined the economies and reduced the living standards of its successor states.[1] It was hoped that the release from control by the center would unleash economic potential, but deep transformational recessions have blocked restoration of ruptured economic ties under the aegis of the Commonwealth of Independent States (CIS). In some CIS countries, as much as half of GDP decrease is attributable to the combination of lower exports to other CIS countries and the inability to obtain imports needed for domestic production (SNG 2000).

Many previous interrepublican ties were economically unwarranted and their artificial conservation by government action would interfere with needed restructuring (Shishkov 1996). The newly independent states, euphoric over their independence, sought to assert their own needs and solve their own problems. There has been hostility toward creation of transnational bodies and disinclination to coordinate economic policy (Garnett

Table 20.1. Percent of Foreign Trade with Other CIS Countries

| | 1994 | | 1996 | | 1999 | |
	Exports	Imports	Exports	Imports	Exports	Imports
Azerbaijan	43	62	46	35	28	31
Armenia	73	52	46	34	24	22
Belarus	59	68	67	66	61	64
Georgia	54	60	65	39	48	38
Kazakhstan	58	60	54	70	26	45
Kirghizia	66	66	78	58	41	46
Moldova	72	73	68	61	54	40
RUSSIA	21	27	18	31	14	27
Tajikistan	23	42	43	57	47	76
Turkmenistan	76	51	67	30	-	-
Uzbekistan	68	54	21	32	-	-
Ukraine	55	73	51	63	28	58

Source: SNG (1996: 96; 2000: 3).

1995). Moreover, several countries aspire to reorient their international ties away from Russia and toward Western Europe and the United States, in part out of distrust. Nevertheless, amidst disappointed expectations, the realization has emerged that some economic reintegration is critical to growth.

Declining Trade

According to official estimates, Russian trade in 1991 with other Soviet republics was greater than its total foreign trade today. Russian trade with the other CIS countries has fallen from $115 billion in 1991 to about $30 billion in 1999.[2] Trade among CIS countries has declined by over 70 percent from its level during the Soviet era. By 1993, intra-CIS trade fell to only $118 billion, compared with $210 billion two years before, and further reduction occurred throughout the 1990s.

Table 20.2. Russian Trade with CIS and Non-CIS Countries, 1996–1999 (percent of previous year)

	1996	1997	1998	1999
Within CIS				
Exports	108.3	105.6	82.4	76.5
Imports	104.2	97.9	79.5	71.4
Outside CIS				
Exports	108.1	97.3	84.2	100.9
Imports	94.1	123.8	83.1	67.7

Source: SNG (1999, 2000).

The share of foreign trade of CIS countries attributable to mutual trade declined from 53 percent in 1992 to only 31 percent in 1998. After 1998 the total exports of the CIS countries fell considerably, and the share of these reduced exports going to other CIS countries in 1999 dropped to only about 20 percent (see Table 20.1). Russian trade with CIS countries did recover somewhat after 1994, reaching a peak of $31 billion in 1997 before falling again (see Table 20.2).[3] The CIS share of Russian foreign trade shrank to below 20 percent in 1999, compared to 65 percent in 1991.[4] On the whole, trade among CIS countries is characterized by an excess of imports over exports. Thus export interests may conflict with the creation of mutual markets for the CIS.[5]

Reintegration Policies

The countries now participating in the CIS began in mid-1993 to consider ways to reintegrate economically. However, despite numerous agreements, little has been implemented.[6]

In September 1993, the Treaty of Formation of the Economic Union of the CIS was signed. Its stated goal was a united economic area based on the following principles:

(1)   free movement of goods and services;
(2)   free movement of labor and capital;
(3)   protection of property rights; and
(4)   contracts without nationalistic biases.

A complementary agreement was approved to support cooperation among enterprises in different CIS countries without regard to the form of enterprise ownership. Implementation required improvements in the legal institutions of the CIS countries. Progress, as in the economic integration of Western Europe, would occur in stages: a multilateral free trade zone, a customs union, a common market, and full economic and monetary union.

In April 1994, the Agreement for a Free Trade Zone called for gradual elimination of tariffs and quotas, unification of customs regulations, and unimpeded transit. An important goal was to facilitate the use of the national currencies as a means of payment among the CIS countries. The Interstate Bank of the CIS agreed upon by the Council of the Heads of States of the CIS was meant to establish a multilateral system of payments among the central banks within the CIS.

The impossibility of rapid integration became evident in 1995, when subregional groupings within the CIS emerged. In 1996 Russia, Belarus, Kazakhstan, and Kirghizia signed the Treaty of Deepening of Integration in Economic and Humanitarian Fields. The aim was a stage-by-stage integration of the member states. Tajikistan signed the treaty in 1999. A high degree of integration was envisaged, but yet to be realized, for the union of Belarus and Russia created in 1997 and modified in December 1999. Uzbekistan, Kazakhstan, and Kirghizia signed the Treaty of Creation of a Unified Economic Space in April 1994; Tajikistan also signed in 1998. In 1998 these four countries formed the Central Asian Economic Association. In 1997 Georgia, Ukraine, Azerbaijan, and Moldova decided to create an informal association, now known as GUUAM, which Uzbekistan joined in 1999.

Recommendations

There are two sides to achieving increased economic integration. The most obvious is mutual abolition of barriers to the movement of goods, services, and productive factors. The other is the development of legal mechanisms within each country that are compatible with one another. Also vital are the mechanisms of cross-national cooperation—including the CIS itself.

The institutional and legal foundations of economic integration established by the CIS agreements need to be consolidated. The Economic Court of the CIS should be amply funded to accelerate its activities. The branch-industry coordination institutions of the CIS could coordinate policies to further economic reform and restructuring within CIS countries, encouraging the emergence of CIS-based multinational enterprises.

Rapid formation of a full economic union is not feasible. Customs regulations could effectively be undone by noncompliance by neighboring countries, either in law or in practice. Thus, each successive stage of integration must be introduced with careful forethought and should embrace only prepared countries.

Movement toward a payments union, entailing mutual convertibility of all national currencies on a continual basis, will necessarily be slow (Grinberg and Lubsky 1995). The strengthening of national currencies, the development of the national financial markets, and the coordination of the monetary policies are all prerequisites for stable exchange rates with rigid limits of deviations, as in the European Payments Union of 1950-1958. A stabilization fund in hard currencies would be needed.

Attention should be given to infrastructural development to facilitate trade. This includes investment in transport and communication, the strengthening of trade finance, trade fairs, and aiding the development of direct ties among enterprises from different republics.

Cooperation within subregional economic groupings has proven feasible, and could be continued. However, efforts at the subregional level should involve coordination at the CIS level to ensure that the authority of the CIS is not jeopardized.

Conclusion

Economic growth in Russia, as well as the other countries of the CIS, would be facilitated by increased economic integration. Creating conditions in which the CIS countries favor one another's goods would cushion adjustment to international competition. However, such a policy should not be implemented too liberally, for in the long run it could become an obstacle to industrial development. It is at least equally important to harmonize legal frameworks and improve payments mechanisms.

Without deliberate policy, further economic disintegration may occur. A cautious, deliberate approach will be necessary because supranational bodies are easily seen to encroach upon the sovereign rights of member countries. Although the disintegration of the former Soviet Union was rapid, economic reintegration will be slow, even with sound economic policies.

Notes

1. The combined GDP of the CIS countries declined about 40 percent from 1992 to 1999; investment fell 71 percent, retail trade 28 percent, industrial production 46 percent, and agricultural output 36 percent (SNG 2000).

2. *Kommersant Daily*, October 20, 1993; *Voprosy ekonomiki*, 1999, 12: 101.

3. *Voprosy ekonomiki*, 1995, 10: 72.

4. Ibid.

5. *Ekonomika i zhizn*, 2000, 6: 1.

6. According to the available data for 1999, over 54 percent of trade operations between Russia and Belarus were barter exchanges (*Finansovyie izvestiia*, December 12, 1999).

References

Garnett, Sherman. 1995. "Iskushenyie integraziei." *Nauchnyie doklady Moskovskogo Tsentra Karnegi* 1: 6.

Grinberg, Ruslan S., and M. S. Lubsky. 1995. "Vzaimnyie raschety stran SNG: Problemy i vozmozhnyie resheniia." *Problemy prognozirovaniia* 1: 51-62.

Shishkov, Yuri. 1996. "Ternistyi put Rossii v mirovuiu ekonomiku." *Rossiiskii ekonomicheskii zhurnal* 1: 31.

Sodruzhestvo Nezavisimykh Gosudarstv (SNG). 1996. *Kratkii spravochnik predvaritelnikh statisticheskikh itogov 1996.* Moscow: Statkomitet SNG.

———. 1999. *Statisticheskii spravochnik 1998 godu.* Moscow: Statkomitet SNG.

———. 2000. *Statisticheskii spravochnik 1999 godu.* Moscow: Statkomitet SNG.

21

Agriculture

Geliy Shmeliov, Bruce McWilliams, John Giraldez, and Alexander Vedrashko

Russian agriculture has adapted poorly to the new economic environment. Total farm output at the end of the 1990s was less than two-thirds that of 1992. Rural unemployment is high, and farm incomes have fallen to below half the national average.[1] Deterioration in health care, education, law enforcement, transportation, and welfare services has intensified the social distress in rural areas. As a consequence of poorer diet (Table 21.1), as much as half of Russia's children may be underdeveloped mentally or physically due to malnourishment.[2]

Soviet-era state-owned farms have been transformed into worker-owned corporations that still require government support to survive. The current policy controversy is how to proceed from there. At one pole, the collapse of the reorganized farms is welcomed so that "real privatization" can proceed with the emergence of independent private farms. However, rural political leaders and the agricultural bloc in the federal parliament (Duma) are wary of radical change. Most farm workers do not expect to benefit from

Table 21.1. Per Capita Food Consumption Indices, 1990–1997

	1990	1991	1992	1993	1994	1995	1996	1997
Meat products	100	92	80	79	76	73	68	67
Dairy products	100	90	73	76	72	66	60	59
Eggs	100	103	94	90	85	77	72	72
Sugar	100	81	64	66	66	68	72	68
Potatoes	100	106	111	120	115	117	118	123
Cereal products	100	101	105	104	104	104	98	99

Source: OECD Secretariat (1998).

reform. They are uncertain about the quality of land they would receive and are afraid of losing the social-economic security, such as housing, pension, and health care (Brooks et al. 1996). Heads of these farms, employing outmoded practices, remain focused on maintaining relations with federal and local government so as to obtain needed subsidies.[3] Amidst inflated hopes, independent private farms have not flourished.[4] Support for a return to Soviet-style central control remains strong in the farming areas.

After providing an overview of the historical background and current environment for Russian agriculture, this chapter addresses six key problem areas: domestic demand, international trade, market infrastructure, property rights, finance and insurance, and diffusion of technology. The focus is the role of government in accommodating the transition.

Background

Soviet agriculture was based primarily on two types of large enterprises, *sovkhoz* (state farms) and *kolkhoz* (collective farms). The *sovkhoz* were run like Soviet factories, filling orders with prices and quantities set by Moscow. The *kolkhoz* not only filled output orders dictated by government but also produced output for sale in response to demand on the open market. There were also interfarm enterprises (known as *mezhkhoz*), which were joint ventures between farm and nonfarm enterprises mostly for food processing.

Family gardens or "household plots" were also prevalent. Farm workers were allotted private plots on which they grew crops and occasionally raised livestock. In addition, many nonfarmers, both urban and rural, cultivated fruits and vegetables on their own plots. Some advantaged urban dwellers grew food on the grounds of their dachas. Dachas and gardens for urban families became more widespread in the late 1980s. All of these household plots were small, generally ranging from a minuscule 0.04 hectares up to 0.3 hectares.

New Forms of Organization

After the Soviet collapse, the government transferred land and other assets to farmers who lived and worked on state and collective farms. By 1994, land deeds were distributed to over 50 million Russians (Wegren and Belenkiy 1998). Almost 300,000 independent private farms were created, and more than 15 million families have title to household plots. Also, the entire agri-industrial complex (food storage and processing, farm machinery, fertilizer) has been privatized.

Most of the privatized Soviet farms are closed joint-stock companies in which land and other assets belong to the enterprise, which in turn is owned by shareholders.[5] The worker-owners in these newly formed farm corporations can sell, lease, and bequeath their shares, but other farm members have right of first refusal, and land must stay in agricultural production. Production by these enterprises has steadily declined in the 1990s, and by 1997 they produced about a third of previous levels.

Independent private farms became possible only after the fall of the Soviet regime (Durgin 1994). At the beginning of 1997, the median size was less than 20 hectares, and the mean was 44 hectares, with 8 percent above 100 hectares (MAF, annual). While at the inception of shock therapy independent private farms were seen as the wave of the future, they have not been very successful and their numbers declined in the late 1990s.

Household plots account for a rising share of national agricultural output, helping prevent starvation among low-income families. In 1998

Table 21.2. Share of Household Plot Production, Selected Crops, 1990–1998 (percent)

	1990	1991	1992	1993	1994	1995	1996	1997	1998
All Vegetables	30	46	55	65	67	73	77	76	80
Potatoes	66	72	78	82	88	90	90	91	91
Fruit	51	65	69	69	77	77	79	80	-
Meat	25	37	35	40	43	49	52	55	57
Milk	25	26	31	35	39	41	45	47	48
Eggs	22	22	26	27	29	30	31	30	30
Wool	25	28	32	35	37	43	46	51	55

Source: Goskomstat (annual).

they produced over 90 percent of potatoes and four-fifths of other vegetables (Table 21.2). The number of urban families with household plots, mostly production for subsistence, more than doubled from the late 1980s to over 22 million by 1995. The surge in output from household plots is driven not by the dynamics of efficiency, but rather by the bleak economic conditions: high unemployment, low income, meager pensions, and wage arrears.

Price Shock

In the Soviet era, the state invested heavily in agriculture and made food supply a high priority (Markish and Cook 1991).[6] Agriculture was sustained by a price structure that, ignoring underlying supply and demand conditions, set farm input prices low and output prices high.[7] With the introduction of a market system, the dramatic shift in the price structure was as devastating as the reduction in government funding.

The prices of agricultural inputs have risen much more than the prices of produce (Goskomstat 1998). Rising indebtedness and lack of liquidity have also forced farmers to reduce purchases of fertilizer and other inputs. They are caught in a vicious circle as depressed harvests, sales, and income further reduce ability to purchase inputs for the following season. While the

Table 21.3. Input Use of Farm Enterprises, 1990–1998

	1990	1991	1992	1993	1994	1995	1996	1997	1998
Agricultural	100	100	99	97	99	97	97	97	95
Mineral	100	102	87	43	21	15	15	15	11
Compound	100	91	67	62	44	35	23	16	-
Gasoline	100	94	84	55	33	30	26	-	-

Source: Goskomstat (annual).

strong agrarian bloc won substantial subsidies for agriculture in the early 1990s, the amount of support steeply declined after 1995 (Wegren 1998). The use of fertilizer is only a ninth of 1990 input levels, and fuel use is about a third (Table 21.3). Farm investments have also declined substantially, and there has been a one-third decline in the stock of farm equipment. Cheap, low-quality seeds contribute to yields.

Policy Agenda

Domestic Demand

During the transition in Russia, incomes deteriorated while consumer subsidies were cut. These, together with the distribution of land for gardens and dachas to the urban population, have led to a dramatic increase in the share of homegrown food in household consumption and steadily declining food purchases throughout the 1990s.[8] Clearly, overall economic growth is vital to the recovery in demand for farm products. Since the poor spend a higher percentage of their incomes on food, government policies that promote a more equal distribution of income and supplements for the poor can boost domestic demand.

The decline of the food processing industry directly reduces demand for farm output. While farm production has severely deteriorated, the decline in the food processing industry has been even more dramatic. Output for most processed foods is only one-third to one-half of 1990 levels, and often lower (Table 21.4). Production of canned goods, for example, has declined

Table 21.4. Food Industry Production Indices, 1990–1998

	1990	1991	1992	1993	1994	1995	1996	1997	1998
Bread	100	91	94	84	75	62	56	49	44
Canned Goods	100	85	65	55	34	30	26	26	-
Cheese	100	86	65	68	62	48	42	36	39
Meats	100	88	72	62	50	37	29	22	20

Source: Goskomstat (annual) and Ministry of Agriculture and Food.

by nearly three-quarters. Much of this may be explained by inferior quality compared with imports, and by the lower costs of home-garden production. As a result, consumers prefer to make their own preserved products at home or purchase imported goods. The future of Russia's processing industry depends on its ability to produce higher-quality processed goods that can compete against foreign imports. Foreign direct investment can provide not only the needed capital, but also managerial and technological skills to help build this industry.

Many farms have created their own processing facilities because this reduces the transaction costs for selling their product, creates higher value-added products, and allows farms to innovate and adapt technologies to their needs. Voluntary integration of the production of processed goods with a farm enterprise can be beneficial. However, in an effort to increase the demand for farm products in their areas, some local governments have given former collective farms control over local food-processing firms (Melyukhina and Serova 1995). If processors are simply forced to purchase products from regional collective farms, these farms do not have incentives to supply high-quality agricultural goods, thereby jeopardizing the final sales of processed products.

Similarly, some local governments set quotas that must be met before produce can be shipped to other localities, and sometimes even impose export tariffs on such shipments. These restrictions reduce potential gains in efficiency from specialization and the ability of farmers to establish regular marketing channels. Restrictions on interregional trade increase the vulnerability of consumers and the processing industry by exposing them to local fluctuations in agricultural production. Promoting interregional trade helps stabilize and increase domestic agricultural supply, thereby reducing reliance on foreign suppliers.

International Trade

Food and agricultural imports in 1997 were 5.4 times greater than exports (MAF 1998). The precipitous decline in the exchange value of the ruble early in the fall of 1998 further eroded living standards and reduced imports, including food products.[9] The declining purchasing power was exacerbated by a backlog in foodstuffs from international humanitarian help.

Better trading arrangements with other countries can increase the demand for Russian products by compensating for the lack of domestic demand. After the Soviet Union's collapse, many of Russia's economic ties were broken. To promote links between Russia and the other successor states of the Soviet Union, the Commonwealth of Independent States was established in 1991. The Agreement on a Common Agricultural Market was signed in 1997, but much needs to be done to facilitate further trade flows with these countries.

Trade arrangements with Western Europe leave Russia at a disadvantage. The Partnership and Co-operation Agreement (PCA) with the European Union (EU) ostensibly guarantees that agricultural goods and processed food traded between Russia and the EU are free of qualitative restrictions. However, Russia is still on the EU's list of nonmarket economies, which weakens Russia's bargaining position in trade disputes. Moreover, large agricultural subsidies in the EU artificially lower the prices of European food products and prevent prices from reflecting natural comparative advantage. Reductions in subsidies to European producers would invariably boost Russian agricultural exports and reduce imports.

Although Russia formally applied for membership in the World Trade Organization in 1994, it has not yet been granted. Russia has been granted conditional most-favored-nation status with the U.S., but is still hindered by being designated a nonmarket economy. Russia has granted preferential treatment to China, Cuba, Vietnam, and Mongolia. However, the lack of progress in developing trade agreements with Central and Eastern European countries other than Romania and Slovenia limits the potential for increasing trade with its neighbors.

Government export subsidies and import restrictions, which were supported by the Minister of Agriculture (Semenov 1999), may incite trade disputes and affect international relations. These policies also reduce the efficiency of the agricultural sector by undermining the incentives to reform unproductive former collective farms.

Market Infrastructure

The transition of the agricultural sector to a market economy requires not only the privatization of productive activities, but also a supporting infrastructure that facilitates transactions between input suppliers, the agricultural sector, and final consumers. Improving the infrastructure requires stemming criminal activities, investing in transportation and storage facilities, reducing monopolistic supply of inputs, and disseminating pertinent market information. These conditions have not been adequately met in Russia.

Criminal involvement is pervasive in many of the market activities in Russia. High priority should be given to eliminating payoffs to organized crime that restrict access to important urban markets. Local and city governments can boost produce distribution by ensuring ample space and facilities for farmers to sell their products free of criminal intimidation. Organized crime frequently interferes in the transportation of agricultural goods and control middlemen, while government officials often demand bribes or favors. These activities not only create hazards, they artificially add costs and reduce the revenues that serve to finance and motivate agricultural production. These barriers can hurt a large farm corporation, but they can kill an independent private farm or discourage its creation.

To enhance the mobility of goods, the government must help finance rural transportation infrastructure. Regulation of railway pricing is also vital, especially in areas where alternative modes of transportation are unavailable or excessively expensive. Some local governments set prices for railway transport so high that use of the rails is prohibitive for farmers.

Despite the reduction in agricultural output, there is still a shortage of storage space. This is the result of agri-food warehouses being used for other purposes, shortage of storage on farms, and lack of specialized storage for fruits and vegetables. The absence of financing for increasing storage facilities depresses prices at times of harvest. The consequence is reduced farmer earnings and decreased stability in the domestic supply of products to consumers and processors, which increases reliance on foreign imports.

Much of the old system of supply continues, and there is little brand competition for chemical and other inputs. High transaction costs, such as the transportation costs discussed above, and lack of information about alternatives, contribute to monopolistic regional markets for inputs.

For trade to occur and transactions to be efficient, all parties need accurate data on prices and product availability. Government should facilitate the private transfer of such information through mass media channels. This would reduce price differentials between regions, erode the power of local monopolies, reduce firm costs and uncertainties, and encourage more exchanges to take place (Melyukhina and Serova 1995). The dissemination of price-data information places producers in a better negotiating position with processors and distributors, who tend to have better information. It also shows producers how prices adjust to changes in supply and demand, giving them a better understanding of how a free-market economy functions. Finally, by establishing institutions to gather this data, one can monitor the impact of policies and the performance of the agriculture and food sector. Regional wholesale markets also provide a mechanism for transmitting information and provide a location for transactions to occur. Federal and local governments should provide the necessary organizational assistance for creating these markets.[10]

Property Rights

Many see the primary objective of agricultural reform in Russia as dismantling large former collective farms, with smaller private farms and household plots providing the basis for future agriculture (IFC 1998; OECD 1998). Though appealing to some Western advisers, such a strategy is not socially or politically feasible (Semenov 1999), and is economically hard to defend since farms tend to be large in countries where land is abundant. It may be argued that large farms are necessary in Russia to achieve productive efficiency in the use of labor and machinery, to gain economies of scale in marketing, and to facilitate the financing of investment (Wegren 1998).

Clear and protected property rights are important for motivating efficiency and facilitating change.[11] In other words, two conditions must be met for effective property rights: to identify who has rights to what property, and to create the legal framework and enforcement mechanisms to protect these rights.

Most agricultural land in Russia is owned by former *kolkhoz* in which individual farmers formally own shares. The meaning of these shares is ambiguous, and they are difficult to convert into property and cannot be used as collateral. Ordinary shareholders have little power to affect farm policy and change managers.

If clear property rights are transferred directly to individuals, the question of optimal size and organization of Russian farms can be resolved, at least in part, through individual or group initiatives and market transfer of ownership. A model for doing this has been developed in Nizhny Novgorod Province (IFC 1995). On the large Soviet-era farms, land and other property were valued, and each member received shares based on years of work and other considerations. Members used these shares to bid in an auction of parcels of land and other property, thus distributing the property fairly and according to the preferences of the bidders. The members could use their new land or other property in whatever way they liked: to start their own independent farm; to rent their land to another farmer; or to invest their land as a share of a new company organized by an individual or group.

As a result, large farms were usually divided into several smaller farms more specialized in production. Few members used their shares to start independent private farms. The success of these restructured farms has been generally positive. The absence of guaranteed employment allowed management to improve worker productivity. Initial results showed that crop harvests on these farms were, on average, 30 percent higher than the average for Nizhny Novgorod Province, although many continued to perform poorly.

The Nizhny Novgorod experiments provide one model for restructuring the former collective farms. The federal government should continue to disseminate information about experiments like these and facilitate the restructuring process.

Some top farm managers who started independent private farms gained superior equipment and land during the reorganization and privatization in 1991 and 1992. Others who wanted to separate from former collective farms were typically allocated low-quality land (Melyukhina and Serova 1995). Shareholders faced with few alternatives can also be pressured by the management to sell their shares to the corporation for a nominal amount. To the extent that the transition process has allowed insiders to use their positions to take advantage of the changing environment, the reforms have been not only inequitable but have often retarded development. There must be prohibitions against conflicts of interest and clear guidelines to reduce discretion in administrative decisions. There also must be full disclosure of decisions and fair and open competition regarding the distribution of resources. To make administrators accountable, procedures must be established to investigate complaints and discipline irresponsible administrators.

Independent private farms are more likely to have the flexibility to innovate and change than do farms under collective management. This does not mean that all aspects of collective activity should be dropped. Cooperative operations provide various social benefits as well as economies of scale. For example, purchasing of inputs, renting, storing and marketing of outputs may be done cooperatively, even if farm operations are private.

In addition, collective bargaining units are very important in rural areas for getting government decision makers to recognize their needs and fund projects in their areas. In the current political environment, people feel more confident about receiving government subsidies if they are part of a collective.

Reluctance to create independent private farms throughout Russia continues to be exacerbated by insecurity regarding property rights. The 1993 constitution permits the sale of land, and a 1996 presidential decree (On Guarantees of Constitutional Rights of Citizens to Land) specifies that land can be freely rented. However, the legislation does not establish effective sale mechanisms with state guarantees of future ownership. A Land Code must be created that develops mechanisms for transfer of collective land into independent private ownership and for permanent exchange (sale) or temporary use (rent) of property, and must formulate procedures for enforcing this law. This code should facilitate the emergence of real estate and agricultural land markets, registering titles to property and permitting the mortgage of land. The police and courts need to be isolated from political interference and provided with sufficient funding to investigate violations of the code (Gordon 1997) and reduce corruptive influences.

Amidst economic crisis, land prices may be distorted. Moreover, the sale of land is of great concern to those who work the land generally, since they do not have the capital to purchase it. Empirical observations in Central and East European countries suggest that when market imperfections are large, renting or leasing land provided longer leases as transition progressed, information distribution improved, and market and institutional instability declined (Macours and Swinnen 1999).

A further benefit of private ownership is that it creates incentives for efficient land and cost management practices, since owners want to preserve value and reduce production costs. For example, owners may practice erosion control, more limited use of chemical insecticides, and improved disposal of animal and industrial wastes than was common in the Soviet era. In this way, market forces provide some environmental control in agricultural activities which the state could not previously penetrate.

Table 21.5. Yield per Hectare, Selected Crops, 1990–1998

	1990	1991	1992	1993	1994	1995	1996	1997	1998
Rye	100	80	89	75	75	61	70	91	42
Winter Wheat	100	83	78	77	66	50	53	68	48
Spring Wheat	100	81	115	99	90	89	95	119	66
Sugar Beets	100	79	81	86	57	80	69	67	60
Sunflowers	100	90	86	75	65	82	57	63	58

Source: Ministry of Agriculture and Food.

Finance and Insurance

Due to declining yields and unfavorable prices, farmers are unable to finance future investments in land and machinery after they have paid their production costs. Lack of credit can prevent them from meeting even immediate needs for quality seeds, fertilizer, and fuel. This inability to invest adequately in agriculture reduces future farm productivity (Table 21.5) and output, which further reduces farm revenues and future ability to invest. Therefore, the agricultural sector has found itself in a downward spiral of investment, productivity, and output. Processors, traders, and merchants also lack access to capital to do business, causing breaks in marketing channels and diminishing demand for raw agricultural outputs.

While direct government subsidies to the agricultural sector allow minimal investment in agriculture and mitigate some of the consequences of the adverse factors that affect profitability, they suppress incentives to improve productivity on farms. Unfortunately, during the transition period, financial institutions require very high collateral as a result of a lack of clear property rights, nonfunctional asset (land) markets, high inflation, risk and uncertainty during transition. As discussed in Chapter 17, one remedy is to create development banks for agriculture that would subsidize interest rates for loans from private banks, and, if necessary, provide loans directly to farmers. Loan guarantee programs can also increase the supply of funds for borrowers by reducing the risk on lending institutions. The programs would need to be designed to reduce moral hazard and expedite closing or reorganization of unprofitable farms.

When approving government credit assistance, authorities have given preference to former collective farms. In years of poor harvest, independent private farms receive less government support for crop losses than do collectives. Moreover, there is no government program to provide infrastructure, such as electricity and road access, to independent private farms. Equal treatment and access to finance would increase the efficiency of private farm operations.

Income risks related to fluctuations in price and weather also hinder agricultural investment. Price risks can be reduced by the development of an integrated futures market throughout the nation. Risks from adverse weather may be alleviated by creating a crop insurance program. Such a program could be administered by the private sector and backed by the government, with the premiums paid by the farmers. In the long run, income risks may be reduced through a program in which farmers contribute to the program in good years and receive assistance in bad years.

Diffusion of Technology

The breakdown of the Soviet Union and the ensuing economic crisis have resulted in a knowledge vacuum in Russia's agricultural sector. Funding for education and research has been cut drastically. The networks between universities, research institutes, and the government have been broken, which is reflected in the sharp reductions in conferences and circulation of journals.

The system for agricultural research and its dissemination has fundamental weaknesses. These include lack of communication and collaboration among research institutes, and failure to focus on economic efficiency and product quality. Inexperience in market-oriented agricultural economics and management hinders organizational change and the creation of new production strategies to meet the needs of private farming. There is also a need to boost expertise in agroecology and biotechnology to facilitate innovations that serve local needs. These innovations may include existing agricultural technologies in other countries, particularly in basic animal nutrition and seed selection (World Bank 1998).

The new competitive environment in agriculture requires that farmers and processors learn advanced farm production and processing practices in order to succeed. They also need to become more sophisticated in management and marketing. Agribusiness programs must be developed, and accessibility to these programs should be government supported. Extension services must expand to include training and dissemination of information in farm production, processing, management, and marketing.

Conclusion

It is a Herculean task to establish a dynamic market-based agricultural sector. The Russian agricultural sector was a disaster waiting to happen given past dependence on government support, a distorted price structure, and development in remote and infertile locations. Persistent macroeconomic depression, a shrinking food processing industry, and subsidized farm production abroad are all retarding demand. Property rights regarding land ownership and governance of privatized farm enterprises are weak due to lack of legal definition and state enforcement. In many areas of the country, access to markets is controlled by organized crime. Transport and storage infrastructure is insufficient, while transport fees are often prohibitive. Investment is thwarted by unavailability of financing. Private institutions, such as marketing networks, futures markets, and insurance, have not developed sufficiently.

In the 1990s attempts to cure these problems and reform the agricultural sector have been hindered by the conservative agrarian establishment's resistance to change. The policies of many foreign advisers and international agencies have been driven by ideological imperatives: all collective economic and property structures must be disbanded as government withdraws from involvement in the economy. Effective reform policies would take into account the existing social and economic realities within agriculture, including the distributional consequences and political feasibility of alternative policies.

While it is counterproductive to support obsolete farm enterprises that are indifferent to market requirements, government needs to take an active role. It should, directly or indirectly, invest in transportation and storage facilities; improve research in and disseminate information about agricultural innovations; provide agribusiness courses and extension services to train farmers and processors in the areas of modern production, processing, management, and marketing; support the development of private farm credit institutions; increase access to markets and retention of profits by reducing the influence of organized crime; provide equal treatment to all forms of agricultural enterprises; and clarify legal property rights and create enforcement mechanisms to ensure that these rights are protected.

Notes

1. Soil fertility, irrigated land area, sown area, livestock numbers, and the availability of machine parts have all declined (Goskomstat, annual, and BEA 1998). Between 1990 and 1998, meat production fell by half and milk output dropped by 40 percent. Grain production depends on weather conditions, and between 1994 and 1999 ranged from between 41 and 76 percent of 1990 levels. Employment in agriculture was down 7 percent, and crop yields per hectare have severely declined. (See Tables 21.3 and 21.5.).

2. Based on a report of the International Federation of the Red Cross and Red Crescent Society (Bloomberg newscast, October 22, 1998). At Russia's request, the United States and the European Union agreed to supply Russia with $1 billion in food aid in 1999 (Reuters, March 19, 1999). In 1989, the average Russian diet was comparable to that of Western countries (Serova 1995). However, since 1990, per capita food consumption has declined for most products. While potato consumption has increased by around 20 percent, consumption of meat products has declined by 30 percent, milk and dairy products by 40 percent, vegetables by 10 percent, and fruits and berries by around 20 percent.

3. The Soviet Union invested heavily in agricultural capital during the 1970s, and during the 1980s it provided large subsidies so that consumer food prices could be kept low (Serova 1995).

4. Independent private farms represented only 6 percent of agricultural land use in 1997 (MAF, annual). In terms of select crop production, independent private farms represented 6.6 percent of grains, 11 percent of sunflowers, 4 percent of sugar, 1 percent of potatoes, and 1.8 percent of vegetables produced (Goskomstat, annual).

5. A small number of agricultural cooperatives have also been formed (OECD 1998).

6. From the early 1960s to the late 1980s, gross agricultural output rose 72 percent, compared with a 30 percent population growth. In 1990, per capita meat consumption reached 70 kilograms, and the amount of beef consumption was higher than in Western Europe (Shend 1993).

7. For example, "acting rationally, given the relative prices they faced," Soviet farms commonly fed bread to cattle in the face of shortages of livestock feed and subsidized bread prices (Bromley 1993, 6).

8. Liefert (1996) notes that much of the decline in farm output is attributable to a sharp drop in animal products, which he views as a normal adjustment to removal of price supports and declining income. However, the fall in output is more widespread and deeper than would be suggested by this view.

9. Imports from non-CIS countries were down 47.9 percent during January-April 1999 compared with the same period the previous year. Imports of meat and poultry were 22 percent, medicine were 33 percent, and machinery and equipment were 66 percent of their values over the same period in 1998 (Ministry of Economy 1999).

10. For example, wholesale markets have been opened by the EU's Tacis program in Oryel and Pokhvistnevo (Samara Oblast) in close cooperation with local governments. They are distributing this information through a Central Memory Unit at the Ministry of Agriculture (Tacis 1999).

11. The ability of the market in the agricultural sphere, and elsewhere, to promote efficiency and exchange requires property rights that are fully specified, exclusive, transferable, and effectively enforced (Randall 1987). Full specification defines the restrictions on owners as well as penalties for violations. Exclusivity assures that the benefits and penalties of an action fall on the

owner. Transferability allows ownership change to enable the property to move to its highest value use.

References

Bromley, Daniel W. 1993. "Creating Market Economies from Command Economies." *Economic Issues* 121. Madison: University of Wisconsin.

Brooks, K., D. Krylatykh, Z. Lerman, A. Petrikov and V. Uzun, 1996. "Agricultural Reform in Russia: A View from the Farm Level," *World Bank Discussion Papers* 327. Washington, D.C.: World Bank.

Bureau of Economic Analysis (BEA). 1998. *Survey of Economic Policy in Russia.* Moscow: BEA.

Durgin, Frank. 1994. "Russia's Private Farm Movement?" *Soviet and Post-Soviet Review* 21.

Gordon, Henry F. 1997. "The Role of Government in a Market-Oriented Cereals Sector: Price Stabilization and Income Support." Chapter 4 in Lawrence D. Smith and Neil Spooner, eds. *Cereals Sector Reform in the Former Soviet Union and Central and Eastern Europe.* Oxon, UK: CAB International.

Goskomstat of Russia. 1998. *Consumer Prices in Russia.* Moscow.

Goskomstat of Russia. Annual. *Agriculture in Russia.* Moscow.

International Finance Corporation (IFC). 1998. *Monitoring Russian Reorganized Farms.* Unpublished report. Washington, DC.

International Finance Corporation (IFC). 1995. *Land Privatization and Farm Reorganization in Russia.* Washington, DC: International Finance Corporation.

Liefert, William M. 1996. "Russian Food Security is Not Threatened." *The Food Systems Policy Roundtable Journal.*

Markish, Yuri and Edward Cook. 1991. "Investment in Agriculture and Food Sectors." *USSR Agriculture and Trade Report: Situation and Outlook Series.* Washington, DC: U.S. Department of Agriculture, Economic Research Service.

Macours, Karen and Johan Swinnen. 1999. "Patterns of Agrarian Transition: A Comparison of Agricultural Output and Labor Productivity Changes in Central and Eastern Europe, the Former Soviet Union, and East Asia." Policy Research Group Working Paper No. 19. Department of Agricultural Economics, Katholieke Universiteit Leuven.

Melyukhina, O., and E. Serova. 1995. "On the Problem of Monopolism in the Sphere of Feed Processing." *Voprosy ekonomiki.*

Ministry of Agriculture and Food of Russia (MAF). Annual. *Production and Economic Figures for the Agroindustrial Complex in Russia.*

———. 1998. *Socio-economic Indicators in CIS Countries.* Department of Economics.

Ministry of Economy of Russia. 1999. *On Current Situation in the Economy of the Russian Federation for the Period of January - April 1999 and Forecast Until the End of 1999.*

Organization for Economic Co-operation and Development (OECD). 1998. *Agricultural Polices in non-OECD Member Countries, Monitoring and Evaluation 1998,* CCNM/AGR/TD (98) 40. Paris: OECD.

Randall, A. 1987. *Resource Economics.* New York: John Wiley & Son.

Semenov, Viktor. 1999. "Novy kurs agrarnoy politiki," *Ekonomist,* 1.

Serova, E. 1995. "Prerequisites and Essence of Contemporary Agrarian Reform in Russia." *Voprosy ekonomiki* (1).

Shend, Jaclyn Y. 1993. *Agricultural Statistics of the Former USSR Republics and the Baltic States: Statistical Bulletin Number 863.* Washington, DC: U.S. Department of Agriculture, Economic Research Service.

Tacis. 1999. "Replication of former successful Tacis projects in Russia." http://europa.eu.int/comm/dg1a/tacis/results/results_rus _success.html.

Wegren, Stephen K. 1998. *Agriculture and the State in Soviet and Post-Soviet Russia.* Pittsburgh: University of Pittsburgh Press.

Wegren, Stephen K. and Vladimir R. Belenkiy. 1998. "The Political Economy of the Russian Land Market." *Problems of Post-Communism,* 45 (4).

World Bank. 1998. *Transforming Agricultural Research Systems in Transition Economies: The Case of Russia.* Discussion Paper No. 396. Washington, DC.

22

The Coal Industry

Alexander Arbatov and Edit Kranner

The Russian coal sector mirrors the economic disarray of the entire nation. Restructuring began in 1992 amidst expectations inflated by Western advisers, who cavalierly applied free-market principles. Russian officials, intent on shielding the sector from market discipline, implemented privatization halfheartedly.

During the Soviet era, coal mining was considered strategically important to economic growth. Poorly conceived directives, however, resulted in an excess of mines, many in highly remote locations, including the Arctic Circle. At the time of the dissolution of the USSR, over 60 percent of electric power was generated by domestic coal, and Russia itself was the world's third largest coal producer.

The experience of many industrialized countries suggests that many years of intensive government involvement are inevitable. The British and French provided aid primarily in the form of severance payments, while the Germans concentrated on expanding demand for German coal. In each case, there was already a highly developed market infrastructure, relatively abundant job opportunities, and mobile labor (Anderson 1995; Radetzki 1995; Ashworth 1986).

Most mines would be unable to survive on their own if subjected to market conditions. While subsidies have been steadily declining as a percentage of GDP since the early 1990s, they continue to represent a significant portion of industry revenue.[1] Virtually all mines will either have to be closed or undergo comprehensive modernization. Both conditional subsidies and job-creation programs are needed.

Background

The coal sector was highly centralized prior to restructuring. All significant decisions were made in Moscow and implemented in 164 coal communities spread out over 17 coal regions. Government and management were one and the same. Workers belonged to the Communist Party Workers Union,[2] which provided health and vacation benefits.

In March 1993, government management was transformed into a state coal company, Rosugol (Russian Coal). Rosugol oversaw 28 regional coal companies known as "ugols." These are regional umbrellas for individual mines and mine-support facilities. In addition to the coal companies, approximately 10 "independent" coal structures have existed in Russia. These large, well-positioned mines and coal-preparation plants work directly with the Ministry of Fuel and Energy, bypassing Rosugol.

Rosugol maintained a strong hold until December 1997, when it was disbanded by presidential decree. Regional and local managers, who previously lacked access to information concerning their own customers and finance, were now being asked to budget and design enterprise strategies. Lack of transparency further contributed to the failure to genuinely decentralize operations. Funds disbursed at the federal level were not sufficiently tracked at regional and local levels.

Rosugol classified all mines into four categories: "viable," "not viable," "viable and likely to remain viable," and "viable and not likely to remain viable."[3] This classification was the single most defining step taken on the tumultuous path toward sector restructuring. For a long time it was kept secret from local managers, the unions, and journalists. Once revealed, the classification was shocking to local mine managers, workers, and even many federal officials who had not been trained or raised in an economic setting where financial priority was ever given to an enterprise. Well into 1994, officials and workers held little belief that traditional federal coal funding would actually lessen.

Rosugol announced in late 1993 that 42 nonviable mines would be closed, commencing that year. What would later become clear was that the list would be expanded to include the mines that were "viable and not likely to remain viable," and totaled over 100 closings.

In 1992, it was estimated that Russia maintained 201 underground mines and 102 surface mines. By the end of 1997 there were considerably less, approximately 164 underground mines and 74 surface mines (USAID 1998). During the course of restructuring, up to half of the mines are expected to close by 2002.

Production and Demand

Coal represents over 20 percent of Russia's primary thermal energy supply. About two-thirds of production is thermal coal (heat, power generation), and coking coal (steel production) represents the other third. While coal reserves, which exceed 200 billion tons, are sufficient for centuries of production, half these reserves remain in isolated regions of the country in severe climatic conditions.[4] Proven reserves of 20.9 billion tons account for upward of 8 percent of proven reserves worldwide. Production reached its peak in 1988 at 417.1 million tons. Throughout the 1980s, coal production averaged 380 million tons per year. Production is down approximately 50 percent since 1988.

Demand has fallen dramatically because of declining industrial production. Both industrial and residential demand are expected to fall further due to increased use of gas and oil as well as increased energy efficiency. Yet, there may be a rebound from an anticipated buildup of light production and small industry, as well as Japan and Europe's continued reliance on coal (USAID 1998). These forecasts, however, also anticipate significant modernization and an improved federal transport, tax, and finance infrastructure to support a growing industry. Expectations that a growing portion of coal-powered facilities will be converted to the use of natural gas further contribute to doubt on increased demand for Russian coal in the near future.

Another question for the future is whether electric power plants will rely, to a greater or lesser extent, on coal. The answer depends on environmental considerations. The conventional methods of coal burning and processing in Russia are unsatisfactory. Due to a lack of attention to the modernization of coal mines, the industry is falling into a state beyond repair. Coal authorities continue to fight for increased federal support aimed at modernization and building new mines. A 1995 government commission on coal mining called for the development and implementation of means to reduce atmospheric emissions, reclaim land, and provide economic incentives for environmental improvements. Ecologically sensitive innovations would raise the demand for coal. Development of such technologies, common in the West, requires industry-wide support with government providing at least a coordinating role. In addition, assistance with technology transfers is a promising area where developed countries can provide aid.

Social Assets

Less than half of those employed in the coal industry are engaged directly in coal production. The majority are occupied in the social facilities owned by the coal companies (World Bank 1994). A 1992 presidential decree mandated that these public services be transferred to municipal control. Housing, health care, roads, boilers, kindergartens (day cares), academic institutes, small groceries and shops, water and sewage, electricity, and repair and maintenance facilities are no longer recipients of federal subsidies directed through the coal industry. In the wake of these transfers, assets have either fallen into disrepair or have been poorly maintained by municipalities.

Sector reluctance, coal communities' growing social needs in the wake of restructuring, and lack of municipal experience in managing social assets delayed actual industry release of asset management until well into 1996. The delay in transfer provided managers the opportunity to identify and retain more valuable assets while transferring from municipal oversight those assets in greater disrepair or with little privatization potential. Rosugol, regional coal concerns, and mine enterprise managers were privy to this opportunity. There has been significant misuse of funds during transition, since managers at all levels have been permitted to allocate funds in a nontransparent manner.

While any restructuring involves significant social costs, coal restructuring has had a particularly adverse impact. Workers have not received the advance notice required by law,[5] coal subsidies have not been effectively used to provide better social protection for those who have lost their jobs, and the coal labor unions have failed to defend the interests of the workers affected by mine closures.

Social services transferred from coal companies to municipalities have deteriorated, nonminers have been inadequately protected from the impact of mine closures by the existing social safety net, and the present institutional arrangements do not ensure an equitable allocation or reliable distribution of subsidies. Finally, miners are ill-informed about their rights and the restructuring program, and mining communities have little trust in the present system, particularly for allocating and distributing subsidies.

Western Reform Strategy

In 1989 the United States started to provide assistance to the coal industry. What struck U.S. representatives was the consistent Soviet requests for knowledge and information, rather than funding. While the original scope of the aid was in the areas of health and safety, by 1992 USAID was also involved, with a wider mandate to include industry-restructuring issues. USAID, along with the privately funded Partners in Economic Reform, has made vital contributions to aid the changing coal sector, particularly in human terms.

However, the program had two failings (USAID 1998). First was the resistance of some U.S. officials to recognize the importance of Russian industry, notably its energy sector, as a starting place for overall economic and political reform. The second element was what often appeared to be U.S. congressional whim. A number of congressional gestures stymied legitimate implementation of simple, important assistance measures for Russia. These trickled down to on-the-ground assistance activities already underway in Russia and gave great pause to some useful assistance efforts, much to the dismay of their Russian counterparts.

Accessing capital not only to purchase coal equipment, but to finance coal operations, has proven to be difficult. Unlike other energy sectors including oil and gas, coal does not attract domestic or foreign private investment. Most coal managers remain ignorant of the steps required to secure financing in a market setting. Valuation of assets, breakdown of labor and production costs, and financial forecasts are important parts of a market-financing process that has yet to become systemic.

The World Bank made two loans to the coal sector in 1996 totaling $525 million. An additional $800 million was approved in 1997. The World Bank's thorough study of production, transport, and demand provides a useful foundation for determining which mines should be closed and which could be revitalized with prudent investment (World Bank 1994). However, the study was limited in conception. There was little evaluation of the effects of widespread closures, and government-managed restructuring was not considered. Market forces presumably would automatically compel closures and downsizing.

Conditional Subsidies

After agriculture, coal has been Russia's most subsidized sector. Between 1992 and 1997, upward of $1.6 trillion was spent by the government to support the coal industry (USAID 1998). In 1996, coal support totaled 2.1 percent of the federal budget. This follows the traditional structure of state support to Soviet industries, subsidizing not only actual industry costs, but related social and community business costs ("ancillary support") which, under a market setting, should be the responsibility of local government or the private sector. These government subsidies, which impose a large burden on the federal budget, are lacking in economic rationale and ultimately deter needed restructuring. Western advisers have urged an end to these subsidies, thereby letting the market drive restructuring. However, given the devastating consequences of such action and the political clout of miners, outright suspension of subsidies is not feasible.[6]

Mining conditions throughout Russia are incredibly harsh, reminiscent of U.S. "pre-modernization" conditions of the 1930s and 1940s. Inherently dangerous mining conditions have worsened with the aging of equipment and neglect of maintenance and repair. Russia has one of the highest rates in the world for coal sector–related deaths and injuries, notably the loss of limbs. World experience has shown that investment in safety improvement results in cost savings, as medical and other expenses resulting from these injuries are dramatically reduced.

Subsidies must be made conditional, so that they serve as a tool for restructuring. A set of criteria is needed for companies to qualify to receive subsidies (decreasing over time). Such a system could expedite mine closures and improve productivity.[7] For example, companies receiving subsidies could be required to close those mines that the World Bank analysis demonstrated to be exceptionally unproductive. There should also be specified productivity growth goals. The development of effective marketing departments could be included in the conditions for subsidies. A well-designed system would create incentives for managers and hold them accountable for their use of funds (Bernstam and MacCurdy 1996).

Job-Creation Programs

Most frustrating about the coal mine closing process has been the lack of notice for workers and lack of information available to federal authorities as to the order of closings or the national mine-closing plan. Not until 1997 was there even minimal record keeping of closed mines and laid-off workers. More than 300,000 people left the coal sector between 1993 and 1997 (USAID 1998).[8] Over 30,000 workers have relocated within Russia and taken up alternative employment.

Many coal miners work off-shift as drivers, handymen, and teachers. This results in a workforce of decreasing loyalty and increased tax evasion. Where coal workers have sought their legal entitlements, they have often been faced with employer nonpayment of benefits, or thick bureaucracy which repeatedly defers them to other agencies until they give up their search. Virtually every week, some type of coal strike is waged. Whether it is a large strike at the federal level where miners converge on Moscow, a regional or local enterprise strike, or a mine section strike where as few as five workers stop work underground and conduct a mine "sit-in," the tool of striking is practically the only negotiating tool with any leverage for coal workers. The main issue plaguing the sector continues to be worker nonpayment, but strikes calling for improved mine-safety conditions or changed mine management are not uncommon. Managers find they are similarly trapped in an industrial environment where enforcement of worker responsibility is virtually nonexistent.

Job-retraining and creation programs have been disorganized and not necessarily oriented toward Russia's emerging market.[9] In 1993-1994, Rosugol offered training programs that encouraged coal-mining futures for young graduates. By 1995, many of the coal institutes were reoriented toward business training. However, a lack of knowledgeable teachers and questionable local markets left students to learn on their own.

In the meantime, coal managers and municipal authorities were receiving, through Rosugol and regional authorities respectively, funds earmarked for local job-creation programs. The reality of these programs was again compromised by the actions of those responsible for implementing the funds. Coal managers repeatedly sought to develop their mines, viable or not. City managers sought to rejuvenate dilapidated textile, chemical, and furniture factories that operated during the Soviet era but had no market for their products in Russia's new economy. Both types of managers have focused on creating a large quantity of jobs, disregarding market demand and worker training.

The most notorious example of this mentality has been demonstrated in regions where local managers urge federal funding for textile and clothing factories. Managers see these factories as places where women, often deemed unemployable in coal regions, can use their sewing skills productively. The reality of this proposal is that existing infrastructure to support the factories is crumbling, equipment is old (reminiscent of U.S. machinery of the 1920s), material is expensive and needs to be transported to the regions, and market demand for Russian-designed and manufactured clothing is very low.

A number of programs which have received partial federal funding have addressed the issue of relocating unemployed coal-sector workers, especially in the north, to other regions. For example, there are programs to relocate Vorkutan (Arctic) miners to Tula (Moscow region) and Rostov (southern Russia). However, the average relocation cost was $16,000 per person in 1994 and has risen substantially since then. Moreover, relocation may not be feasible given the acute housing shortage (Tchernina 1994).[10]

Since there is considerable overlap of skills in construction and mining, miners could be redeployed to improve physical infrastructure for economic development.[11] Lack of usable roads prevents food and other products from reaching the market (Dyker 1992). With subsidies to railroads reduced or discontinued, trucking is becoming increasingly crucial for many industries, and bus transport will become more important for intercity travel, once people can better afford to travel again.

Because past mining practices have resulted in severe water pollution and extensive landscape destruction, restoration projects could temporarily employ many dismissed miners in areas without economic potential. Another potential area for employment growth is housing construction.

Conclusion

The rapid rate at which Russian coal mines are being closed must be accommodated. Unemployment and severance benefits, which help to overcome resistance to layoffs, will not suffice. Direct measures are needed:

turning subsidies into devices to speed restructuring; job-creation programs, particularly for transferring miners to the construction of infrastructure; and ecologically sound innovations in coal use.

Adjustment measures should be applied in a more open fashion. Effective monitoring of government support, with findings subject to public scrutiny, is essential. Leadership from the national government is needed to overcome the resistance of miners fearing the worst. It is also necessary to win the support of and surmount the corruption of the trade unions and local governments. In addition, government regulation of transport charges, support for improvements in transportation infrastructure, and protection of transportation from costly criminal interference are all critical.

Success in the coal industry is especially crucial, as this sector has imposed such a large burden on the federal budget. The example of an effective transition program for the coal industry would give economic reform a boost.

Notes

1. In 1993, 77 percent of coal-sector costs were federally funded; by 1997, support had been reduced to approximately 25 percent of industry costs (USAID 1998).

2. Currently three trade unions represent the coal workers of Russia. The independent trade union NPG is a renegade union that began as the "coal workers' collective" at local mines from 1989 through 1991. Approximately 20 percent of Russian coal workers belong to NPG. There is also the Independent Coal Workers Union, which follows the traditional state structure where both workers and managers hold membership. The union oversees distribution of health and vacation benefits and is an arm of the government, working closely with Rosugol. Finally, the Union of Mine Engineers is affiliated with NPG but maintains separate union management at the local level. This offshoot of NPG was intended to cater to nonpolitical mine engineers seeking improved work conditions.

3. Beginning in 1993, a series of documents were published by Rosugol, the Ministry of Fuel and Energy, and various coal institutes on industry

restructuring. *Basic Trends*, published in July 1994, is the foundation for industry-restructuring strategy.

4. Prospects vary greatly by region. In the Tula-Moscow Basin, for example, virtually no mines have potential because of the poor nature of the deposits. The Kuzbass coal region in western Siberia is Russia's largest, yet it is thousands of kilometers away from its consumption centers and export stations. The Pechora Basin, in the Russian Arctic, is also remotely located in a difficult environment. Transport costs are decisive for other distant mines as well (USAID 1998).

5. Under Russian law, workers must be given a minimum of three months' notice.

6. There are almost a million coal-sector employees. Together with their families and communities, they constitute a powerful political force.

7. Output per worker in Russian coal mines is far lower than in developed Western countries. For example, productivity in the United Kingdom is three times as high as in Russia (World Bank 1994).

8. A 1995 breakdown of how workers would fare upon the closing of their mine predicted that: 30-40 percent would require social and other assistance; 10-15 percent would remain at the mine during closing; 10 percent would find work at local mines or preparation plants; 30 percent would retire; and 12 percent would find work in other sectors. A second study projected that 40 percent of a mine's workforce would be absorbed by other mine enterprises (USAID 1998). The reality during 1995-1996 was that workers initially laid off were employed more readily at nearby mine sites, yet mine positions were no longer available to workers laid off later in 1996 and into 1997.

9. Until the economic depression is over, there will be few job openings, and starting a private business is not a viable option for most. Few miners are in a position to invest in a business. Most savings were lost during the post-1991 inflation, and few even own their own homes. Unlike the situation in other Eastern European countries, such as Hungary or Poland, where there was a small but functioning private sector, Russians had no experience before 1991 as owners of legal businesses.

10. Those employed in coal mining and other industries considered strategically important during the Soviet era were assured heavily subsidized or free housing.

11. Construction projects could be the focus of reemployment programs in most coal basins. However, in remote regions where the entire economy is dependent on coal mining, it would make no sense to build new economic infrastructure after mines are closed.

References

Anderson, Kym. 1995. "The Political Economy of Coal Subsidies in Europe." *Energy Policy* 23(6): 485-496.

Ashworth, William. 1986. *The History of the British Coal Industry (Volume 5), 1946-1982: The Nationalized Industry.* Oxford: Clarendon Press.

Bernstam, Michael S., and Thomas E. MacCurdy. 1996. *Interenterprise Debt and the Russian Coal Industry.* Washington, DC: U.S. Agency for International Development.

Dyker, David A. 1992. *Restructuring the Soviet Economy.* New York: Routledge.

Fischer, Stanley, and Jacob Frenkel. 1992. "Key Issues of Soviet Economic Reform: Macroeconomic Issues of Soviet Reform." *American Economic Review* 82(2): 37-42.

Fischer, Stanley, and Alan Gelb. 1991. "The Process of Socialist Economic Transformation." *Journal of Economic Perspectives* 5(4): 91-105.

Peterson, D. J. 1993. *Troubled Lands: The Legacy of Soviet Environmental Destruction.* Boulder, CO: Westview Press.

Radetzki, Marian. 1995. "Elimination of West European Coal Subsidies: Implications for Coal Production and Coal Imports." *Energy Policy* 23(6): 509-518.

Sachs, Jeffrey D. 1992. "Privatization in Russia: Some Lessons from Eastern Europe." *American Economic Review* 82(2): 43-48.

Svejnar, Jan. 1991. "Microeconomic Issues in the Transition to a Market Economy." *Journal of Economic Perspectives* 5(4): 123-138.

Tchernina, Natalia V. 1994. "Unemployment and the Emergence of Poverty during Economic Reform in Russia." *International Labor Review* 133(5-6): 597-611.

United States Agency for International Development (USAID). 1998. *U.S. Assistance to Russian Coal.* Washington, DC: USAID.

World Bank. 1994. *Russian Federation Restructuring the Coal Industry: Putting People First*, Volumes I and II. Report No. 13187-RU. Washington, DC.

23

Energy Efficiency

Eric Martinot and Vladimir Usiyevich

Higher energy prices, lower subsidies, and privatization should have resulted in more efficient energy use in Russia. But enterprises and households have not been responsive to vast and profitable opportunities to improve energy efficiency. Without support and initiative from governments at municipal, regional, and federal levels, responses to market incentives may take decades. In the meantime, many enterprises, households, and municipal governments are overwhelmed by high energy costs. The situation in the residential sector has changed little since 1992. In industry, some larger enterprises had finally begun to finance energy-efficiency improvements by 1998, but the macroeconomic turmoil of late 1998 put a halt to these types of investments.

This chapter examines the role of government in improving energy efficiency in both the industrial and residential sectors. Among the important issues it considers are physical infrastructure for energy metering, legal and financial institutions, strengthened managerial and regulatory skills, and government support for market intermediation.

Industry

Typical energy intensities in Russian industry were 20 to 100 percent higher than in Western countries in 1990, and the gap has increased since then (Cooper and Schipper 1992; IEA 1995). Inefficient energy use resulted from well-known features of the former Soviet system: enterprise managers lacked incentives to minimize costs and to innovate; energy was often wasted, or even dumped, to maintain future allocations; and design institutes were separated from production, inhibiting technological advance (Nove 1986). In addition, energy was priced extremely low.

A wide variety of energy-efficiency improvements could drastically lower energy intensities (Office of Technology Assessment 1993; Kogan 1993; Evans 1996). Some of these improvements require replacement of entire production processes. For example, for the steel industry to be competitive, steel rolling must be replaced with the more efficient process of continuous casting. In 1991 the latter produced only 20 percent of steel output, compared with 90 percent or more in other countries, including Japan. Ironically, the Soviet Union invented this technology and licensed it to Japan, where diffusion was rapid (J. Cooper 1991).

Other gains in energy efficiency can be achieved through small incremental investments. Examples include better accounting and management of energy flows, automatic thermostats, secondary process-heat recovery, reduction of steam and pressurized air leakages, better heat-pipe insulation, improved boiler-combustion controls and boiler tuning, lighting-control equipment, and addition of variable-speed drives to motors. The technologies involved pose no problems for Russian engineers. And these investments can be very profitable; payback times range from a few months to a few years for most investments.

To take advantage of these opportunities, managers must think in cost-minimizing terms, analyze investment returns, and borrow capital. Managers also need to learn how to present investment proposals and business plans to financial institutions. But Soviet managers were unfamiliar with the concepts of cost of capital and rate of return because capital was allocated on the basis of planning and political priorities.

Moreover, the capacity for creative, independent thinking was suppressed in the Soviet era since managers followed plans dictated from above. Interviews and case studies corroborate the importance of fostering "new mentalities" among enterprise managers (Martinot 1995; Evans and Legro 1997).

Inexperience related to business planning, cost minimization, innovation, and finance are compounded by lack of information regarding costs and benefits of energy-efficiency measures. In the West, cost estimation is a mature field with many established databases from which to draw. In Russia, there is little historical experience on which to base cost estimates. In the Soviet era, information was centralized among authorities in Moscow, and enterprise managers did not directly contact foreign suppliers. Informal information networks now operate through personal contacts. Cost savings are difficult to judge because unmetered heat consumption and a lack of energy-accounting practices obscure energy-consumption baselines.

Many enterprises could invest in cogeneration to become independent power producers. Energy costs from cogeneration using combined-cycle gas turbines can be significantly less than the costs of purchased energy. A federal law allowing independent power producers to operate and sell surplus power back into the electric system was adopted in 1996. But practical implementation of the law, including the proper legal framework, regulatory oversight by regional energy commissions, and contractual models, has yet to be developed. Inadequate oversight means that utilities wield considerable power. One enterprise that wanted to install a combined-cycle gas turbine was threatened with being cut off from the electricity grid by the Moscow power utility (Martinot 1995).

Similarly, inefficient heat production can result from a lack of appropriate regulation at the municipal level. Many enterprises find it cheaper to produce their own heat than to purchase heat from a common municipal network. Conversely, existing industrial boilers may be less efficient than municipal utility boilers, but continue to operate because enterprises cannot purchase network heat. Uncoordinated heat-supply expansion may result in technically and economically inefficient outcomes.

Proper heat-pricing and heat-purchase agreements are needed to achieve least-cost solutions.

Another primary problem is financing. Through 1998 it was rare for a bank to loan funds for more than two years. The situation immediately after August 1998 was even worse. Credit risks increase because information about the financial condition of a particular borrower is difficult to determine in the absence of established financial disclosure norms. Compounding this problem is a legacy of disinformation from the Soviet era, when deceit was considered ordinary and necessary for enterprise operations (Nove 1986).

The Moskovitch automobile factory in Moscow, which was closed in 1996 but later partially reopened, illustrates some of these problems and opportunities (Martinot 1995). The factory, which in 1993 produced 120,000 cars, was one of the largest automobile plants in Russia. Space-heating costs alone, including several buildings above one million cubic meters in volume, represented more than one-third of total plant energy costs. Electric motors represented 50 to 60 percent of total electricity consumption, a common figure in Russian industry. According to the plant energy engineer, energy costs represented up to 12 percent of total production costs in 1993, depending upon production volume and time of year. From 1993 to 1995, electricity prices had risen by a factor of two and heat prices had risen by a factor of eight.

Energy-efficiency opportunities identified by engineers at the Moskvitch plant included: variable-speed ventilation systems, automatic control systems for both heat and peak electricity usage, hot-water temperature regulators, and more efficient natural-gas burners. The chief energy engineer was particularly interested in reducing heat consumption and reducing peak electric power demand (for which a premium was paid). He had a good idea of what technologies to use, had made estimates of potential energy savings, and had gathered technical information from several foreign and domestic firms.

However, the chief energy engineer still did not have an accurate idea of the costs of such improvements nor of the rates of return on investment. He did not have either outside financing or support from senior plant management to finance the improvements out-of-pocket. The plant had difficulty securing loans because production was decreasing and future demand was uncertain, in part due to high prices stemming from inefficient production processes. In fact, the plant had trouble simply meeting its payroll. As it turned out, demand for Moskvitch cars fell so drastically that the plant was forced to close, at least temporarily, despite the fact that the Moskvitch was one of the most commonly purchased cars at the end of the Soviet era.

Russian managers are overwhelmed with problems in marketing products, obtaining production inputs, getting paid by customers, and simply meeting payrolls. In relation to these concerns, attempting to cut energy costs is a low priority. Yet saving energy can offer a positive cash flow immediately or in a very short time, and is vital for improving competitiveness of Russian industry.

Housing

During the Soviet era, housing construction was driven by quantitative plan targets with little or no attention to producing energy-efficient buildings. Moreover, despite the frigid climate, very low energy prices meant that costs of construction always overshadowed heating costs. Inadequate building maintenance and poor heating controls seriously aggravated energy losses. Boris Nemtsov, the ill-fated first deputy prime minister who sought in 1997 and 1998 to transfer the burden of housing utility costs from government to private owners, stressed that the legacy of energy inefficiency was jeopardizing the entire reform program.

Energy-efficiency opportunities are largest for space heat and hot water because these typically account for two-thirds to three-quarters of residential energy consumption. Demonstration projects and analyses have shown that energy-efficiency improvements and better heating controls can reduce energy costs of apartment buildings by 25 percent or more with payback times of five years or less (Nekrasov et al. 1993; Kazakevicius et al. 1996; Martinot 1997; Martinot 1998b).

Higher residential energy costs have caused severe budget pressures on municipal governments, which continue to subsidize housing and utility costs even after apartment privatization (albeit with help from federal allowances). Costs for heat and hot-water averaged $30 to $50 per month for a typical apartment in 1995, about 25 to 40 percent of the average monthly wage. Typical subsidies averaged 70 to 80 percent of actual costs at the end of 1996 (Freinkman and Starodubrovskaya 1996). Municipal governments throughout Russia were typically spending 30 to 45 percent of their *total* municipal budgets on these subsidies (World Bank 1996a). In response, municipal governments have been reducing utility services. Social surveys have shown growing dissatisfaction with housing and energy services, including inadequate heating and hot-water supply (Guzanova and Diachenko 1996).

A federal government decree mandates gradual phaseout of subsidies by 2003, which will have a severe impact on households. Without subsidies, housing and utility costs could reach 30 to 40 percent of average household income. A burden on municipal governments will also remain because of housing allowances for low-income households, which will dramatically increase as housing costs become a larger share of household income.

Despite these pressures, privatization and high energy prices have not reduced energy usage in apartment buildings. Energy-efficiency improvements are practically ruled out by current conditions (Martinot 1997). The main challenges include:

(1) Municipal responsibility. For the most part, the institutional and management structures associated with responsibility for buildings have not changed at all after privatization. Generally, this means that municipal governments, through municipal housing maintenance organizations, are still responsible for building operation, maintenance, and capital improvements.

(2) Homeowner associations. Most energy-efficiency measures require changes to the common areas and equipment of buildings, not to individual apartments, and thus require a collective decision-making mechanism. But residents of apartment buildings can be collectively responsible for their building only after they organize into a homeowner association. Although

the necessary federal legislation was passed in 1993, effective legal frameworks have been slow in emerging and very few homeowner associations have formed. Residents are reluctant to assume responsibility for a building that could require costly repairs. Once an association forms, the financial losses resulting from households that do not pay their utility bills become the responsibility of the association (rather than the municipal government, local utility company, or an enterprise), and thus are shared by all households within the building. Also lacking are guidelines and decision-making models of how homeowner associations should function.

(3) Metering. Heat, hot water, and gas are not metered in apartment buildings. Without meters, households do not pay for consumption according to actual use, but instead pay a fixed monthly amount based on the size of their dwelling, the number of registered inhabitants, and the type of appliances present (i.e., stove, water heater, and bath). Households face zero marginal cost for their energy consumption and thus have no incentive to conserve or invest. Although building-level metering is a necessary first step, apartment-level metering would create a larger range of conservation incentives. But apartment-level metering poses special difficulties because of the physical piping arrangements in Russian buildings and because of the need for more costly meter reading and billing systems.

(4) Controls. During the Soviet era, radiators were installed without adjustable valves. The standard method of temperature control was to open a window, even in the dead of winter, because radiators lacked adjustable valves. In household surveys, virtually all respondents wanted radiator regulators. In addition, entire buildings can be over- or underheated because heat-supply levels are determined by the operators of central heat-supply plants, and there are no building-level controls that residents can adjust.

(5) Finance. The lack of financing for households, homeowner associations, and real estate developers is a serious obstacle. Banks are not willing to lend without adequate collateral and guarantee mechanisms, but homeowner associations have few assets. The institutional problem of how to secure a collective loan with individual property requires that new laws be enacted. In order to obtain financing, households must also have good information about technical opportunities, costs and benefits, and realistic

managerial and technical capabilities for specifying, contracting, and supervising building improvements.

(6) Social heterogeneity. There is often a high degree of variation in socioeconomic status and household income among households in the same apartment building. In the Soviet era, building occupancy was generally assigned without regard to the socioeconomic status or income of households. Consequently, buildings now house an essentially random mixture of socioeconomic groups. If the required majority of households in a homeowner association collectively decides to invest in energy efficiency, lower-income households in the same building will be forced to pay their share of renovation costs. If low-income residents are unable or unwilling to pay, the other households may end up trying to evict these low-income households, producing a difficult social situation.

(7) Regulation. Municipal utility regulations are deficient. For example, the basic institutional question of who purchases, owns, and maintains heat meters in buildings has not been resolved. Administrative and regulatory structures will need to be created to bill households according to actual consumption once meters are installed. District-heating companies will need to be regulated to permit buildings to vary their heat consumption autonomously, which may necessitate technical or operational changes in the district-heating system itself.

Government Leadership

Government has a role in supporting "market intermediation" related to energy usage. Such intermediations would introduce knowledge, services, and financing to overcome the efficiency barriers discussed above. The intermediaries would provide political, bureaucratic, and legal functions (see Figure 22.1) that were unnecessary in the Soviet era but crucial today (Usiyevich 1993).

In the United States, market intermediations for energy efficiency have taken several specific forms. Examples include tax breaks for energy-service companies; special regulatory incentives that give intermediation tasks to existing regulated organizations (such as electric power utilities and demand-side management programs); laws allowing independent power producers which have spawned "project developer" intermediaries; and appliance and equipment labeling standards. Other policies include direct provision of information to consumers and manufacturers, taxes and subsidies, credit services, enhancement of distribution systems, and direct government participation in equipment manufacture.

These same intermediation policies are relevant for Russia. In particular, energy-service companies are one of the most important potential vehicles (Martinot 1998a). Energy-service companies provide the project evaluation and implementation services, purchasing, financing, and experience necessary to undertake energy-efficiency investments in industry. They often provide a "shared-savings" arrangement with their client (also called "performance contracting"), which reduces risks and encourages enterprises to undertake energy-efficiency investments.

Many existing structures also can act as market intermediaries: departments or agencies of municipal and regional administrations, nonprofit organizations, electric power utilities, and enterprise associations. Information and business intermediaries have already grown in importance, including the nongovernmental Center for Energy Efficiency in Moscow (Chandler et al. 1996). In the future, Russian banks may also be significant intermediaries offering project evaluation and financing mechanisms. Independent power producers were allowed starting with the 1996 Russian federal law "On Energy Efficiency." Other federal and regional policies have established "energy-efficiency funds" to finance industrial conversion to energy-efficient products (IEA 1996).

Government programs can also develop human and institutional capabilities. Examples include business-plan training, training in energy management, and entrepreneurship for energy-service businesses (Evans and Legro 1997). Programs should target engineers, managers, and local government officials. There is also a need to develop the role of regional energy commissions throughout Russia. These commissions can play a role in establishing mechanisms and regulations to encourage and support energy-efficiency activities, including regulating independent power pro-

Figure 22.1. Market Intermediations

Securing the support of government officials
Finding and matching potential investment and joint-venture partners
Arranging sources of finance and engineering financing schemes
Evaluating and verifying information about partners and projects
Obtaining information about technologies and understanding markets
Identifying potential investment projects
Estimating the costs, benefits, and risks of investment projects
Packaging projects for public or private investors
Securing credit and performance guarantees
Developing licensing arrangements
Negotiating and writing contracts
Engendering trust among project participants
Obtaining necessary licenses and government approvals
Preparing technical specifications and bidding documents
Bidding and selecting bids for equipment and installation services
Managing, supervising, monitoring, and evaluating projects

---

ducers. Thus far, these commissions have had little staff or expertise to carry out their responsibilities.

Municipal governments may save on housing subsidies by making investments to improve energy efficiency of apartment buildings before they are privatized. If an investment is made in a building that is expected to become private property before investment costs are fully recovered, then there should be mechanisms for the government to recover investment costs from the future owners. Heat meters are a good place to start investing, and municipal governments in Ukraine have begun to do this.

In one of the first examples of municipal investment in energy efficiency, the World Bank in 1996 signed a 300 million dollar loan with six municipal governments in Russia to improve the energy efficiency of apartment buildings (World Bank 1996a). The objective was to reduce the municipalities' financial burden from housing that was being transferred from enterprise to municipal ownership. The energy-efficiency investments have aggregate payback times of less than five years. With a 15-year loan term, the cities expect positive financial returns from the loan immediately after installation of the measures.

Municipal governments need to develop administrative systems for consumption-based metering and billing in the residential sector, along with regulations to specify a new system of consumption-based energy tariffs. With building-level or apartment-level metering, a database of building characteristics must be created in order to allocate building-level heat-meter readings among all households within a building. An agency must be created, equipped, and trained to read heat meters and calculate heat payments on a monthly or annual basis. New administrative mechanisms must incorporate calculated payments into household energy bills. New municipal regulations must give appropriate authority and budgets to the new agencies. Without new regulations, district-heating companies are not likely to allow changes in consumption that will require changes to their systems. Regional energy commissions may also need to approve the transformation of residential heating tariffs from a per-square-meter to a per-gigacalorie basis.

Government policies should promote homeowner associations as vehicles for improving energy efficiency. Studies have shown that home-owner associations in the former Soviet Union need access to organizational, legal, financial, and technical advice. Public advisory centers are one way to provide this support. In a test activity, the Lithuanian Ministry of Construction and Urban Development helped four homeowner associations go through a process of borrowing from commercial banks and implementing energy-efficiency improvements. Direct assistance was provided to the associations at each step in the process, including: (1) inviting associations to take the loan, (2) obtaining a mandate from association members, (3) gathering technical and procedural information, (4) preparing a proposal that identified options and their respective costs and benefits, (5) choosing a course of action and inviting bids from contractors, (6) selecting a bid, (7) negotiating with contractors, (8) negotiating with banks, and (9) overseeing construction and installation.

The activities in this project illustrate the kinds of support homeowner associations require (World Bank 1996b).

Public education campaigns are important for educating households about energy efficiency. Experiences of homeowner associations could be publicized through radio or television interviews of association members. New homeowner associations need to become aware of technological opportunities and the possibilities for credit. Understanding of management issues is crucial since energy-efficiency projects require so many kinds of expertise.

Policies to strengthen legal and market institutions will assist energy-efficiency investments along with all forms of investment. Standards are needed for contracting, accounting, and performing credit ratings. Regulations should provide strict procedures for financial audits of enterprises so that the financing risks for bank loans are reduced. In particular, stronger contract law would reduce the risks faced by energy-service companies and facilitate "performance contracting."

It is the responsibility of government to provide the balanced macro-economic policies necessary to make available long-term credit. Government could also institute a variety of "carrots and sticks," including tax incentives for investments in energy conservation and penalties for wasteful energy use. Market-determined energy prices, elimination of subsidies, and privatization of enterprises and apartments are all important so that market forces can promote efficiency. However, the market operating by itself will bring about only sluggish improvement. Government leadership would accelerate gains in energy efficiency in factories and homes.

References

Chandler, William U., John W. Parker, Igor Bashmakov, Jaroslav Marousek, Slavomir Pasierb, and Zhou Dadi. 1996. *Energy Efficiency Centers: Experiences in the Transition Economies.* PNNL-10965. Washington, DC: Pacific Northwest National Laboratory.

Cooper, Caron R., and Lee Schipper. 1992. "The Efficiency of Energy Use in the USSR—An International Perspective." *Energy, the International Journal* 17(1): 1–24.

Cooper, Julian. 1991. "Soviet Technology and the Potential of Joint Ventures," in Alan B. Sherr, Ivan S. Korolev, Igor P. Faminsky, Tatiana M. Artemova, and Evgeniya L. Yakovleva, eds., *International Joint Ventures: Soviet and Western Perspectives.* Pp. 37–56. New York: Quorum Books.

Evans, Meredydd. 1996. *Russian Business Opportunities in Energy Efficiency and Renewable Energy.* PNNL-11154. Washington, DC: Pacific Northwest National Laboratory.

Evans, Meredydd, and Susan Legro. 1997. "Business Planning: A Key to Energy Efficiency in Russia." *Proceedings from the ECEEE 1997 Summer Study on Sustainable Energy Opportunities for a Greater Europe.* Prague and Copenhagen: European Council for an Energy-Efficient Economy.

Freinkman, Lev M., and Irina Starodubrovskaya. 1996. *Restructuring of Enterprise Social Assets in Russia: Trends, Problems, Possible Solutions.* Policy Research Working Paper No. 1635. Washington, DC: World Bank.

Guzanova, Alla K. 1998. *The Housing Market in the Russian Federation: Privatization and Its Implications for Market Development.* Policy Research Working Paper No. 1891. Washington, DC: World Bank.

International Energy Agency (IEA). 1995. *Energy Policies of the Russian Federation.* Paris: OECD.

International Energy Agency (IEA). 1996. *Perspectives on Energy Efficiency in Russia: Regional Approaches.* Proceedings of a conference sponsored by the Russian Ministry of Fuel and Energy and the Chelyabinsk regional administration, September 25–26, 1996. Paris: OECD.

Kazakevicius, Edas, Lee Schipper, and Stephen Meyers. 1996. *The Residential Space Heating Problem in Lithuania.* Berkeley, CA: Lawrence Berkeley National Laboratory.

Kogan, Yuri. 1993. "Assessment of Power Saving Potential in Russia." Moscow: Khrzhizhanovsky Power Engineering Institute.

Martinot, Eric. 1995. "Energy Efficiency and Renewable Energy in Russia: Perspectives and Problems of International Technology Transfer and Investment." Ph.D. diss., University of California, Berkeley.

———. 1997. *Investments to Improve the Energy Efficiency of Existing Residential Buildings in Countries of the Former Soviet Union.* Studies of Economies in Transformation 24. Washington, DC: World Bank.

———. 1998a. "Energy Efficiency and Renewable Energy in Russia: Transaction Barriers, Market Intermediation, and Capacity Building." *Energy Policy* 26(11): 905–915.

———. 1998b. "Energy Efficiency and Housing-Sector Transitions in Russia." *Perspectives in Energy* 4: 295–310.

Nekrasov, A. S., I. N. Borisova, Y. S. Kretinina, T. M. Polyanskaya, L. F. Suzdaltseva, and S. A. Voronina. 1993. "Russia's Energy System: Development Alternatives." *Studies on Russian Economic Development* 4(6): 477–513.

Nove, Alex. 1986. *The Soviet Economic System.* Boston: Allen & Unwin.

Office of Technology Assessment, U.S. Congress. 1993. *Energy Efficiency Technologies for Central and Eastern Europe.* Report No. OTA-E-562. Washington, DC: U.S. Government Printing Office.

Usiyevich, Vladimir A. 1993. "The Trigger Mechanism of Energy Saving: Institutional and Economical Aspects." *AVOK Journal* 3/4: 12–13.

World Bank. 1996a. *Russian Federation Enterprise Housing Divestiture Project.* Staff Appraisal Report. Washington, DC: World Bank.

World Bank. 1996b. *Lithuania Energy Efficiency/Housing Pilot Project.* Staff Appraisal Report. Washington, DC: World Bank.

24

Real Estate Markets

Dwight Jaffee and Olga Kaganova

Soviet central planning has left some of its worst legacy in real estate, especially urban housing. Significant improvements will require changes in the policies of local governments and further development of market institutions.

During most of the years of central planning, housing construction was a low priority. There were long waiting lists for small, low-quality apartments in poorly maintained buildings. Nominal rents remained fixed at levels virtually unchanged from those set by Stalin in 1928. Far below the market clearing value, the typical level of rent relative to income averaged about 2.5 percent in the USSR in the 1980s (Renaud 1992), compared with a typical value in the West of about 33 percent.

The size of the housing stock in Russia is well below Western standards. For example, adjusted for population, Sweden has twice as many housing units as Russia. The housing stock is meager even compared with many other former Soviet bloc countries, such as Hungary and Estonia (UN-ECE 1994). In Russia's major cities there are about 1.3 families per housing unit (World Bank 1995). The acute shortage of housing and the low level of affordability are reflected in very high prices relative to income (Struyk 1996). The level of residential construction is now only half what it was in the late 1980s.

There is now an absence of clear institutions regarding private land ownership, bankruptcy, foreclosure, and eviction. This makes it virtually impossible to use real estate as collateral for borrowing investment funds. At the same time, there is minimal experience with any form of market financial intermediation, the proliferation of private banks notwithstanding. Even the term "real estate finance" is sometimes translated into Russian as "real estate subsidies."

This chapter is divided into two main parts. Part One describes in further detail the current status of the real estate market. Part Two offers numerous recommendations to accelerate real estate investment.

Current Status of the Real Estate Market

Privatization

Privatization of real estate has progressed furthest in the housing sector as state-owned housing is transferred to individual citizens and to private enterprises. For the country as a whole, at least half of the housing stock has thus far been privatized (Klepikova et al. 1995).

The extent of the privatization of existing commercial and industrial buildings is not known in general. In St. Petersburg about 25 percent of total floor area in commercial buildings and premises was privatized by the end of 1996 (Kaganova 1998).

No urban land was privatized until recently, with the lone exception of small plots of land allocated to families for single-family homes or privatized by families living in already existing single-family homes. In 1995, after three years of repeated attempts, the privatization of land sites underneath privatized enterprises finally began by means of land purchases by enterprises. By December 1995, about 1,300 enterprises across Russia had completed land purchases, and another 2,300 enterprises had submitted applications (Limonov 1996). By the end of 1997, the share of privately owned city territory varied from 0.2 to 17.5 percent in six surveyed cities (Kaganova 1999). However, the process of land privatization is limited since Moscow and other regions, ignoring the constitution and presidential decrees, allow only long-term land leases.

Urban Housing Markets

There are striking geographical differences in housing markets, in part a reflection of sharp differences in municipal policies. According to a 1994 survey of several cities, mean income of nonpensioner households varies from about 5 to 21 percent of mean home price (Struyk 1996). For a sample of six cities, Kaganova (1999) found that annual turnover rates (sales as a percent of privately owned housing stock) range from 5.0 percent to 8.7 percent, with new homes built accounting for from 19.4 to 49.3 percent of sales of existing homes.[1] Fees for infrastructure and other costs imposed by cities ranged from 9 to 33 percent of the total cost of housing development.

Initially most residences (apartments) offered for sale were provided by persons planning to emigrate. Currently, the supply primarily represents the redistribution of wealth and migration within Russia. Families leasing out their own residences account for at least 2 percent of the housing stock (Struyk 1996). Investments in rental residential properties have yet to occur in any significant amount.

New construction of housing is primarily of two types. First, there are high-rise apartments in multiapartment blocs laid out in the Soviet era. Second, there are single-family luxury houses, a type of residential development without precedent except for the dachas of the nomenclatura. A less prevalent third type is townhouses which are meant primarily for foreign residents. Demand for entire buildings for renovation is growing in the center of St. Petersburg, and presumably central Moscow as well. A building to be renovated, with tenants already relocated, commands a higher price per square meter than a high-quality apartment in an unrenovated building (Kaganova 1995).

Housing prices are highest in Moscow. A typical three-room apartment of 70 square meters (750 square feet) sells for about $80,000. Apartments renovated to Western standards cost several hundred thousand.[2] Prices in St. Petersburg are about half those in Moscow for local-quality apartments, and about a third as much for Western-standard apartments. Given the low family incomes, a home purchase is out of the question for most Russians, especially given the absence of mortgages.

Due to the absence of institutional lending, prepayment by future homeowners is the primary source of finance for housing construction, while in commercial real estate, construction equity investment is very high. A recent study found that in Moscow and Rostov-on-Don, about two-thirds of projects are financed 100 percent with the developers' own funds (Kaganova 1996). Much of the inflow of capital may be illicit in origin, since construction offers a way to launder money.

Commercial Real Estate

The market for commercial properties is very active: the annual turnover rate (sales as a percent of privately owned stock) is around 40 percent in some cities. Office rentals are also active. It is common knowledge that rental rates on office and other commercial space are impacted by the cost of mafia protection, at least in big cities.

Office space at Western standards of quality is usually in reconstructed or new privately owned buildings and exists only in major cities. Its supply consists largely of business centers that function as foreign enclaves providing telecommunication facilities, apartment or hotel rooms, restaurants, and garages. In addition, there are three types of local-quality space: (1) low-quality office buildings, often poorly managed, belonging to privatized enterprises; (2) premises used as income properties by municipal agencies; and (3) premises occupied rent-free by public institutions (state research institutes, state universities, defense institutions, etc.) which rent out part of their space to obtain revenue. These leases are often legally questionable since the premises are actually owned by the city or the state.

New businesses and foreign companies desire offices in prestigious central districts, but many office buildings are located far away from the center and are often in industrial zones. The difficulties in obtaining land sites limit the ability of private developers to fill this gap.

In Moscow the average net rent for offices of Western standards was about $825 per square meter in January 1996 with a total occupancy cost of about $1,050, ranking the city sixth highest in the world for office rents. Rental rates are substantially less in other Russian cities.[3]

The cities themselves are the largest owners of commercial and other nonresidential properties. In St. Petersburg, authorities of inner-city districts hold about 13,000 active lease contracts on nonresidential premises, and about another 10,000 contracts are held by other city authorities. There is still no private management for municipal properties. Lease terms are standardized and rents are calculated by a formula or, for smaller spaces, are determined by officials who often can be bribed. The municipalities are not responsive to market conditions, either losing revenue because of below-market rents or losing tenants because of rents and terms less attractive than those offered by private owners. Only St. Petersburg has begun implementing more objective methods (mass appraisal) for setting up rent rates for municipal commercial property.

Retail space is generally less expensive than office space, unlike in cities with developed real estate markets. There are several reasons. First, demand for retail space is a function of the public's overall purchasing power, which is low. Second, in the process of privatization restrictions were imposed on many retail and service-sector premises with respect to permitted activities. Third, the commercial real estate market is still a long way from equilibrium, and the unsatisfied demand for office space exceeds that for retail space.

Industrial Property

In all industrialized Russian cities, industrial buildings and warehouses are available for lease or purchase as the result of privatization. Vacancy rates are high because of the economic depression as well as lack of fit to the requirements of potential renters. In St. Petersburg the typical annual rent for industrial properties is from $30 to $60 per square meter.

Land Markets

As should be clear from our discussion of privatization, the market for urban land is very thin and consists mostly of family owned sites zoned for housing or gardening. As a rule, such sites are not provided with a full set of utilities (sewage, gas, electricity, water, etc.), making them unsuitable for construction. As one would expect, turnover of land sales on sites privatized by enterprises is high in some cities; we discuss later the potential consequences of allowing the privatization of industrial land in the absence of other privatized urban land.

Proposals

Real estate markets depend on the ability to exercise and transfer well-defined property rights. In the current context, property rights require that Russian law guarantee: (1) the rights of owners of individual residential apartments, and the rights of enterprises and developers holding long-term land leases, to make appropriate use of owned, or leased, real property; and (2) the right to sell, rent, and mortgage these property rights. Property rights are not meaningful unless there are clear and effective mechanisms to ensure that local authorities, courts, and police are willing and able to enforce these rights. One basic component is an effective system of property recording (title registration).

Legislation passed in the last several years has helped to clarify property rights, but contradictions remain at various levels of Russian law, and implementation has not been consistent or strict. Although the constitution states that land relations are regulated by federal law, primarily through the land code, many presidential decrees challenge this constitutional provision by addressing a number of areas related to land rights and registration. Also, although the constitution states that juridical entities may own land in fee simple, and privatization laws state the same, many cities in Russia, including Moscow, refuse to grant anything but land leases.

Municipal Policies

Municipal policies should be changed to take into account the reality that private funds are now the main source of construction and reconstruction financing. Authorities in many cities, including Moscow and St. Petersburg, do not sufficiently realize that the private investor/developer of today and the municipal contractor of Soviet times are not the same and need to be treated differently. Currently, the authorities offer investors contractual relations for a construction period, and the prototypes for these investment contracts are contracts with hired contractors. Investment contracts assign no property rights to investors and allow the cities to dissolve the contract unilaterally, should the developer violate the terms.

The official policy of many cities is to attract as much foreign investment into real estate development as possible. The mayors of Moscow and St. Petersburg travel across the world to market their cities. Nevertheless, the total number of projects with foreign participation and the amounts of investment are surprisingly small. Even in Moscow, with its high real estate prices and office construction boom in 1995, foreign investment is negligible.

A study conducted by Kaganova (1995) of St. Petersburg in 1995 identified the main obstacles to foreign investors: (1) lack of secure property rights during the construction period, since titles and long-term land lease agreements are available only after construction is completed; (2) unreliable real property registration systems; and (3) uncertainty concerning the expense requirements imposed by the city. A less frequently cited concern was the general political and economic instability in Russia.

Russian investors are apparently less concerned about these problems, although the absence of mortgageable rights during construction is an issue for them as well. The courage of Russians to invest under uncertain and unclear conditions can presumably be explained by their relative inexperience and, in some cases, the priority of money laundering over investment return.

The Russian construction industry remains highly inefficient, with a great deal of power remaining with the large *kombinat* enterprises inherited from the Soviet past. Their power lies in relationships with the municipal agencies that provide land and construction approval, and in priority access to construction materials, both from established networks and from direct control (vertical integration). To increase competition in the construction industry, new entrants should have equal access to land, building permits, and construction materials.

Property Registration and Professional Services

Many countries are offering technical assistance to federal and municipal governments and to private business and professional organizations. While generally constructive, this assistance can undermine efficiency and fairness when local circumstances differ from those under which recommended models evolved. Technical advice is often contradictory as well.

The recording of real property and the guaranteeing of title are important illustrations. Under the European model,[4] a government registrar checks the validity of each property transfer before recording it. The government then takes responsibility to guarantee title. If someone were to establish the validity of a conflicting claim, then the government would resolve the conflict according to law and pay any and all compensatory damages.

There is a strong rationale for favoring instead the American system. Rapid privatization over geographically vast territories, the rapid development of local markets, and the absence of a strong and effective centralized administrative system are all factors in the evolution of the American system which exists in Russia today. These factors may be interpreted as typical for a "frontier society."[5]

The American system relies less on government and more on the market. Government recording of transactions is done without the registrar establishing the validity of the recorded documents other than to check that they are notarized. The recordings are voluntary, and the government bears no responsibility. Private title insurance is the mechanism for ensuring the validity of ownership transfers and other property rights. In practice, the American system is faster but more expensive for users than the European system.

St. Petersburg now has a European system but without legislation specifying how the government should adjudicate conflicts and provide compensatory payments. Thus privately provided title insurance is developing as well, leaving St. Petersburg with a slow and expensive hybrid.[6] Even more to the point, real property registration remains unreliable. The evolution of this unsatisfactory hybrid model has so far been ignored by legislators at both the federal and municipal levels.

Land Policy

Under central planning, construction was primarily on the existing perimeters of cities. Like a tree's cross section, the urban structure of Russian cities reflects alternating periods of residential and industrial construction that mirror changes in central planning emphasis. Considerations of commuting time and energy efficiency played little role.[7] For many years, large-scale, high-rise housing construction was assigned to raw land remote from the city centers. Old industrial lands located close to the city center have yet to be recycled. This spatial evolution of cities reflects the absence of a land market as an instrument of land redevelopment (Bertaud and Renaud 1997). As a result, transport systems are lengthy and costly to operate.

Currently, there is a municipal monopoly on land, which allows the authorities to dictate to developers both the financial terms on which lots are provided and the location of projects. The administrative mechanism for allocating sites is not sufficiently sensitive to market demand. In these circumstances, bribery can be rationalized as a mechanism for making officials attentive to the market. Further development of the housing and building market in the absence of land privatization may proceed under two negative scenarios.

Scenario one: local authorities block land privatization and the private ownership of land other than individual housing tracts. The inertia of the bureaucratic patterns will continue to push urban development to land leases of raw land (with bribed exclusions). Given the shift to a system in which users pay for infrastructure operating costs, this scenario will impose high costs on the final consumers. Once better land becomes available, there will be a rapid decline in market values for improvements built in bad locations.

Scenario two: local authorities allow the privatization of lands controlled by privatized enterprises, while other land follows scenario one. This situation would result in construction activity on industrial lands converted to housing use.

Rational and prudent development of Russian urban real estate requires that municipal land policy be more sensitive to market demand. Cities should direct development toward more central locations and introduce mechanisms that are responsive to locational preferences.

Public Utilities

The location of new construction in city outskirts is largely predetermined by the technologies of the urban utilities developed during the Soviet era. These technologies are behind those available in developed Western cities. The further evolution of Russian cities depends critically on the transformation of the outmoded urban utility systems.

The centralized supply systems do not now provide individual metering or adjustments for heat, water, and gas. These systems are costly to build and operate and have sizable internal losses. Moreover, because they are monopolies which are often privatized, these enterprises lack incentives to improve efficiency and the quality of service.

A new policy of capital financing and the management of public utilities is needed. Eliminating monopolies and creating incentives for new technologies should be key. However, in view of the political influence of monopolies and urban utilities, such a policy may be difficult to implement.

Real Estate Finance

It is not surprising that mortgages did not exist in the Soviet era. Since most housing was owned by the state or by enterprises that were owned by the state, Russian households did retain important entitlements and rights of bequest regarding their primary housing units as well as their dachas (summer houses), but these entitlements also made eviction difficult and thus precluded the use of real estate assets as mortgage collateral.

A system of real estate finance is needed to fund the construction of new structures and to finance the purchase of existing properties. As with many of the proposals made here, a consistent set of laws is needed in a number of known areas: property rights, collateral, eviction, and foreclosure. In addition, it is now apparent that the Russian banking industry is unlikely to take the lead in creating a mortgage market. Their attention is focused on highly profitable, short-run, trading markets. Jaffee and Renaud (1996) offer an alternative strategy: a government-sponsored mortgage credit institute could take the initiative that the commercial banks have failed to provide.

Conclusion

Economic depression, political uncertainty, and a lawless environment are jeopardizing the functioning of real estate markets. Moreover, real estate finance is primitive, limiting the potential for real estate investment. Nevertheless, further legislation and more realistic municipal policies could strengthen construction activity in a manner responsive to social needs. Property rights need to be clearly established, property registration must be reliable, policies regarding utilities revamped, and both land ownership and land leases made more available to developers.

Improvements in the real estate sector are important for the entire economy. New housing and commercial construction would stimulate aggregate output through a macroeconomic multiplier. More housing would also facilitate relocation of the population to the relatively more prosperous urban areas, allowing workers to be more productive and earn higher wages. New commercial construction would enhance the productive capacity of the economy. Also, a developed mortgage system for real estate would provide financial assets with positive real rates of return, which would help bolster private savings and thereby strengthen the underpinnings for noninflationary growth.

Notes

1. Not all new housing construction was for sale. Some portion was built from public funds for various state programs.

2. Data are from a fall 1995 survey by Kaganova (1996). In Moscow, most apartments sold for between $950 and $1,330 per square meter for local-quality apartments, and $3,000 to $4,500 for those of Western standards.

3. In St. Petersburg, annual rents in 1995 for local-quality offices ranged from $190 to $370 per square meter compared with $370 to $800 for Western-standard offices (Kaganova 1996).

4. The conventional view among real estate economists is that the European model (or Australian or Torrens model) is more progressive, though reportedly the European system was disbanded in several American cities because of its inefficiency.

5. Implications of the "frontier society" to real estate were outlined by Peter Colwell during an on-line conference on land and real estate issues sponsored by the World Bank (November–December 1998).

6. In mid-1995, registration of an apartment sale in St. Petersburg took, in the best case, two days, at a cost of 0.2 to 0.4 percent of the sale price, with title insurance costing another 1 to 3 percent (Kaganova 1996). In the United States, recording of a home sale would take minutes and cost 0.05 to 0.08 percent, while title insurance would cost another 0.6 to 0.8 percent.

7. Bertaud and Renaud (1997) found this pattern to be common in other socialist countries as well.

References

Bertaud, Alain, and Bertrand Renaud. 1997. "Socialist Cities without Land Markets." *Journal of Urban Economics* 41(1): 137–151.

Jaffee, Dwight, and Bertrand Renaud. 1996. "Strategies to Develop Mortgage Markets in Transition Economies." Paper presented at the European Financial Management Association annual meeting.

Kaganova, Olga. 1995. "Reconstruction of Central St. Petersburg." Report of World Bank Working Group. Washington, DC: World Bank.

———. 1996. *Russian Home Building in Transition*. Washington, DC: The Urban Institute.

————. 1998. "Urban Real Estate Markets in Russia: The Current Stage." *Real Estate Issues* 23(2): 30–35.

————. ed. 1999. *Monitoring Indicators of Land and Real Estate Reform in Russian Cities.* Washington, DC, and Moscow: The Urban Institute and the Institute for Urban Economics.

Klepikova, Elena, Nadezhda Kosareva, and Andrei Suchkov. 1995. *Structure of Housing Finance: Country Report.* Moscow: Institute for Urban Economics.

Limonov, Leonid. 1996. "Land Buy-Outs by Privatized Enterprises and Property Markets Development in Russia." Paper presented at the 1996 AREUEA International Real Estate Conference, Orlando, FL, May 23-25.

Renaud, Bertrand. 1992. "The Housing System of the Former Soviet Union: Why Do the Soviets Need Housing Markets?" *Housing Policy Debate* 3(3): 877-899.

Struyk, Raymond. 1996. "The Long Road to the Market," in R. Struyk, ed., *Economic Restructuring of the Former Soviet Bloc. The Case of Housing.* Pp. 1–69. Washington, DC: The Urban Institute Press.

UN-ECE. 1994. *Annual Bulletin of Housing and Building Statistics.*

World Bank. 1995. *Russian Housing Reform and Privatization: Strategy and Transition Issues*, Vol. 1: Main Report. Washington, DC: World Bank.

25

Management of Public Holdings

Alexander D. Nekipelov

Amidst the rush to privatize the Russian economy, the management of public assets has been neglected. Sound policies are needed to deter abuses and strengthen the economy.

Although privatization has proceeded rapidly, most economic assets in Russia remain publicly owned. The government (the public) typically retains ownership shares in industrial enterprises even after they are "privatized," with the public stake often above 50 percent. Most of the largest enterprises have not been privatized at all. Moreover, extensive government ownership is likely to persist, for widespread disillusionment has caused a slowing in the pace of privatization.

Public utilities, public transport, and public health and education remain in the "command sphere." Federal or local executive power controls day-to-day operations, parliament determines budgets, and prior organizational structures remain largely intact. Despite drastic reductions in funding, these areas of the economy have experienced relatively less mismanagement. Abuse has been more prevalent among enterprises that operate in the "market sphere." Decontrol has made their assets easy targets for pilfering by managers, bureaucrats, and collectives—frequently in league with mafia operatives, both brutal and sophisticated. This "pumping out of resources" from the public sector is still the most profitable economic activity of the emerging private sector.

The crisis is most acute among large enterprises in the industrial sector. Here privatization has been less successful than for small enterprises such as retail stores, restaurants, and small-size providers of consumer and business services. In the industrial sector, output has declined drastically to only about a third of its level of a few years ago, though industrial employment has actually fallen very little. The mass of redundant workers exerts political pressure for highly inflationary government rescue— subsidies and loans, orders, and both the toleration and liquidation of enormous interenterprise debt.

The proposal developed here is concerned with improving the management of public (and semipublic) business enterprises, primarily manufacturing and other large industrial enterprises. These are former state enterprises that have been transferred to the market sector or have the potential to be transferred.[1]

Public Wealth Funds

Many former state enterprises have been reconstituted as joint-stock companies in which the federal government retains stock. The existence of government-owned stock suggests the creation of public entities to serve as the custodians of this stock. We shall call these new entities public wealth funds. Their design and operation would follow forms familiar in modern Western economies.

The public wealth funds would be given legal ownership of the government holdings in joint-stock enterprises. In addition, the funds would become the owners of those state enterprises in the market sphere that have been neither privatized nor turned over to regional or municipal authorities. The public wealth funds, acting in the interests of the Russian citizenry as a whole, would be insulated as much as possible from partisan or political interests.

Turning all government stock holdings over to the funds would end the widespread cross-ownership that results when public enterprises own stock in other public enterprises. This would immediately clarify responsibility for abuses and establish an institutional mechanism to reorganize the management of public assets so as to promote economic growth.

Narrowly defined, the mission of the funds would be to maximize the long-term value of their holdings. The broader goal would be to remedy maladies stemming from the reform process, including the collapse of domestic production, the arrears crisis, and the accumulation of redundant workers. But these objectives cannot be realized by the funds' efforts alone. The funds must act in conjunction with an overall program for economic transition. Otherwise, a quick liquidation in pursuit of profit maximization could accelerate the deindustrialization of Russia.

To be sure, the funds could become corrupted and obstruct progressive change. To avoid this will require clarity of purpose; broad support from legal authorities, including law enforcement; substantial financial resources; able and dedicated personnel; and strong performance incentives. The specific functions of the funds must be carefully designed, clearly specified by legislation, and conscientiously implemented. Care must be taken to ensure that existing control structures are not removed before the funds are capable of exercising effective oversight. Otherwise, lack of accountability could be exacerbated.

The establishment of multiple funds, rather than a single fund, would prevent a new centralization of power reminiscent of Gosplan. Competition among the funds would spur performance. Separate funds would be established in different areas of the country, distributing power to the local and regional levels. Alternative funds competing in the same regions or in the same industries would provide a basis for identifying which funds were not well run. Such information is essential for uncovering corruption and adjusting the policies governing fund operations.

Five Key Issues

Relationship to Enterprises

The public wealth funds shall be prohibited from acting in a manner that restores the previous system of central control. They will not be permitted to set production quotas or otherwise interfere in day-to-day operations. Rather, the funds will reinforce the corporate form of enterprise governance.

Combining the functions of a holding company and an investment company, the funds will pursue the goal of maximizing the value of their assets. Investments will be scrutinized to ensure that expected rates of return, adjusted for risk, exceed the cost of capital (i.e., the return from alternative investments). The funds would oppose efforts by enterprises to retain earnings if this condition is not met.

In accordance with corporate governance, the board of directors of each enterprise will select and oversee management and set long-range policy, including choice of partners, major investment decisions, and reorganizations and closings. Thus the funds will exercise their influence through their representatives on the board.

The funds will participate along with other stockholders in voting to select the board and may designate professionals employed by the funds to serve as directors. For those public enterprises in which a fund's interest is over 50 percent, it will have unilateral control over board selection, though it will consult with other stockholders. Indeed, if stockholding is otherwise dispersed, even a 10 percent minority interest could give a fund dominant control over selection of the board.

As a matter of highest priority, the funds will work to upgrade the quality of managers. To fulfill its responsibilities to the owners, namely the Russian citizenry, the funds will insist that the managers of each enterprise undertake needed restructuring and maximize long-run profits.

Public enterprises are now mostly forms of "collective units" oriented toward consumption by managers and workers, rather than toward economic efficiency. The funds, in demanding profit maximization, would pressure public enterprises to respond to market signals. In the final analysis, the funds will have had a positive impact if they are able to force enterprises to participate in open markets.

Relationship to Executive Power

The funds would operate without subordination to the executive power. The branch ministries would relinquish their authority over public enterprises operating in the market sphere. This is necessary to protect the autonomy of both the funds and those public enterprises in which the funds have an interest.

Ending the involvement of branch ministries would stop their lobbying within the government for their own interests and the partisan interests of the respective industries. Another benefit would be to halt the battles between different levels of executive power concerning the right to control public assets, including the spoils from privatization. Ideally, less involvement in individual enterprises would facilitate focus on structural issues in the transition to a market economy.

Forcing hasty privatization would cease. Rather the funds would strengthen the corporate structure of enterprises, making them more suitable for eventual privatization. Selling off underpriced assets would contradict the goal of maximizing the value of fund assets.

Personnel

Institutions are not constructed instantly; it takes time and attention to build structures of accountability and coordination. Thus the initial selection of a board of governors to oversee each fund is crucial. An independent commission should be empowered to choose the governors on the basis of criteria to assure impartiality, integrity, and competence.

Legislated "sunshine provisions" are necessary to assure transparency of operations. Strict standards should require disclosure of holdings of governors and staff, and prohibit conflicts of interest. Salary information should be made public.

To facilitate recruitment of well-trained professionals, salary levels should be comparable to those of the private sector. There should be not only incentives to motivate exceptional performance but also procedures to facilitate timely dismissals.

To minimize risk that the funds would obstruct needed restructuring, orientation toward long-run profit is essential. This will require commitment from managers who are chosen for their ability and integrity. Hence it is important that compensation be tied to fund profits. Only by maximizing profits would managers and workers obtain resources to reward themselves.

Profits

A capital account for each fund will be established at the central bank so that the central bank can monitor operations and enforce honest disclosure. Fund dividends and proceeds from sales of ownership shares are to be deposited in this account. The rate of interest on the cash balance will be the same as the rate charged by the central bank on short-term borrowing by member banks.

The inflow and outflow of funds to the capital account will be a matter of public record. The funds will be used for investment, including portfolio investments and the founding of new companies.

Fund profits, including capital gains, would be subject to taxation. The purpose would be to help finance in a noninflationary manner the government budget, including the subsidies and credits called for by industrial policy.

Privatization

Competition among the funds and profit-based remuneration will not ensure that the funds will cut waste and innovate in the determined manner of profit-motivated individual owners. There may be political interference in decisions, recruitment, and dismissals.

Provision should be made for experimenting with partial and total private ownership of the funds. If a fund issues stock, then its market valuation will signal performance. This will create added pressure for efficiency and profits, especially if shares are owned by managers and other employees. By issuing stock, the funds would also be able to seek added resources from capital markets. Such designs may attract substantial foreign capital, perhaps with guarantees from Western governments.

Judgment of the relative merits of private and public funds should be made on the basis of performance. Whether private or public, they should be liquidated if they fail, providing automatic evaluation on the basis of survival of the fittest. For the comparisons to be meaningful, private and public funds would have to be comparable in their makeup and treated equally by government. Before deciding which funds to privatize, the candidates could be divided into matched pairs, and then one of each pair would be selected for privatization. A full evaluation of performance would include growth, export performance, product innovation, technological upgrading, success in redeploying redundant workers, and various social and environmental considerations.

A cautious and flexible approach to privatizing the funds would be prudent. The transfer to private owners of public assets priced well below real long-term values has outraged most Russians and exacerbates economic inequality. Furthermore, private enterprises are less able to shield themselves from mafia encroachment. Ownership shares in the funds could gradually be sold to private stockholders as warranted by experience.

Industrial Policy

The funds could facilitate implementation of industrial policy. Indeed, "public development corporation" might a more appropriate name than public wealth fund.

The funds could be used to channel and evaluate subsidies and loans for retraining and restructuring. This would provide a convenient mechanism for setting up the funds. In order to receive government assistance, enterprises would be required to join a fund. It would provide an added spur to reform if an enterprise had to meet the demands of the fund before joining.

The funds could eventually function like modern conglomerates. As is common in modern Western economies, the fund would monitor subsidiary enterprises. It would also marshal resources, leveraging the best legal, accounting, financial, and managerial expertise.

It should be noted, however, that Soviet experience showed that the advantage of size should not be overestimated. Western experience also has shown that it is difficult to manage huge conglomerates efficiently.

In Western capitalist countries, mergers sometimes turn out to be disappointing. Thus, prudent consideration must be given to the size of funds in order that they remain competitive in national and world markets.

The allocation of enterprises among the funds is crucial. The funds could buy and sell enterprises to each other, subject to restrictions to preserve competition. No one fund would be allowed to control more than a certain fraction of an industry. Enterprises would be aggregated to aid development of marketing capacity. Vertical and horizontal integration of production may also be important. For example, the funds could be required to acquire enterprises in a manner that would permit redeployment of skilled workers, such as moving coal miners into subway construction.

Care must be taken not to squeeze out private competition. The funds must not be allowed to monopolize credit, inhibiting private investment. They could be assigned an active role in promoting competition, with monies earmarked for breaking up monopolies and supporting new enterprises.

Russian industrial enterprises are in weak condition, and efforts by the funds to reinforce market discipline might further intensify "market shock." Revitalization of Russian industry will require new resources, an improved economic environment, and large-scale layoffs. Clearly, better managers will not be enough, nor will privatization or piecemeal measures that coddle public enterprises. Instead, broadly conceived industrial policy should be applied. This should include: conscientious enforcement of a rational scheme of tariffs and taxes to support domestic production; public investment in physical capital both to increase productivity and to stimulate employment; public investment in human resources and institutional development to provide the legal, accounting, and managerial foundations for a lawful market economy; and temporary and measured use of subsidies and favorable credit terms.

A reorganization of control over public (and semipublic) business enterprises is urgently needed. Although not necessarily a privatization initiative, establishing public wealth funds would help enterprises function in a market environment. The funds would upgrade managerial performance and normalize the moral climate, bolstering public support for a market economy. In the long run, the funds could evolve from being public watchdogs to being dynamic corporations, either publicly or privately owned.

Note

1. In theory, enterprises in a market system (private, semipublic, or public) strive to maximize the profits of their owners and derive income solely from the lawful sale of goods and services at prices determined by competition—without being shielded from the sink-or-swim discipline of the market. But economic conditions and policy options are complex. Market competition is a matter of degree, and privatization surely does not guarantee efficient operation. Moreover, a system of market-determined prices does not require private ownership.

26

Human Capital

Michael D. Intriligator, Serguey Braguinsky, and Vitaly Shvydko

Russia's potential to be a leader in information technology and other advanced technologies has been largely overlooked. With the right government leadership, Russia could benefit greatly from its rich heritage in science and universal education. The challenge is to create a comparative advantage out of Russian human capital.

Scientific Heritage

Russia's formidable science establishment made the country a leader in technologies ranging from metallurgy to computer software. The concentration of resources by command methods paved the way for good results in certain technological branches of the Russian economy. This applies, in particular, to space technologies, aircraft building, precision instruments, and development of new materials. The former Soviet Union had also achieved a high level of development not only in mass education but also in fundamental research. This development entailed an extensive network of research institutes and experimental laboratories and the coordination of their activities on a national level.

The high quality of human capital needed for the success of these research efforts was attained, first, by guaranteeing the labor force a high level of general education, and, second, by creating a special system of nonmarket incentives for the country's intellectual elite. In 1990 less than 3 percent of workers had not graduated from high school, and 20 percent of the workforce had completed higher education. The Russian Federation had 200 university and college students per 10,000 of population, comparable to most developed nations. In 1985 there were more than 1.2 million research workers, and there were almost 2 million other technical personnel. These workers enjoyed an above-average standard of living guaranteed by the state. This was especially true for research centers and production facilities specializing in nuclear and space technologies and in the development and production of arms. Many lived in elite self-sufficient communities separated from the rest of the country. In addition to high social status and many fringe benefits, they received salaries several times higher than those of the rest of the workforce.

Post-Soviet Deterioration

With the demise of the planned economy, government abruptly cut its expenditures on research while expenditure on public education declined by over 50 percent. R&D as a percentage of Russia's GDP shrank from 2 percent in 1990 to about 0.7 percent in 1995 (*Nauka v Rossii v tsifrakh,* March 1996, 102; *Finansovyie izvestiya,* May 5, 1998). Moreover, in the mid-1990s less than 40 percent of budget allotments for research institutes were actually distributed (*Nezavisimaya gazeta*, July 17, 1996).

In the 1990s the sharpest declines in new hiring were recorded in fundamental science and related sectors and in those sectors linked to information technologies. Moreover, the number of people leaving jobs in these sectors has consistently far outpaced those newly hired. As a result, the number of personnel engaged in research and research-related activity, which had reached its peak in the mid-1980s, declined by almost half by 1998. Many researchers only formally retain their jobs at institutes and research centers, while their main source of income and economic activity resides elsewhere.

The relative size of incomes of employees engaged in research-related spheres has fallen far below the average. A large proportion now have incomes below the official subsistence level (Ushkalov and Malaha 1999, 50–51). Comparing real wages across industries, in October 1997 the share of personnel receiving wages below the official poverty line stood at 32 percent for the research sector and 49 percent for the education sector, while it was 17.5 percent for the industrial sector as a whole.

Over one million Russians, disproportionately highly educated, have emigrated over the past 10 years (*Ekspert*, 2000, Nos. 1–2, 73). Many of these émigrés had formed the core of Russian research institutes and were attracted to job opportunities in the United States, Canada, Israel, and Germany. Israel alone has received on a permanent basis more than 13,000 scientists (*Moscow Times*, August 7, 1999, 10). On average, 7 percent of researchers employed in military research institutes and laboratories had resigned from their position each year during the 1990s. Out of this number, 1 out of 7 emigrated (*Expert 2000*, No. 12). The number who have left Russia on a temporary basis to perform contracted research exceeds the number of officially recorded cases of emigration by several fold (Ushkalov and Malaha 1999, 71).

Impediments and Policies

Government expenditure on fundamental research is not only small but inefficiently allocated. It is spread across thousands of institutes and research centers without any hope of providing adequate financing to any one of them. As a result, many institutes and centers have ceased meaningful research. With effective government leadership, the principal research institutes, including those of the Russian Academy of Sciences and those of the Russian atomic, military, and space programs, could provide the people, facilities, and ideas for commercializing a role for Russia in super-computers, computer software, pattern recognition, advanced communications, lasers, plasma fusion, biotechnology, and elsewhere.

Government support could be focused on the development of key projects where Russia has special potential. These projects could serve as demonstration projects or incubators for related technologies, leading to further development of the knowledge sectors of the economy. Examples would include technologies that have already been developed at Russian research institutes and that are now in pilot-plant operation.

There are many areas where Russia has a technological lead. One exciting example is a method for the incineration of wastes that turns garbage into fuel without environmental pollution. Called superadiabatic combustion, it has been perfected at the Institute of Chemical Physics of the Russian Academy of Sciences. Another example is a new technique for identification of mineral deposits using pattern-recognition techniques as developed at the International Institute for Earthquake Prediction Theory and Mathematical Geophysics in Moscow. Others examples include new technologies in producing petroleum products based on catalysis processes, the development of new composite materials, and biotechnology.

A serious obstacle to commercialization of research is insecurity of property rights. Property rights and business contracts in Russia today are guaranteed and enforced not so much by public institutions, but rather by private protection teams and corrupt insider rings. Their judicial norms have little in common with economic reality, and, accordingly, they are treated with contempt not only by businesses, but even by the authorities themselves. Actual interactions among economic agents are based on unwritten rules of the economic game that are enforced by the threat of unorganized but nevertheless quite effective reprisals against deviators by criminal elements. These rules that have arisen spontaneously largely determine the realm and the degree of competition in any industry. They also regulate relations within economic groupings, among them, and between private agents and the government (Braguinsky 1999). While such an economic order does not prevent the export of mineral resources from Russia, it presents an insurmountable hurdle to starting new projects that require longer-term investment. The problem is not simply the shortage of money for investment.

Some high-tech firms base their commercial activities outside of Russia. An example is the Russian venture business ParaGraph, which has developed new software for optical character reading of handwriting. Its headquarters is officially the Bahamas and its marketing division is in California, while research and production is in Russia.

Although many research centers have been reduced to a state of near total collapse, there has been some commercial success with software projects, nuclear physics and physics of extremely low temperatures, organic chemistry, pharmacology, and modern optics. For example, Minnesot˄ Mining and Manufacturing (3-M) has 28 contracts for joint research with Russian institutions.

Information Technology

Human capital–intensive industries that are currently attracting particular attention worldwide are those related to information technology (IT). Consider the example of India, which has evolved in the past decade to become a major center for computer software development. When you call a technical support number, there is a good chance the expert on the other end of the line is sitting in front of a computer terminal in Bangalore. This is a precedent that could apply to Russia as well, which would be starting from a much more significant base of expertise than that of India.

The Russian market for IT-related products and the demand for experts in this field have shown some visible signs of recovery in the past couple of years despite the generally depressed state of the economy. *Kommersant Dengi* (February 9, 2000) reported a notable increase in vacancies in computer-related areas, mass communications, and IT businesses. The firms are offering quite attractive salaries by Russian standards. At the same time, programmers are still inexpensive, with monthly salary ranging from $200 to $700 a month (Fukolova 2000).

One of the leading companies in this industry is IBS (Information Business Systems), headed by 40-year-old Anatoly Karachinsky. It has undertaken projects for the central bank of Russia, Gazprom, and Lukoil. IBS employs more than 400 people, and its 1999 sales exceeded $50 million (Nefedov 2000). According to a senior vice president of IBS, in the early 1990s most IT projects in large businesses in Russia were undertaken with a view to "stealing money," presumably through a kickback system, with the efficiency of the project a secondary issue at best. He claims that the situation has changed dramatically in recent years, with kickback cases now being extremely rare.

The IT industry in Russia remains in its infancy stage. Nearly all projects carried are targeted at the domestic market. This feature is characteristic not only of IT but of virtually all new businesses in Russia, with the exception of the resource-extraction sector. What this means in macroeconomic terms is that the source of new income for the country as a whole basically continues to be the foreign demand for Russian resources, while the IT industry currently competes only for the demand generated by the proceeds from those exports.

One more problem that was also noted in the interview of the vice president of IBS is the general lack of long-term financing that impedes the development of the human capital–intensive industries in general. The programs devised by Russian programmers dominate the Russian market on the level of individual programs, but as to higher-level operating systems, Russian products cannot compete against Sun Microsystems, Oracle, and other major international players. The main reason, as seen from the IBS perspective, is not a lack of high-quality programmers, but the absence of long-term economic stability and funding for large investment projects (Nefedov 2000).

Many Western and joint-venture companies that show interest in IT-related projects in Russia at the present moment have been set up or at least intend to use the expertise of former Russians who have immigrated to the West. This is the same path as had been followed by India: first many of its gifted and educated people immigrated to the United Kingdom and the United States, and then they set up firms that started employing the human capital remaining in India. Thus, the so-called "brain drain," although it does have some negative short-term effects, can also represent a powerful way to bring human and financial capital together.

General Issues

Many of the policy measures that are needed to revive the human capital–intensive sector in Russia are badly needed to promote Russia's overall economic development. These include the creation of market institutions (see, for example, Braguinsky and Yavlinsky 2000). Crucial are contacts and access to global markets, capital access and financing mechanisms, a social capital approach to economic development, protection of shareholder rights, good accounting regulations, and an entrepreneurial culture.

Russians, including Russian émigrés of various generations, have developed a class of new business people who reject the values of "robber barons" and desire to make modern creative businesses inside Russia. The opening up of the country has already created the potential for transnational business operations, for which no borders exist between Russia and the West. So far, this business has kept almost all of its financial resources abroad and it has raised investment funds and paid taxes outside of Russia. However, the production processes and the psychology of these business people remain rooted in Russia. Mostly represented by offshore-registered financial and investment firms, these businesses currently control most of Russian exports and some key elements of its transport facilities. The main missing pieces could be provided through appropriate technical assistance.

Russia requires appropriate financial institutions, including access to investment and working capital both nationally and internationally. It would benefit from technical assistance, especially to commercialize the various products and services from its research-and-development sector. One important source is the EU's TACIS program of technical assistance to the Commonwealth of Independent States. Financing and marketing would be facilitated by joint ventures with international firms. One path for the exploitation of Russian science is collaboration with Israeli companies since many of them already rely on Russian scientists and engineers.

It is important to disseminate information on the research inherited from the former Soviet Union that can be commercialized. It is difficult to obtain reliable information as to what technology is available and who has the property rights. The government should assist in creating a database, or at least make sure that the information is made publicly available. Given that most research has been carried out and is still being carried out in military-related institutions, government must take an active role.

Conclusion

To integrate itself into the world economy after the breakup of the Soviet Union, Russia has relied on the resource-extraction sector, which is made up of industries with a very low share of value added from human capital. Given its heritage, Russia has a latent comparative advantage in the use of human capital. Coincidentally, high tech has been the focus of attention in developed nations for the past decade, composing the core of the "new economy," including information technology. But the realities of the transition economy and government policies introduced so far have been so unfriendly to Russia's latent comparative advantage that no actual development could be forthcoming regardless of its potential.

If proper conditions for its development can be secured, knowledge-based development in general and information technology in particular could lead to the revival of the Russian economy and accelerate its integration into the world economy. Indeed, with proper internal policies and external support, Russia has a chance to become one of the fastest growing emerging-market economies. Such knowledge areas, rather than mineral extraction or the old smokestack industries, represent the greatest potential sources of growth.

References

Braguinsky, Serguey. 1999. "Enforcement of Property Rights during the Russian Transition." *The Journal of Legal Studies* 28(2): 515–544.

Braguinsky, Serguey, and Grigory Yavlinsky. 2000. *Incentives and Institutions: The Transition to a Market Economy in Russia*. Princeton: Princeton University Press.

Fukolova, Y. 2000. "Inzhenery, vperiod!" *Kommersant Dengi*, February 9.

Nefedov, Paul. 2000. "Yesli partnyory ne possorilis' v hode proekta – eto uzhe uspeh." *Vedomosti*, February 2.

Ushkalov, Igor., and Irina Malaha. 1999. "Utechka umov: masshtaby, prichiny, posledstviia." Moscow: Editorial URSS.

27

Reform Agenda

Economic Transition Group

This chapter offers a broad range of specific recommendations. They were prepared in consultation with the Economic Transition Group (ETG), an international network of economists established to promote a balanced approach to economic transition in Russia. (Chapter 2 provides background on the group and a list of ETG participants.) Those who contributed to this chapter include:

Leonid Abalkin, Irma Adelman, Georgi Arbatov, Oleg Bogomolov, Alberto Chilosi, Sergei Glaziev, Ruslan C. Grinberg, Lawrence R. Klein, Michael D. Intriligator, Viktor V. Ivanter, Nicholas N. Kozlov, Dmitri S. Lvov, Valery L. Makarov, Robert McIntyre, Alexander D. Nekipelov, Marshall Pomer, Geoffrey Shepherd, Martin K. Spechler, Lance Taylor, and James Tobin.

Other economists also provided useful comments, including A. A. Anfino-gentova, Dmitri Chernavsky, Alan Gelb, Peter M. Holmes, Jeffrey Miller, Grigori Pirogov, L. I. Tatarkin, Rafael Tsvylev, K. K. Valtukh, and Viktor Volkonsky.

Our recommendations are organized as a five-point reform agenda to improve the environment for private enterprise and yield a distribution of economic benefits compatible with stable democracy:

(1) **Institutional Infrastructure.**
     Upgrade market institutions and strengthen government capability to fashion and implement economic policies.

(2) **Decriminalization.**
     Root out corruption and improve the legal and moral climate.

(3) **Growth-Oriented Policy.**
     Establish a favorable macroeconomic context.

(4) **Restructuring and Competition.**
     Implement prudent development policy.

(5) **Social Contract.**
     Meet the basic social needs for a stable democracy.

1. Institutional Infrastructure.

It is the responsibility of both the federal and local governments to establish and coordinate public and private institutions required for a market economy. *Property Rights* need to be well-defined and legally protected. *Financial Institutions* necessitate a high degree of government regulation and prudential oversight. *Tax Compliance* is essential to provide government with needed resources without jeopardizing the soundness of the currency. To meet the challenges of transition and development, a *Development Council* is needed to improve government management of the economy. A revamped *Civil Service Commission* and a strengthened *Audit Chamber* would bolster competence and integrity. A key aim is to ensure that the rules of the market are laid down clearly and predictably and applied transparently.

Property Rights

1.1 Codify strong, stable, and transferable property rights for individuals and corporations, both domestic and foreign.

1.2 Strengthen the legal system and police protection to ensure that private property and business revenues are protected from criminal intrusion. (See **Decriminalization.**)

1.3 Establish mechanisms to allow the state and private parties to sue for the return of property rights acquired illegally.

1.4 Return to workers ownership shares acquired by managers who, refusing to pay wages that were due, pressured employees to sell their ownership shares.

1.5 Reduce licensing fees and eliminate licensing of business activities that do not pose a risk to health or safety.

1.6 Strengthen government responsibility for recording ownership (and transfer) of real estate and for assignment of assets as collateral.

1.7 Ensure that government contracts and asset sales are made on the basis of open bidding and are subject to public review. (See *Bankruptcy* and *Privatization.*)

1.8 Develop liaison with regional and local governments to encourage "reform experiments" and facilitate replication of successes.

Financial Institutions

1.9 Tighten central bank regulation of financial institutions, including investment funds.

1.10 Ensure proper prudential control of banks, including requirements of adequate collateral in the form of income-earning assets, to limit risk of improper and unproductive loans.

1.11 Require banks to utilize a certain proportion of their capital to fund productive investment or to contribute capital to government lending institutions (i.e., development banks and Home Mortgage Agencies).

1.12 Ensure safe registry of stocks and bonds, either by licensing such activity or by establishing government agencies for this purpose.

1.13 Require stock-ownership registration by either a public agency or by an entirely independent private body.

1.14 Increase the power of the Federal Securities Commission to require disclosure, stem fraud, and ensure shareholder rights, thereby up-grading corporate governance and encouraging investment.

1.15 Establish a premier stock exchange with strict disclosure require-ments, rigorous accounting standards, and certified independent auditing.

1.16 For equities listed on the premier exchange, require that all trans-actions go through the exchange and be immediately publicized via a "ticker tape" mechanism.

Tax Compliance

1.17 Reduce rates on businesses not involved in exploitation of natural resources. (See *Industrial Policy* and *Public Finance*.)

1.18 Streamline the tax system, eliminating "nuisance taxes."

1.19 Establish modern accounting and auditing standards.

1.20   Improve the salaries and training of tax collectors and vigorously prosecute malfeasance.

1.21   Enforce especially strict requirements on disclosing revenues (and their distribution) from oil, gas, and other mineral resources. (See *Public Finance*.)

Development Council

1.22   Form a Development Council to improve the design and implementation of economic policies.

1.23   Designate a top government official (president, prime minister, or a deputy prime minister) as head; include the chair of the central bank, key ministers, and legislative leaders as council members.

1.24   Staff with well-paid professionals who would formulate policies in a nonpartisan fashion and evaluate their implementation.

1.25   Enforce stringent rules regarding conflict of interest and require public disclosure of council members' personal and family assets.

1.26   Actively promote, via the president and other members of the Development Council, a positive business ethic, rewarding law-abiding, investment-oriented enterprises with public attention that could enhance demand for their products.

Civil Service Commission

1.27   Establish a Civil Service Commission, with substantial autonomy from elected officials, to eliminate unneeded employment and to elevate standards of recruitment, compensation, and promotion.

1.28   Select commission directors by presidential nomination and parliamentary approval, initially setting terms of varying lengths to provide continuity.

1.29   Minimize political appointments and insulate government hiring,
promotion, and termination from politics.

1.30   Consolidate and terminate unnecessary agencies and activities; eliminate unnecessary inspections and other red tape that add to the cost
of Russian-made goods.

1.31   Reduce government employment to below its level at the end of the
Soviet period.

1.32   Link pay to performance and make salaries for key employees more
competitive with the private sector.

Audit Chamber

1.33   Increase the resources and investigative powers of the Audit Chamber (counterpart to the U.S. Government Accounting Office).

1.34   Require that government agencies organize their records and documents to comply with approved standards.

1.35   Monitor public administrators for misconduct and impose heavy
penalties for wrongdoing.

1.36   Publish auditing results in periodical bulletins.

1.37   Allow public to purchase photocopies of unpublished materials.

2. Decriminalization.

A corrupt and criminalized economic system has emerged in Russia. *Government Disclosure*, strengthened *Investigative Powers* and tougher *Sanctions* are all needed. **Growth-Oriented Policy** and an equitable **Social Contract** would also build allegiance to ethical standards.

Government Disclosure

2.1   Enforce strict requirements on disclosing revenues and expenditures for government at all levels.

2.2   Establish modern auditing to ensure high standards of accounting and accountability for abuse.

2.3   Require high standards of accounting and auditing for property assets on public balance sheets. (See *Audit Chamber*.)

2.4   Implement safeguards to ensure that privatization does not result in transfer of assets to criminal structures.

2.5   Abrogate fraudulent privatizations.

2.6   Require disclosure of second jobs held by government employees and prohibit potential conflicts of interest.

Investigative Powers

2.7   Broaden parliamentary responsibility to advise and consent on major presidential appointments.

2.8   Empower parliament to establish special investigative task forces with subpoena powers and police protection.

2.9   Provide both the Audit Chamber and the Development Council the authority and resources to demand full disclosure from ministries and enterprises that receive substantial subsidies.

Sanctions

2.10   Enact and enforce severe penalties for extortion, bribery, and interference with judicial process.

2.11   Increase sanctions and prosecution for managerial malfeasance, such as asset stripping and corrupt diversion of funds.

2.12   Increase funding for police, prosecutors, and courts.

2.13   Expand police protection for law-enforcement officials, prosecutors, judges, and key witnesses.

2.14   Institute mechanisms to encourage cooperation with prosecutors, including plea bargaining and grants of immunity, witness support programs, and free legal representation for victims.

2.15   Fund special law-enforcement programs to address mafia infiltration in critical areas of the economy, including banking, transport of goods, gas and oil pipelines, and customs.

2.16   Provide both the Audit Chamber and the Development Council the authority to initiate suspension and prosecution of corrupt officials.

2.17   Establish procedures for private complainants to win enhanced compensatory awards in cases where watchdog agencies failed to address wrongdoing.

3. Growth-Oriented Policy.

Expansionary macroeconomic policy is needed to create employment and reduce overdependence on exports of unprocessed or minimally processed raw materials. *Investment Stimulus* would enhance demand and improve productivity. *Capital Controls and Monetary Policy* should reduce capital flight, limit inflow of unstable short-term capital, and provide an environment that would allow interest rates to stabilize at moderate levels.

Investment Stimulus

3.1   Increase public investment in needed infrastructure for transporting Russian goods, including storage facilities for farm produce now subject to high rates of spoilage.

3.2   Establish an autonomous self-financing mortgage agency (Home Mortgage Agency) both to provide home mortgages and to purchase such mortgages from original lenders.

3.3   Allow accelerated depreciation and make other changes to the tax code to encourage investment in new facilities and technology.

3.4   Discourage foreign aid in the form of credits for the purchases of foreign goods, except for purchases of investment goods leading to upgraded technology. (See *Industrial Policy*.)

3.5   Welcome foreign aid that raises investment in Russian production (finance for investment projects and guarantees for foreign investors) and infrastructure (risk insurance and interest subsidies for development bonds).

Capital Controls and Monetary Policy

3.6   Tighten controls on capital flight and enforce severe penalties, including seizure of assets.

3.7   Tax currency conversion (Tobin Tax) to dampen volatility of short-term capital flows and to reduce hoarding of foreign currency.

3.8   Limit real appreciation of the ruble in order to bolster demand for Russian production.

3.9   Do not allow monetary policy to contribute to accelerating inflation, but set moderate inflation targets and avoid rapid disinflation.

4. Restructuring and Competition.

Government initiatives to expedite restructuring and promote economic development must be well designed and carefully implemented to ensure that market discipline is maintained. Government should foster new competing enterprises, including joint ventures that facilitate transfer of administrative and technological know-how. Effective *Industrial Policy* requires strict definition of priorities, transparency, and measurement of results. A substantial degree of temporary *Tariff Protection* may be justified if the real exchange rate continues to appreciate. Until financial institutions grow in assets and become more oriented toward financing expansion of business, *Development Loans* are needed. *Privatization, Bankruptcy, Arrears,* and *Price Regulation* must be managed deliberately and responsibly. Increased *Energy Efficiency* would make Russian industry more competitive. *Public Wealth Funds* and a *Management Council* are potentially useful innovations. Judicious support for *Science and R&D* is important to promote technological advance, especially if there is an emphasis on practical application.

Industrial Policy

4.1   Establish criteria that are not firm-specific and minimize discretion of officials to aid individual firms.

4.2   Do not provide financial assistance for investment unless business owners are at risk if investments prove unsuccessful.

4.3   Make support of targeted industries time-limited and conditional on evidence of success.

4.4   Implement strict accounting requirements, including rigorous audits, and enforce severe penalties to prevent improper diversion of any development loans. (See *Audit Chamber*.)

4.5   Until strong economic growth resumes, reinstate export duties on energy and metals to lower domestic costs and thereby improve competitiveness of industry. (See *Public Finance* for another rationale.)

4.6   Until this sector of the economy is more mature, temporarily reduce tax rates on manufacturers of final consumer goods. (See *Tax Compliance*.)

4.7   Eliminate bureaucratic red tape on foreign investment other than to enforce commitments by strategic investors (see *Privatization*) and to ensure that foreign investment is not geared toward eliminating Russian competitors.

4.8   Make judicious use of domestic content requirements to promote use of Russian capital goods in conjunction with the Production Sharing Law and to encourage manufacturing of finished goods. (See *Trade Policy and Exchange Rates*.)

4.9   Experiment with indicative planning of the sort done in postwar Europe and Japan to coordinate expanded industrial output and, perhaps more importantly, create positive expectations that will encourage private investment.

4.10   Reduce unnecessary licensing and reporting requirements, especially so as not to inhibit formation of new businesses. (See *Civil Service Commission.*)

4.11   Establish quality-control inspection and certification for manufactured commodities with large export potential.

4.12   Help inform Russian firms regarding standards, testing, and certification regimes in foreign markets.

4.13   Conduct export promotion fairs.

4.14   Negotiate with other governments and international agencies to ensure unbiased treatment in the world market for Russian producers, including farmers.

4.15   To ensure awareness of opportunity costs, assess the effects on the rest of the economy of support for each assisted sector.

Tariff Protection

4.16   Limit the scope of tariff protection unless there is substantial real appreciation of the ruble and continued high levels of unemployment.

4.17   Make tariff rates highly predictable and ensure that tariffs cannot be suddenly raised to suit failing firms.

4.18   Consider in particular the use of high tariffs to encourage investment in auto and aircraft manufacturing.

4.19   Make any tariff protection conditional on progress in industrial restructuring and specify phased reduction in rates.

4.20   Do not allow tariff exemptions for privileged importers.

Development Loans

4.21   Fund development loan agencies (development banks) and eliminate all direct and indirect subsidies other than development loans.

4.22   Limit development loans in accordance with policy targets and make loans conditional on evidence of effective investment.

4.23   Rather than directly supply development loans, rely on interest subsidies for loans from private banks so that market discipline prevails.

4.24   Audit development loans to ensure they do not abet capital flight or the accumulation of financial assets.

4.25   Involve the World Bank, the European Bank for Reconstruction and Development, and other international institutions as partners.

Privatization

4.26   Privatize further only when it would improve the long-run financial position of the government and expedite economic restructuring.

4.27   Ensure open competitive bidding and fully disclose the terms of any privatization.

4.28   Restructure enterprises prior to privatization auctions to reduce uncertainty and attract greater investor interest.

4.29   Where appropriate, require that asset transfers be conditional on further investment (strategic investors).

4.30   Abrogate sales of enterprises to strategic investors in cases of failure to honor investment commitments.

4.31   Where abuse is evident and the government would benefit, reverse transfers of assets under the "loans-for-shares" program.

Bankruptcy

4.32   Increase the powers of the Federal Bankruptcy Agency to ensure that assets are liquidated by trustees free of conflict of interest. Ensure that all interested parties have the equal right to learn about and bid on assets liquidated through bankruptcy.

4.33   Revamp procedures to speed liquidation of insolvent businesses.

4.34   Reestablish public ownership in the case of insolvent enterprises that exploit natural resources if they have economic potential.

4.35   Give regulatory agencies the authority to initiate and carry out bankruptcy proceedings, but reserve for the Federal Bankruptcy Agency the power to review and override decisions in the case of abuse.

4.36   Ensure that local government takeovers of insolvent enterprises (e.g., Zil by the city of Moscow) do not undo market discipline.

Arrears

4.37 Grant the Federal Bankruptcy Agency the power to implement an arrears settlement to reduce mutual indebtedness while minimizing erosion of market discipline.

4.38 In any arrears settlement, reward enterprises that have been responsible in making tax payments.

4.39 Expedite bankruptcy proceedings against enterprises that remain insolvent after arrears settlement—full liquidation or reorganization with debt reduction and partial liquidation.

Price Regulation

4.40 Strengthen price regulation and auditing standards for utilities and railroads.

4.41 Regulate prices of basic commodities supplied under monopolistic conditions and ensure that regulated prices are market clearing.

Energy Efficiency

4.42 Require, where economical, metering of heat and power for individual apartment units.

4.43 Require utilities to purchase at economic value surplus heat and power co-generated by industrial enterprises.

Public Wealth Funds

4.44 Establish public wealth funds to act as owners of state-owned enterprises and as owners of state-held shares in partially privatized enterprises.

4.45 Operate similarly to head offices of conglomerates—selecting and overseeing management of individual enterprises, assisting with finance, and providing liaison with strategic investors.

4.46 Link compensation to performance by tying a portion of managerial compensation to future profits (e.g., stock options).

4.47 Allocate assets among the funds in a manner that contributes to competition; ensure that one fund does not control an entire industry.

4.48 Authorize the funds, as a potential vehicle for careful privatization, to sell shares of stock to the public when economic conditions are such that the government can expect to get fair value.

4.49 Ensure that state shareholdings deliver economic returns so that shareholdings are not used as a covert subsidy mechanism.

Management Council

4.50 Establish a Management Council to promote a business ethic that is law-abiding and investment-oriented.

4.51 Draw on international technical assistance for staff and promote creative emulation of leading foreign enterprises.

4.52 Offer competent, modestly priced management consulting to businesses of all sizes.

4.53   Assemble and disseminate information to encourage innovation in marketing, R&D, and employee incentives.

4.54   Publicize examples of successful restructuring and growth.

Science and R&D

4.55   Orient science policy toward practical application and the dissemination of technology.

4.56   Specify priority research areas to circumvent permanent loss of technological capacity.

4.57   Establish transparent mechanisms for allocating and monitoring government support.

4.58   Ensure reasonable salaries for promising young scientists in priority fields.

4.59   Close research institutes that are unproductive.

4.60   Create outreach programs and R&D partnerships at universities and research institutes to stimulate technological progress.

5. Social Contract.

Only government can ensure that the benefits of the new economic order are shared, which would improve the moral climate and fortify respect for democracy. Expanded *Social Services* would ease transition and expedite restructuring. The system of *Public Finance* requires overhaul.

Social Services

5.1 Increase funding for education and health care.

5.2 Improve disclosure and accountability for expenditures.

5.3 Maintain regulation of price and quality of medical goods and services, and do not attempt total commercialization of health care.

5.4 Complete government takeover of responsibility for social services previously supplied by state-owned enterprises (e.g., health care, education, and child care).

5.5 Ensure that social guarantees provided to the poor and pensioners are adjusted for inflation.

5.6 Put more educational resources into creating a professional class of public and private administrators/managers, and establish links between universities and the Civil Service Commission.

5.7 To reduce public opposition to downsizing, guarantee reasonable benefits to laid-off older workers, and provide retraining and relocation assistance.

5.8 To stem malnourishment of children and the elderly, ensure adequate low-cost supplies of basic foodstuffs.

Public Finance

5.9 Concentrate high-rate taxation on natural resources and luxuries including imports of alcohol and tobacco.

5.10   Establish low-rate taxation on retail sales and incomes so that businesses and individuals get accustomed to paying taxes.

5.11   Continue export duties on energy and other natural resources until other mechanisms are in place to capture fully economic rents. (See *Industrial Policy*.)

5.12   To complement taxes on natural resources, use competitive bidding for concessions, with extensive safeguards to ensure fair pricing.

5.13   Decentralize property taxation and remove other disincentives to the privatization of real estate owned by local governments.

5.14   Intensify enforcement, increase penalties, and eliminate loopholes to stem avoidance of personal income taxes by the wealthy.

5.15   Impose significant real estate taxes on personal residences with a high market value.

5.16   Raise the threshold for wage income not subject to taxation.

Call for Action

Failure to implement the type of recommendations presented above is not due simply to neglect or the power of vested interests in Russia. Western governments, the IMF, and the World Bank have pressured the Russian government to be passive. The Economic Transition Group, supportive of more activist policy, has sought to counter this international pressure. A public statement issued in June of 2000 was endorsed by the heads of eight major economic institutes within the Russian Academy of Sciences and by three American Nobel laureates in economics. This statement parallels the five-point reform agenda presented above:[1]

AGENDA FOR ECONOMIC REFORM IN RUSSIA

Despite predictions of doom, devaluation of the ruble has stimulated Russian production, and the rebound in world oil and gas prices have improved government finances. However, the challenges of recovery, transition, and development remain.

We, Russian and American economists, agree with Russia's new President, Vladimir Putin, that the state must be strengthened in order to play a more active role in the economy. We would also like to emphasize that both the quality of Russian life and the prospects for economic development depend on ensuring civil liberties, a free press, and a democratic system of government. Economic reform is needed to create a more favorable environment both for entrepreneurs and employed labor. To this end, we wish to offer a five-point agenda:

1. Institutional Infrastructure.
Government has the responsibility to eliminate distortions in the market mechanism and to establish and maintain the institutional infrastructure of a genuine market economy. It is imperative that the federal government, along with local governments, rationalize property rights, reorient large- and medium-size enterprises from asset stripping to net-worth maximization, and introduce modern systems of accounting, finance, and insurance. Government, including the central bank, should stringently oversee private financial institutions and ensure that savings are channeled into investment. It is urgent to upgrade the ability of the Russian government to fashion and implement economic policy. Measures should be taken to insulate hiring and promotion from politics and ensure high standards of recruitment.

2. Decriminalization.
Criminals have filled the institutional vacuum with corrupt officials and mafia control. As President Putin has emphasized, the rule of law must be solidified in order to increase allegiance to standards of ethical behavior

and to provide a business climate that would stimulate investment. Extortion and bribery must be prosecuted irrespective of the officials involved, and penalties should be severe. Government policies should be tailored to mitigate economic causes of corruption such as substandard pay for public officials, high transaction costs, and a Byzantine tax system.

3. Growth-Oriented Policy.

Economic growth should be the primary goal of macroeconomic policy. Overly zealous monetary and fiscal restrictions to bring inflation to near zero are counterproductive. Within economically justified limits, the government should bolster purchasing power through more adequate pensions and restoration of a portion of the savings lost as a result of sustained inflation and the financial collapse of 1998. Government should pay more attention to rebuilding social overhead capital. A substantial program to upgrade roads and other physical infrastructure would boost demand for Russian goods while enhancing the private sector's competitive potential. Concerted action should be taken against illegal capital flight. Cleaning balance sheets of mutual overdue debts would greatly improve the financial position of the real sector. To increase investment in new facilities and technologies, the government must help develop mortgages and permit accelerated depreciation of industrial investment. Judicious subsidizing of interest payments on development loans would increase private investment.

4. Restructuring and Competition.

During transition, government involvement in the economy is needed on a microeconomic level. Proper industrial policy would avoid undue interference with market discipline. The federal government should encourage the growth of new competing enterprises, including those with local government participation and joint ventures drawing on foreign capital. Government assistance is needed for Russia to realize its potential in the information economy, biotechnology, and other high-tech spheres. Until steady growth resumes, selective import tariffs conditional on industrial performance could be introduced. Government has to regulate the prices of basic commodities supplied under monopolistic conditions, being careful that prices are market clearing and ensuring removal of barriers to fresh sources of supply. It is important prior to future privatization auctions to restructure enterprises and overhaul their finances. Privatizations that have been carried out in violation of the law should be reconsidered.

5. Social Contract.

Only government can ensure that the benefits of the new economic order are shared fairly, which is vital to improve the moral climate and fortify respect for democracy. Health care, education and public services should be allocated more resources. Pensions for the elderly are meager and must not be allowed to lag behind inflation. A law on guaranteed subsistence, including rent subsidies for low-income households, may be mandatory to overcome mass poverty. To reduce income differentiation and mitigate social tensions, well-enforced progressive taxation is needed. There should be substantial real estate taxes on personal residences with high market value. High taxes on extractive industries would ensure that the Russian people as a whole are the main beneficiaries of the export of natural resources.

Successful transition requires a realistic and balanced economic program. The five-point agenda, if implemented responsibly, would ensure a prosperous and equitable future for the Russian people.

Note

1. The signatories are: Leonid Abalkin, Irma Adelman, Georgi Arbatov, Oleg Bogomolov, Marshall I. Goldman, Michael D. Intriligator, Victor V. Ivanter, Lawrence R. Klein, Dmitri S. Lvov, Valery L. Makarov, Franco Modigliani, Alexander D. Nekipelov, Douglass North, Nikolai I. Petrakov, Marshall Pomer, Natalia M. Rimashevskaya, Stepan A. Sitarian, Lance Taylor. (Signatories support the principles of the statement and its general outline without necessarily agreeing with every detail.) Published in *Nezavisimaya gazeta* on June 9, 2000.

Statistical Appendix

The primary source for this appendix is the *Survey on Economic Policy in Russia in 1997*, Bureau of Economic Analysis, Moscow, 1998. Consult this publication for further details on variable definitions and data sources. Most of the series were originally obtained from the Russian Government Statistical Agency (Goskomstat), which endeavored to include the underground economy. The data have been updated using *Russian Economic Trends: Monthly Update*, Russian-European Centre for Economic Policy, Moscow, October 2000 in combination with the historical data base constructed by the Russian-European Centre for Economic Policy (http://www.hhs.se/site/ret/exceldb/default.htm).

Note: Pre-1998 ruble values are expressed in new rubles. On January 1, 1998 the currency was redenominated: one new ruble was made equal to 1,000 pre-1998 rubles.

Contents

Table A1. Gross Domestic Product (billions of rubles)

	1990	1991	1992	1993	1994	1995	1996	1997	1998	1999
GDP	0.644	1.399	19.01	171.5	610.7	1541	2146	2479	2696	4546
Constant prices	100	95.0	81.2	74.2	64.8	62.1	60.0	60.5	57.6	59.4
Percentage change	*-3.0*	*-5.0*	*-14.5*	*-8.7*	*-12.7*	*-4.1*	*-3.4*	*0.9*	*-4.9*	*3.2*
Personal consumption	0.289	0.506	5.175	55.07	239.3	664.8	950.1	1124	1340	2200
Constant prices	100	89.4	52.4	60.1	64.5	60.3	58.8	60.8	57.6	49.4
Investment (commercial and public)	0.249	0.210	2.670	27.13	108.8	267.0	376.0	408.8	402.4	659.3
Constant prices	100	85.0	51.0	44.9	34.1	30.7	25.1	23.9	22.3	23.3

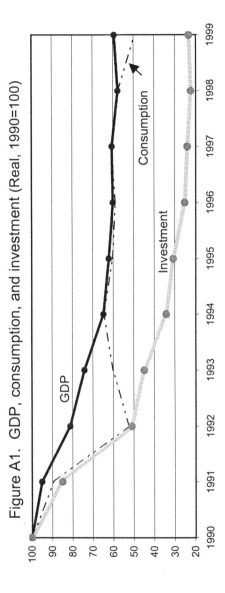

Figure A1. GDP, consumption, and investment (Real, 1990=100)

Table A2. Income and employment

	1990	1991	1992	1993	1994	1995	1996	1997	1998	1999
Personal income per capita (rubles monthly)	-	0.465	3.975	44.81	206.4	514.9	765.1	931.7	997.6	1587
Constant prices (1991=100)	-	100	49.3	59.1	68.2	58.3	58.8	62.5	52.9	44.2
Average wage (rubles monthly)	0.303	0.548	5.995	58.66	220.4	472.0	790.0	950.0	1095	1581
Constant prices (1991=100)	103.1	100	65.7	69.7	63.7	46.9	53.5	56.1	50.3	39.1
Employment (millions)	75.3	73.8	72.1	70.9	68.5	66.4	65.9	64.7	63.6	64.0
Unemployed (millions, ILO concept)	-	-	3.594	4.160	5.478	6.431	7.002	7.843	8.587	9.300
Unemployment Rate (%)	-	-	*4.7*	*5.5*	*7.4*	*8.5*	*9.6*	*10.8*	*11.9*	*12.6*

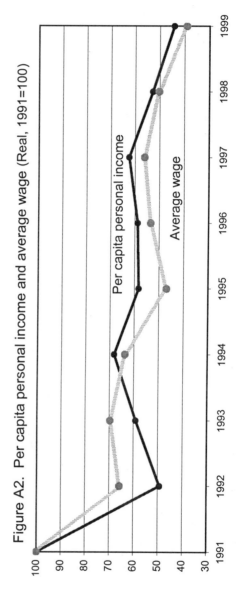

Figure A2. Per capita personal income and average wage (Real, 1991=100)

Table A3. Output by sector

	1990	1991	1992	1993	1994	1995	1996	1997	1998	1999
Industrial production	100	92.0	75.5	64.8	51.3	49.6	47.6	48.5	46.0	49.8
Electricity	100	98.7	96.2	91.3	83.5	82.2	80.8	79.5	78.8	80.6
Natural Gas	100	100.3	99.9	96.4	94.6	92.9	93.7	89.2	92.3	92.1
Crude Oil	100	89.3	77.0	68.2	61.3	58.9	57.8	58.7	58.1	58.3
Coal	100	89.4	85.3	77.4	68.7	66.6	64.5	61.8	58.7	63.0
Construction volume	100	98.0	62.7	57.7	41.9	39.4	33.0	30.9	29.3	30.9
Housing construction (millions of square meters completed)	61.7	49.4	41.5	41.8	39.2	41.0	34.3	32.7	30.7	32.0
Agricultural output	100	95.4	86.5	82.7	72.8	66.9	63.5	64.5	56.0	57.3
Transportation volume (billions of tons-kilometers)	5891	5457	4698	4158	3567	3537	3374	3256	3169	3338
Railway shipments (millions of tons)	2140	1957	1632	1346	1054	1025	908.6	886.8	834.2	945.0

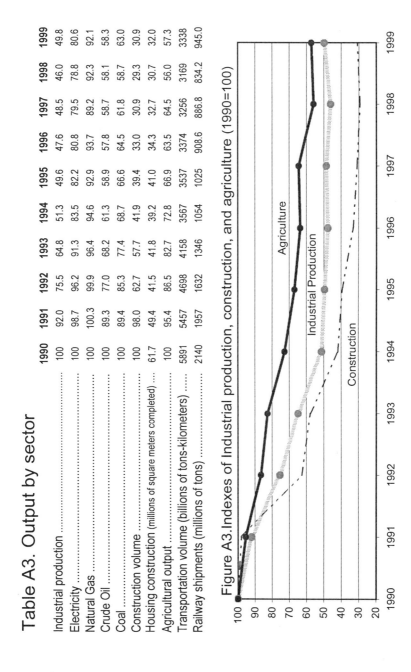

Figure A3. Indexes of Industrial production, construction, and agriculture (1990=100)

Table A4. Foreign trade and direct investment (billions of US dollars)

	1990	1991	1992	1993	1994	1995	1996	1997	1998	1999
Merchandise exports	71.1	50.9	53.6	59.6	68.1	81.1	88.6	88.2	74.2	75.1
Oil and oil products	-	-	-	-	-	17.3	23.1	21.9	14.5	18.8
Gas	-	-	-	-	-	10.8	15.8	16.4	13.3	11.4
Merchandise imports	81.8	44.5	43.0	44.3	50.5	60.8	68.8	73.7	59.1	40.2
Machinery and equipment	36.3	15.8	13.9	9.1	13.6	15.8	14.6	18.5	15.6	9.9
Trade balance	*-10.7*	*6.4*	*10.6*	*15.3*	*17.6*	*20.2*	*19.8*	*14.5*	*15.1*	*34.9*
Foreign direct investment into Russia	-	-	-	-	0.640	2.016	2.479	6.639	2.761	2.890

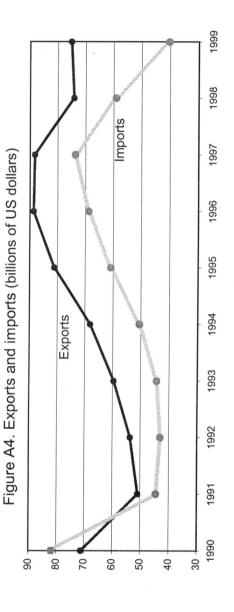

Figure A4. Exports and imports (billions of US dollars)

Table A5. Prices (end of year, December 1997=100)

	1990	1991	1992	1993	1994	1995	1996	1997	1998	1999
Consumer price index (CPI)	0.016	0.041	1.080	10.15	31.98	73.97	90.09	100	184.4	251.7
Inflation rate (%)		*160*	*2509*	*840*	*215*	*131*	*21.8*	*11.0*	*84.4*	*36.5*
Food and beverages	0.020	0.047	1.226	11.10	34.86	77.90	91.66	100	196.0	266.4
Nonfood goods	0.022	0.068	1.819	13.50	36.31	78.53	92.51	100	199.5	277.7
Paid services	0.003	0.005	0.110	2.660	16.56	55.01	81.63	100	118.3	158.5
Industrial producer price index (PPI)	0.016	0.041	1.080	10.10	32.00	74.10	93.00	100	123.2	206.2
Inflation rate (%)		*156*	*2534*	*835*	*217*	*132*	*25.5*	*7.5*	*23.2*	*67.4*

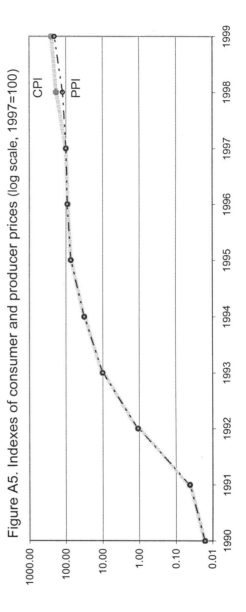

Figure A5. Indexes of consumer and producer prices (log scale, 1997=100)

Table A6. Government budget (IMF definition, billions of rubles)

	1990	1991	1992	1993	1994	1995	1996	1997	1998	1999
Federal government										
Revenues	-	-	-	25.50	86.30	201.0	253.8	311.6	273.0	606.0
Expenditures	-	-	-	35.40	146.4	286.2	427.1	494.8	407.2	680.2
Interest payments	-	-	-	-	-	54.60	124.5	117.8	106.8	162.6
Percent of GDP	-	-	-	-	-	*3.5*	*5.8*	*4.7*	*4.0*	*3.6*
Deficit	-	-	-	9.9	60.1	85.2	173.3	183.2	134.2	74.2
Percent of GDP	-	-	-	*5.8*	*9.8*	*5.4*	*7.9*	*7.0*	*5.0*	*1.7*
Regional and local government										
Revenues	-	-	-	28.70	116.1	238.4	321.2	410.4	395.5	647.9
Expenditures	-	-	-	26.80	113.4	247.0	342.8	446.9	407.1	648.9
Deficit (surplus)	-	-	-	(1.9)	(2.7)	8.6	21.6	36.5	11.7	1.0
Percent of GDP	-	-	-	*-1.1*	*-0.4*	*0.5*	*1.0*	*1.4*	*0.4*	*0.0*

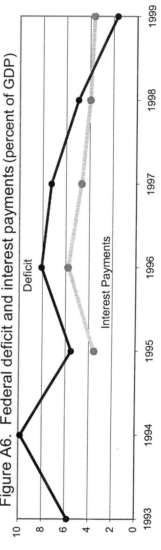

Figure A6. Federal deficit and interest payments (percent of GDP)

Table A7. Monetary factors (end of year)

	1990	1991	1992	1993	1994	1995	1996	1997	1998	1999
CBR refinance rate	20	20	80	210	180	185	110	32	60	57
Interbank rate (%)				275	207	190.4	47.6	21.0	50.6	14.8
Currency in circulation (billions of rubles)	0.079	0.191	1.678	13.28	35.70	80.80	103.8	130.4	187.8	266.5
Percent of GDP	*12.3*	*13.7*	*8.8*	*7.7*	*5.8*	*5.2*	*4.8*	*5.2*	*7.0*	*6.0*
Monetary base (billions of rubles)			2.235	16.69	48.00	103.8	130.9	164.5	210.4	324.3
Percent of GDP			*11.8*	*9.7*	*7.9*	*6.7*	*6.1*	*6.5*	*7.8*	*7.2*
Moscow Times (MT) stock index (August 31, 1994=100)					147	133	372	815	357	1398
MT $ stock index (In dollars; August 31, 1994=100)					94.1	64.0	148.4	302.7	38.4	114.6
Exchange Rate (MICEX, Rubles/US dollar)		0.169	0.415	1.247	3.550	4.640	5.570	5.974	21.14	26.96
Average exchange rate for year		0.058	0.222	0.933	2.205	4.562	5.126	5.785	9.965	24.84
Real exchange rate (Dec.1994=100, avg. for Dec.)		3353.6	343.21	112.32	100	60.5	61.4	60.4	112.3	111.3
Gross international reserves (billions of US dollars)					6.5	17.2	15.3	17.8	12.2	12.5

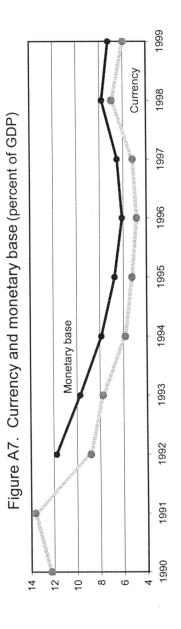

Figure A7. Currency and monetary base (percent of GDP)

Index

Abalkin, Leonid, 11, 44, 57, 58, 61,
154, 163, 413, 434, 453
Abramovich, Roman, 244, 247
Adelman, Irma, 12, 34, 57, 110, 117,
126, 131-133, 413, 434, 453
Aeroflot, 244, 282
Aganbegyan, Abel, 146-149, 151,
152, 160-162
Aggregate demand, 271, 273,
275-277, 315, 316
Agrarian bloc, 337
Agriculture, 10, 245, 254, 333-349
decollectivization, 10, 78
policies in other countries, 53, 78,
124, 176
private farms, 333-335, 342-344
Soviet, 143
Aircraft industry, 281-284
Alekperov, Vagit, 244, 247
Andropov, Yuri, 144, 146, 148
Anfinogentova, A. A., 413
Arbatov, Alexander, 15, 57
Arbatov, Georgi, 5, 6, 13, 57, 413,
434
Argentina, 109
Arrears crisis
interenterprise arrears, 36, 115,
191, 195, 197, 219
tax arrears, 43, 194, 219, 292
wage arrears, 62, 192, 219, 241,
251, 252, 336
Arrow, Kenneth J., xx, 12, 24, 27, 44,
58, 85, 159, 453
Åslund, Anders, 3, 6, 7, 43, 57, 153,
162, 171, 246
Audit Chamber, 414, 418-420, 422
Automobile industry, 283
See also China; auto industry *and*
Ukraine; auto industry

Bankruptcy, 30, 41
Federal Bankruptcy Agency, 424,
425
lack of historical precedent, 100,
110, 143, 272, 311, 424
real estate, 380
Banks, 39, 108, 127, 195, 221-231,
415
regulation of, 39, 70, 128, 182, 222
See also Oligarchs
Barter, 98-100
Belarus, 149, 163, 326, 328, 330
Belousov, Andrei, 13, 157, 199, 453
Berezovsky, Boris, 242, 244, 247
Berliner, Joseph, 142, 160, 245
Bernstam, Michael S., 14, 221, 232,
359, 453
Black market, 26, 145, 153, 234
Boeing, 281, 282, 294, 295
Bogdanov, Vladimir, 244, 247
Bogomolov, Oleg, 6, 11, 43, 53,
55-58, 413, 434, 453
Bolivia, 109
Bolshevik example, xiv, xxii, 159,
175
Brada, Josef C., 5, 43
Braguinsky, Serguey, 16, 203,
205-207, 218, 219, 245, 246,
403, 406, 409, 453
Brazil, 8, 283, 295
Brezhnev era, 145
Brezhnev, Leonid, 144, 145, 148, 234
Bush, George H, xiv, 163
Canada, 68, 405
Capital controls, 62, 309, 421
Capital flight, 275
causes of, 32, 207
consequences of, 242, 287, 292
estimates, 193, 292, 318

Contributors

Leonid Abalkin	Institute of Economics, Russian Academy of Sciences (RAS)
Irma Adelman	University of California, Berkeley
Alexander Arbatov	Committee for Natural Resources, RAS
Georgi Arbatov	USA-Canada Institute, RAS
Kenneth J. Arrow	Stanford University
Andrei Belousov	Institute of Economic Forecasting, RAS
Michael Bernstam	Hoover Institution
Oleg Bogomolov	Institute of International Economic and Political Studies, RAS
Serguey Braguinsky	Yokohama City University
David Ellerman	World Bank
Yevgeny Gavrilenkov	Bureau of Economic Analysis, Moscow
John Giraldez	Agriculture and Agri-Food Canada, Government of Canada
Sergei Glaziev	Federal Council of Russian Federation
Svetlana P. Glinkina	Institute of International Economic and Political Studies, RAS
Mikhail Gorbachev	Gorbachev Foundation
Andrei Grigoriev	Kompaniya
Ruslan S. Grinberg	Institute of International Economic and Political Studies, RAS
Michael D. Intriligator	University of California, Los Angeles

Dwight Jaffee	University of California, Berkeley
Olga Kaganova	Urban Institute
Lawrence R. Klein	University of Pennsylvania
Edit Kranner	University of Kentucky
Dmitri Kuvalin	Institute of Economic Forecasting, RAS
Eric Martinot	Tufts University
Bruce McWilliams	University of California, Berkeley
Stanislav Menshikov	University of Aalborg, Denmark
Vladimir Mikhalev	World Institute for Development Economics Research (WIDER)
Alexander D. Nekipelov	Institute of International Economic and Political Studies, RAS
Victor M. Polterovich	Central Economics and Mathematics Institute, RAS
Marshall Pomer	Macroeconomic Policy Institute
Geliy Shmeliov	Russian Agricultural Academy
Vitaly Shvydko	Institute of Oriental Studies, RAS
Andrei Sitnikov	Institute of Systems Analysis, Moscow
Joseph E. Stiglitz	Stanford University
Lance Taylor	New School for Social Research
James Tobin	Yale University
Vladimir Usiyevich	World Bank
Alexander Vedrashko	University of California, Berkeley
Vakhtang Yakobidze	Kompaniya